Trouble at the Mill

Trouble at the Mill

Factory Law and the Emergence of the Labour Question in Late Nineteenth-Century Bombay

Aditya Sarkar

OXFORD
UNIVERSITY PRESS

OXFORD
UNIVERSITY PRESS

Oxford University Press is a department of the University of Oxford. It furthers the University's objective of excellence in research, scholarship, and education by publishing worldwide. Oxford is a registered trademark of Oxford University Press in the UK and in certain other countries.

Published in India by
Oxford University Press
2/11 Ground Floor, Ansari Road, Daryaganj, New Delhi 110 002, India

First Edition published in 2018

ISBN-13 (print edition): 978-0-19-947442-4
ISBN-10 (print edition): 0-19-947442-7

ISBN-13 (eBook): 978-0-19-909329-8
ISBN-10 (eBook): 0-19-909329-6

Typeset in Dante MT Std 10.5/13
by Tranistics Data Technologies, Kolkata 700 091
Printed in India by Replika Press Pvt. Ltd

For my parents
Tanika Sarkar and Sumit Sarkar

Contents

Acknowledgements

Many institutions have enabled the work that has gone into the making of this book. The idea behind it was initially formed during my early years of post-graduate training at Jawaharlal Nehru University in New Delhi, India. A scholarship from the Felix Trust enabled my PhD training at the School of Oriental and African Studies (SOAS) in London, UK. A post-doctoral fellowship at the Centre for Modern Indian Studies in University of Goettingen, Germany, and subsequent employment at the University of Warwick, UK, have made continuing research possible. I am grateful to the staff and management of various libraries and research institutions for their support: the Maharashtra State Archives, Mumbai, India; the Oriental and India Office Collection at the British Library, London; the Indian Merchants' Chamber Library, Mumbai; the National Archives of India, New Delhi; the Nehru Memorial Museum and Library, New Delhi; the Central Secretariat Library, New Delhi; the School of Oriental and African Studies Library, London; the Centre for Education and Documentation, Mumbai; the Centre for South Asian Studies, University of Cambridge, UK; the Modern Records Centre at the University of Warwick; the V.V. Giri National Labour Institute, Noida, India; the Gokhale Institute of Politics and Economics, Pune, India; and the National Library in Kolkata, India.

I am very grateful to Oxford University Press, India, for its support, which has been instrumental to the publication of this book. I am grateful to the anonymous reviewers of this book as well as of other publications which prepared the base for it, and I also thank my PhD examiners, Claude Markovits and Jon Wilson, for their detailed comments, which helped immensely in turning a dissertation into a book.

Many mentors and teachers have made this book possible. In particular, I owe a deep debt to Peter Robb, who supervised my PhD research at SOAS. His lucid interventions helped to discipline and organize an often flailing set of arguments into some sort of cohesion, and his insights into labour history and state policy deeply influenced the ways in which I conceived of the overall structure of the argument. This book would not have been possible but for his kindness, encouragement, and truly enviable patience. I am grateful to Neeladri Bhattacharya, whose supervision of my pre-doctoral research at the Centre for Historical Studies in Jawaharlal Nehru University was crucial in defining my interests. I am also indebted to Ravi Ahuja, for formulating historical and theoretical arguments about labour history which have deeply influenced my own thinking. I am still profoundly marked by the teaching I was lucky enough to encounter during my undergraduate and graduate studies, particularly in courses taught by Upinder Singh, Neeladri Bhattacharya, Madhavan Palat, Radhika Singha, Sabyasachi Bhattacharya, and Pratap Bhanu Mehta. I owe a great deal to the two institutions which formed me into a historian, University of Delhi and Jawaharlal Nehru University—both, sadly, now suffering the crippling pressures exerted by the political forces dominant in present-day India, as free intellectual enquiry continues to be encircled, threatened, and punished.

The work and insights of Prabhu Mohapatra and Chitra Joshi, as well as their encouragement, have meant a great deal to me. I have benefited immensely from my exchanges with them, and with many other scholars who have played a role in setting out and debating a future for Indian labour history, particularly Dilip Simeon, Jairus Banaji, Samita Sen, Gopalan Balachandran, Rana Behal, Naveen Chander, Shahana Bhattacharya, Nitin Sinha, and Nitin Varma. The Association of Indian Labour Historians, for many years, has played an indispensable role in stimulating exchanges between scholars researching histories of work, and, like many others working in the field of labour history, I have benefited immensely from the conversations it has enabled.

Inevitably, it is impossible to list all the people who have, at one point or another, shaped this book, and of the intellectual exchanges, conversations, and friendships that have been important to me over the years. An incomplete list of thanks for friendships, interlocutions, critical support, or enabling insights would include: John Game, Franziska Roy, Pradip Kumar Datta, Shipra Nigam, Jayeeta Sharma, Camille Buat, Nitin Sinha, Nitin Varma, Sunalini Kumar, Priya Ranjan, Ben Smith, Erica Wald, Prabhu Mohapatra, Vanessa Caru, Chitra Joshi, Rana Behal, Samita Sen, Dilip Simeon, Jonathan Saha, Uditi Sen, Lara Choksey, Aditya Pant, Angad Singh Chowdhry, Partha Prathim Shil, Rachna Singh, Mahesh Gopalan, Mekhola Gomes, Mandakini Devasher Surie, Samiksha Sehrawat, Shahana Bhattacharya, Rahul Govind, Layli Uddin, Antara Datta, Mukul Mangalik, Harry, Achin Vanaik, Sanjukta Sunderason, Sarah Hodges, Mrinmoyee Majumdar, Sebastian Schwecke, Sarah Hodges, Parismita Singh, Claire Midgley, David Arnold, Stefan Tetzlaff, Manu Sehgal, David Mayer, Gargi Chakrabarty, Meghna Deka, Robert Rehman Raman, Vidhya Raveendranathan, Medha Saxena, Ravi Kant, Shankar Ramaswami, Marcel van der Linden, Priyamvada Gopal, Razak Khan, Aparna Kapadia, Enrique Martino, Ali Raza, Sumeet Mhaskar, Michaela Dimmers, Charles Walton, Sikandar Kumar, Gopalan Balachandran, Anupama Rao, Srirupa Roy, Lalit Vachani, Sourit Bhattacharya, Laura Schwartz, Anna Hajkova, Bodhisattva Kar, Benjamin Zachariah, Meera Viswanathan, Parismita Singh, Jahnavi Phalkey, Ravi Vasudevan, Indivar Kamtekar, Beli, Joerg, Maja, Carolyn Steedman, Maxine Berg, Sulekha Sanyal, David Hardiman, Bikram Ghosh, Pronoti Datta, Deepak Rao, Joya Chatterji, Carrie Heitmeyer, Henrique Espada, Abhinandita Mathur, Tara Puri, Onni Gust, Benoit Dillet, John Thomas, Srirupa Roy, Lalit Vachani, Atishi Marlena, Ankita Pandey, Somak Biswas, Claude Markovits, Parita Mukta, Jon Wilson, and Ajay Gandhi.

There are some enduring friendships which have been particularly crucial in sustaining both this book and myself over the years. Akhila Yechury, Dhivya Janarthanan, Rukmini Barua, Anish Vanaik, Liz Davies, Ahmad Azhar, John Game, and Naveen Chander have, in different ways, been vital sources of support in good and bad times, and equally vital in shaping my sense of the world.

I will always miss Joachim Sailer, whose warmth and generosity deeply enriched my life in the brief time I knew him, and from whom I learned so much both directly and indirectly. I miss Praful Bidwai and Robi Chatterji, who went too early. I will always be saddened by the knowledge that my aunt, Sipra Sarkar, and my grandmother, Sukumari Bhattacharji, did not live to see this book.

I dearly miss Mike Marqusee, who passed away in 2015. Mike's several extraordinary books are a source of constant wonder as well as nourishment for me, and so were the warmth of his friendship, the almost absurdly capacious character of his mind, and his open-hearted relationship with the world. Mike, and his comrade and partner Liz Davies, were a home away from home for me in London. Liz and Mike's political commitments offer a model of what a socialist politics to learn from might look like: open, democratic, and profound.

Anna Sailer has shaped the point of view of this book in more ways than one, and her thought has decisively influenced my own. I feel immensely lucky that her life and mine converged so serendipitously eight years ago. It was the luckiest historical accident I have ever known.

This book is dedicated to my parents, Tanika and Sumit Sarkar. They have goaded, cajoled, and pushed this book into existence; but for them it would never have been begun, let alone completed. Their courage and integrity are, for me, models of how to live and think, in good times and dark. For their love and support, I owe them more than I can say.

Introduction

In 1881, the Government of British India passed a Factory Act, the first of its kind in the subcontinent. This Act produced the first official definition of 'factories' in modern Indian history, as workplaces using steam power and regularly employing over 100 workers. It imposed certain minimal restrictions upon the freedom of employers in a limited range of industrial workplaces, and invested factory workers, most explicitly children, with a slim set of immunities and entitlements. In 1891, the Factory Act was amended: factories were redefined as workplaces employing over fifty workers; the upper age limit of legal 'protection' was raised; weekly holidays were established; and women millworkers were brought within its ambit.[1] In its own time, factory law was experienced as a minor official initiative, but it connected with some of the most potent ideological debates and political oppositions of the age.

This book takes these two pieces of labour legislation as an entry point into the history of 'industrial relations' (the term did not yet exist in its present sense) in colonial India in the last quarter of the nineteenth century. To this end, it combines legal and social history in a way that diverges from most studies of Indian workers. It identifies an emergent 'factory question' built on the problem of protective labour legislation. The cotton mill industry of Bombay (present-day Mumbai), long familiar to labour historians as one of the nodal points of modern Indian capitalism, is the principal focal point of this investigation.

These claims need, however, to be qualified at the outset. While this is a book about law and regulation, it is neither a legislative nor a policy history. While it is preoccupied with the history of factory legislation, it does not offer a full narrative that takes this as its 'object'. And while the book focuses on Bombay's cotton mills, it contains significant departures both from the city and its major industry.

A more precise description of my intentions and strategies in writing this book is therefore needed. Briefly put, I *follow* late nineteenth-century factory law, constituted as a mobile, shifting set of practices and texts, in and out of various interlinked domains. These comprise ideological debate, social reform, commercial politics, lawmaking, administrative practice, and working-class struggle. Rather than a predefined object of study, factory regulation serves as a connective device, linking apparently heterogeneous realms of social experience.

The big theme tackled by the book is best rendered as the emergence of a 'labour question'. I mean this in a very particular sense, as a set of relations and conflicts which crystallized around the problem of work regulation. My claim is that the late nineteenth century witnessed the emergence of two kinds of industrial relations regime in Bombay: first, a domain of labour legislation that was by definition regulatory; second, a domain of strikes and industrial conflicts that demonstrated the limits of law, but was also anchored precisely in the problem of regulation. Mapping the rhythms and relations of forces in this sequence allows us to reassemble some of the connections between law, social relations of domination, and emerging forms of workers' resistance.

This book stands somewhat askew to the dominant themes of Indian labour history since it seeks to introduce new problems rather than directly join existing debates. Some of the key issues in existing traditions of research—migration patterns, the authority of mill jobbers, the politics of the neighbourhood, and the nature of working-class consciousness—are dealt with very lightly. Conversely, I raise a number of questions which have only rarely been thematized by labour historians—the ideologies of factory reform, the politics of factory commissions, the routines of factory inspection, and the earliest waves of strike action in the cotton textile industry. I have, therefore, made certain very specific thematic choices. These are best apprehended through some preliminary reflection on the narrative structure of the book, which is neither transparent nor arbitrary.

It is a narrative that begins with a set of three speculatively posited founding moments. The first, which occupies the second part of this Introduction, is a brief conspectus of the history of factory legislation in Britain in the first half of the nineteenth century, which delineates some of the contours of the specific policy tradition that bore upon the factory question at its point of emergence in India. The second is the elaboration of a reformism addressed to factory questions in India, which I trace through the figure of Mary Carpenter, the Unitarian social activist whose journeys to India, and associations with Indian reformers set on similar paths, placed factory reform upon the agenda of colonial legislation. The third is the antagonism, in the 1870s, between the textile capitalisms of Lancashire and Bombay, the *political* dimensions of which, I argue, outweighed their more commonly identified economic rivalry as an operative context for Indian factory legislation.

In Chapter 1, I attempt a parallel staging of the latter two narratives—Mary Carpenter's social activism and the tension between metropolitan and Indian variants of textile capitalism—as determinants of the (initial) contours of factory law. This entails an analysis of factory reform both as a broad ideological agenda addressed to British India at large, which Carpenter and her associates played the major role in formulating, and as a singular problem focused exclusively on the textile industry of Bombay, which was Lancashire's contribution. The first chapter, therefore, traces the movement of factory law from general principle to singular problem, and establishes Bombay as the privileged locus of debates and conflicts around legislation.

Chapter 2 explores the passage of factory law from policy proposal to statute book through the mediation of Bombay's first Factory Commission and the interventions of Sorabji Shahpurji Bengali, the prominent Parsi social activist who led the middle-class agitation for factory reform after Mary Carpenter's departure. It also considers, at some length, the framing and implications of the provisions of the Factory Act of 1881. Taken as a whole, the opening chapters of the book stage the geographical movements and displacements which have to be understood in order to locate the early history of Indian factory legislation. Beginning in Georgian and Victorian Britain, they trace the movement of the idea of factory legislation—in both its reformist and economic dimensions—into India, and specifically into Bombay. The implication of this is that in the late nineteenth century, Indian factory law emerged as a specifically Bombay-based regulatory field, and this in turn was dependent upon a number of contingent factors.

Chapters 3 and 4 explore some of the key practices of early factory regulation in Bombay on a microhistorical scale. They are best comprehended as forays into 'the life of a law'. Chapter 3 explores the administration of factory law as expressed through the work of inspection. The 'intrusion' of factory inspectors upon the domain of the workplace, I argue, entailed accommodations with, but also posed threats to, the sovereignty of employers within 'the hidden abode of production'.[2] I establish the dynamics of the tripartite relations between employers, inspectors, and workers through detailed microhistorical analysis: a dispute over the fencing of dangerous mill machinery, the accidental death of a young labourer in a factory outside the purview of law, and the conflict between civic officials and a provincial employer of mill labour are identified as staging posts for the tensions inherent in the working of the Factory Act. One of the three incidents I discuss took place outside Bombay city, and another was unconnected to the textile industry. Rather than compromising the unity of analysis, I believe these 'digressions' beyond the Bombay mill industry serve to establish the 'limits' of my enquiry in a precise sense. They enable us to see the frontiers of factory law not as given accomplishments, but as *problems* continually faced and renegotiated by the protagonists of this narrative.

Chapter 4 extends these microhistorical considerations of 'small' events into the domain most emphatically marked out as a province of factory law—the regulation of child labour in mills. The establishment of age-based requirements for factory labour, I argue, generated significant tensions in the life of the first Factory Act. These tensions developed on the basis of the uncertainties of age determination, which gave rise to a problematic bureaucracy of medical inspection, which in turn came into repeated conflict with the Factory Department. Through two case studies, both involving the dilemmas attendant upon the medical certification of mill children, I develop an argument about the ways in which law and illegality sustained each other. I also track a symptomatic shift within the legal and administrative discourses of factory law through a close reading of these episodes. The first of the controversies around certification involved administrative anxieties around the incipient disturbance of relations between the state and industrial capitalists, something portended by a doctor claiming 'unwarranted' fees for medical inspection. The second case, practically identical in its details, disclosed a new worry—the illegitimate extortion of fees from mill children. The question of the 'proper subject' of factory law—employers or (child) workers—therefore is interwoven with these small episodes of administrative 'malpractice'.

A parenthetical remark. The chapters just mentioned are concerned, primarily, with the tensions and torsions within the structure of factory regulation that emerged with the enactment of law. However, these are 'internal' tensions in a very precise sense. Despite the focus on elements that discommoded and modified the rhythms of factory law, the overarching story is one of the (temporary) emergence of a relatively stable structure of routine, everyday administration. The fact that this is permeated with cracks and fissures does not make the emergent system of industrial relations under the aegis of factory law unstructured or indeterminate. The cracks I identify, for the most part, were internal to the very stability of this structure: they were internal or 'inherent' transgressions, rather than deliberate and effective subversions.

The industrial relations of the late 1880s and 1890s, the subject of the last two chapters of the book, clarify this point. It was only in the light of the conflicts of the 1890s—most clearly manifest in successive waves of industrial strikes—that the preceding industrial relations appeared stable and manageable. In other words, this stability was a truth produced retroactively by the turbulence of class struggle that emerged in the 1890s. Chapters 5 and 6 are concerned with the new relations, produced through the pressure of crises of wage payment and the social reproduction of the workforce, that bound a newly anxious colonial state, a crisis-ridden capitalist bloc, and a working class that turned increasingly to militant protest in a time of profound economic trouble. The strike wave of the early 1890s concludes Chapter 5.

The final chapter offers a detailed reconsideration of the effects of bubonic plague in fin-de-siècle Bombay. This is a familiar episode for historians of Bombay, and has been the source of rich investigations of medico-social techniques of control, as well as of popular resistance. My contribution is to situate the plague crisis within the history of industrial labour as the incubator of an unprecedented experience of industrial conflict in 1897, when hierarchies and dispositions of authority in the mills were momentarily overturned and subsequently configured in new ways.

The theme that runs through the last two chapters is not factory law as such but the larger problem of labour regulation, which, I suggest, was posed both from above, in the form of new techniques of social control, and from below, in the form of working-class protests and demands that centred on the regulation of modes of wage payment. The problem of wage payment, I suggest, was *structurally* excluded from the scope of factory legislation from the outset. This very absence became the trigger for momentous social conflict.

Factory law and industrial conflict, then, are situated in my analysis as the two components of a labour question that emerged in the late nineteenth century, defined at its base by the problem of social regulation. This binary division of the realm of 'regulation' can also be rendered, more precisely, as a three-part sequence. This would take the form of tracing the movement of regulation from idea (the founding of factory law) to practice (the routines of factory inspection) to site of conflict (the strike waves of the 1890s). Yet another conceptualization could render this movement as the foundation, operation, and collapse of a putative order of industrial relations in the late nineteenth century. These framing devices are not mutually exclusive: indeed, they imply one another, and each is implicit in the structure of the argument.

Setting the Stage: A Brief History of Factory Law in Britain

> In place of the pompous catalogue of the 'inalienable rights of man' comes the modest Magna Charta [*sic*] of a legally limited working day, which shall make clear 'when the time the worker sells is ended, and when his own begins'.
>
> —Karl Marx, *Capital*, vol. I (London, 1976)

> The new situation created by the Industrial Revelation was boldly met by the statesmen of the day with a wave of Acts, such as Tory Acts, Factory Acts, Satisfactory Acts and Unsatisfactory Acts. The most soothing of these enacted that children under five years of age who worked all day in factories should have meals (at night). This was a Good Thing, as it enabled them to work much faster.
>
> —W.C. Sellar and R.J. Yeatman, *1066 and All That* (London, 1930)

The debates initiated in the provincial and colonial legislatures of India in the 1870s, which culminated in the Factory Acts of 1881 and 1891, drew upon and reformulated English legal precedent. India experienced the pressures of legislation as part of the British Empire, as factory law followed master–servant legislation into the domain of codified imperial labour law.[3] From the 1870s, Parliament and various organized campaigns within Britain closely monitored, and more than occasionally directed, an evolving debate over the need for protective factory law and its possible modalities in a colonial context.

It is important to remember, however, that this reliance upon the British precedent was unique neither to India nor to the Empire. The basic trajectory that governed the installation of protective factory regimes in various parts of the world by the late nineteenth century had, in its main outlines, been mapped out by the early experiments in the United Kingdom (UK), a detail consonant with the British dominance in global industry that marked this entire period, and also with Britain's status as the pioneer and, for a long time, the dominant industrial power in the world. British experiences of factory regulation, then, acquired a modular form, with components that could apparently be reassembled with slight modifications and transplanted in other contexts, either by effective force or by the force of example.

The trajectory of British factory legislation itself was governed by a nervous, shifting relationship between labour militancy, business strategies, and state-driven paternalism.[4] In their global (and particularly colonial) translation across the course of a century, however, these contingent experiences were necessarily elided, and a confusing narrative became a cogent history that retroactively created its own logic of progression, its own explanatory frames, its own necessity. What had emerged at the confluence of many struggles and negotiations became, through a process of radical simplification, a model, to be adapted or adopted according to need.

British factory legislation was inaugurated on the initiative of Sir Robert Peel, pioneer textile capitalist, prominent politician, and grandfather, in a strictly biological sense, of modern English Conservatism.[5] Peel, apparently struck by the dismal conditions of work in his own factories, introduced and stewarded the passage of the Health and Morals of Apprentices Act in 1802, which sought to safeguard factory children—at this stage mainly parish apprentices sent up from workhouses in London to work in up-country, isolated rural mills—from the perils of overwork and 'moral corruption'.[6] He followed this up with another bill in 1815, inspired in part by Robert Owen's philanthropic, proto-socialist activism, which painfully inched its way into law in 1819. In effect, besides mandating rudimentary sanitary arrangements, the first two Factory Acts limited the hours of work for children, defined as between nine and sixteen years of age, to twelve a day.[7] Local magistrates were given the power to appoint independent unpaid inspectors, but no coherent machinery of enforcement was established.[8]

During the turbulent 1820s, as working-class movements and the push for parliamentary reform and suffrage gathered pace, the mantle of factory reform passed from the Tories.[9] The Radical statesman John Hobhouse shepherded two more Factory Acts through Parliament in 1825 and 1831. The 1825 Act reduced the weekly working hours of children from seventy-two to sixty-nine, and the 1831 Act introduced a new category, 'young persons', comprising thirteen–eighteen-year-olds who were brought within the ambit of limited working hours.[10] An important new principle was established parallel to this: magistrates who were proprietors of mills or related to proprietors were declared incapable of adjudicating under the Act.[11]

In the 1830s, the movement for factory reform began to strike deeper roots in the popular politics of the time, especially in the aftermath of the Reform Act of 1832. An unusual alliance of Radicals and Tories—led initially by Michael Sadler and the independent reformer Richard Oastler, and drawing grassroots support from working-class Short Time Committees—sought the extension of factory law to adult workers. Sadler's electoral defeat to Macaulay in the Newark parliamentary election of 1832 was a brief setback, but the rising Tory politician Anthony Ashley-Cooper (at the time known as Lord Ashley, and later the Earl of Shaftesbury) took up cudgels on behalf of factory reform, providing the cause of factory legislation with its most energetic and durable spokesman.[12] Capitalists' opposition to the short-time movement was given a fillip by the Whig victory in 1832. The revised Factory Act of 1833, modified from Ashley's original programme by Lord Althorp (one of the architects of the Reform Act) refused to legislate for adult workers, focusing on children and 'young persons'. The 1833 Act owed much to the support of large manufacturers in new industrial towns, who used regulation to undercut competition from smaller manufacturers operating rural water-powered mills.[13] As Howard Marvel argues, the 1833 Act was, in effect, a Whig coup, watering down Ashley's proposals in the interests of large textile manufacturers.

Nevertheless, it was a piece of legislation of immense historical significance. As Marx observed, the history of factory legislation in any real and effective sense dates to the 1833 Act.[14] This was in large part because it finally set in motion an organized machinery of factory inspection. This ran in tandem with the official investigations of 1832 and 1833, which made working lives and conditions of work newly visible in the public sphere. In addition to the Factory Commissioners, medical experts and independent investigators like Peter Gaskell—who, in a sense, anticipated the later investigations of Engels and Mayhew in the 1840s—built up a powerful body of public opinion against the abuse of workers' bodies and lives through overwork and appalling working conditions. One of the consequences of this was the beginning of a sequence of extensions of factory regulation beyond the textile factories to which their operation had hitherto been limited. Printworks were regulated for the first time in 1845, and between 1860 and 1878 the remit of factory legislation would expand to cover, among others, bleaching and dye works, hosiery and lace factories, potteries, brick and tile works, and a range of smaller workshops.[15]

A major consequence of the expansion of factory-based capitalism, and the slew of investigations that attended it, was the production of a vigorous critique of women's industrial work, which was condemned as much for the moral 'corruption' it produced as for its exploitative dimensions.[16] The Mines Act of 1842, another initiative spurred by Ashley, took such concern to its logical limits, excluding women from mining labour altogether, and playing, according to many feminist historians, a pivotal role in enforcing a gendered notion of industrial work that rested upon the figure of the male breadwinner.[17]

Industrial struggles around the question of factory legislation continued in the late 1830s and 1840s. Parliamentary and administrative initiatives, the working-class agitation for a 'general working day' of ten hours, and the strategies of employers intersected to extend factory law. In 1844, at the initiative of Ashley, who headed a new Factory Committee in 1840, yet another Factory Act was passed, following the Mines Act in restricting the working hours of women. A new category of vulnerable workers was thus produced in the 1840s. For workers engaged in the short-time movement, this represented an oblique triumph. While Parliament refused—as it did through the century—to legislate for adult male workers, the restriction of the labour of women, children, and young persons, most dramatically in the textile industry, had the effect of reducing working hours in general, and effectively creating a 'normal' twelve-hour day. Women and children comprised the bulk of the labour force in the early cotton industry. If their work was restricted, it effectively restricted the hours of work in the mill as a whole. This accounts for a persistent peculiarity of the history of factory law in Britain—the frequent separation between the question of the restriction of working hours in itself (which, by the end of the century, was held by many economists and politicians to be a good thing for industry) and the explicit regulation of adult male labour, which was included within factory legislation only in the realm of accidents.[18]

It is no coincidence that the struggles over factory legislation were most bitter in the heyday of Chartism, and generally ran parallel to a sustained upsurge in artisanal, plebeian, and industrial working-class politics. The short-time committees effected a direct link between this world and that of factory regulation, though their political alliances may well have led them towards Toryism and Parliamentary Radicalism rather than the independent world of popular politics that Thompson describes. At the same time, the question of factory regulation was bathed in the democratic politics that dominated the 1830s and 1840s: the Tolpuddle martyrs took their secret oath of union allegiance a year after Althorp's Act (and were convicted and deported for it), and the Chartists were to formulate the demand for universal male suffrage shortly afterwards. Anchored in these contexts, the meaning of factory regulation was radically ambivalent. A top-down measure of regulation in its conception, it intersected, through an osmotic process, with movements from below.

In 1847, the intrusion of state power upon industrial relationships was intensified further. Ashley shepherded yet another bill through Parliament that further restricted working hours, to ten in the day for women and young persons, a measure that by implication restricted the working hours of *all* workers. Huge celebrations broke out in the mill districts: '[B]roadsheets elaborately and expensively printed in black and gold setting out the terms of the new Act and commemorating the leaders of the struggle were widely distributed.'[19] Ashley's stock soared among short-time agitators: it was never to be higher among workers than it briefly was at this time.

A sustained employer offensive in the late 1840s confronted this changed state of industrial relations. Driven by the economic crisis of 1846–7, and perhaps emboldened by the collapse of Chartism, mill owners launched what Marx described as a 'revolt of capital', slashing wages in anticipation of the coming reduction of hours.[20] For the first time, many mill owners also began to work their labourers in shifts, thereby instituting a substantially new industrial practice and managing, as a result, to keep their factories open for as long as eighteen hours. This generated fresh opportunities for evasion and made the work of factory inspectors extremely difficult, though some of them, like Leonard Horner, responded aggressively, instituting a series of prosecutions that went against normal inspectorial caution.[21]

In the midst of these fractious times, Ashley struck a compromise that hurt his reputation among workers badly. This took the form of yet another piece of legislation. In return for the concession of a fixed working day for women, children, and young persons (whereby they could only be worked between six in the morning and six in the evening on weekdays, and till two in the afternoon on Saturdays), he agreed to a reduction in compulsory mealtimes, effectively extending the working week from fifty-eight to sixty hours.[22] This was the fulcrum of the Factory Act of 1850, the seventh piece of protective legislation in the century, and the fourth since 1833. This was the climax of the formative and pivotal period of factory legislation, the two decades between 1830 and 1850, which witnessed the birth of most of the patterns of regulation that were to persist through the century.

Between the 1850s and the 1880s, the pace of legislation slowed, though its scope was extended. Non-textile factories were brought within its remit, again in large measure as a consequence of the parliamentary activism of Ashley, who had in the meantime become the seventh Earl of Shaftesbury. After the Children's Employment Commission of 1863–5 revealed the extent of child labour in factories that did not use steam power (which, till that point, had been a necessary condition for the operation of factory law), factories were redefined as any premises constituting 'one trade establishment' in which fifty or more persons were employed, irrespective of the kind of power used. This was given legal form by the Workshop Regulation Act of 1867.[23] In 1875–6, the Home Secretary, Viscount Cross, successfully argued for the consolidation of existing factory and workshop laws, which led to the enactment of a Factory and Workshop (Consolidation) Act in 1878.[24] This, more or less, was how matters stood when factory legislation for India began to acquire the status of an official imperative.

Factory legislation in Britain, then, emerged within a complicated matrix of industrial tensions, political debate, administrative practice, and official investigation. It evoked hopes and apprehensions that were promiscuously distributed across the social field, appearing at times as a reflex of industrial competition among mill owners, at other times as an adjunct to working-class agitation, and at other times still as state-authored commands which 'balanced' the claims of capital and labour. The polyvalent meanings factory law offered to its many interlocutors are perhaps best rendered with reference to Marx's *Capital*, where the section on factory legislation is bookended by two statements that apparently contradict one another. At the beginning of the section, Marx declares that 'nothing is more characteristic of the spirit of capital than the history of the English Factory Acts between 1833 and 1864'.[25] At the end of the chapter, he describes factory legislation as 'the modest Magna Charta [*sic*] of a legally limited working day'.[26] Both these meanings are, then, immanent within the codes of factory law. They establish its status as a field of force that could be appropriated, in opposed ways, by employers and workers alike.

What did the principle of state intervention in industrial relations imply? Most obviously, it signalled an expanded sense of the capacities and responsibilities of the state, increasingly mediated through a highly organized bureaucratic apparatus. Two dimensions, both of Benthamite provenance, are relevant here. First, the extension of the logic of officially commissioned enquiry moving through discrete stages: the identification of the problem, the amassing of empirical evidence, the weighing and evaluation of the official knowledge thus produced, and its eventual translation into legal doctrine.[27] This was an administrative tradition that travelled overseas with colonial rule, and would be played out in significant ways in the Indian context, where a long tradition of state-organized official investigation of industrial labour was initiated with the Bombay Factory Commission of 1875.

The second dimension was the establishment of a highly centralized, and *expert*, professional bureaucracy that would execute and monitor such law. The principle of regularized inspection that was instituted by law in 1833 was typical of this. The state expanded its powers by intruding upon a domain of 'free' interaction between employers and workers. Originally piecemeal social interventions were thus knitted into a putative logic of social *policy*, defined by new kinds of bureaucratic expertise, which began to acquire its fullest form in the mid-Victorian era.

For the most part, inspectors preferred to avoid open confrontation with powerful industrialists, opting for 'negotiated compliance' instead.[28] However, as the conflict between mill owners and inspectors generated by the ten hours' controversy demonstrates, at particular moments of tension relations could become more fractious, and a basically conciliatory 'regulatory style' could break down.

The experience of factory legislation in nineteenth-century Britain thus produced a specific model of lawmaking, and a lawmaking and social policy, both of which would be modified within the colonial context. It also bore the weight of a profound ideological tension, between the principle of protecting the vulnerable and the principle of non-interference with adult male labour. A speech in 1891 by Lord Salisbury, once Secretary of State for India and at that time the Prime Minister, renders this tension eloquently.

> Our rule is, with respect to the labour of those who are unprotected, women and children, Parliament is right to interfere; that with respect to all the causes that affect the health of the community Parliament has the right to interfere with industry; but that with the ordinary labour of the adult man Parliament has not a right to interfere. And I believe that if you once leave that solid ground of principle, *if you once pass the rubicon that separates you from the domain of Socialism*, you will part with your commercial and industrial supremacy, and some decades or generations hence will shrink back to your old ground with all that lost for which you once might have struggled.[29]

Salisbury said this at a gathering of the Associated Chambers of Commerce, in the context of a revival of militant trade union activity directed at achieving an eight-hour day. These phrases also attest a durable worry about the possibility of *containing* the meanings of factory legislation, and thus mastering an unruly discursive and ideological field. To define the adult male as a legitimate recipient of 'protection' would, given the ways in which discourses of 'protection' were shaped by gender and childhood, involve crossing the line between paternalist protection and the recognition of a right, open to being politically deployed.

The principle of non-interference with adult male labour was a key component of debates throughout the century. In this light, legislation for the factory child, the principal focus of early Victorian legislation, appears not principally as a necessary humanitarian intervention (which it was) but, more significantly, as a desperate attempt to forestall the possibility that the principle of legislation might slide beyond its 'natural' boundaries and infect the world of 'free' labour. The master and the adult male factory 'hand', in the terms of this philosophy, were to be bound by nothing except a mutual contract.

Of all the motifs that made up the arsenal of Free Trade ideology in the nineteenth century, few were as durable as this. It organized and generalized the interests of capitalist employers. It cut through the industrial working class, which, despite the prominence of political campaigns for the restriction of the working day, was necessarily ambivalent about the pecuniary consequences of legislative interference with hours of labour. Parliamentarians, including Lord Shaftesbury, who explicitly claimed to represent the interests of workers, balked at any direct intervention in this terrain. It is noteworthy that the most radical proposal Shaftesbury ever forced through Parliament, in 1847, achieved legislative restriction of the hours worked by adult men obliquely rather than directly, through the protection of 'vulnerable' categories of worker: women and children. Such protection was extensive enough to prevent men as well as women and young persons' from working beyond the stipulated time, but the point is that till the twentieth century, in both metropole and colony, this could *only* be permitted to happen obliquely.

Seen in economic terms, this was a somewhat incongruous preoccupation. Factory legislation for women and children, in a number of occupations, had pushed down working hours in general. As Hobsbawm has pointed out, by the last quarter of the nineteenth century the restriction of working hours had entered legislative and public common sense, and this involved the lessening of work hours for adult men as well.[30] However, the *symbolic* importance of 'non-interference' with adult male labour had a weight of its own. Besides protecting the material interests of employers, the denial of legislative protection to adult male labourers played a specific ideological role. The separation of 'able' from 'vulnerable' workers, along the axes of age and gender, sought to prevent factory protection from acquiring the status of a general principle covering all workers.

In the long run this produced a deeply bifurcated structure of industrial relations. Factory regulation became an exercise chiefly in the identification and amelioration of *vulnerability*, and its destined subjects were always those who were deemed unable to protect themselves. Inspectors and magistrates became de facto spokespersons for the 'voiceless', a profoundly ambiguous identity that contained both the possibility of socially 'progressive' official activism and the hierarchies and dependencies embedded in this. The only universal claim to protection that all workers enjoyed, irrespective of the minute gradations of vulnerability, was in the realm of accidents and safety. Other than this, real and potential grievances that could affect all classes of workers—wages being the most obviously crucial of these—were largely left untouched by law. The identification of vulnerability thus became simultaneously the anchor, the function, and the absolute limit of the operations of 'protection'. As it marked out the domains which could be legitimately 'protected', it also marked out the domain of employer freedom.

All this rested on an ideology of free labour and of freely contracted relations between 'masters and men'. This, as Robert Steinfeld has argued persuasively, was in essence a fiction. The world of legally untrammelled industrial relations posited by free-trade ideology never really existed, since labour markets have always been regulated in some manner or another. Freedom of contract for labourers through most of the nineteenth century meant freedom at the point of entry, and emphatically not at the point of exit. This was sustained by statutes and common-law practices enforced by magistrates, which compelled the 'specific performance' of labour contracts and contained punitive injunctions against breaches. It was the articulation of prolonged workers' agitations and legislative changes between the 1850s and 1870s—significantly, at the same time as the extension of factory law—that finally terminated nonpecuniary compulsions to work. The Arcadian world of free labour that dominated political economy and political discourse, therefore, was ironically produced and sustained by the very state interference that it was supposed to be the antithesis to. It was never, contrary to its organizing myth, a field defined by a spontaneous social contract, but was instead always overdetermined by state intervention.[31]

Implications

R.K. Das' description of the decades before the First World War, as the 'regulation period' in the history of Indian labour, inadvertently stumbles upon the crucial problem that attends their reconstruction.[32] Factory law was conceived, implemented, and spread from metropole to colony in an era when Free Trade acted as a hegemonic ideology, structuring not only the foundations of commercial and industrial practice but also the discourses of both justification and opposition. A simple example will suffice: Lancashire's and Bombay's capitalists each accused the other of violating the basic tenets of Free Trade. The free movement of commodities and the equality of terms of trade—Lancashire's siren calls—were counterposed to the insistence, on the part of Bombay's textile capitalists and their allies, upon the freedom of the relations between employers and employed at the point of production. Conversely, each side interpreted the strength of the other as an effect of the 'protection' it enjoyed, the word being as opprobrious as any in the discourse of the age. The opposed positions were, at this level, contrasting interpretations of the same principle, each unassailable within its own terms.

In an era when the right to economic freedom—construed in very particular ways—was an article of faith, state intervention could only be justified negatively, as 'regulation' preventing the worst excesses of the capitalist system from coming to fruit. The debilitating physical and social consequences of industrial production enabled regulation as a necessary evil: the dominant problem, then, had to be the *limitation* of regulation. In Chapter 2 of this book, I take stock of a suggestion made by W.O. Meade-King, a factory inspector brought over to India from Britain, to the effect that the number of workers employed should play no role in the definition of a factory. This was passed over in embarrassed silence by contemporary policymakers, and, as a matter of fact, *never* passed into law: its realization seems as impossible today as it did in the 1880s. Indian worlds of labour have generally been bewilderingly diverse. They make any attempt at full regulation look like Borges' fabled map, which sought a 1:1 correspondence with the world. Yet, this is not a self-evident truth and it has precise consequences. It is not self-evident because a fuller regulation of employer practice might well have released social tensions difficult to anticipate and regulate, and, therefore, threatening from the perspective of any sort of state order in a capitalist society. It has consequences because every exclusion, however 'minor', can galvanize a range of creative strategies on the part of capital. Douglas Haynes writes of employers' strategies in small textile units in western India immediately after Independence, a time when the drive to regulate capitalist production and 'protect' workers was probably stronger than it has ever been in modern Indian history. The weaver-capitalists Haynes writes of, however, managed to circumvent factory legislation by building walls within their workshops and registering different sets of machines between different legal 'occupiers'. Thus, dozens of miniscule 'factories', each registered as a different enterprise, functioned within what were actually integrated production units.[33]

The practical obstacles to a fuller factory regulation, then, often seemed insurmountable even in the time apparently conducive to it. And in the present, across the world and especially sharply in India, the drift of policymaking is in the opposite direction, as the very principle of legal immunities for workers appears terminally threatened. In the historical period surveyed here, the dynamic curiously resembles the present day, despite the end of old ideals of laissez-faire (from which the currently hegemonic system, often called 'neoliberalism', diverges in key aspects).[34] Non-regulation itself appeared as a positive good in the decades dominated by laissez-faire ideology and practice: in India, the decades between the 1870s and the 1910s. It could only be sustained as such, though, if the worst excesses of industrial capitalism could somehow be curbed, and the fiction of freedom supplemented by the fiction of social progress. It would, of course, be crude to see this as a concrete, continuous *strategy* on the part of either capital or state, for this suggests a level of cynicism that does not allow for ideological self-deception as a living, generative practice of capitalist social life, and reduces it to *mere* illusion or error. Viewed individually, each state-led decision about the factory in late Victorian Bombay (and India) was governed by specific imperatives, animated by unique points of view and capable of a range of inflexions. The regularities, which emerge when these decisions are put in relation, however, are far from accidental.

Nineteenth-century factory law imposed barriers to the employment of those who were liable to be more easily exploited. It prescribed standards of safety. It restricted the duration for which labour could legitimately be exploited. It instituted powers and protocols of scrutiny, complaint, adjudication and penalty against employers. These were not arbitrary decisions; they flowed from the potentials and constraints of factory law as a legal, administrative, and discursive *form*. Factory legislation is governed by a certain internal teleology: it seeks to establish 'industrial relations' as a stable body of rules tending to an idealized harmony between worker and employer, adjudicated by the state. The operation is delicate, for it not only delegitimizes certain forms of exploitation but legitimizes others—if violations of the law are named and made visible, employers' freedoms within the boundaries of the law are rendered absolute and, therefore, do not need to be named as such. It not only concretely identifies a finite set of impermissible violations, but also renders the background to this set abstract. Thus, a vast array of exploitative practices is naturalized, and becomes integrated into the smooth functioning of capitalist orders, as common sense, 'the way things are'. Absences of illegality are rendered into absences of conflict, and thereby into proofs of consent and consensus.

Yet this necessarily fails. At an empirical level, new ways of circumventing legal regulation have never been hard to devise. Haynes' example is a perfect instance of this. Another, more germane to the historical period discussed in this book, is the very establishment of 'protected' forms of labouring experience—the working child under twelve years of age, working women, and legally defined factories with over 100 workers. These declare lines of inclusion and exclusion which are imprecise and hard to police. How is age to be determined? Under what conditions can one workplace be stably assimilated to the category 'factory' and another denied this status? Additionally, the very regulation of standards *within* the 'line of protection' often tends to intensify the exploitation of those who stand outside it, thus regularly triggering challenges to, or reconsiderations of, the limits of law. The fullness of regulation is limited by the principle of exclusion.

This principle of exclusion may be viewed in two ways. Debates over factory law largely addressed the problem of which kinds of workplaces and workers might plausibly, and practically, be brought within the purview of the law. Yet, this was silently underpinned by another kind of decision about inclusion/exclusion: what were the areas of working-class social experience which it might be permissible to regulate through legal means? At this stage, it may be useful to briefly introduce a distinction between the problem of law and the problem of social regulation.

Social regulation has to be conceived as something distinct from law and from what the state did/does—even though in practice the two domains often overlap. Custom regulates, borders regulate, family regulates, and so, of course, does the very fact of employment. The regulations intrinsic to these forms of social life may or may not correspond with the law: the latter may 'interfere' with them, reinforce them, cancel them, or be resisted by them. Within this matrix of social relations of regulation, law's *initial* function is the separation of the domains of the formal and informal, public and private. It is the decision about which domains belong to the province of law and which stand outside it that initiates law's entry into a given matrix of relations—field, factory, school, family, sexuality, or prison. This is not the only, nor necessarily the principal, function of law in its varied social contexts. It is, however, always the *first* function, since it precedes all others. Law makes the cut and draws the line which constitutes its separation from—and determines its effectivity in regulating—the field of social practice.

Factory law spelt out a schedule of immunities and putative obligations that feebly governed the everyday practices of industrial employment. It shackled itself, however, to the gates of the factory, and refused to follow workers into their homes and neighbourhoods. The social reproduction of the mill workforce was regulated by the 'free' play of market forces. In practice, this meant coterminous regulation by family budgets, the prices of foodgrains, moneylenders' interest, and rent paid to landlords who often doubled as employers—in short, the financial calculations that were adjoined to the everyday social relations of workers. Social reproduction was systematically separated from the domain of law and emerged as the domain of 'informal' practices (figured as such precisely because of the legal fiction that hived off public and private, formal and informal domains of practice).[35]

The problem of wages, however, stood at the fountainhead of the problem of social reproduction. Wages were the great exception to the legal field of force that composed the formal regulation of factory work. Here the sovereignty of employers, construed in contemporary ideology as the freedom of relations between employers and employed (in other words, a variant of contractual freedom), was unquestionable. In other words, the issue of remuneration, more likely than any other to provoke conflicts of interest between workers and employers, was boxed into the realm of strictly *private* relations that were *internal* to mill work, beyond the scope of public regulation. In the nineteenth century, the payment of wages and the employment of adult male labour were the two classical instances of laissez-faire in industrial labour relations. Drawing upon a British principle that had effectively been universalized across the world, legal systems regulating industrial labour were premised upon the legal fiction of faith in the absolute autonomy of the relations between employers and workers. But while the public regulation of male labour remained a constant, disturbing presence on the margins of factory regulation (indeed making its way into the domain of law in 1911, when legislative protection was extended to adult men), factory workers' wages, till the end of the First World War and the shift in regulatory *epistemes* and repertoires in the 1920s, remained outside the purview of state control.[36]

So the principle of exclusion runs, 'organically', through the formulation of protective labour legislation. Something like factory law, therefore, has to appear in the very shape of its concrete impossibility. If it really were possible to anticipate every single breach of law in advance, to prescribe correctives and preventives for each body broken on a machine, each coin pocketed from a monthly payment by an intermediary, or each underage child hidden in a sack of cotton wool, we would be back with Borges' map. If, further, law were to extend to all dimensions of the work relationship and engross all the forms of 'social regulation' structuring working-class life, it would lose its coherence. Alternatively, we would already be in a realm beyond capitalist exploitation and, therefore, beyond the remit of law as regulation, which has to presuppose the regularity, if not the ubiquity, of violation. So decisions about legitimate forms of exclusion are a permanent feature of law. But if the principle of exclusion is stable, its content is not—it is, on the contrary, perpetually a shifting ground of contestation. There is a structural impossibility at work here, which means that the law formalizes its own failure or its own lack of 'fullness'.

Marx conceived of factory law as the moment when capital encounters a blockage in its relations with labour, when the worker appears as subject rather than object (or, more accurately, a subject precisely *because* he is absolutely objectified). The worker confronts his master with demands that regulate the terms of his exploitation: 'You can exploit me this far and no further,' he says. This, obviously enough, cannot be transposed directly to actual historical contexts: this is not its purpose. Rather, such a narrative acts in a Hegelian manner or, alternatively, as a 'legal fiction'—it 'posits the presuppositions' which *have to be at work* for factory law and, indeed, factory relations to exist in the first place. The paradox of this relationship is summed up by Marx in a fleeting allusion in a section of *Capital*, where he speaks of the inscription of workers' resistance in the very state that was 'ruled by landlord and capitalist'.[37] This accounts for the peculiar character of 'progressive' laws and institutions such as those which establish workers' rights (Bourdieu describes these as 'the left hand of the state').[38] At its most fundamental level, then, 'protective' labour legislation materializes a problem inherent in all forms of social balance instituted by states that are determined by the rights of property and moved by the needs of capital. It is the very form of a certain structural impossibility within capitalist orders.

Notes

1. John Rae, 'The New East India Factory Act', *The Economic Journal* 1, no. 4 (December 1891): 803–6; D.A. Barker, 'Factory Legislation in India', *The Economic Journal* 21, no. 84 (December 1911): 643–8.
2. Karl Marx, *Capital: A Critique of Political Economy*, vol. 1, chapter 6 (Harmondsworth: Penguin Books), 1976.
3. See Douglas Hay and Paul Craven (eds), *Masters, Servants and Magistrates in Britain and the Empire, 1562–1955* (Chapel Hill, 2004) for the most extensive survey available of the transmission of master–servant law through the British Empire.
4. See M.W. Thomas, *The Early Factory Legislation: A Study in Legislative and Administrative Evolution* (Leigh-On-Sea: Thames Bank Publishing, 1948); B.L. Hutchins and A. Harrison, *A History of Factory Legislation* (London: P.S. King & Son, 1903); D. Greer and J.W. Nicolson, *The Factory Acts in Ireland: 1802–1914* (Dublin: Four Courts Press, 2003); Paul Mantoux, *The Industrial Revolution in the Eighteenth Century* (London: Methuen Press, 1928).
5. His son, whom he imaginatively named after himself, went on to become Prime Minister, presiding over the dismemberment of old Toryism and the emergence of a new, politically coherent Conservative Party.
6. Thomas, *The Early Factory Legislation*, pp. 10–12.
7. George Henry Wood, 'Factory Legislation, Considered with Reference to the Wages, & c., of the Operatives Protected Thereby', *Journal of the Royal Statistical Society* 65, no. 2 (June 1902): 285.

8. Thomas, *The Early Factory Legislation*, pp. 17–27.

9. Thomas, *The Early Factory Legislation*, pp. 14–46; see also E.P. Thompson, *The Making of the English Working Class* (New York: Pantheon, 1963).

10. Wood, 'Factory Legislation', pp. 285–6.

11. Thomas, *The Early Factory Legislation*, pp. 27–30.

12. J.L. Hammond and Barbara Hammond, *Lord Shaftesbury* (London: Constable, 1923); Georgina Battiscombe, *Shaftesbury* (London: Constable, 1974), pp. 77–92.

13. Howard Marvel, 'Factory Regulation: A Reinterpretation of the Early English Experience', *Journal of Law and Economics* 20, no. 2, (October 1977): 379–402. Also Peter Mandler, 'Cain and Abel: Two Aristocrats and the Early Victorian Factory Acts', *The Historical Journal* 27, no. 1 (March 1984): 83–109. Mandler argues that the interventions of the Tory Ashley and the Whig Morpeth in the 1830s, both in support of factory legislation, signal a conjunctural fluidity of ideological positions, as old certainties and anchors of political identity dissolved, and the leading younger votaries of either political persuasion found themselves confronted with new choices for which party precedent had not prepared them.

14. Marx, *Capital*, p. 390.

15. Wood, 'Factory Legislation', pp. 284–6.

16. Patricia Johnson, *Hidden Hands: Working-Class Women and Victorian Social-Problem Fiction* (Athens: Ohio University Press, 2001), pp. 19–45.

17. The precise effects of mining regulation, however, have been disputed within feminist historical studies: see Jane Humphries, 'Protective Legislation, the Capitalist State and Working-Class Men: The Case of the 1842 Mines Regulation Act', in *On Work: Historical, Comparative and Theoretical Approaches*, edited by R.E. Pahl (Oxford: Blackwell, 1988), pp. 95–125.

18. Greer and Nicolson, *The Factory Acts*, pp. 68–70.

19. Thomas, *The Early Factory Legislation*, p. 297.

20. For a good discussion of the more conflictual dimensions of the mill owner–inspector relationship, see David MacGregor, *Hegel, Marx and the English State* (Toronto: Westview Press, 1992).

21. MacGregor, *Hegel, Marx and the English State*, pp. 204–72.

22. Thomas, *The Early Factory Legislation*, pp. 313–14.

23. Greer and Nicolson, *The Factory Acts*, p. 50; Wood, 'Factory Legislation', p. 285.

24. Greer and Nicolson, *The Factory Acts*; Wood, 'Factory Legislation', pp. 60–6

25. Marx, *Capital*, vol. I, p. 390.

26. Marx, *Capital*, vol. I, p. 416.

27. The logic of such knowledge production, it must be remembered, had implications that went far beyond the realm of pure administration. It is no

coincidence that factory commissions and Parliamentary Blue Books—the classic prototypes of an official industrial literature—emerged at the same time as two other new literary forms: the independent investigator's report (the classic examples being Engels and Mayhew) and the industrial novel, which reached its apogee with Dickens' *Hard Times* and Elizabeth Gaskell's *Mary Barton*.

28. P.W.J. Bartrip and P.T. Fenn, 'The Evolution of Regulatory Style in the Nineteenth Century British Inspectorate', *Journal of Law and Society* 10, no. 2 (winter 1983): 201–22.

29. *Times*, 5 March 1891 [emphasis mine].

30. Eric Hobsbawm, *Industry and Empire: An Economic History of Britain since 1750* (New York: The New Press, 1968), p. 101.

31. Robert Steinfeld, *Coercion, Contract and Free Labour in the Nineteenth Century* (Cambridge: Cambridge University Press, 2001).

32. R.K. Das, *Factory Labour in India* (Berlin, 1923), pp. 184–5.

33. Douglas E. Haynes, *Small-Town Capitalism in Western India: Artisans, Merchants, and the Making of the Informal Economy, 1870–1960* (Cambridge: Cambridge University Press, 2012), pp. 287–90.

34. See Philip Mirowski, *Never Let a Serious Crisis Go to Waste: How Neoliberalism Survived the Financial Meltdown* (London: Verso, 2013) for a compelling recent account of the ideological make-up and novelty of modern neoliberal thinking.

35. This line of analysis is consonant with that offered, in a different context, by Prabhu Mohapatra in *Situating the Renewal: Reflections on Labour Studies in India* (Noida: V.V. Giri National Labour Institute, 1998).

36. Interestingly, this was not the case in work regimes where the 'formal' freedoms of the labourer were more ambiguous. The legal regulation of wage levels, for instance, became a feature of plantation labour legislation in India when, at the same time, a similar concession to the interests of factory workers was unthinkable. Workers in tea plantations in Assam were always more bound by non-economic forces, and it was precisely in muted recognition of this that they were granted a minimum wage. Intervention into wages, housing, food, and shelter could, within this matrix, be plausibly construed as an index of unfreedom.

37. Marx, *Capital*, vol. I, chapter 10.

38. Pierre Bourdieu, *Acts of Resistance: Against the Tyranny of the Market* (New York: The New Press, 1998), chapter 1.

PART I

THE BIRTH OF FACTORY REGULATION

1

Imperial Entanglements

In the second half of the 1870s, the prospect of a Factory Act for India entered debates around colonial policymaking. Proposals to limit the hours of work in Indian factories and to limit the employment of children and women emerged in both metropole and colony. As contemporaries debated the utility of these proposals, sharply opposed arguments also crystallized over their provenance. As such, the historical question of the 'origins' of factory legislation was already present in late nineteenth-century debate.

While factory regulation would fade out of historical discussions of Indian labour in the twentieth century, contemporary scholarship still bears the mark of earlier arguments. It is possible to present two explanations of the passage of factory law which have each, in contrasting ways, inserted themselves into the 'common sense' of historical accounts of Indian labour relations. Taken in combination, these offer a shadowy outline of the field of force that governed the 'factory question' at its inception in colonial India.

The first of these emphasizes individual, reformist efforts. To begin with, there is a remark made by the great British social historians of the Industrial Revolution, John and Barbara Hammond, in their 1925 biography of Lord Shaftesbury: 'Shaftesbury had one further success, for, after several vain attempts, he secured at last a Factory Act for India.'[1] Here Indian factory legislation appears as a consequence of the earlier campaigns for British factory reform. But contemporaries equally drew attention to another person's exertions. On 30 July 1875, Lord Salisbury, the Secretary of State for India, explained his decision to push for Indian factory reform in these terms: 'I was induced to take this course by the efforts of a lady whose name cannot be mentioned without honour among all who are interested in moral progress and philanthropic effort in India—I mean Miss Carpenter.'[2] Mary Carpenter, the Unitarian social activist who established the principle of Ragged Schools for the 'improvement' of British street children in 1846 and spearheaded the campaign for juvenile reformatory and industrial education in Britain, was often acknowledged as the real progenitor of the Factory Act. She had made four visits to India between 1866 and 1875, initially to campaign for institutional arrangements for women's education, a reformist schedule which eventually swelled to also engross a 'half-time' Factory Act with educational provisions for child workers.

The other explanation of factory legislation in India focuses on Lancashire and Bombay as centres of two increasingly antagonistic textile capitalisms, one metropolitan and the other colonial. This line of interpretation can be traced back to the first public discussions of the question of factory law in India. For instance, in December 1878 the Bombay newspaper *Native Opinion* bemoaned the Factory Bill that had just been introduced in the Imperial Legislative Council, and accused its initiators of seeking to 'gladden Manchester'.[3] On the same day, another newspaper, the *Gujarat Mitra*, suggested that S.S. Bengali (the reformer who introduced the Bill, and a major protagonist in the following chapter) had taken the burden of preparing the provisions in order to 'save Europeans from the odium of advocating it in Manchester's interests'.[4]

In the late nineteenth century, the identification of Lancashire's economic self-interest at the base of Indian factory legislation served several purposes. It helped unite Indian capitalists around a common enemy; it played an important role in the emerging nationalist critique of the colonial economy; and it helped legitimize the extremely exploitative labour practices of Bombay's mill owners. Some of the historical work on the politics of business and early nationalism—for instance, Bipan Chandra's important work on economic nationalism—has acknowledged the crucial role of Bombay's resistance to Lancashire's demands for factory regulation in the 1870s, and explained the ineffectiveness of the Factory Act of 1881 in these terms.[5] Other accounts, such as the business and labour histories written between the 1920s and the 1970s, see the Factory Act simply as a capitulation to Lancashire's economic interests. The precise coordinates of explanation vary; what remains constant is the identification of factory legislation, in a more or less direct manner, with the imperatives of commercial tensions in the age of Empire.

Existing accounts of the emergence of factory law are clearly insufficient. On the one hand, we have a story of influential individuals 'making history' on the basis of their best intentions. On the other, we have the work of capital conceived as conspiracy. In the existing scholarship, the two trajectories of understanding never meet and are never placed in relation to one another.

These historical perspectives are hobbled less by their 'errors' than by their casual character. The historiography of Indian industrial labour has concentrated chiefly on the period after the First World War, which is understandable, given the intensity of workers' movements between the 1920s and Independence. The nineteenth century appears as a backcloth to this narrative, and factory law is relegated to the margins because of its evident weaknesses and the failures that attended its implementation. The corollary of this is that these inadequacies have not been probed in order to yield new historical problems. The most sustained accounts of factory law, therefore, are to be found in much earlier work, such as the books written by J.C. Kydd, S.G. Panandikar, R.K. Das, and Ahmad Mukhtar. These tend to be rigidly teleological accounts of progress and/or failure, evaluative rather than exploratory.

What all this implies for the history of factory law is a fragmented tradition of mostly secondary or casual observations, and laundry lists of unconnected 'causes' and 'results' of factory legislation. The problem this chapter poses, then, is one of historical determination. It is clear that the adventure of social reform and the growth of commercial hostilities both, in some sense, 'determined' factory legislation. But what does this mean? If we take 'determination' in Raymond Williams' sense (as a force that sets limits and exerts pressures), what precisely were the relationships between Mary Carpenter's activism, Lancashire's and Bombay's animosities, and the passage of factory law in 1881?[6] What enabled these determinations, and how did they, in turn, generate or constrain the meanings of factory law?

Methodologically, this chapter starts with a simple proposition: social reform and commercial rivalry exhibit two modes of imperial entanglement which lie at the base of the emergence of factory regulation in India. Both Mary Carpenter's activism and Lancashire's advocacy of factory legislation were made possible by the new terms of imperial power that bore on post-Mutiny India. Parliament was more directly involved in the administration of Indian affairs. This was also an era when the telegraph and the expansion of steam-shipping intensified traffic between the British and Indian centres of Empire (Whitehall and Calcutta [present-day Kolkata]), and enabled speedier movement of people, capital, commands, and ideas. At the same time, as Karuna Mantena has pointed out, post-Mutiny colonial rule was marked by escalating worries about interventions that might transform the texture of Indian social relations and practices, an attitude that was flanked by an advancing conservatism.[7]

The second half of the nineteenth century was an age marked by a tremendous global expansion of capitalism. Methods of accumulation and investment, modes of labour control, developments in technology, and competition among imperial powers for land, markets, workers, and materials knitted much of the globe into similar patterns of unequal and dependent relations. At the same time, the passage from 'the age of Capital' to 'the age of Empire' in the 1870s, to use Hobsbawm's terms, was marked by continual strains, both in the sphere of capitalist growth (the long economic slump between 1873 and 1896) and in the stability of colonial domination (the Indian revolt in 1857 marked this most emphatically).

This global pattern of 'uneven development' left profound traces upon the imperial entanglements this chapter is concerned with. In the first place, Mary Carpenter's interventions were indicative of a growing concern in Britain with the 'rescue' of the downtrodden, which took paternalist forms within the frames of both domestic and imperial politics. Indian social reform offered new routes of moral action and social intervention. India became available as a 'field of endeavour' through the encouragement—and the circumscriptions—of imperial and colonial administration. If certain sets of admissible social concerns were thus generated (such as the fate of impoverished and delinquent children, or the condition of women, or the effects of modern industry), ways of intervening were strictly defined. Overtly proselytizing activity, for instance, was discouraged, as was the passage of social legislation through imperial fiat.

The tensions between Lancashire and Bombay, too, bore traces of the fractures within imperial capitalism. The restriction of Bombay's mill capitalism was enabled by parliamentary interventions into Indian affairs: tariff and factory regulation arrived, I shall argue, as a *plausible* rather than an *effective* answer to Lancashire's own problems. Yet, in a time of famine, unrest, and military adventurism (such as the British campaigns in Afghanistan), Indian revenues posed a problem. This delayed and weakened the Free Trade policies sought by Lancashire. The other side of this was the growth of Bombay's cotton mill industry from the mid-1870s. Here, a different sort of battle over 'Free Trade' was played out with regard to colonial intervention in an emerging industry.

These simultaneous drives to enforce and limit imperial intervention, I suggest, lie at the base of one of the peculiarities of Indian factory regulation. There was a pattern common to both the entanglements of social reform and the politics of economic rivalry. Both Mary Carpenter's reform agenda and Lancashire's campaign clearly exerted decisive force upon Indian factory law, in the sense that they were squarely responsible for its passage. At the same time, the actual framing of the Factory Act, caught up in contestations between state, capital, and social reform at provincial, Indian, and imperial levels, eventually bore very little correspondence with either reformist desires or the imperatives of trade rivalry. Therefore, the story I tell about the emergence of factory legislation is one of prime movers and, at the same time, of continual mediation. In other words, it is a story about the *simultaneous* strength and weakness of the forces that underpinned legislation. And, as all histories at some level are, this is a story of unintended consequences and their logics.

Mary Carpenter and India: The Tensions of Factory Reform

Mary Carpenter's interventions were consequential because they made up the most coherent ideological justification for Indian factory legislation, though the system that emerged was very different from the reform she had envisaged. I begin, therefore, by trying to identify the historical conjuncture in which Carpenter intervened. I then turn to an account of her increasingly difficult relationship with the British state and to her subsequent involvement in colonial reform projects in India. This is followed by an analysis of her activism in the cause of Indian reform, which traces the emergence of a putative imperial public sphere around the questions raised by Carpenter. This lengthy but necessary digression serves as a basis for a consideration of Carpenter's entanglements with what can be broadly called the cause of Indian labour reform, an agenda that came to hinge on the prospect of an Indian Factory Act.

Mary Carpenter before India

Carpenter, in common with other middle-class women who led lives devoted to social activism and reform, cut an uneasy figure in mid-nineteenth-century Britain. Her personal and ideological choices have to be framed against the background of the larger social dynamics that unfolded in her lifetime. Her times were marked by an efflorescence of ideologies of domesticity and womanly virtue. The frontiers of these ideologies, as Catherine Hall has shown, were partly maintained by a crusading Evangelicalism, but they found a range of subtler inflexions.[8] Carpenter's persistent anxieties, expressed in letters and diaries, about her role, destiny, and *value* in the larger world were consonant with the moral concerns that dominated these decades. Her proud evocations of personal achievements in a greater Cause, haunted always by the spectre of their ultimate nullity and meaninglessness, make sense only against this larger backdrop.

Her personal decision to lead a life of spinsterhood upon independent and inherited means was, as Seth Koven has argued, a difficult choice to maintain within the ideological constraints of the time, which tied women's virtue closely to marriage and family.[9] Britain, during and after the Napoleonic wars, witnessed the flowering of publicly sanctioned moralities that fixed a determinate range of possible social functions upon women at a time of occupational and social flux. Domestic order, founded upon marriage and child-rearing, was the pivot of this moral order.

At the same time, a contradictory consciousness could be bred, and generalized, in the midst of the social dynamics fostered by industrialization. Educational opportunities for women expanded in the nineteenth century, and schools that fostered hegemonic ideas of domesticity could, in a contrary dimension, also expand the sphere of desires and aspirations. As recent feminist history has illustrated, women entered the arts, literature, and, in a broad sense, pedagogy through the deployment (and acceptance) of rhetorics of gender-based skill and competency.[10] Seth Koven and Sonya Michel use the term 'maternalism' to describe the most powerful of these rhetorics: women in Western Europe and the United States, they argue, could draw upon ideologically naturalized invocations of motherly love and care to justify lives spent in voluntary social activism. A life spent working with voluntary associations aimed at social and moral 'uplift' could, in Koven's words, 'counterbalance anxieties about spinsters as dangerous and redundant burdens on families and society'.[11]

A vocation based upon pastoral care, then, was a particularly seemly burden for an independent woman to bear, with the absence of family being compensated by the transferring of domestic responsibilities outward into the public domain. An extract from Carpenter's account of her first Indian voyage, describing her visit to the Surat Lunatic Asylum in October 1866, can be read as a coded vindication of her own 'specially' gendered vocation of social care:

> The only unsatisfactory part of the asylum is that allotted to women, and there ... the great want was evident of well trained, respectable *female* officials. However clever and well-qualified male officials may be—however devoted to their duty, and anxious to discharge it well—they *cannot* understand ... the work of a woman, any more than one of the other sex can do the work of a man. Our Heavenly Father has created the two sexes with different powers, and for different spheres of work, in His world. One cannot take the duties of the other without disturbing the order of His providence. A man cannot comprehend the proper work of the woman.[12]

As the works of feminist historians such as Koven, Michel, and Clark suggest, this line of argument transferred the realm of feminine domesticity from the private to the public sphere. The separation, in material reality as well as in ideological doctrines, of a privatized 'feminine' domestic sphere and a 'male' public sphere was blurred by this invocation of feminine virtue. It assumed naturally and divinely ordained states of gendered being, but suggested that the very capacities that justified the domestic role of women had a role to play within the quintessentially male world of policymaking in zones of intervention, such as child-moulding, where nurture and care were the keywords. This 'maternalism', which translated the mothering functions of women into specific areas of state intervention, was an important component of Carpenter's activity. It functioned as self-legitimation for a middle-class woman making the difficult choice of public life, with few role models and guidelines to follow. Her argument about feminine capacity justified the occupation of a segment of the public realm by women, whose special abilities made them peculiarly suited to vocations of care and nurture.[13]

Where precisely were these public vocations sought? The dislocations produced by the expansion of industrial capitalism lay at their heart. Voluntary associations and individuals addressed these dislocations in a number of ways: 'rescuing' women and children from the perils of overwork, disease, and 'moral degeneracy' in the form of the temptation of sexual promiscuity; exposing the horrors of the new kinds of work through investigation and analysis of industrial conditions in factories, mines, and workshops; constructing welfare nets for people living and working on the margins of society and facing the temptations of crime; and expanding various kinds of instruction (formal schools, basic literacy, prison instruction, and industrial and reformatory education) across this social field.

In a period marked by crises of existing structures of poor relief and the slow development of a usually parsimonious state-designed 'social policy', the ideology of 'improvement' through voluntary effort filled a void. Welfare for the growing numbers of people who worked in (or were excluded from) the new occupations produced by industrialization was by the 1840s and 1850s a vast and complex question. Measures of social control and amelioration devised by paternalist employers no longer had the same reach as before. Direct forms of intervention that mediated the explosive terrain of industrial relations were increasingly unavoidable. This required, in the first place, an enormous accumulation of knowledge, and for this the state deployed not only the services of its paid investigators, but also of a growing number of independent experts who were concerned with problems of social control.

All this can be comprehended as part of the inexorable and necessary expansion of the British state in a century of unprecedented social transformation. Yet, this would have the misleading effect of rendering a fractious process in overly neutral terms. Carpenter's own life, her ideological moorings and her social activism, in fact, bear witness to a profound political torsion in the world of reform. A possible, if speculative, entry point into this is her Unitarianism.

Unitarian congregations, such as the one Carpenter was born into in Bristol in 1807, were deeply marked by the transformation of late-eighteenth-century traditions of radical, dissenting Christianity in the first quarter of the nineteenth century. Unitarians, in common with the many other inflexions of Dissenting Christianity, suffered the burdens of the Test Acts: they were debarred from Parliament and military vocations on the basis of their faith. Their energies thus flowed into expanding middle-class professions such as education, law, journalism, and commerce. They also not infrequently flowed into dissident political activism, notably in the aftermath of the French Revolution and in the context of the Napoleonic Wars. Prominent Unitarians like Richard Price, Anna Laetitia Barbauld, and William Frend campaigned for religious toleration, the abolition of slavery, political liberty, and parliamentary reform. Lant Carpenter, Mary's father, was representative enough of these trends to welcome a major Indian social reformer, Rammohun Roy, to Bristol towards the end of his life. Roy was also acquainted with the London-based William Frend, a dissident during the Napoleonic Wars and, therefore, on the far left of the British political spectrum. Mary Carpenter was a young woman when Roy visited her family: he was to die and be buried in Bristol, and Carpenter would acknowledge his influence all her life. Such choices and connections, in a Britain increasingly saturated with xenophobia and empire-mongering, indicate that the Carpenters stood at an oblique angle to the dominant ideologies of their time.

In the 1830s, though, Unitarianism was reshaped by the paradoxes of the settlement achieved over religious toleration and parliamentary reform. Freed from legal discrimination, many Unitarians—especially the large number concentrated in expanding bourgeois vocations—were tamed of their democratic and theological heterodoxies, such as campaigns for the disestablishment of churches, and the framing of more extensive conceptions of liberty. Unitarianism, more than many other pillars of reforming dissent, was increasingly folded within establishment politics and values.

This produced precise patterns of accommodation with state power, new for people from dissenting faiths. This very newness may indeed have been a source for the enthusiasm with which wealthy or prominent Unitarians embraced the service of state and bureaucracy. Another source, undoubtedly, was the tradition of activism and social service, now unmoored from its erstwhile radical contexts. Carpenter herself may have been representative of this trend. She was apparently deeply affected by the Bristol riots of 1832, where a prominent opponent of parliamentary reform had been attacked by a plebeian crowd.[14] Like other incidents of its kind, this made the immensity of social distances suddenly visible, which, as a middle-class Christian humanitarian, Carpenter was horrified by. She could account for incidents like this only through a narrative of absolute social degradation among the 'perishing and dangerous classes', her term for the poorest social strata produced by industrialization.

In the 1830s, social reform underwent a Benthamite transformation. Practices and ideologies of social intervention, which had earlier been anchored in radical activism, were now increasingly folded within the bureaucratic circuits of organized social care where knowledge was produced, assembled, tabulated, and mobilized. Independent professional expertise was engrossed within social policy, which was administered through departments like the Poor Law councils and, perhaps most prominently in the 1830s and 1840s, the Factory Inspectorate. Social reform, thus, moved from individual conscience and radical agitation into the political and ideological establishment. The state, rather than the Dissenting congregation, became the focus of latter-day reformist and social-ameliorist activity. This marked a political *displacement* of activist energies, as confrontations with the emerging social and political order were substituted by state-administered compensations for the consequences of industrial capitalism. As she came of age as a social worker in the 1830s and became an increasingly prominent public figure after establishing the first Ragged Schools in the 1840s, Carpenter's itinerary in public life bore witness to these ideological and political changes in the landscapes of Dissent.

Crucial to this was the emergence, from the 1830s, of an improving agenda centred around prisons, reformatories, workhouses, industrial schools, and factories. Discipline and meliorism were combined in these initiatives. Early attempts at amelioration of the conditions of the new working classes came predominantly from paternalist employers. This was a very literal paternalism, where the responsibilities and powers of care were privatized in the hands of putatively benevolent individuals. Early mill owners in Britain, setting up large enterprises in predominantly rural districts in the North, often invested in a kind of disciplinary paternalism, where the imperatives of an exploitative and extractive capitalism were frequently married to a range of disciplinary-welfarist thrusts, centring on education, housing, and food. The inherent instability of this form of intervention was demonstrated by the intensified miseries that contemporary chroniclers described in the lives of the labouring poor through the course of the nineteenth century.

By the second quarter of the nineteenth century, the paternalist nerve within early industrial capitalism was largely exhausted, and the growth of monster industrial towns like the Manchester of Gaskell's *Mary Barton* or the London of Dickens and Mayhew were more obviously characteristic of the brave new world of industry. The sight of the wasted and stooped bodies of children and infants became the ground for a discourse of moral horror for spokesmen across a wide ideological spectrum. The Factory Act of 1833 traced the lineaments of this new ideology of concern: children were to be protected from industrial overwork, and their time away from the factory was to be deployed in an alternative form of discipline—the school. The Factory Act was simultaneously a piece of industrial legislation and a pedagogic intervention.

However, in an era increasingly dominated by ideas of Free Trade, such state-based paternalism had a clear limit. The efflorescence of 'voluntary effort' through the Victorian period in a sense marks this limit. Arguably, though, it would be more precise to view this limit as a point at which bureaucratic organization and voluntary effort recurrently met and corresponded. Many of the most significant social initiatives of the time came from women like Carpenter, whose campaigns of public advocacy had begun with the establishment of a Ragged School for street children in Bristol in 1846, and expanded with the establishment of two reformatories. One of these, named Red Lodge, would remain her abiding personal preoccupation through her life, and she would try to put her ideas about moral reformation into practice here, often, as commentators have remarked, with signal failure.[15]

The pattern of her interventions—rescuing fallen children from the moral and physical perils of transgression—found its conceptual anchor in a publication, in 1851, that would remain among her best known. This rudimentary sociology, which perhaps forms part of the genealogy of better-known conceptualizations (lumpenproletariat, underclass), was illuminatingly titled *Reformatory Schools for the Children of the Perishing and Dangerous Classes and for Juvenile Offenders*. Carpenter identified two locations of social danger and vulnerability. The first group she described were those who 'have not yet fallen into actual crime, but who are almost certain from their ignorance, destitution, and the circumstances in which they are growing up, to do so; - these form the *perishing classes*'.[16] Set below this, in more or less terminal stages of social and moral degeneracy, were the 'dangerous classes' who had already fallen to temptation, 'whose hand is against every man'.[17] The question was salvation and the answer was the cultivation of habits of enterprise, sobriety, and responsibility through systematic education directed specifically at them, through a multiplicity of disciplinary forms and institutions. In *Our Convicts*, she defined her programme as one of enlightenment through 'the institution of intermediate establishments between the prisons and the world'.[18]

In the 1850s, her campaigns were built on an understanding that some degree of state support was necessary, given the scale of the problems she addressed. Her advocacy became more strident and, with some initial hesitation, she became an accomplished public speaker and articulate propagandist.[19] She was consulted with respect and deference by parliamentary committees upon social questions, and she exercised significant influence upon the making of two connected pieces of social legislation: provision for juvenile reformatories in 1854 and provision for industrial education in 1857. Through the 1850s, in collaboration with like-minded reformers, most prominently Matthew Davenport-Hill, she organized campaigns and conferences in which an ameliorative policy towards 'the children of the perishing and dangerous classes' was devised.[20]

The interventions made by Carpenter—the publication of numerous volumes of social investigation, the testimonies offered to parliamentary committees on issues dear to her heart, the formulation of ideas of social control—were realized in the form of state intervention, and her activism, therefore, was repeatedly knitted into a Benthamite agenda sustained by bureaucratic power. Her concerns repeated those of a state that, in the course of prolonged industrial transformation and political turmoil, apprehended social dislocation and conflict everywhere. Carpenter grew up and worked in a rapidly industrializing nation, and her forms of social intervention explored the underbelly of the new social logics unleashed by industrial capitalism. She understood and articulated her concerns as exercises in the salvation of the wretched, a mission that defined, for her, the meaning of achievement and social commitment. She became, consequently, both a social campaigner and a social investigator.

Her entanglements with state authority, however, left subtle wounds. Despite her efforts, upon the passage of reformatory law, all juvenile offenders continued to be sent to prison for a fortnight, and exposed to the 'demoralizing influence of adult criminals'. She understood this as the biggest impediment both to effective prison reform and to the moral reformation of young delinquents. Between 1854 and 1860, her energies had been most enthusiastically lavished upon her project of girls' reformatory education at Red Lodge. Through the exercise of its powers of funding and inspection, however, the state wrested away control of the reformatory in 1860.[21] She seems to have acutely felt the humiliation of a visit by the first inspector of schools, Sydney Turner, in 1854, who expressed scepticism about her ability to manage her charges.[22] The personal, maternal, quasi-pastoral 'care' Carpenter had exerted was consequently, in her dearest experiment, replaced by a male bureaucracy of welfare.

The immediate consequences of this are difficult to distil from available evidence, but the details do establish the persistence of a difficult relationship, made out of symbiosis and suspicion in equal measure, between Carpenter and the mid-Victorian state. As Seth Koven has pointed out, Carpenter was always suspicious of state intervention, and accepted welfare schemes initiated and funded by the state as an 'unfortunate necessity'.[23] Her independently conceived initiatives were, however, drawn ineluctably into the expanding policy frameworks and bureaucratic powers of the Victorian state, and thus found expression in forms that lay beyond her purview. Her evident capacity to influence state policy was matched by her equally evident practical powerlessness. In a sense, Carpenter's dilemma marked a crisis—one of many—in the long accommodation between bureaucratic regulation and voluntary philanthropic activity. It was an ironic consummation of the association between activist Unitarianism and state power.

These tensions had important implications. Mary Carpenter's particular gloss on social policy corresponds with the emergent age of the workhouse. The moral imagination which derives a norm of social engineering from a series of quasi-penal institutions is best understood in this context. Carpenter was by no means a 'representative' figure: the single woman reformer commanded legitimacy within the Victorian world, but could not traverse it without cutting a somewhat unusual figure. However, the shape taken by her imagination of social reform was marked in very determinate ways by the limits imposed by the times. Industrial capitalism wedded social reform to social control, and Carpenter's humanitarian activism, enfolded as it was into circuits of state-led penal institution-building, was driven to continually imagine disciplinary mechanisms that produced normative labouring subjects.

Mary Carpenter and India

It was at these crossroads that Carpenter conceived the Indian project that took up the best part of her last years. In significant ways, this drew her into relationships with state power that replicated, in modified form, her British experiences. Here, again, her independent activism was already formulated within a pre-existing project, in this case the extension of the techniques of social control and amelioration from metropole to colony.

India, for Carpenter, began as a personal mission. Her activism there can partly be understood as an outgrowth of her missionary inheritance, which resounded in all her interventions at home and abroad. They also function as an instance of colonial discourses on the move. At the most obvious level, after all, her interventions can be read as an attempt to transfer her social-activist energies to India, where, as she put it, 'there was a *vast field of new enterprise* awaiting anyone who should go without prejudice or preconceived ideas'.[24] She elaborated further: 'A new field is about to open to me … one in which my natural powers will have free scope.'[25] The force of these words stemmed from the fact that British imperial power could make thinkable, and even natural, such an overseas investment of her 'natural powers'. 'Other sheep I have,' she added sententiously, 'which are not of this fold.'[26] Her attempts to locate this strayed flock were ultimately a route for the insertion of British social concerns into Indian policy.

Nevertheless, India was a personal mission in ways that went beyond this apparently nonchalant assumption of colonial mastery.[27]

By the early 1860s, as Koven has observed, Carpenter's influence upon social reform in Britain was running up against its limits.[28] Crusades of social amelioration that were personally and lovingly conceived were absorbed into the impersonal rhythms of an expanding bureaucracy, and Carpenter was unable to influence the texture, as distinct from the formal structure, of reform.

As her powers within her own country seemed to dim, Carpenter's thoughts turned to India. This turn was sustained by several visits to England by English-educated Indians, some of whom had earlier associations with the family, and some of whom were interested in or had converted to Christianity. The first of these visitors, in 1860, was J.C. Ganguly, a Bengali Brahmin convert to Christianity, whose address at the Unitarian chapel in Bristol 'inspired us all with very warm interest and desire to help him'.[29] In 1864, Satyendranath Tagore and Manmohan Ghose, two young Brahmos who were studying in London for the Indian Civil Service Examination and who went on to play active roles in Indian public life, visited Carpenter in Bristol. Ghose visited her again in 1866. They invited her to visit India to investigate, and perhaps help improve, the state of female education. The encounter clearly affected her powerfully, and she recorded, in a diary entry at the beginning of 1864, her 'solemn resolve' to 'devote my heart and soul and strength to the elevation of the women of India. ... I shall obey the remarkable call which has been given me so unexpectedly'.[30]

Carpenter's subsequent diary entries about the impending Indian campaign were tinged with romance and even intrigue. On 12 January 1864, she wrote: 'Without any present and apparent change of plan I shall watch openings, devote myself to perfecting my present work, and ... gain information and prepare in every way for my great object, going to India to prepare the Christian work for the women.'[31] On 14 February 1864: 'Now that my poor little forsaken ones are cared for here, I may go to the others and help them. ... Should I never return, heaven will be as near to me as that region from here.' At the beginning of 1866, we find her confessing to herself in transports of ecstasy:

> A grand and new life appears opening upon me. Heavenly Father, by tokens drawn from the marvelous workings of Thy providence, I believe that Thou hast destined for me the unspeakable privilege before leaving this world, of going to our distant India, and there working with the

> spirits of my beloved father and the noble Rajah for the elevation of women, and perhaps also for the planting of a pure Christianity. Thou knowest, O Father, that I have never withheld anything from Thee, since I first offered to Thee all my powers and myself.[32]

These lines denote a feeling of excitement, of religious ecstasy that could not be subsequently expressed in public life. (Carpenter was always punctiliously sensitive to charges of overt missionary activity, especially in a country whose cultural differences from Britain were as frequently remarked upon as India.) They also suggest an immense personal breakthrough, an irrevocable decision. They can be read, too, as signs of the strain of achievement as much as of its triumph: her anxious, repetitive invocations of her higher Purpose seem sometimes almost to function as self-admonition.

Carpenter's introduction to India, as recorded in her account of her first voyage in 1866–7, signalled mixed feelings. Her visit to India was, she wrote, undertaken not 'with any intention of special work there, but as a proof of friendly sympathy'. On 26 September 1866, shortly after she arrived in Bombay, this desire was peremptorily, if politely, interrupted by an official summons. 'It was, then, with great astonishment, and at first with some regret, that I received the following official document, which was handed to me on this day.'[33] This consisted of two letters from the government, requisitioning her assistance, respectfully but insistently, on questions of education, reformatories, and convict discipline. This correspondence was copied to the inspector general of prisons, the inspector general of the medical department, the officers in charge of lunatic asylums, and the inspector general of hospitals.[34] It was evident, wrote Carpenter, recalling her regret, 'that my journey must include a much more extended sphere than I had hitherto contemplated'. An opportunity, however, 'so courteously given of studying the different institutions of this country must not be lost'.[35]

Carpenter's 'astonishment' should make us pause. She brought with her to India letters of introduction from some major contemporary public figures, including Lord Cranborne, then the Secretary of State for India, and Florence Nightingale. Her friends in India had communicated with Bartle Frere, the Governor of Bombay, who had invited her to stay at his marine bungalow. Her expertise on questions of social discipline and rehabilitation was consequential to colonial administrators for whom memories of the Mutiny were still fresh. At the same time, Carpenter insists, in the pages that follow this account, on the absence of any stable anchors to hold on to in India and on the feeling that she was exploring uncharted territory, and it might be fruitful to take this insistence—which perhaps betokens her libidinal investment in the adventure of her project—seriously.[36]

Carpenter, in her reflections upon her Indian campaign, always interpreted it as a chapter in a meaningful spiritual Bildungsroman. 'I have always hitherto been led aright,' she wrote in a letter to a friend shortly before her departure for India, 'and never did I see such reason for my course as now, or such hope. If I neglect such an opening for good, I should feel myself sinning against my conscience and inner light.'[37] However, as the episode just narrated illustrates, she was always also bound to a calling that was more profane, which issued from government departments and official meeting rooms and offices both in Britain and in India. Her spiritual quest and duty was translated into the practical task of the social investigation of institutions. Equally, the field of her endeavours expanded in unexpected ways. There is no evidence that she intended to separately investigate schools, prisons, and reformatories in India prior to the letters she received upon arrival in Bombay, and she had more than once reiterated that her principal concern was the moral and practical 'elevation' of Indian women. By the end of her travels in India in 1875, however, she had developed projects of institutional reform aimed at juvenile offenders, prison discipline, and factory regulation—all involvements pivoting, as we shall see, on ideas of disciplined labour.

At the very beginning of her journeys in India, then, Carpenter was uneasily poised between projects of state intervention and independent, salvationist (though not proselytizing) activity. The same tension had defined the relationship between her activism in Britain and the extension of social controls by the state. Her early experiences in India mark a distinct historical moment, when connections forged between private philanthropy and public policy were transferred from metropole to colony. She began her campaigns to India as a solitary, if influential, traveller, without, as she reiterated, a pre-set agenda. After the letters from the government reached her, she repressed the regret she claimed to feel and wrote to England asking for copies of Acts of Parliament and reports on schooling, reformatory, and industrial education. By the end of her first visit, she was writing to the government and individual statesmen in Britain, offering recipes for social intervention—schooling, industrial training, the fostering of habits of labour—that were congruent with the concerns that inflected national and imperial policymaking.

These concerns were essentially disciplinary. Carpenter travelled from a country that had witnessed intense class conflict and moral panic to one that had recently witnessed a mass revolt against imperial power. Her interventions were all marked by the twin projects of 'improvement' and 'discipline'. Optimism about the possibility of 'reclaiming' potentially 'dangerous' segments of the labouring poor from the squalid existences they eked out was tensely balanced by a strong belief in the exercise of harsh disciplinary methods to effect this reformation.

'I love India as a mother loves her child,' Carpenter declared in a letter to Keshab Chandra Sen in 1870, and there is no reason to doubt her sincerity.[38] In practice, this love manifested itself in an obsessive concern with the confinement, segregation, and productive employment of juvenile delinquents, and, in a more general sense, the children of the labouring poor. In her advocacy of social reform, Carpenter sought to substitute graduated schemes of discipline and moral reformation for punishment, in a line of reasoning that can be traced back to Pentonville Prison.[39]

This leads on to a rather obvious Foucauldian point: from the outset, Carpenter's visit to India was caught up in disciplinary strategies that were executed by bureaucratic apparatuses. Correspondingly, her own salvationist concerns with India (and, as Burton has observed, the consummation of her 'family romance' with colonial reform), predicated upon sincere professions of motherly love, were ineluctably drawn into officially administered policies of social control and discipline. This was an outgrowth of the 'maternalism' described by Koven and Michel: if the public realm of socially ameliorative policymaking belonged by right to women, on account of their capacities to love, care, and nurture, then the maternal love felt by Carpenter needed to be translated effectively into the vocabulary of social control. Love and discipline, then, were the twin logics that bisected her activism. Her maternalist endeavours were invariably expressed as labours of love, and equally invariably produced disciplinary recipes. While horrified by the brutality of some of the discipline she observed—for instance, the shackling of prisoners with irons in jails—Carpenter was, nonetheless, an advocate of firm disciplinary controls and precise measurements of the labour, leisure, and instruction that would mould or reform the boys, girls, prisoners, and workers she turned her energies to. Discipline was the mechanism whereby love was translated into law.

Carpenter always saw state intervention as a necessary, though sometimes regrettable, *supplement* to the voluntary charitable and reformist activity of enlightened elites. Her visits to India produced policy prescriptions that materialized in statute law, but she lavished her energies more enthusiastically upon the cultivation of circles of reformers. Her decision to visit India was, of course, already mediated by the intervention of Bengali Brahmo reformism. While in Calcutta, she actively sought the company of Brahmos, in particular Keshab Chandra Sen, leader of the more influential wing of the movement.[40] The mutual fascination that had bound her father and his church to Rammohun Roy, in a sense, was repeated in Carpenter's close relationship with Sen. Carpenter summed up the theological basis of this fascination in a letter written from Calcutta, where she praised 'the beliefs and devotion of those who had abandoned ideology, and had made the doctrine of the unity and spirituality of God the basis of an important moral and religious reform'.[41]

Carpenter, like her father, saw the Brahmos as, effectively, proto-Unitarian. Her theological affinities, however, were of secondary importance, and what drew her principally to the Brahmos, as to other reform-minded elites in other parts of India, was the commitment to social change based on the building of new kinds of pedagogic institutions. In Bombay, Ahmedabad, Surat, and Madras (present-day Chennai), she searched for men who shared her ideas about institutional reform and female education, and found them among Hindu, Parsi, and Jewish reforming and philanthropic elites and among adventurous European and Indian doctors, teachers, and prison administrators.[42]

While in India, Carpenter closely studied and associated with disciplinary and pedagogic movements that spoke to her concerns. She was a particularly vocal advocate of 'female normal schools' or schools to train women teachers. Carpenter was enthusiastic about the few Indian experiments in this field, but identified a key problem in the exclusively male instruction and management of such institutions. She recommended, therefore, that the Government of India import women teachers from England who could superintend the initial experiments in female education. She procured financial assistance from the Government of India for the establishment of female normal schools in Bombay and Ahmedabad, and upon her second visit to India in 1868 offered to fill what she saw as the key role of the Superintendent of the Female Normal School in Bombay.[43] As Claire Midgley points out, the effect of the financial assistance received from the colonial government was that the experiments in the training of women teachers became, against Carpenter's wishes, exercises in colonial education rather than independent efforts backed by government aid.[44] In this respect, too, the tensions between voluntary initiative and state-led social control, which had troubled Carpenter in Britain, were re-elaborated in a colonial context.

Such experiments were limited in number and scope, though, and Carpenter seems to have suffered some disappointment at their slowness and inefficacy. At the conclusion of her third visit to Bombay in 1870, she seems to have decided that 'she would have more opportunity of promoting the cause to which she had devoted herself by general influence at home, than by the actual establishment or conduct of institutions in India itself'.[45]

Upon a suggestion by Keshab Chandra Sen, who visited her in Bristol in the summer of 1870, Carpenter decided to assemble an association of like-minded people, responding to 'the obvious need of some means of communication between English and Native fellow-subjects who were interested in promoting Social Reform in India'.[46] In September, a large public meeting at Bristol inaugurated the National Indian Association (NIA), which was set up with the twin objectives of promoting English interest in Indian social questions through publications and campaigns, and of helping reformist Indian visitors to England to 'study its institutions, and enter into its society'.[47]

At the most basic level, this was a movement in the direction of a putative imperial public sphere, assembled from different projects and ideas of social reform in India and sympathetic currents within England. It was based on the desire for an imperial connection that stood at a distance from the official channels of power, even as it battened on them. This was an alternative mediator of social change and control, one made possible by the imperial connection but burrowing, as it were, beneath its coercive and regulatory apparatuses to forge different connections based on assumptions of equality in association.

The NIA had its headquarters, naturally, at Bristol, where Carpenter exercised close controls over its functions, principal among which were the organization of public meetings and the publication of a monthly journal.[48] Branches of the association soon sprang up in London, Leeds, Liverpool, and several other large cities. Of equal importance to Carpenter, however, was the establishment of corresponding branches within India in many of the places she had visited—Calcutta (present-day Kolkata) and its suburbs, Bombay, Poona (present-day Pune), Ahmedabad, Madras, and Ranchi.[49]

Over the next seven years, the last of her life, Carpenter drew on the collective resources of the NIA and her own clout with lawmaking circles to push for programmes of social reform dear to her heart, and to encourage and sometimes finance projects within India that met the requisite criteria. Above all, the NIA was an instrument to facilitate encounters between 'progressive' Indians and their sympathizers in Britain, by exposing the former to the homes and institutions of the latter.

The Factory as Improvement: Mary Carpenter, Sasipada Banerjee, and the Reformist Agenda

While in Bombay in February 1867, Carpenter hunted down a workshop where *kinkhab*, or gold-plated thread, was produced. Having seen several 'splendid specimens' of this work at the Paris Exhibition, she wanted to see the place where it was produced, which, she seems to have assumed, would correspond to her understanding of a factory. What she encountered was a rude shock:

> After passing through the better streets, we threaded our way through narrow lanes, in vain looking for anything like a factory; at last we stopped at a common poor-looking house, and with difficulty ascended some stairs to a miserable loft; so this was the factory! Four looms were at work there, of so primitive a construction, and clumsy a make, that if one could have been transported to Paris along with its workers, it would have been among the greatest curiosities of the Exhibition. The men and lads who were employed there as draw-boys, in their semi-nude and uncivilized condition, totally ignorant, seemed beings of another sphere from those for whom their manufacture was intended. The merchants buy the gold thread and silk, and pay these men trifling wages, on which

> they can barely subsist. One clever bright little fellow, with shaven head, laughed with intense glee at so strange a sight as English ladies in that secluded loft; another boy of fourteen was so clever that he had already mastered the whole art, and could weave as well as a man. These bright lads were growing up immured in this loft, without any education, or opportunity of improvement.[50]

Nine years later, at a speech in Royston where she campaigned for a Factory Act for India, Carpenter was to expound on this encounter in more graphic detail, as reported by the NIA's journal:

> There were two persons at each loom, entirely naked, one of whom, a boy, seemed lost in wonder and astonishment at the visitors—he had never seen such before in his life. The wages of these poor people—she was really afraid to tell them—was not more than 2s 6d. a week, barely enough to hold body and soul together. And if any special occasion occurred, and they were compelled to borrow from the masters, these advanced them money and kept them in a sort of bondage in consequence, because they could not leave them on account of debt. In this way the poor people were kept enslaved all their lives. She inquired if it would not be possible to introduce some better machines, and induce some persons of enterprise to conduct such a valuable manufacture, and it was thought to be impracticable, owing to the conditions which existed between employer and employed.[51]

There were more horrific revelations in the house next door, which was home to an oil-factory:

> [The] seed was crushed in a gigantic cumbersome press, requiring far more labour than our machinery. We ventured into the interior of this house, where a woman, removing a quantity of clothing from a sort of hammock, disclosed a young baby to us; the cramped position it was in, explained to me why most of the babies I see in the schools have such narrow chests. We had that morning a most instructive glimpse of the native in the lower circles of society.[52]

So, Carpenter was horrified, in the first place, at the opacity of industry: a factory could be located in a house, hidden entirely from public view, even in its identity as a workplace. These passages are marked by a potential tension. In her recollections of this first encounter with the labouring poor in India, Carpenter expressed an acute comprehension of the concrete conditions that bound them to exhausting and debilitating occupations. Her remarks articulated the simultaneous materialization and *de*materialization of labour in the process of production: the beauty of the manufacture both incarnated and concealed brutal conditions of labour. The 'relations between employer and employed' do not admit of a change in these structures of exploitation: for Carpenter, the answer lies in a change in the heart of those relations—but in what direction? The answer is summed up in the last sentence. 'The native in the lower circles of society' is offered as a concrete, material being, but also as a *category*, with heuristic as well as descriptive value. The first moment is subsumed within and sutured by the second—the appropriate answers are to be found within a theory of civilization, and the task is one of instruction and improvement, physical amelioration and moral uplift.

Such surroundings were horrific to Carpenter, not only for their plainly oppressive character, but also for the moral, *civilizational* deficit they seemed to signal. The answer, as she saw it, lay in the spread of factory industry, not simply as a productive force but also as a civilizing mission. The factory, in the ability it had to cluster people together within a compressed space under 'enlightened' supervision, could furnish the materials for rehabilitation and moral reformation. Carpenter encountered in India, perhaps more intensely than she had ever done in England, an excitement at the social transformations heralded by what was only embryonically an industrial culture. The 'enlightenment' promised by modern factory production proper, on this plane, lay in the growth and consolidation of recognizable and designated units of industrial production, presumably marked out physically from their surroundings.

Carpenter's descriptions of the factories (in the 'English' sense) that she had occasion to visit in India volubly expressed this enchantment. At Surat, shortly after her disturbing encounter with the industrial garret in Bombay, she visited a cotton-spinning factory:

> The manager of this factory is one of those men whom one may proudly recognize as a true Englishman, in whatever part of the world one may find him. He had brought the iron framework of the factory from England, and had himself erected the whole building with native labour. When the masons were afraid of going up the high chimney in the course of erection, he went up himself, and they confidingly followed him. In fact, he bore the same testimony that I had received from many, that the natives work well under the English, if treated with kindness;—they fully recognize the superiority of the British character, and yield

> to its guidance with willingness … a number of women and children of low condition were employed, who thus obtained valuable training, as well as the means of improving their condition. It required very great patience and forbearance to bring them into any degree of order, and to induce them to attend with regularity, as all of us can understand who have been accustomed to work with a similar class at home. Yet it was astonishing what an improvement they made after a time, and this was a sufficient recompense to a worthy manager. He much regretted that a Factory Act is not in operation in India, that the children may be taught to read as well as to work.[53]

In the recollections of India that she shared with her audience at Royston in 1875, Carpenter described a similar experience, this time at a cotton factory in Bombay:

> It was an excellent building, and the worthy superintendent was a Lancashire man. On entering she was perfectly astonished, and said to the superintendent: 'Why, this is a little bit of Lancashire transported to India!' The arrangements were well organized and beautifully carried out, as they would have been in England. The Superintendent spoke very highly of them too. They had not quite as much strength, he said, as the English, they could not work as many hours, or do quite as much, but they could do the work as well. (Applause). This superintendent thought he had a mission to accomplish as well as his regular work, and he said, in his opinion, cotton factories were doing as much almost as Christianity for India. He had people working for him who had been in the lowest stage of degradation, but he had raised them to a position of usefulness; and he took delight in taking little boys whom he found running in the streets, and teaching them how to gain a livelihood. When she saw such a work being carried out she felt proud of her country, and thought that a number of such Englishmen would do good to India.[54]

The modern factory, then, transplanted the industrial virtues of Britain upon Indian soil. Carpenter's approval of the Englishness of the two managers she mentions in these passages is worth remarking on: it signalled a conviction that such 'Englishness' could be learnt by example (the Surat manager leading the masons, the 'mission' the Bombay manager so fervently believed in). The replication of English skills, techniques, and values, in a new terrain of industry, would furnish the materials for moral regeneration. Carpenter was a committed supporter of Indian efforts to stimulate capitalist production, in significant contrast to the manufacturing lobby in Lancashire, which also sought an Indian Factory Act.

Factories represent a *telos* in the logical structure of Carpenter's convictions about Indian reform, and consequently also in the strategies advocated or endorsed by the NIA. The discipline of labour runs in a continuous line through the advocacy of reformatories, industrial schools, and factory reform. If prisons and reformatories produce the rehabilitation of the transgressors and the 'fallen' through a life disciplined and made useful by labour, industrial schools confer skills that equip people for lives in stations appropriate to them. Basic education is an adjunct to this, and the wheel turns full circle at the highest stage of this structure—factory regulation. If the other forms of discipline were pedagogic strategies equipping their subjects for normal working lives within the confines of their class, factory work, the evidence of the English precedent suggested, liberated children from overwork to subject them to the new discipline of schooling.

A mutually reinforcing relationship between work, education, and 'civilization', passing through a sequence of institutional forms that would themselves have to be moulded in humanitarian-disciplinarian ways, sat at the centre of Carpenter's thoughts on India. Correspondingly, she began to keep a close watch on experiments in the reform of incipient working-class populations in India. Through the network of the NIA, she reported and applauded labour-reform initiatives that bore affinities to her own projects and ideas. A brief resume of some of the more striking of these experiments is in order at this juncture. Conceived by different men at different places in the course of the 1860s and 1870s, these experiments were loosely knitted, by the discursive agency of Carpenter and her colleagues, into a tentative forecast of paternalist proposals for the regulation of industrial capitalism.

The first was an experiment begun in 1863 by Arthur Crawford, Senior Assistant Judge at Ratnagiri in Bombay Presidency. Crawford (subsequently to achieve notoriety as a lavishly extravagant Municipal Commissioner of Bombay, between 1865 and 1871) set up a School of Industry at Ratnagiri. The following year saw this develop into a large enterprise, the Ratnagiri Saw Mills Company, which rapidly came to employ hundreds of workmen, engaged in extensive work for railways, reclamations, and a number of public undertakings—investments which boomed during the share mania of the early 1860s. The industrial school remained on the premises of the factory, taking in apprentice boys of all castes, aged between seven and fifteen. These boys were employed as regular wage-labourers in the factory, but their remuneration was made subject to two hours of schooling every day. Wages were paid according to skill, and deducted if a boy failed to attend school.[55]

The enterprise's subsequent fortunes were chequered: it succumbed to the crash that followed the share mania of the mid-1860s, was bailed out of bankruptcy by seven local entrepreneurs, and finally became a government institution in 1879. Crawford's commitment to industrial education, however, was retained by his successors through these oscillations. Students entered the school on probation for a month, at the end of which, 'should their work be worth it', they received Re 1, which was to gradually rise 'as their work increases in value' to a monthly wage of Rs 8.[56] A series of operations can be seen at work here: a programme of education, a regime of wage-discipline, a system of incentives and penalties, a logic of skilling and training for a life of industrial labour. The continuity between school and factory was central: the discipline of one was meant to flow seamlessly into the discipline of the other. Schooling built up an industrial worker, and work 'educated' a boy into habits of discipline and productivity.

The Association also offered 'sympathy and pecuniary support' to an Industrial School at Ranchi, which 'asserted the duty of enabling neglected boys to be able to maintain themselves through honest labour, and of giving them some simple instruction'.[57] Womesh Chandra Sen, the headmaster of a government school at Ranchi in Chhota Nagpur, referred to Carpenter's strategy of compelling the education of street children in Certified Industrial Schools in Britain. He also expressed the wish 'to see something done for the factory men' and advocated an organization of factory proprietors for the purpose of 'giving education to their servants'.[58]

The most consequential of these experiments, however, took place in Bengal. This experiment mediated one of the closest of Carpenter's Indian friendships, with the Brahmo reformer Sasipada Banerjee. It is in some of the episodes of this association that we find the first articulations of a cogently conceived idea of factory reform in India, and more generally of a reformist programme around industrial labour.

Sasipada Banerjee, at the time he met Carpenter at a mutual Brahmo acquaintance's house in Calcutta in the winter of 1866, was a twenty-six-year-old aspirant reformer who worked in the town of his birth, Baranagar, a northern suburb of Calcutta on the eastern bank of the Hooghly River. A flourishing weaving centre under Dutch administration in the eighteenth century, the town fell on bad days as English competition drove weavers out of business. The Borneo Jute Company's Mill, opened in 1859, seemed to the young Banerjee to hold the promise of some kind of revitalized prosperity. By the beginning of the 1870s, some 4,000-odd labourers, many of them from weaving castes, had found employment in the factory, consolidating a large, superficially homogeneous working-class population in what had until recently been a de-industrialized backwater.[59] In 1879, writing in *Bharat-Sramajibi*, the cheap Bengali monthly he had set up in 1874 to communicate moral advice and instruction to Baranagar's workers, Banerjee reflected on the significance of the turn in Baranagar's industrial fortunes. He asked, rhetorically, whether the inhabitants of other ex-weaving centres could be similarly rescued.

> Is there no way out for them? There is—and it lies in the hands of rich zamindars and moneylenders. If … they import machinery from England, and set up factories for making cloth … five or six thousand workers could find employment in each one.[60]

There are, of course, ways in which Banerjee's diagnosis differs mildly from Carpenter's: what the latter saw as a project of salvation, the former saw as a recipe for the restoration of lost craft traditions, pride, and livelihoods. The two understandings, however, corresponded with each other in their optimism about the transforming powers of industrial production. The Borneo Company, at the time, was one of the largest in India. In a country still unmarked by large-scale factory production, but where such a development was anticipated by many modernizing reformers, it could be held up as an easily replicable model. It was precisely the limited extent of factory production that allowed the construction of such putatively universal industrial imaginaries.

The new working-class neighbourhoods that had sprung up in the wake of the establishment of the Borneo Jute Mill were the grounds for what Dipesh Chakrabarty, in a detailed reconstruction, has pinpointed as the beginning of industrial labour reform in Bengal, and perhaps in India. It was not the first experiment of its kind, as we have seen, but, in large measure due to Mary Carpenter's efforts, it was the first project that sought its own generalization. It was also the first labour-reform initiative among industrial workers that was to receive widespread publicity in some elite and high political circles. It also served as an early basis for the demand for a Factory Act.

Banerjee initially attracted Carpenter's attention not because of his role as fledgling labour reformer, but because he had set up a girls' school in the face of intense opposition from the upper-caste Hindu orthodoxy from which he had been excommunicated for his Brahmoism.[61] Carpenter, however, came to be more attracted by another of his projects—an evening school, composed of two rooms, that he had set up for the education of workers in a corner of the girls' school. The company had doubled the mill's workload in 1864, and the emergence of a large working-class population with distinct modes of sociality was of some consequence to employers and reformers such as Banerjee alike. In a letter to Carpenter in 1867, Banerjee wrote with distress about the tendency of drunken working people to 'become vicious' and neglect 'their duties as men'.[62] Carpenter herself drew attention to the nature of modern industrial progress in Baranagar:

> The influx of money into this town is very great, numbers thus obtaining good regular wages who were previously in receipt of small precarious earnings only. But this increase of the resources of our inhabitants has not hitherto been productive solely of good effects. These people are quite content with what we should deem a low, miserable way of living, in poor huts; they are without any education, nor have they the wants of civilized life; they spend their money, therefore, in vicious indulgences.[63]

As Dipesh Chakrabarty observes, the Borneo Company's proposal, in 1866 and 1867, to open a school on the premises of the factory was probably a response to the growing need for a coherent system of labour discipline. The demands of labour discipline and moral reform, in the event, soon animated each other. Banerjee, backed by Carpenter (who had made contacts among some of the Company's officials), was able to set up his school effectively as an extension of the mill itself. The manager of the company inaugurated the school in 1869, which gave

Banerjee some of the impetus for an expanded programme of moral instruction among workers.

Banerjee's initiatives from the late 1860s, under Carpenter's tutelage, marked a very precise shift in the direction of social reform in Baranagar. Banerjee had been initiated into reformist activism by a temperance movement aimed chiefly at 'reclaiming' high-caste Hindus from the temptations of alcohol.[64] Carpenter's influence pushed him to concentrate his activities exclusively among the labouring poor. In another letter written to Carpenter in February 1867, Banerjee described the tactics he deployed to influence factory workers: 'I have made a plan of collecting as many men of the factory as I can collect on Sundays, and giving them advices in simple Bengally, so as to make them better men, good fathers and loving husbands ... we should try to go into the circles of the working people.'[65] This didactic method seems to have attracted support from the employers of the mill and, obviously, from Carpenter.

The years between 1869 and 1874 saw a flurry of activity, as a number of experiments in social reform cropped up under Banerjee's supervision, initially with the financial aid of the Borneo Company. These included several night schools for workers; an 'Anna Bank', modelled on penny banks in England, where workers were encouraged to become depositors; a savings bank; and two journals, the *Barahanagar Samachar* in 1873 and the *Bharat Sramajibi* in 1874. The journals instructed their audience, composed of the labouring poor, in values appropriate to their station. The *Bharat Sramajibi*, which amassed a large readership among workers and their families, was closely modelled on *The British Workman*. It contained advice for workers on the values of thrift, education, and temperance; inspirational stories of success through toil and sacrifice (Richard Arkwright's example was much cited); and essays celebrating the British government.[66]

Clearly, the poor, rather than the affluent, were now the principal targets of paternalist reform. This shift was symbolized best by the transformation of the Temperance Society into a Workingmen's Club in 1870.[67] This was conceived by Banerjee principally as a space of instruction, where the values of docility and patience were to be cultivated through lectures, educational programmes, and the cultivation of certain values (discipline, perseverance, thrift) that were reminiscent of Samuel Smiles' *Self-Help* (1859). It drew upon similar experiments in England, and Chakrabarty makes the persuasive suggestion that the importation of such institutions was critical for Banerjee's success in acquiring assistance from local Europeans and the Borneo Company. His own resources, in common with many contemporary reformers, were straitened.

Banerjee organized a 'pleasure excursion of working men' in December 1873 on the occasion of the fourth anniversary of the Workingmen's Club. The workers assembled at his house, they went together to the Barrackpore Club and the government school building, and he gathered them together in a park to lecture them about the merits of Canning's government. The meeting ended with songs in praise of Victoria, and of the government's educational initiatives. Subsequently, the meeting, under Banerjee's stewardship, adopted four resolutions. First, they deplored intemperance. Second, they expressed gratitude to the Borneo Company 'for the support which they are giving to upwards of six thousand of people'. Third, they expressed gratitude to the government of Bengal for its system of primary education. Finally, they expressed gratitude to the 'friends, well-wishers and supporters of mass education here and in England'.[68] Banerjee thus articulated a common theme of the age—the importance of creating a sober, industrious, and self-improving working man who would harness the productive forces of society and observe social peace. A culture of common sociality had to be fashioned with the materials at hand, which in Banerjee's case were his own good relations with the Borneo Company and Mary Carpenter's active support.

However, it might not be insignificant that Banerjee's own project, which operated entirely within the digits of social control, was construed by its opponents as a measure to 'disturb society'. The very idea of an activist intervention into the lives of the poor, however conservative in its orientation, could be changed into a signifier of discord. 'Self-help', insofar as it promoted collective activity on the part of workers, could be a double-edged instrument of social change. It appears that the very attempt to organize workers within a culture of common sociality evoked strong conservative protests within Baranagar. There is no direct evidence, but a speech Banerjee made in 1871 works as a negative proof:

> [A] loud cry is raised against me that I am disturbing society—setting class against class. Let them cry; I shall go on ... I have been trying to teach them (the working men) that labour is honourable, not to bring

disorder and confusion among them, but to bring class and class in sympathy with each other.[69]

As Dipesh Chakrabarty points out, the very scanty evidence that is available suggests that some jute workers in Baranagar, at least, followed paths of action that militated against such projects of social control. The evidence of Noderchand, a weaver in the mill since 1870, before the Factory Commission in 1890 demonstrates that workers 'resorted to the courts for wages and won their cases'. By the time of his testimony, Banerjee's experiments had, in any case, died a young death, and Noderchand spoke vaguely of a school that had once existed, but which factory children did not, by and large, attend on account of their intense fatigue.[70]

For Carpenter, at least, Banerjee's activity had no such disturbing implications, and her support and advocacy played the pivotal role in elevating him to the status of a public figure of some consequence. In 1871, Banerjee visited her in England along with his wife (who thus acquired the fame and notoriety of becoming apparently the first Brahmin woman to cross the ocean, an act that led to the loss of caste). This was a journey sponsored and facilitated by Carpenter and was one of NIA's first initiatives: under their aegis, Banerjee travelled across England and Scotland making speeches on the reformers' agenda in India.

The symbiosis of the two branches—imperial and colonial—of Carpenter's reformist network is evident here. The Association helped finance Banerjee's reformist activity and organized his travel to the metropolis, as it had done for Keshab Chandra Sen before him. Banerjee, in turn, quickly played his role in expanding the Association's formal, registered presence in the UK. He spoke at Birmingham, Walsall, Manchester, Leeds, Sheffield, Glasgow, and Edinburgh. At each of these places, branches of the NIA were set up immediately after his tour. Banerjee spoke only at Workingmen's Clubs in the UK. As Chakrabarty suggests, such a choice had implicit, if not explicit, political meaning at a time when the nation was witnessing the most serious outburst of organized working-class protest since Chartism.[71]

At Leeds, Banerjee spoke at the invitation of the Social Science Association, another project with which Carpenter was involved. It is here that we find the first major public articulation of the need for factory reform in India. Banerjee, speaking of the importance of elementary popular education for the masses, stressed the need for two kinds of schooling: training to provide basic literacy, and industrial schools providing technical education to 'raise the character and position of the working man'.[72] India was clearly a country marked by immense poverty, want, crime, and a chaotic dispersal of the sources of these problems. For Banerjee, as for Carpenter, education offered the solution to these problems—not as empowerment and self-organization, which would have been a dangerously radical idea for middle-class reformers to grapple with, but as a means of alleviating absolute impoverishment and misery, and of transforming a population apparently prone to crime and vagrancy into a disciplined and contented body of subjects. Schooling for the poor on a large scale in a huge and chaotic country, however, posed problems of management and administration. One of the possible ways around this, according to Banerjee, was to make use of the immense accumulations of human labour in the relatively ordered space of factories:

> In places of business where many children and young men work together to earn their livelihood, the influences of education and enlightenment can more easily make their way, than by any individual attempt to bring together the children for the sake of education only … factories have been established … in different parts of the country. … In all these places there are materials for mass education, if only schools could be opened to carry out the object. It is a subject worthy of the attention of the capitalists, for by educating these workmen they would not only raise a low and degraded people, but also improve their own resources; for the more educated and skilled the assistants, the better would be the work obtained by them.[73]

Banerjee was making an appeal to the conscience of industrial capitalists that would be echoed several times over the next decade by like-minded reformers. However, he also indicated his awareness that 'without the interference of Government, without some legislative enactment, the work of education cannot spread extensively among the factory people'.[74] He spoke of his own beloved project for the education and moral uplift of factory workers at Baranagar. However, he also expressed his disappointment at the limitations of this project, since there was no administrative system to enforce it, nothing that *compelled* workers into schools. It was in this context that he couched his demand for a Factory Act, drawing upon the experience of England, where over the decades between 1833 and 1870 half-time factory legislation for children and compulsory schooling had, legally at least, been knitted together.

The purpose of such schooling, for Banerjee as for Carpenter, was rhetorically linked to a civilizing project aimed at fostering social peace and suturing the social wounds that could grow from deprivation. This was its negative, defensive agenda: educate workers and they will be content and obedient. It was also linked to a positive economy of production: the education and uplift of factory workers would deliver a content and disciplined workforce into the hands of its employers. The problems of drinking, indiscipline, and insubordination could be resolved through a voluntary compact of state, employers, and reformist activity, and this would enhance the productive capacities of workers. Factory reform was thus marked out as part of a larger disciplinary project. This clearly drew on one aspect of the experience of factory law in England—that part of it which embodied the dream of a contented, competently educated, but also a basically quiescent and docile working-class population. This opened up possibilities for the creation of docile bodies, and balanced entitlements with social duty and obedience.

The incipient philosophies of industrial relations just investigated contained a common point of departure: the possibilities of the factory as a vehicle of pedagogy. This had a metaphoric sense—of civilizational uplift through industry, of the inculcation of the values of effort and learning through work—and a literal sense, in which the factory, because it amassed large numbers within a common space and discipline, provided a catchment pool for schooling. Two strategies, in alliance but also in tension with one another, appeared in the campaign mounted by Mary Carpenter and the NIA. The first, much closer to Carpenter's heart and congruent with the expansively paternalist practices she applauded, cast employers and voluntary benefactors in the role of dispensers of the civilization and discipline needed for the maintenance of social order. Workers were to be taught their proper place and role, but through the kindness of compulsory and charitable education, training in skills, work incentives, medical assistance, and institutions of self-help (savings banks, libraries, workingmen's institutes, excursions, and cheap educational newspapers). Efforts like Sasipada Banerjee's were steps in this direction.

The other scheme, which was always conceived as a supplement to the first, was factory legislation aimed solely at the working child. This, as Banerjee emphasized at Leeds and as Carpenter repeatedly put it in issues of the Association's journal in the 1870s, was the only way of instituting education at the centre of factory children's lives. The English precedent, where the installation of a half-time Act was linked to the establishment of factory schools, served as the model for this programme. Factory legislation, therefore, was understood as an instrument of enlightenment and discipline simultaneously. The Factory Act came to occupy an increasingly insistent place in Carpenter's programme, as the culmination of the logical triad that began with the prison and passed through the reformatory and the industrial school.

In functional terms, this could be conceived as a parcelling out of the responsibilities of social reproduction between employers and the state. The state would provide the legal constraints that would release the space for factory education, and an enlightened stratum of paternalist employers, assisted by voluntary workers and philanthropists, would administer the correct doses of moral instruction and encouragement. The smoothness of this projected alliance was, however, disturbed before it had begun. The practices of employers did little to encourage the belief that they were interested in educating and 'civilizing' their charges. By the late 1870s, for instance, the Borneo Jute Company had broken off its relations with Banerjee and was no longer funding his initiatives. The library he had established for workers was closed down in 1879, and shortly afterwards the factory school was converted into a warehouse.[75]

In Bombay, matters were much more extreme. The industry boomed in the 1870s, and a large clutch of new mills seemed to spring up every year. In May 1876, Carpenter addressed her Association upon her return from India. Here she expressed dissatisfaction with the management of Bombay's factories, pointing to the evidence collected by the Factory Commission, which established the near-universal absence of education, the fact that labourers, including children, were subjected to gruelling overwork, sometimes fatally, and drawing unfavourable comparisons with prisons, where prisoners never worked over ten hours a day.[76]

The anxiety that the 'civilization' induced by harmonious industrial relations was not going to transpire made the Association offer an ambitious proposal to Bombay's mill owners in 1878. Praising the mill industry for its modernizing impetus and the employment it provided, the Association pleaded for 'patient investment' in the primary education of children between eight and fifteen years of age.

> If each mill owner employing a number of boys in his mill were to enter into a sort of contract with the Bombay Branch of the National Indian Association, that body will voluntarily undertake to organize a regular system for the education of boys eight to fourteen years old, and to have the entire charge of appointing teachers, making the necessary arrangements, and having a regular and periodical inspection of and report on the progress, for all which the mill owner in his turn should agree to pay to the Branch every year a certain reasonable sum to be fixed hereafter.[77]

The association went on to suggest that the boys should be schooled and worked in shifts of six or ten from each department, so that the working of the school would go on unhindered. The proposal concluded with a fervent appeal to the 'humane instincts' of the mill owners, but the proposal was not accepted.[78] Each experience of this kind must have brought bitter lessons of its own and made the idea of a voluntary philanthropic compact between mill owners and reformers seem more and more distant.

Between 1874 and 1877, Carpenter repeatedly put forth her programme of reform before statesmen and public figures. Her advocacy of a string of reforms—juvenile reformatories, prison discipline, female education, industrial schools, and factory regulation—had, before her death in 1877, managed to garner some fairly influential sympathy. The question of factory legislation for India was far from settled in any form at this point, and the likelihood of regulation, in the face of a belligerent Bombay cotton lobby, seemed faint. However, Carpenter's interventions—and, equally important, the interventions she mediated—did manage, to a certain extent, to determine the trajectory of discussion by articulating a range of problems that the protagonists of later debates had to accept as consequential: overwork, the need for a half-time Act, and education.

So a cogent ideological programme of 'improvement' structured the emergence of Indian factory law as an idea. The benefits of restricted working hours—generally conceived as a measure directed solely at factory children—were seen to be instructive. The discipline of the factory was to be regulated and cut down in order to accommodate the discipline of moral and educational instruction, which, in turn, would (*a*) produce enlightened workers and (*b*) sustain social order and harmony. The third dimension of factory law—protection against the exploitation of employers—was secondary to this, and factory law, within this ideological framework, represented a virtuous confluence of voluntary philanthropy, employer paternalism, and state regulation. In its actual course, as will be seen, this bore only a thin, formal resemblance to the law as it actually emerged, as statute and as practice. Carpenter's intervention is best understood as a thick ideological thread that twisted its way through the course of factory legislation and thinned out in its relations with other forces.

Bombay and Lancashire: Commercial Competition and the Factory Act

In 1892, the *Indian Textile Journal*, mouthpiece of the Bombay cotton-textile industry, carried an article entitled 'The Cotton Trade Humanitarian Thermometer'. This juxtaposed the ebb and flow of Lancashire's interest in the working hours of Bombay's mills to the state of dividends in the cotton trade.

> +20 per cent: 'Leave India alone, let every country mind its own business, India has a right to work as she likes.
>
> +10 per cent: 'It is a question whether India should not have Factory Acts applied. We are all part and parcel of one empire, and there is no reason why she should be unshackled while we are heavily handicapped …
>
> −5%: 'The state of affairs in India is really scandalous. Slavery is really the position of mill employees who are worked to early graves for mere pittances, and these even are reduced by numerous fines. Humanity cries aloud for redress, and if the Indian Government will not interfere the Home Government must be speedily made to put a stop to this disgraceful and hideous abuse.[79]

This was a witty variant on a theme that Bombay's mill owners had played on since the mid-1870s: factory legislation in India was explained in terms of the Lancashire cotton lobby's desire to stifle competition from the Bombay mill industry. Manchester's thieving ways, dressed up in the garb of Free Trade and humanitarian concern, were seen as a sufficient explanation of the project of factory reform in India. It was an explanation which proved to have immense lasting power, played a significant role in crystallizing a kind of business nationalism in the late nineteenth and early twentieth century in India, and inserted itself into a number of subsequent historical accounts of factory legislation.[80]

In terms of 'real' historical consequences, there can be little doubt that the passage of factory legislation by the Government of India was in large measure motivated by Lancashire. The *form* of this pressure, however, needs to be precisely elucidated. In this context, it might be helpful to flag an observation about the gap between the legislative restrictions sought by Manchester and the actual shape of factory legislation in India, which, it is clear, made virtually no difference to the economic rivalry between Bombay and Lancashire. Bodies of employers (and occasionally workers whom they organized under their tutelage) demanded, sporadically in the 1870s and more aggressively in the late 1880s, the legislative restriction of the working hours of Indian factories. The working time of factories, however, was barely regulated by the enactments of 1881 and 1891, which aimed at the protection of discrete minorities—women and children—within the workplace. General working hours, indeed, were not touched until much later, in 1911. Manchester had little to do with that piece of law: it was, rather, a response to public campaigns and working-class agitations against the inordinately long hours of work made possible by the use of electric light in mills.

So at the time that factory legislation as a project was being conceived for India—the 1870s—Manchester's interventions were consequential in a purely *nominal* sense. In other words, the *fact* of protective legislation owed something to British textile-capitalist interventions, but its *content* was shaped by entirely different forces. The actual passage of factory legislation in 1881 and 1891 belied Manchester's hopes: at the very least, then, there was a significant gap between the demands of commercial rivalry and the objectives of legislation.

This discrepancy is partly accounted for by the operation of other forces—the nature of the British precedent in factory legislation, the imperial–humanitarian interventions brokered by Mary Carpenter, and struggles over factory regulation that emerged within Bombay (which I take up in the following chapter). But it also points to an important dimension of Indian factory law that is not usually given its due weight. To put it plainly: the actual economic interests of Manchester, conceived in terms of the health of the textile export trade, were *not* the motivating force behind factory legislation. Instead, there existed a complex political field-of-force where the demand for factory legislation played an important role that, nevertheless, was largely *rhetorical*.

The question of factory legislation must be situated within the context of the major demand made by Manchester in the 1870s—Indian tariff reform. Historians generally agree that the period between 1874 and 1882 saw the imposition of virtual Free Trade upon India, under the stewardship of Salisbury as Secretary of State, and of Lords Northbrook, Lytton, and Ripon as Viceroys of India.[81] This principally took the form of the repeal of protective duties levied on cotton piece goods imports into India by the colonial government, under pressure from the India Office, which in turn was under pressure from Lancashire.

As Ira Klein has pointed out, economic historians studying India in this period have often converted Gallagher and Robinson's influential notion of an 'Imperialism of Free Trade' into, effectively, a theory of the imperialism of Manchester Free Traders, implicitly assuming that the Free Trade policies imposed on India between 1874 and 1896 (before financial exigencies rolled them back) derived from Lancashire's interests in the global export trade.[82] Klein remarks that economic nationalist critiques of British policy, which emerged at this time, describe 'an Indian economic landscape dotted with the bones of Indian entrepreneurs who tried to break the Manchester monopoly'.[83]

By the mid-1870s, as Klein puts it, the mid-Victorian economic boom, which had begun in the 1850s, was 'thudding to a close'.[84] A prolonged slowing of Manchester's cotton textile trade was one of the principal signifiers of this decline. With the emergence of other industrializations on the Continent and in the United States, the export trade was subject to unprecedented foreign competition. The emerging cotton textile industry in Bombay, financed and run principally by wealthy or upwardly mobile Indian entrepreneurs (in contrast to the predominance of European capital elsewhere in the country), was one of the sources of this challenge.

This challenge was restricted to one part of the international market in cotton exports—the trade in coarse fabrics. In 1876,

Colonel Raynsford Jackson, the Chairman of the Associated Bodies of Employers and Workmen of the Cotton Manufacturing Districts, expressed alarm at the fact that exports to Bombay had halved in the space of a year.[85] Meetings of cotton manufacturers and the Manchester Chamber of Commerce regularly passed resolutions deploring this loss of trade, and businessmen expressed their worry that fairly soon Indian mills might be able to spin finer counts of cotton than they had been doing. This would mean, they calculated, a potential loss of two-thirds of Lancashire's trade in piece goods if, as they anticipated, Bombay mills were likely to shift their production from coarse to medium-grade cloth.[86] Sir Richard Temple, who had been the Finance Member of the Governor General's Council between 1868 and 1874, Lieutenant Governor of Bengal under Northbrook, and who later served as the Governor of Bombay, addressed Manchester businessmen in extremely commercial–patriotic terms some five years later, shortly after his return from India, on the same issue. Deploying a rhetoric that Manchester was bound to respond to, he bemoaned the fact that Bombay was turning out 'excellent articles' and gaining markets 'which, as a patriotic Englishman, I should say rather belong to Manchester', listing the Persian Gulf, South-Eastern Arabia, East Africa, and East Asia as areas of competition.[87]

This aggressive and insecure idiom, which deliberately exaggerated the consequences of Bombay competition, marked a shift in the nature of the Manchester Free Traders' relationship with India. Radical liberal propagandists of Free Trade, headed by Cobden and Bright, had always been keenly interested in questions of Indian development. They had the ear of the Government of India on matters of economic 'improvement' (which consisted chiefly of recipes for transport and agricultural reform) and education, and rejected, on partly ideological grounds, any direct political involvement.[88] By the mid-1870s, as Klein points out, the 'community of interest between Manchester and the Indian administration was breaking down', and Manchester began to use overt political pressure, in the form of a ceaseless flow of public meetings, deputations, petitions, and newspaper propaganda, to influence colonial policy.[89]

At the same time, capitalist interests within India were beginning to organize their own defences against 'the imperialism of free trade'. Several of the Indian Chambers of Commerce—especially Bombay and Madras—had been known to actively support and push for the retention of cotton import duties.[90] This sharpened the hostility of Lancashire capitalists towards their Bombay counterparts.

This came to a head in 1874 over the question of tariff reform. Lancashire manufacturers petitioned Whitehall for the removal of the 5 per cent duty levied on the import of coarse piece goods into India. This set the stage for a controversy between the Secretary of State, Salisbury, and the Viceroy, Northbrook. As Salisbury admitted in private, his reasons for backing tariff reform were entirely political. It is no coincidence, perhaps, that the Conservatives had wrested Manchester from the Liberals in the 1874 elections: this would have made Salisbury all the keener to please cotton manufacturers. Most of all, he wanted a swiftly executed reform, a single stroke to knock down tariff walls. He was aware of the growing weight of middle-class, business-friendly public opinion in India, especially in Bombay, and anticipated an open clash between Free Trade propagandists and Indian critics of imperialism if the reform were to be delayed.

Northbrook refused to comply with Salisbury's increasingly desperate imperatives, pushing through instead, in August 1875, at a single sitting of his Council, a Tariff Bill that left cotton duties untouched. He introduced, as a sop to Salisbury and Manchester, a countervailing duty on the import of high-quality yarn into India from Egypt and America, which Bombay's manufacturers were beginning to use to produce higher-count cotton goods.[91] As the Chairman of the Tariff Committee set up by Northbrook, A.B. Money argued tariffs provided eighty lakh rupees' worth of revenue at a time of acute financial trouble. There were two paths open if Salisbury's demands were to be met: either to shift the revenue burden on to direct forms of taxation or to attack the cotton duties that affected Manchester's trade alone—a mere 2 per cent of the total revenue from tariffs.[92] The first measure would have involved an intensification of the very financial hardships that Northbrook was committed to avoiding. The second—which was adopted by his successor, Lytton, in 1878–9—would have been tantamount to an open declaration that Indian tariffs were being manipulated in deference to Manchester.[93]

In an emergency measure aimed at persuading Northbrook to reverse his decision, Salisbury deputed the Under-Secretary of State for India, Louis Mallet, to Calcutta in October 1875. Mallet, who unlike Northbrook (or, for that matter, Salisbury himself) was an ideologically committed Free Trader, was also one of the Viceroy's oldest friends. His intermediation failed, and consequently the political nightmares Salisbury entertained were amply realized.

It was in this context that the questions of factory and tariff reforms first intersected. The Factory Commission of 1875 had held its proceedings and published its report shortly before the tariff controversy broke out in full force. Thus, two measures that effectively sought to contain the expansion of Bombay's textile capitalism were envisaged at more or less the same time. There is little evidence of conscious design behind this confluence at this early stage. Mill owners in Bombay, however, thought otherwise, and it is to the moment of Mallet's visit, in a sense, that we can ascribe the origins of the emergence of Bombay's industrial capitalists as an organized political force.

This was because Mallet, while in India in October, decided to visit several of Bombay's factories in the company of a Glasgow cotton spinner named John Robertson. This galvanized the mill-owning community into collective action, and served as the foundational tension that brought a new organization, the Bombay Millowners' Association (BMOA), into being. Outside scrutiny of their industrial practices caused the mill owners of Bombay particular alarm. In an address to Sir Louis Mallet, virtually the founding act of the BMOA, they wrote fretfully that 'no intimation of your intended visit of inspection was given to the owners of the mills, and consequently no preparations were made by them for your reception, or to shew the mills in any other than their ordinary working state'.[94] They added that 'we have no doubt that you were convinced that the representations made by interested persons, or mistaken philanthropists, in England, of the condition and system of work in Indian factories, had been grossly exaggerated'.[95] A similar complaint was registered about the visit of John Robertson:

> [H]is investigations were conducted with such secrecy that, until a few weeks ago, when it became known that he had issued a report, the object of his mission to India had never been suspected.[96]

The idea of outsiders scrutinizing the domain of the factory, so carefully shielded by mill owners from public view, was evidently reprehensible to Bombay's textile capitalists, especially if such scrutiny was organized with a view to legislation. So what appears to have been a decision by the Government of British India to bolster their faltering finances, through the retention and extension of duties, rapidly turned into a fierce contest between the textile capitalists of Bombay and Manchester.

Salisbury, and his successor at the India Office, Cranbrook, received several intimations of alarm from organized Lancashire cotton manufacturing capital in the second half of the 1870s. In February 1878, a deputation from the 'associated committees of employers and workmen' of Lancashire visited the India Office. Colonel Raynsford Jackson, a successful Lancashire manufacturer who led this delegation, 'reluctantly' demanded 'countervailing' excise duties on the production of Bombay's mills as a measure to counter the effect of continued Indian import duties.[97] This was in some ways a fairly heretical demand, given the principles of Free Trade, as 'A Lancashire Manufacturer' reminded Jackson in a letter to the *Times* a week later.[98]

A year later, in February 1879, Cranbrook was approached by a similar deputation, this time from an Association for the Removal of Protection from Indian Manufactures, an organization composed of Manchester merchants and agents, which again demanded the remission of Indian duties.[99] Raynsford Jackson was the spokesman for Lancashire again, and this time he left out his old demand for countervailing excise duties. Cranbrook replied sympathetically, and in this context mentioned the question of factory legislation as a possible panacea to the hardships of Manchester. Factory legislation, in its four-decade journey through Parliament and the courts in England, had come by this time to be seen as something that, in principle at least, could be accepted—indeed, *had* to be accepted—by committed Free Traders as well. To suggest the application of this process to India was, on humanitarian and historical grounds, legitimate, though not free from contestation.

Restrictive factory legislation against Bombay manufacturers was, then, a permissible way in which Salisbury and his government's tariff promises to Lancashire, thwarted by Northbrook and the Government of India, could be redeemed on another stage. In the event, the decision to press for factory legislation was passed through Parliament relatively smoothly in 1879, whereas, on the very same day, 4 April 1879, 'the embarrassments of Indian finance' were declared to be of a magnitude that made the lifting of cotton import duties unfeasible.[100] Factory law for India, then, in one of its dimensions, could serve as a pawn in an intricate political bargaining game between the interests of Whitehall, the British Indian administration, and Lancashire capital.

Upholders of the principle of factory legislation, whatever motives they were propelled by, thus needed to tread carefully and avoid, as far as possible, any direct linkages between the project of factory law and the interests of Lancashire in their rhetoric. If these linkages were made, there were costs to be feared. In late July 1875, having been recently alerted of conditions in Indian factories, Lord Shaftesbury made a long and eloquent intervention in the House of Lords on the question of Indian factory labour.[101] He expressed his desire to give 'the Natives what we most earnestly desire for our own population—the boon of healthy work, healthy homes, and good education', and cited the work of both the NIA, whose journal he had been reading 'for the present month', and of the Factory Commission in Bombay, the evidence produced by which he had found in the journal, to bolster his case.[102] He also made reference to the importance of legislation for Indian factories for Manchester's cotton trade. Salisbury rose to answer the Earl, and one of his comments betrayed an anxiety about possible construals of Shaftesbury's speech:

> I am afraid, however, that my Friend is too sanguine when he says the Natives are with us on this question. That is the precise difficulty with which we have to contend. There may be some persons who can see the thing in the light in which we see it; but generally this proposal is to limit the hours of factory labour is looked upon as a great conspiracy for the purpose of promoting Manchester manufacturers. There is no subject more commonly discussed, and writers in the Native journals dwell on the wickedness of the English, who are trying to stifle Native manufactures in India under the guise of philanthropy. I am, therefore, glad that my Noble friend is coming forward in this matter, for his philanthropy is, at all events, above suspicion; he cannot be suspected of joining in this dark conspiracy, and trying to stifle the infant manufactures of India in the interests of Manchester. I hope that his well-known efforts on behalf of the factory operatives of his own country will show that he is actuated by none but philanthropic motives in desiring that the Government shall take the same measures for the protection of the women and children, the factory operatives of India.[103]

Salisbury knew the strength of the Lancashire campaign for unfettered Free Trade, and the terms in which it was seen in India. Shaftesbury was lending the weight of a tumultuous epoch of English legislative and political history, marked by the advance, through legislature, administration (inspection), and court, of the principle of factory regulation. His philanthropic motives were, so far as we can judge at a distance of over a century, indeed genuine. Salisbury had also corresponded with Mary Carpenter and knew the existence of a campaign for factory legislation by reformers who stood outside the apparatuses of industrial capital, British state, and colonial administration. It was important for the legitimacy of factory legislation as a principle that these independent demands, which linked up ideologically with Shaftesbury's concerns, were kept untarnished by association with Lancashire manufacturing interests.

What, however, was the nature of the association that actually existed, and that was mediated through such rhetoric? Lancashire's *economic* interests do not furnish the material for an adequate story. Was the connection between Manchester and Indian factory reform, then, chiefly ideological, a loop around Free Trade *doxa*? This raises another question: was there actually a relationship between the two principal dimensions of the project of factory reform, the project outlined by Mary Carpenter's campaigns on the one hand and the commercial agenda of Free Trade on the other? This is not a question that can be answered unequivocally. It might be instructive, however, to briefly examine a curious sidelight of the history of factory legislation, one that has gone unnoticed in most histories.

This was an exchange of letters between Carpenter and John Bright in 1876, shortly after Carpenter's return from her last visit to India. Bright was one of the principal luminaries of the Manchester Free Trade movement in its glory days, between the 1840s and the end of the 1850s. He was Cobden's lieutenant and partner in the anti-Corn Law agitation and a Parliamentary Radical who represented Manchester in Parliament between 1847 and 1857. He lost his seat in 1857, as Arthur Silver has shown, principally as a consequence of intense faction-fighting within the once united school of Free Traders, but this defeat was sustained and made real by the advances of a new, revitalized, and hegemonic Conservatism through the 1860s and 1870s.[104] He seems, by the time of his brief correspondence with Carpenter, to have generally fallen behind the emerging trends of politics and statecraft in this period, which ushered in more social interventionism, more welfare, and, famously, Disraeli's takeover of the agenda of electoral reform in 1867.

Carpenter wrote to Bright in 1876, asking for his support in the cause of an extension of the English Factory Acts to India. We do not know what calculations impelled her to approach Bright, but we can guess. In the first place, she must have been galvanized by his long-standing interest in Indian affairs, and the programmes he advocated—agricultural improvement, education, roads, and transport—were, theoretically at least, complementary to her own 'improving' agenda. Beyond this, however, she would also have been aware of the strength that Bright's support would have lent her campaign. There is no indication whatsoever that Carpenter was remotely interested in 'protecting' Manchester interests; however, she could not have been unaware of the strategic advantages of a possible alliance with Britain's leading commercial lobby.

In the event, Bright's reply was curt and even rude, though, in a strange way, also principled. It amounted to a statement of Free Trade social philosophy in its purest form, which was increasingly untenable in domestic policy by the 1870s, and had been forsaken by leading Liberals as well as Conservatives.

> As to a Factory Act in India. It seems to me not to be a subject for the House of Commons, but for the India Government and I should be disposed to object to its being discussed in the House of Commons.
>
> Factory Acts are measures which tell upon industry as the Tariffs of foreign countries do—and if pushed much further will cripple and perhaps destroy it. I hope we may keep from meddling with such delicate matters in India—and be content to leave them to the Government of India.[105]

What makes this exchange interesting is Bright's typical commitment to a complete identification with the doxa of free-trade ideology. The principle of imperial non-intervention in Indian administration, an opposition to tariff reform, *and* an opposition to any kind of protective factory legislation are here tied together within an entirely cogent structure of reasoning. The Manchester interventions (mediated through Whitehall) that I have touched on follow precisely the opposite line of thought: direct imperial intervention in Indian industry, and in social policy, was acceptable because it secured Free Trade in India for Britain. In the next chapter, I demonstrate how the campaign of another meliorist–activist—the Parsi reformer Sorabji Shahpurji Bengali—managed to latch on to *this* strand of free-trade politics, in sharp contrast to Carpenter's failure to obtain Bright's support.

There was no automatic link, therefore, between the verities of free-trade ideology and the establishment of a Factory Act in India. Nor did the exigencies of economic competition compel Manchester to seek the control of Bombay capital by Parliament. I suggest, tentatively, that enquiry into this question is better served by a consideration of the industrial politics and strife 'internal' to Britain, especially Lancashire, from the 1870s.

It was not a happy decade for employers. The long economic depression that was to last nearly till the end of the century had set in. In this context, trade slumped, sometimes mildly, sometimes more violently, for the Lancashire textile industry. Wages and profits were both under threat, and tensions inevitably resulted from this. These were played out in a substantially transformed political terrain.

E.H. Hunt describes the years between the 1867 Reform Act and 1875 as 'a period of remarkable legislative advance'.[106] After Disraeli extended the property basis of the franchise in 1867, a substantial proportion of the male working class had the vote, and this set the political context for the legal changes of the 1870s. Master–servant legislation was finally repealed in 1875, and punitive legal sanctions against breaches of contract by workers were abolished. Strikes, and peaceful picketing, were recognized as legitimate political tactics. Unions were concomitantly recognized as necessary partners in industrial dispute resolution. Correspondingly, parliamentary lobbying within the framework of law and an emphasis on friendly relations between employers and workers became part of the dominant language of industrial relations.[107]

At the same time, collective working-class representation was consolidated, both in the growth of new associations and in parliamentary campaigns. In the cotton industry, the early 1870s saw the emergence of the Factory Acts Reform Committee and its successor, the United Textile Factory Workers Association.[108] Factory legislation was concomitantly amended. In 1872, Anthony Mundella, Member of Parliament for Sheffield and a major figure in the development of methods of conciliation and arbitration in industrial relations, introduced a Factory Acts Amendment Bill to regulate the hours of work of adult women, children, and 'young persons' (below sixteen) in cotton factories.[109]

This passed into law in 1874, reducing the hours of work for the protected categories of worker, prohibiting employment for children below ten (the former limit was eight), and extending half-time protection to fourteen-year-olds.[110]

In the spring of 1872, the Manchester Chamber of Commerce, in its quarterly meeting, reacted to the proposed measure in a two-pronged fashion. They applauded the intent of the Bill—to extend protection to the 'helpless'—but condemned the opportunity taken by adult men to press for a legal reduction of *their* working day.[111] This judgment expressed a deeper anxiety about the consequences of unionization. As an account in the *Quarterly Review* of 1878 observed, 'Before 1872 ... the want of cohesion on the part of the employers exposed them to incessant and systemic attack ... demands for higher wages were unceasingly being made in one form or another upon individual millowners, and the workpeople withdrawn to enforce them.'[112] Despite the language of conciliation that dominated the discourse of both unions and employers in this period, a new terrain for industrial struggle was being mapped out in the 1870s, with workers enjoying both shorter hours and greater legislative protection than they had before.

In 1878, in the context of a downturn in the cotton trade and, incidentally, the consequences of the growth of Bombay, employers of cotton mill labour in various parts of England and Scotland imposed a 10 per cent wage cut. An editorial from the *Times* describes, with suitable horror, the working class response to this. Mills were burnt down, armed workers surrounded their masters' houses and demanded money, and, most serious of all, a massive strike swept Lancashire and spread to Glasgow, causing an enormous loss of profits and capital in an already crisis-ridden industry.[113] 'The working classes,' wrote the editor gravely and sententiously, 'seem to be losing their heads in more than one country at this moment. In Germany, the Socialists ... are peculiarly active; and in America grave fears are excited by the threatening aspect of Communistic bodies.'[114] A letter written by 'A Lancashire Man' to the *Times* three and a half months later has the same air of gloom: 'It is not too much to say that the cotton trade never will, never can be what it once was.'[115] It ends on a note of warning: 'Reconciliation will doubtless, indeed must, at length be arrived at as between capital and labour, the employer and the employed, but with present appearances a long and bitter day of reckoning will intervene.'[116]

Constant fears about the disruption of industrial relations, then, intruded upon the public discourse of the time. Factory legislation, at the same time, was moving ahead in Britain, bringing new categories of labourers under its sway. Law, at one of its poles, could function as a restraining mechanism, to defuse the dangers of militant trade unionism through the piecemeal recognition and/or creation of entitlements. Mundella, who introduced the new Factory Bill, certainly would have had this end in mind—he himself was an employer in the hosiery trade and a pioneer of arbitration schemes between employers and workers.[117] At the same time, the wedding of industrial unrest in 1878 to the demand for an eight-hour day shows that law could perform a very different function in the context of working-class struggle and serve as a reference point for the articulation of new demands for rights.

Seen in the light of these tensions, Lancashire's signature on the text of Indian factory legislation reveals another dimension. Lancashire's industrialists felt besieged by working-class movements and also by the continued advance of protective labour legislation and the demands that crystallized around it. These problems, they continually asserted, were not suffered by their rivals in India. For this reason if for no other, a Factory Act for India was a worthwhile project. The apparent willingness of the India Office to consider factory legislation for India seriously, in the context of its unwillingness to legislate new terms of trade directly, suggests that factory law for India may have been something of a sop conceded to Manchester in lieu of more important concessions. As such, its symbolic value outweighed its practical value.

From the perspective of Lancashire capitalists, on the other hand, factory legislation was always very much a supplementary demand, subordinate to a wider agitation for the transformation of the terms of trade with India. But this agitation itself may not have been premised upon the assumption that a removal of import duties would automatically change the balance of trading power and international market share for the textile industries of Lancashire and Bombay. Many manufacturers had, by the late 1870s, conceded that the market in coarse cotton cloth no longer belonged without challenge to Lancashire.[118] At the same time, the friction that was simmering in the textile industry needed to be addressed. The late 1870s witnessed repeated appeals by employers to workers to understand the exigencies of international trading trouble, highlighting the *externality* of the difficulties that were besieging the industry, and, therefore, driving their wages down. Workers were urged to refocus their energies and concentrate their hostility on their 'real' enemy—the protection offered to Bombay textile manufacturers by the Indian government.[119]

It is symptomatic of this desire that at the meeting in February 1879 where Colonel Raynsford Jackson vehemently denounced the retention of import duties, Elijah Holt presented a massive petition from the textile workers of Blackburn, Lancashire, which had apparently collected 13,672 signatures in two days. The petition said:

> [T]his was not merely a manufacturers' question. The working people of Lancashire looked at it in no such light. If the manufacturers could not carry out their business at a profit, the working men must be sufferers. The working people of Lancashire regarded this tax as one which vitally affected them, and as one which the Government ought to remit at once totally and entirely.[120]

The damage done by Bombay competition to the production of Lancashire textile mills was thus exaggerated at a time when the beginnings of generalized industrial depression were in evidence. Wages and profits were poised against one another, their contradictions brought sharply into focus by a period of economic stress. In such a context, arguments that could solder unity between the interests of employers and workers were welcome. The constant reference to the injustice of duties protecting Bombay mills helped, in a limited way, to externalize industrial tensions and displace the hostilities that stalked the world of textile capital and labour in Britain.

There was, then, a powerful commercial angle to the making of factory legislation in India. This, however, had more to do with a clash of political than of economic interests. Two groups of textile capitalists—in Manchester and in Bombay—exerted influence and pressure upon the governments they addressed, and the fruit of these negotiations was an ambivalent and weak piece of legislation. Manchester got its revenge for the 'protection' enjoyed by Bombay—though in a very watered-down form—in an Act that afforded them little consolation. The Bombay textile lobby, which intervened actively against legislation, succeeded in weakening the Act, but, as I shall argue in the following chapters, this did not free them from emergent tensions within their city's industrial relations.

'Improvement' and 'competition', crudely put, were the mechanisms that effected the enactment of factory law in India in 1881. On the one hand, a doctrine of uplift and civilization through the discipline of the factory, embodied in Carpenter's interventions, provided the basic ideological matrix within which the project of a Factory Act was articulated. On the other hand, factory law also sprang from a complex terrain of commercial rivalry, and, more significantly, anxiety, on the part of the mill owners of both Lancashire and Bombay. At the same time, as factory industry grew in Bombay, the question of protective legislation became part of an ideological tussle within Bombay and marked the introduction of a labour question into the city's politics. In the next chapter, I explore this dynamic and trace the paths followed by factory law from idea to statute book.

Notes

1. J.L. Hammond and Barbara Hammond, *Lord Shaftesbury* (London: Constable, 1923), p. 150.

2. *Hansard's Parliamentary Debates (3rd Series)*, vol. 226, House of Lords, Friday, 30 July 1875.

3. *Native Opinion*, 29 December 1878, *Reports on Native Newspapers in Bombay Presidency* (henceforth *RNP, Bom.*), 1878–9.

4. *Gujarat Mitra*, 29 December 1878, *RNP, Bom.*, 1878–9.

5. Bipan Chandra, *The Rise and Growth of Economic Nationalism in India* (Delhi: People's Publishing House, 1966).

6. Raymond Williams, *Keywords: A Vocabulary of Culture and Society* (New York: Oxford University Press, 1976), pp. 98–102.

7. Karuna Mantena, *Ends of Empire: Henry Maine and the Ends of Liberal Imperialism* (Princeton, 2010).

8. C. Hall, *White, Male and Middle Class* (Cambridge, 1992); G.M. Young, *Portrait of an Age* (Oxford, 1936).

9. Seth Koven, 'Borderlands: Women, Voluntary Action, and Child Welfare in Britain, 1840 to 1914', in *Mothers of a New World: Maternalist Politics and the Emergence of Welfare States*, edited by Seth Koven and Sonya Michel (London, 1993), pp. 94–127.

10. Linda Clark, *Women and Achievement in Nineteenth-Century Europe* (Cambridge: Cambridge University Press, 2008).

11. Koven, 'Borderlands', p. 106.

12. Mary Carpenter, *Six Months in India* (London: Spottiswoode & Co., 1868; henceforth *SMI*), vol. 1, p. 60.

13. See Seth Koven and Sonya Michel, 'Womanly Duties: Maternalist Politics and the Origins of Welfare States in France, Germany, Great Britain and the United States', *The American Historical Review* 95, no. 4 (October, 1990): 1076–108, for a fuller elucidation of this argument.

14. See John Eagles, *The Bristol Riots: Their Causes, Progress and Consequences, by a Citizen* (Bristol, 1832) for a colourful contemporary account of this event. Also J.E. Carpenter, *Life and Work of Mary Carpenter* (London: Macmillan, 1879), p. 29.

15. Koven, 'Borderlands', pp. 99–105.

16. Mary Carpenter, *Reformatory Schools for the Children of the Perishing and Dangerous Classes* (Bristol: C. Gilpin, 1851), p. 2 [emphasis in original].

17. M. Carpenter, *Reformatory Schools*, p. 2.

18. Mary Carpenter, *Our Convicts* (London: Longman, 1864), p. 9.

19. Jo Manton, *Mary Carpenter and the Children of the Streets* (London: Heinemann Educational, 1976); Harriet Warm-Schupf, 'Single Women and Social Reform in Mid-Nineteenth Century England', *Victorian Studies* 17, no. 3 (March 1974): 301–17; Janice Elaine-Schroeder, *The Public Voice in Victorian Feminist Speech and Writing*, unpublished PhD dissertation, University of Alberta, 2002.

20. Koven, 'Borderlands'; J.E. Carpenter, *Life and Work of Mary Carpenter*.

21. Koven, 'Borderlands', p. 103.

22. Koven, 'Borderlands', p. 103.

23. Koven, 'Borderlands', p. 100.

24. J.E. Carpenter, *Life and Work of Mary Carpenter*, p. 298 [emphasis mine].

25. J.E. Carpenter, *Life and Work of Mary Carpenter*, p. 298.

26. J.E. Carpenter, *Life and Work of Mary Carpenter*, p. 298.

27. Claire Midgley argues against Antoinette Burton's reading of Carpenter as an 'imperial feminist' and 'colonial reformer'. She argues that 'we should be alert to instances of cooperation [...] between activists positioned on opposite sides of the colonised/colonising divide'. Claire Midgley, 'Mary Carpenter and the Brahmo Samaj of India: A Transnational Perspective on Social Reform in the Age of Empire', *Women's History Review* 22, no. 3: 363–85.

28. Koven, 'Borderlands', p. 105.

29. A. Burton, 'Fearful Bodies into Disciplined Subjects: Pleasure, Romance, and the Family Drama of Colonial Reform in Mary Carpenter's *Six Months in India*', *Signs* 20, no. 3 (1995): 553.

30. J.E. Carpenter, *Life and Work of Mary Carpenter*, p. 299.

31. J.E. Carpenter, *Life and Work of Mary Carpenter*, p. 299.

32. J.E. Carpenter, *Life and Work of Mary Carpenter*, p. 310.

33. M. Carpenter, *SMI*, vol. 1, p. 23.

34. M. Carpenter, *SMI*, vol. 1, p. 24.

35. M. Carpenter, *SMI*, vol. 1, p. 24.

36. Antoinette Burton offers an analysis of Carpenter's Indian voyage, arguing persuasively that she constructed, and had a strong libidinal investment in, the adventure and the 'family romance' of Indian reform, undergirded by assumptions of colonial and racial mastery and difference. Her argument, however, is chiefly directed against heroic-feminist genealogies that place figures like Carpenter unproblematically within the heritage of women's struggles, and so she tends to see Carpenter principally as an embodiment of colonial discourse, ignoring the tensions of her relationship with the state. See Burton, 'Fearful Bodies into Disciplined Subjects', pp. 545–74. See Midgley, 'Mary Carpenter and the Brahmo Samaj of India', for a more systematic critique of Burton's argument.

37. J.E. Carpenter, *Life and Work of Mary Carpenter*, p. 310.

38. Dipesh Chakrabarty, 'Sasipada Banerjee: A Study in the Nature of the First Contact of the Bengali Bhadralok with the Working Classes of Bengal', *Indian Historical Review* 2, no. 2 (January 1976): 339–64.

39. M. Ignatieff, *A Just Measure of Pain* (New York: Pantheon, 1978); M. Foucault, *Discipline and Punish* (New York: Random House, 1977).

40. J.E. Carpenter, *Life and Work of Mary Carpenter*, pp. 331–56.

41. J.E. Carpenter, *Life and Work of Mary Carpenter*, p. 331.

42. M. Carpenter, *SMI*, vol. 1.

43. J.E. Carpenter, *Life and Work of Mary Carpenter*, p. 365.

44. Midgley, 'Mary Carpenter and the Brahmo Samaj of India', p. 376.

45. J.E. Carpenter, *Life and Work of Mary Carpenter*, p. 376.

46. J.E. Carpenter, *Life and Work of Mary Carpenter*, p. 381.

47. J.E. Carpenter, *Life and Work of Mary Carpenter*, p. 381; *Journal of the National Indian Association, in Aid of Social Progress in India*, no. 1 (January 1871).

48. J.E. Carpenter, *Life and Work of Mary Carpenter*.

49. J.E. Carpenter, *Life and Work of Mary Carpenter*.

50. M. Carpenter, *SMI*, vol. 2, p. 36.

51. *Journal of the National Indian Association*, no. 51 (March 1875): 62–3.

52. M. Carpenter, *SMI*, vol. 2, p. 37.

53. M. Carpenter, *SMI*, vol. 2, pp. 43–4.

54. *Journal of the National Indian Association*, no. 51 (March 1875): 62–3.

55. *Journal of the National Indian Association*, no. 46 (October 1874): 238–42.

56. *Gazetteer of the Bombay Presidency*, vol. 10: *Ratnagiri and Savantvadi*; Government Central Press (Bombay, 1880).

57. *First Annual Report of National Indian Association* (Bristol, 24 November 1871).

58. Letter from W.C. Sen to NIA, 8 August 1870, *Journal of the National Indian Association*, no. 3 (March 1871).

59. *Bharat-Sramajibi* (May–June 1879), edited by Kanailal Chattopadhay, Introduction; *Sasipada Banerjee's Life and Work* (n.a., n.d.); Chakrabarty, 'Sasipada Banerjee'.

60. *Bharat-Sramajibi* (May–June 1879).

61. For a discussion of Banerjee's place in the fairly volatile local politics of Baranagar, and Calcutta more generally, see Chakrabarty,'Sasipada Banerjee' and Albion Rajkumar Banerjee, *An Indian Pathfinder* (Oxford: Kemp Hall Press, 1934).

62. Letter from Sasipada Banerjee, cited in *Journal of the National Indian Association*, no. 1 (January 1871): 36.

63. M. Carpenter, *SMI*, vol. 1, p. 251.

64. Chakrabarty, 'Sasipada Banerjee', p. 340.

65. *Journal of the National Indian Association*, no. 3 (March 1871).

66. See *Journal of the National Indian Association*, no. 12 (December 1871); M. Carpenter, *SMI*; Chakrabarty, 'Sasipada Banerjee' *Bharat Sramajibi*, 1879, *passim*.

67. Sitanath Tattvabhushan, *Sasipada Banerji's Life and Life Work* (Calcutta, 1919).

68. *Indian Daily News*, 11 December 1873, cited in *NIA*, no. 38 (February 1874): 35–8.

69. Cited in Chakrabarty, 'Sasipada Banerjee', p. 355.

70. Chakrabarty, 'Sasipada Banerjee', p. 355; *Report of Indian Factory Commission, 1890* (Calcutta, 1890), p. 86.

71. Chakrabarty,'Sasipada Banerjee', p. 357.

72. Chakrabarty,'Sasipada Banerjee', p. 367.

73. *Journal of the National Indian Association*, no. 12 (December 1871).

74. *Journal of the National Indian Association*, no. 12 (December 1871).

75. Chakrabarty, 'Sasipada Banerjee'.

76. *Journal of the National Indian Association*, no. 68 (August 1876): 230–1.

77. *Journal of the National Indian Association*, no. 91 (July 1878): 277–81.

78. *Journal of the National Indian Association*, no. 91 (July 1878): 277–81.

79. *Indian Textile Journal* 3, no. 27 (December 1892): 52–3.

80. See, for example, S.D. Mehta, *The Cotton Mills of India 1854–1954* (Bombay: Textile Association, 1954) and S.M. Rutnagar, *Bombay Industries: The Cotton Mills: A Review of the Progress of the Textile Industry in Bombay from 1850 to 1926 and the Present Constitution, Management and Financial Position of Spinning and Weaving Factories* (Bombay: The Indian Textile Association Ltd, 1927).

81. Mehta, *The Cotton Mills of India*; Chandra, *The Rise and Growth of Indian Nationalism*, pp. 217–71.

82. I. Klein, 'English Free Traders and Imperial Tariffs', *Modern Asian Studies* 5, no. 3 (1971): 251–71.

83. Klein, 'English Free Traders', p. 251.

84. Klein, 'English Free Traders', p. 260.

85. Report of Special Meeting of Manchester Chamber of Commerce, 29 March 1876, from *Tracts on Trade, Finance, etc.*, 1860–1901, Oriental and India Office Collections, British Library, London (henceforth OIOC).

86. Report of Special Meeting of Manchester Chamber of Commerce, 29 March 1876, from *Tracts on Trade, Finance, etc.*, 1860–1901, OIOC.

87. Address of Sir Richard Temple to the Members of the Manchester Chamber of Commerce on the 'Conditions and Prospects of British India', 15 March 1881, Report of Special Meeting of Manchester Chamber of Commerce, 29 March 1876, from *Tracts on Trade, Finance, etc.*, 1860–1901, OIOC.

88. Arthur Silver, *Manchester Men and Indian Cotton, 1847–1872* (Manchester: Manchester University Press, 1966); Bright to Carpenter, 16 May 1876. *Unitarian Historical Society, Transactions*, 17, no. 4 (April 1982).

89. Klein, 'English Free Traders', p. 251.

90. Klein, 'English Free Traders', speech by George Lord at Special Meeting of the Manchester Chamber of Commerce, 1876.

91. *Annual Report of Bombay Millowners' Association*, 1875, p. 5.

92. Klein, 'English Free Traders'.

93. Lytton abolished cotton duties on twenty-seven categories of coarse cotton imports. As Klein argues, this created massive problems of reclassification and plunged a delicate, 'comprehensive and interlocked' customs system into disorder. This further stimulated Manchester demands for the comprehensive abolition of duties, and also intensified opposition to his policy within India. This opposition was vocally expressed *within* the Viceroy's Council, and Lytton, outvoted, had to use his extraordinary constitutional powers to push through his policy. All of which aggravated the political crisis around tariff reform.

94. *Annual Report of Bombay Millowners' Association*, 1875, p. 52.

95. *Annual Report of Bombay Millowners' Association*, 1875, p. 52.

96. *Annual Report of Bombay Millowners' Association*, 1875, p. 55.

97. *Times*, Friday, 15 February 1878.

98. *Times*, Friday, 22 February 1878.

99. *Times*, Wednesday, 5 February 1879.

100. *Times*, Friday, 15 August 1879.

101. *Hansard's Parliamentary Debates* (henceforth *HPD*): *House of Lords*, 30 July 1875, vol. 226, pp. 209–12.

102. *HPD: House of Lords*, 30 July 1875, vol. 226, p. 212.

103. *HPD: House of Lords*, 30 July 1875, vol. 226, p. 214.

104. Silver, *Manchester Men and Indian Cotton, 1847–1872*.

105. Bright to Carpenter, 16 May 1876, *Unitarian Historical Society, Transactions*, p. 177.

106. E.H. Hunt, *British Labour History 1815–1914*, (London: Weidenfeld and Nicolson, 1981), p. 268.

107. Hunt, *British Labour History*, p. 259.

108. Hunt, *British Labour History*, p. 255.

109. *HPD: House of Commons*, 11 February 1873, vol. 214, p. 283.

110. *HPD: House of Lords*, 9 July 1874, vol. 220, pp. 1326–40.

111. *Times*, 23 April 1872.

112. *Correspondence between the Employers' Association and the Delegates of the Trades Unions, 1877, 1878*, in *Quarterly Review* 146: 292 (October 1878): 485–6.

113. *Times*, 18 May 1878.

114. *Times*, 18 May 1878.

115. *Times*, 2 September 1878.

116. *Times*, 2 September 1878.

117. Hunt, *British Labour History*, p. 282.

118. Report of Special Meeting of Manchester Chamber of Commerce, 29 March 1876, from *Tracts on Trade, Finance, etc.*, 1860–1901, OIOC.

119. *Quarterly Review*, October 1878, pp. 485–519.

120. *Times*, 5 February 1879.

2

The Emergence of Factory Law

Bombay, 1874–81

The development of Indian factory law and the advance of Bombay's industrial capitalism were, through the late nineteenth century, two mutually constitutive historical sequences. The question of factory legislation, in the late nineteenth century, was always overdetermined by the specific conditions of Bombay's cotton textile industry. Yet the reverse movement also took place. It was the British Indian government, rather than the Bombay administration, which eventually introduced factory legislation for all of British India, on the basis of debates which ultimately referred almost solely to Bombay. Inextricably embedded in the growth and problems of Bombay's textile capitalism, factory legislation was, thus, also wrenched out of these immediate contexts, since problems which emerged on a local scale were 'resolved', through legislation, at a more general, pan-Indian level.

In the 1870s, the Bombay textile industry was notable mostly for its frequent crises of managerial corruption, over-subscription, and insolvency in the wake of the speculative cotton boom, and subsequent depression, of the mid-1860s.[1] At one level crises of mismanagement, at a deeper level these were crises of growth. Conflicts between managing agents and shareholders in joint stock firms, which quickly came to dominate Bombay's industrialization, were a staple feature of the industry in its early decades, and expanded as the industry itself did. Questions of legal intervention accompanied the textile mills from their inception, most pronounced perhaps in the emerging sphere of company law, which spelt out legitimate practice. There were two other forms in which legislative 'interference' affected the mills—often acrimoniously—in the 1870s: boiler inspection and cotton frauds regulation. These diverse forms of regulation were rather inadequately backed by executive authority—the manpower afforded to inspecting officers was limited. In this, factory legislation would be no different. However, the earlier forms of regulation involved the scrutiny of raw materials, product quality, and company accounts. The conditions of labour, in contrast, were defended assiduously as a domain, alternately, of 'the freedom of contract' and of the employer's sovereignty.

In the early 1870s, the problem of working conditions in Bombay's textile mills cropped up episodically for official attention. In his *Administration Report* for 1872–3, Major A.T. Moore, Chief Inspector of the Cotton Department, observed that

> [t]he hours of labour … are at present not limited by any Government regulation; the working day is undoubtedly long; the nature of work is fatiguing, whilst women and children are largely employed. … The physical wear and tear of the employed must, therefore, be serious and considerable, whilst it is useless to expect that greater consideration will be shown to the female and juvenile hands by the millowner, husband, or parent in this country, than has been exhibited by and towards the same classes at home.[2]

Moore recommended legislation to fix the hours of labour, referring to 'considerable interest' in the question within Bombay—probably a reference to the concerns stirred up by Mary Carpenter's visit. At the same time, given that there were only ten mills in the city, Moore was confident that 'the regulation could be enforced easily and without extra expense by the officers of this Department'.[3] Moore suggested amending the 1863 Cotton Frauds Act, passed in the initial period of Bombay's industrial growth, to engross protection for factory operatives. He did not seek a Factory Act as such. Labour regulation at this stage, therefore, appeared as a minor element in the state's scrutiny and regulation of Indian capitalism.

The industrial dynamism of these years, however, swiftly inflated the urgency of factory reform. In 1873–4, no fewer than nine new joint stock companies were registered in Bombay.[4] Capital had flooded into the construction of Bombay's urban infrastructure and industrial base during the cotton boom which dominated the early and mid-1860s, and new mill companies were established. The completion of the Suez Canal in 1869 further linked Indian trade to imperial markets in a way that facilitated not only the quicker export of British-made cloth (which ruled out Indian competition in the higher counts of cotton), but also facilitated the purchase and rapid transport of British-made textile machinery by Bombay's mills. Despite the several troughs in investment and profitability after the boom induced by the American Civil War reversed itself, Bombay's mills clearly experienced a secular rise in their fortunes, and by the mid-1870s, were rapidly establishing their foothold in Far Eastern markets. Congruently, smallholding peasants and agricultural labourers from the Konkan coast began flooding into Bombay to seek work in the mills. The new social relations of industrial capitalism, fracturing as they expanded, were increasingly seen as scheduled for a more systematic inspection in the interests of social stability.

J.A. Ballard, Mint Master of Bombay, added his voice to Moore's in 1874, drawing attention to the conditions of employment of women and children in Bombay's factories.[5] Ballard's interventions may have been of some significance in securing government attention towards factory labour: he was a man of considerable influence in Bombay. Besides presiding over the Mint since 1861, he had also become President of the Bombay Port Trust in 1873. He was also the President of the Sassoon Mechanics' Institute, which had been founded in 1847 by Europeans working in the Mint and Dockyard in order to foster technical education. In 1863, the institute received Rs 60,000—a considerable endowment—from David Sassoon, who headed one of the city's most prosperous and 'public-minded' family firms. This elevated the institute's public profile and helped it expand its activities in broader directions, which might perhaps be summed up as the stimulation of public opinion among the city's cosmopolitan social elite.

In early 1875, the Mechanics' Institute, upon Ballard's initiative, announced an essay competition on the subject of the necessity of factory legislation. The prize was duly awarded in June to an essay with the title 'Too Much of Anything is Good for Nothing'. The essay bore interesting ideological inflections in the authorities it cited and in the arguments from political economy and philosophy which it harnessed, to the end of establishing that legislative 'interference is quite consonant with political economy and the rules of government'. The essay made use of the 'dear cost of cheap labour' argument originally formulated by Adam Smith and also cited the maxim that 'freedom of contract to the weak really means freedom to coerce by the strong'. Its author anticipated industrial conflict, until then muted in Bombay's mills, suggesting that economic and physical ill-being would provoke 'the *ultima ratio* of physical force', and also argued, perhaps unusually, that women would be particularly prone to revolt against extreme exploitation, since (here Rousseau was cited) 'it is easy to show that woman has been at the bottom of the greatest revolutions in the world'.[6] The essay concluded with a curious, unsettled invocation of the need to protect from overwork 'those who have minds but do not appear to think, who have tongues but do not appear to speak'.[7] In its own way, this was an eloquent rendering of the anxieties of the socially dominant sections of Bombay society, for whom the advancing visibility of a familiar (yet unfamiliar) industrial working class must have produced precisely such an ambiguous reaction.

At the same time, Indian factory labour, for the first time, became a theme of concern within imperial policy debate. At the end of his report for the half-year ending in October 1874, the Chief Inspector of Factories for the UK, Alexander Redgrave, observed that

> we see a cotton industry springing up in India, extending with rapid strides, and it behooves us here to ask whether that industry is carried on upon the old lines of the cotton manufacture here, and if it is so carried on, as is the common report, by factories making 14 hours a day, it is well that the legislature should step in while the industry is, so to speak, in its infancy, and by wise and moderate regulations stop the growth of habits of long hours, and of the employment of child labour ... looking to what factory legislation has achieved in this country, may we not hope that the native workers of India may be spared the ordeal which our cotton operatives went through in former days, and that they may be permitted to enjoy the blessing of moderate labour, of ample time for rest and meals, and of protection to children of tender years.[8]

Concerns were, simultaneously, voiced by rather weightier figures. In 1874, Lord Salisbury, who had recently been appointed Secretary of State for India, seems to have 'noticed' Moore's report.[9] Thereafter, he wrote to the Government of India, urging it to consider the possibility of factory legislation along British lines. These lines of pressure fused in mid-1875, and on 23 March the Government of Bombay, upon imperial instruction, set up a Bombay Factory Commission, the first enquiry of its kind into the conditions of industrial labour in India.[10]

The Factory Commission was the immediate product of the historical juncture of 1874–5, one in which the interests of metropolitan and Bombay capitalists collided, reformist arguments gained ascendancy, and an industrial capitalism centred on factory production took hold in Bombay. It was the first fully articulated encounter between the colonial state and an emergent Indian industrial capitalism over the question of labour. The proceedings of the Commission, therefore, present a freeze-frame of not only factory conditions but also industrial relations at the beginning of the textile industry's entrenchment as the economic basis of Bombay's capitalism.

The depositions of a few dozen people—mill proprietors and agents, company directors, managers, doctors, engineers, foremen and jobbers, working women and children—are contained in this document. The Commission was designed as a concession to the reforming and commercial interests behind factory legislation, an answer to an increasingly audible question. But if its purpose, seen in this light, was to pave the way for legislation, it was destined to fail from the beginning. Its significance cannot be sought in its immediate practical impact: indeed, its most tangible achievement may have been to impede a Factory Act by six years. Rather, what the Commission produced was, first, specific kinds of *knowledge* about working conditions and, second, the elaboration of certain lines of discourse and argument around the factory question. These would prove consequential in the years to come.

Factory Testimonies: The 1875 Commission

The Government of Bombay faced the pressures of emergent middle-class and business opinion in Bombay in the already fractious battleground of the 1870s. The city politics of Bombay in the 1870s was dominated by conflicts over representation, taxation, and the disposal of municipal finances between the city's ratepayers—an expanding but fractured base of property holders, ranging from merchants and industrialists to small traders and shopkeepers—and the government.[11] These interests were expressed most articulately by the city's industrialists. Accordingly, the government appointed a Commission *both* designed to allow—even produce—ground for debate *and* weighted heavily against the possibility of a positive answer to the question of the need for legislation. The locally situated field of force between state and capital in Bombay, on this occasion as subsequently, showed up the limits of metropolitan pressure. It is interesting that a Commission that would, had the writ of metropolitan interests been supreme, have borne the *duty* of recommending legislation, was composed precisely in a manner that would rule out such a recommendation.

The President of the Commission was F.F. Arbuthnot, the Collector of Bombay, who would reveal himself as sympathetic to factory regulation through the sessions of the Factory Commission. The Secretary was W.O. Moylan, Inspector of Steam Boilers, who, in the 1880s, was to play a significant subsidiary role in the extension of the scope of factory law. Thomas Blaney, Coroner of Bombay and an ardent advocate of factory legislation, also served on the Commission. Along with one of the witnesses before the Commission, Thomas Stevenson Weir (Health Officer of the Bombay Municipality), Blaney had visited a number of mills in 1874, collecting information on sanitation, ventilation, and working hours.[12] Weir's report for 1874 had concluded: 'Legislation … is urgently called for … to protect the lives, if not the health, of those who are employed in the cotton mills in the city.'[13] Blaney, Moylan, and Arbuthnot were the only members of the Commission who could be expected to support a Factory Act.[14]

The Commission, however, was packed with men with material interests in the textile industry. J.K. Bythell was Director of the New Berar Company, which ran cotton presses. Mangaldas Nathubhai, who belonged to a family with old connections to the cotton trade with China, had served on the Legislative Council and was the first Indian in Bombay to be knighted.[15] He had also, till 1870, been the Director and Chairman of the Bombay United Spinning and Weaving Company, one of the largest mill companies on the island.[16] Morarji Goculdas was the Director of another successful spinning and weaving mill; G.A. Kittredge represented a managing agency firm; H. Maxwell was associated with two mill companies; and Dinshaw Manockjee Petit, son of one of the textile industry's pioneers, was perhaps the most powerful industrialist in the city.[17] V.N. Mandlik, Vakil at the High Court and distinguished conservative ideologue, was a staunch supporter of the mill owners' agenda. Petit and Goculdas set the tone that was to dominate the Commission's enquiries in the very first meeting, when

Petit declared that injuries in mills were almost all due to the workmen's own negligence, and Goculdas inveighed against restrictions of working time, claiming that 'some workpeople overstayed their meal hours by 2 hours'.[18]

The Commission's encounters were marked by a particular set of rituals, easily taken for granted, but nevertheless encoding, in subtle ways, the operations of hierarchy and power. The Library Room of the Secretariat defined a zone of conversation, a physical and conceptual space marked by the rituals of social equality. Commissioners and witnesses spoke mostly as equals, free to disagree and argue. Testimonies were weighted both with the force of the concrete evidence they supplied and with the force of the patterns of reasoning they offered. These were men invested with the power of knowing and the knowledge of (different kinds of) power. This applied irrespective of whether the expertise pertained to management, medical knowledge, or engineering, or drew simply from the weight of proprietorship. At one level, more or less half the Commission's proceedings amounted to a conversation between proprietors, directors of companies, mill managers, doctors, and engineers about the best way to administer the lives of mills.

On a few occasions, though, the Commissioners burst the bounds of the Library Room and sallied forth to the mills. Here they summarily interrupted work and picked out a series of men, women, and children. In this, too, there were nuances and hierarchies. Jobbers were interviewed with care, as working men but also as experts in their own field—the recruitment and discipline of workers. The operatives may have had their own forms of expertise to offer, some of which might conceivably have been relevant to the Commission's enquiries—their relationship to machinery, for instance, or their patterns of work and leisure. But more often than not these questions would already have been answered for the Commissioners by their expert witnesses. Workers were picked out casually while at their work, interviewed in groups rather than individually, and the Commissioners only occasionally saw it fit to record their names. Their voices were elicited in pursuit of a very limited set of answers. A single choice, in particular, was persistently set before them, presumably dictating the patterns of their reasoning and their answers: would they prefer to retain their current wages or did they seek greater leisure? The very form of the question encoded a threat and posited a zero-sum relation between wages and leisure.[19]

In addition to this, workers were interviewed by men at times associated with the directorships or proprietorships of the mills they worked in, and, without a doubt, they coded their answers accordingly. The women interviewed at the Manockjee Petit Mill on 26 May, for instance, were interrogated, among others, by their employer.[20] The codes of a specific and unequal social order were thus performed, and elaborated, through these patterns of interrogation.

The Factory Commission eventually delivered a verdict in consonance with its composition. The Commission weighed in against a law, and a separate minute by Nathubhai, seconded by Goculdas, Maxwell, and Petit—the mill owners standing firm as a team—loudly deplored the prospect of legislation.[21] Blaney and Arbuthnot were the only dissenters, and it is probably due to their pressure, as well as to limit the potential damage from an Act, that the Commissioners drew up a rudimentary scheme for legislation should the government decide to press ahead. The principal suggestions were: machinery should be protected, children below eight should not be employed, those between eight and fourteen should work eight hours a day at most, daily hours of labour should be limited to twelve, there should be a weekly holiday, and good drinking water should be provided. It is one of the many absorbing twists of the story of factory legislation that these recommendations gestured to an Act far more generous than the parsimonious statute that was eventually enacted in 1881, and that a general working day for factories was not effected till 1911.

The internal coherence of the Commission, then, stemmed from the logic of existing social hierarchies and powerful vested interests. But if this were all, the document—and the encounters made visible by it—would hold little of interest. The real historical value of the Commission of 1875 is the tension it makes visible, on either side of the policy divide. The Commission's remit forced it to act *as though* the conclusions of its enquiry were not foreordained and were open to modification in the light of empirical evidence. The dominant interests it served may have closed off certain avenues of enquiry completely, but nevertheless could not fully predetermine the nature of the evidence collected and knowledge produced, which spilled out of the confines designated for them.

The evidence and knowledge produced by the Commission operated in a realm that was *public*—however limited this 'public' may have been.

Certainly the agitation for factory reform was not in the nature of a popular movement—workers did not organize in favour of it, and its deliberations occurred within a very bounded realm. Yet several of the witnesses and Commissioners seem to have been persistently aware of—and anxious about the consequences of—the public nature of their words. They were aware that they were speaking in their own names and that their words were not their own property.

The emergent press—both English and vernacular—kept a close watch on the proceedings of the Commission. The *Akhbare Sowdagar*, as early as November 1874, immediately after a new Factory Act came into being in Britain, called for similar legislation in India, remarking that a working day from 7.00 a.m. to 5.30 p.m. was sufficient.[22] This was a more radical solution to the question of the length of the working day than any offered by either the Commissioner or witnesses. Shortly after the Factory Commission was appointed, the *Jam-e-Jamshed* issued, from the other side of the divide, a forceful statement. This attacked Lancashire's recent appeal to the Secretary of State, which had called for control of the working hours of women and children in Bombay's factories, following upon the failed attempt to abolish duties on cotton imports into India.[23]

Equally significant was the fact that the newspaper situated the very act of appointing a Commission within a continuum of diabolical moves initiated by Manchester.[24] On the following day, the *Yajdan Parast* made a practical suggestion to the mill owners: if they wanted to forestall legislation, they should get together and supply all the information and arguments they had to the Commission.[25] The lines of confrontation, then, were being drawn up in the public realm before the Commission had even begun its enquiries. This was to intensify through the two months that the Commission held its meetings and gathered testimonies.

Through the period of the Commission's enquiry, Bombay's major newspapers kept a strict watch on its enquiries, applauding, for the most part, arguments and evidence against legislation, and pouncing upon evidence in favour of it as biased and inaccurate. Simultaneously, anxious refutations of the grimmer pieces of evidence were offered. Contrasts were drawn between work in the mills and the lower-paid and more oppressive work performed outside them. The millworkers were constantly presented as happy, well fed, and contented with their conditions of work.[26] It seems that these were arguments and evidence arranged in a particular manner to attract the attention of the Commissioners and make the case against legislation better than the witnesses could do. Simultaneously, the evidence of the Commission was carefully scrutinized by local newspapers.[27]

At the same time, such newspapers, deeply hostile to the cause of labour legislation, nevertheless had to take the proceedings of the Commission seriously. This small but important shift installed the Commission as a legitimate jury for the adjudication of factory conditions, and the pro-business press thus had to reformulate its strategies. This had to do with the presence of a small but vocal group of publications, such as the *Rast Goftar*, the *Dnyanodyaya*, and the *Akhbare Sowdagar*, which with varying degrees of consistency supported legislation and used the Commission as a court of appeal. The establishment of the Commission, and its investigations, thus set in motion particular ways of mobilizing evidence and initiating rhetorical strategies on both sides of the fence.

Throughout the sessions of the Commission between March and June, intriguing relationships were formed between the collection of evidence and the public realm represented in the world of journalism in Bombay. Consider, for instance, the case of Joseph Sharpe, a year into his job as engineer to the Apollo Press at the time of his interview by the Commission, on 2 June. Sharpe provided the following evidence: there were no privies, workers had no time for meals through a working day that could last over sixteen hours in the busy season, six-year-olds were employed at the press, and the work involved the inhalation of dangerous cotton dust. The workers at a press, he claimed, worked 'ten times as hard' as millworkers. He thought legislation enjoining Sunday closing was necessary, and at one point suggested a six-hour day.[28] A week after this, he wrote a panicky letter to the Commission, changing his tone entirely. He accepted that he had recommended legislation for women and children and for Sunday closing. But he also insisted that 'the coolies overwork themselves' and would consider it a great hardship if their working hours were restricted.

The context for this was a report in the *Bombay Gazette* on 5 June, cited by the hapless Sharpe in his note of clarification. The newspaper applauded Sharpe's evidence, mobilizing it in its continuing advocacy of factory legislation for Bombay.[29] His testimony was swiftly woven into a public, polemical context, and this was the source of his worry. He needed to struggle to establish mastery over his own words; they could become weapons in someone else's war. We do not know if Sharpe kept his job.

In another instance, J.K. Bythell, who attended very few of the Commission's meetings and had to resign on the grounds of ill health, responded, with an extremely agitated and anxious letter, to the successive disclosures by the Commission's interviews of the plight of cotton-press workers, of which Sharpe's evidence was only one instance. Bythell, Director of a press presumably not unlike the ones being castigated in the unfolding text of the Commission, issued an eventually successful plea against interference with presses, claiming that the workers were 'naturally extremely anxious to work early and late to make as much money as they can', immediately after stating that two shifts were employed and nobody really had to work through both night and day.[30] Two contradictory statements, then, buttressed a single claim: 'Men who are compelled to take six or eight months' rest annually, may work overtime, I think, for three months or so, without much injury to health.'[31]

Within the proceedings of the Commission, sometimes the patterns of question and answer virtually amount to catechism. This response by 'six women interviewed at the mill' was phrased as a formula, and it is unlikely to be a direct rendition of their words: 'Any diminution of working hours, as it would be attended with loss of income, would not be satisfactory.'[32] In another encounter, the Commissioners asked some children at the Girgaum printing press if they wanted four holidays in a month. The children responded affirmatively. Instantly, a Commissioner cross-examined: 'But would you like to get four holidays if you were to get reduced pay?' The answer, doubtless to most of the Commissioners' gratification and relief, was 'No, then we would not like any holidays.'[33]

In another exchange, the catechism failed. Bhana Naik, employed as foreman (*muccadam*) at Manockjee Petit's mill, vacillated when pressed to decide between wages and holidays. The questioner, after a couple of indecisive answers, urged: 'You must consider and tell us, would it be a good thing to get four holidays a month, instead of two, though you might lose two days' wages?' The foreman's reply continued to frustrate the questioner, though: 'Yes, it would be a good thing, but the loss of 4 days' pay would be a serious matter to some of us poor operatives.'[34]

The choice anxiously urged upon the worker—to choose between wages and 'free' time—was implicitly refused.

Roles sometimes could be reversed, and the questioned rather than the questioner could seek the 'correct' answer to the problem at hand. Consider the following—again, catechistic—conversation. Motiram Bhagubhoy, general manager of the Frere and Mazagaon Spinning and Weaving Company, was asked if he would allow factory children time off to go to school. He responded aggressively. 'Do you mean that if there are 100 children employed in the mill, that all the children should be sent to school at the same time?' The questioner hastily retracted the question: 'No, no, that is not necessary.' The witness drove the point home triumphantly: 'Of course, if all the children are sent away to the school, how could the work be carried out?'[35]

Given the effective marginalization of pro-legislation voices which nonetheless could be raised vocally in the sessions, it was not entirely surprising that these exchanges could sometimes take on fierce tones of hostility. Consider two instances. In the first, Rao Bahadur Becherdas Ambaidas, proprietor of a Gujarat mill, answered the question of dietary arrangements for his millhands—as many mill owners did—with the response that he did not have a shed where they could eat. Instead, they ate 'in the shade of big trees', where it is 'very pleasant'. Ambaidas, however, was aggressively cross-examined by one of the Commissioners, probably Blaney. Would he, too, eat in the shade of trees? He replied that he would, and frequently did. One of the Commissioners then asked him whether he would do so even if it rained—the implication being that his employees had no choice but to do so. This exchange bordered on open mutual hostility.[36]

More bitter still was an exchange involving Thomas Stevenson Weir, who emphatically stated before the Commission that work for more than six hours in a cotton mill was bound to damage the health of children. A Commissioner took it upon himself to acrimoniously remind Weir, at this point, of his role as Municipal Health Officer, working in a department where work was heavy and children were employed.[37] Now Weir, at this stage, was the prime agitator for factory legislation in Bombay, and his comrade-in-arms was Blaney. What he was being told, in effect, was that, given his acceptance of and collusion with similar labour practices, he had no right to represent the cause of factory workers.

The implications of the discursive trajectory of the Commission were perhaps most strikingly elaborated in the interrogation of M.N. Banaji, a young, rising mill director associated with the New Great Eastern Mills, who was later to serve on the Bombay Factory Commission of 1884.[38] Questioned about machinery, Banaji accepted that there should be adequate distance between machines in a mill as a general principle. He claimed that no legislation was needed to protect workers, since there were 'no real dangers' of accidents. Simultaneously, he was forced to acknowledge that *were* there real dangers, legislation 'would do good'.[39] In a similar vein, he claimed that children were actually employed on light work for very short hours in the Bombay mills—tacitly conceding that had they really suffered serious exploitation and danger, they would have merited legislative protection. His general views on factory legislation are worth quoting at length:

> The cotton manufacturing industry is still in its infancy. ... The mill-owners of Bombay have not hitherto conducted their business in so careless a manner, or in a manner so prejudicial to the interests of the operatives as to necessitate the introduction of a Factory Act; on the contrary, they have conduced to the establishment of a healthy local trade since the crisis of 1865;[40] and have immensely contributed to the happiness and contentment of a large class of poor people, and such industry ought to be encouraged and not restricted by legislative enactment.[41]

On the surface, then, we have a series of disavowals that correspond closely to—but articulate with more force—those made by all mill owner–witnesses before the Commission. But consider Banaji's anxious repetition of his premises: there were *no* dangers of accident, mill owners had *not* behaved irresponsibly or cruelly towards workers, and children were *not* overworked. In each of these cases, the denial was, from Banaji's immediate perspective, rational and necessary—in order to ward off factory legislation, it was necessary to disprove its grounds. At the same time, though, an alternative template was marked out by this very process of disavowal—Banaji had to concede that *if his assessments were not true, if conditions in factories genuinely required reform on the grounds of workers' interests, legislation would be merited*. A significant shift had already been made, almost imperceptibly—the mill owner had to clamber on to the ground of workers' interests and needs in order to substantiate his argument. The very process of disavowal, in other words, staked out the space for a possible legal intervention. The *need* for legislation acquired, ironically through the words of a witness adamantly opposed to it, extremely material referents: machines, air and ventilation, working time, fatigue, and the age of working children.

The pattern of Banaji's answers can be extrapolated to the trajectory of the Commission's enquiries at large. As the Commission moved towards the negative answer made inevitable by the terms of its composition, the outlines of an *alternative* scenario emerged with force. The process of disavowal produced, through the act of negation, the structure of a positive avowal. It is important to remember that if the 1875 Commission produced all the grounds for the rejection of the Act, it simultaneously produced more or less all the grounds and arguments for the Act that eventually emerged in 1881. It could hardly be claimed, after all, that factory conditions in 1881 were so very different from those in 1875. Tacitly, therefore, the evidence of a Commission that on the whole worked extremely hard to negate grounds for legislation ironically became the very foundation of the legislation it negated.

Further, if it is true that the connections of most Commissioners and witnesses alike to the mill industry in Bombay furnished the material basis of interests that precluded the recommendation of factory legislation to the government, these interests could never be the final, or even a primary, court of appeal in the arguments as they actually unfolded. Like Banaji, the Commission in general had to accord primacy to the interests of workers over capital in its discourse. Legislation could *only* be vetoed on the ground that workers neither sought nor needed it. Factory legislation may have been an affront to the commercial interests of Maxwell, Goculdas, Bythell, Petit, and Nathubhai, as to those of a large number of their witnesses, but the importance of this constantly had to be played down.

The Commission elicited—had to elicit—the voice of the worker to reinforce its legitimacy. This was not inconsequential. Three jobbers and foremen, five or six boys, six women, and a press labourer were interviewed by the Commission towards the end of its enquiries.[42] This set in motion an entirely new *mode* of investigation of labour. The 1875 Commission interviewed workers only as an aside: their evidence seems to have made little difference to the final recommendations. But they needed to be consulted nevertheless, as people with a stake in their own future. In an industry that was by then over two decades old, this was a novel departure.

So the 1875 Commission undermined, by its very existence, the idea that regulation could be comfortably decided as a finished, mutually enhancing compact between state and capital. In the structure of the Commission's enquiries, the mill owner is on trial; the labourer, as it were, stands on witness. By the operation of a strange dialectic, this reversed not only the usual patterns of industrial relations, but also the actual material configuration of circumstances that made up the Factory Commission. The Commission, after all, can at some level be understood, in Marxist terms, as a moment where the state embodied the interests of 'social capital'—indeed, how else is one to understand a two-month conversation principally involving mill owners, directors, agents, managers, and shareholders? But given the remit of the Commission, the situation was not merely one in which capital managerially interrogated labour, but one where it interrogated *itself through labour*. So what the labourers interviewed by the Commissioners had to say served not only as a statement of needs and dilemmas, but also as a running commentary on the system of industrial relationships they and their employers (their interlocutors) were mutually locked in.

Three of the worker-witnesses, Assur Veerjee, Syed Tyab Ali, and Bhana Naik, were jobbers and foremen. They were interviewed with more care than other workers. As historians of the Bombay cotton industry have noted, the jobber occupied a distinct, ambiguous, and shifting position within the relationships of the mill: supplying labour, playing a managerial and supervisory role at the point of production, and being paid wages well above average levels in the mill.[43] Like the managers and engineers who were interviewed, the jobber was implicitly invested with a certain (subsidiary) expertise. He was also designated to speak *for* the workers he supplied and headed: Did they get tired? Did they want holidays? Was special legislation for women and children needed? Important gradations within working-class identity were thus given a particular twist by the patterns of questioning: the 'ordinary workers' interviewed by the Commission, principally women and children, were asked no such universalizing questions. Their role seems to have been to speak for themselves alone. Jobbers and foremen, by contrast, were asked to speak for the needs and interests of their class, but often in their capacity as sub-managers of work and recruitment. There was an interesting internal tension here: the jobber, invested with double agency, was singled out as the one representative of the working class with the capacity to generalize the experiences of millworkers.

A significant feature of the Factory Commission was the evidence it gathered on wages. This evidence does not allow us to reconstruct a reliable schedule of earnings in the mill industry in the 1870s: these varied from mill to mill, and between different categories of workers. Bhana Naik, a muccadam at Manockjee Petit's mill, was paid Rs 100 a month,[44] and Syed Tyab Ali, another muccadam, was paid Rs 60–80 a month.[45] An ordinary skilled labourer like Rama Antoba, working at the Scott Press, was paid Rs 15 in the slack season and Rs 50 in the busy season (this range, however, was due to the peculiar working schedule of cotton presses, with their long slack months and their frenetic and exhausting peak season).[46] The evidence of the factory owners and managers suggests a wide wage differential *within* the category of skilled labourers, generally upward of Rs 15, and often significantly higher. But all the children and women interviewed received wages between Rs 4 and Rs 7 a month.[47] This was despite the fact that the women often worked as long as the men did. Further, this wage scale, below Rs 10–15 a month, seems to have applied more or less across the board to unskilled labour in factories, to man, woman, or child.

The limits of the Commission's enquiry in addressing these matters were evident. Its basic sphere of investigation was limited, by the remit of the proposed factory legislation, to child labour, hours of work, the protection of machinery, and the provision of a weekly holiday. These were not insignificant recommendations—the last was to be a staple demand of the Millhands' Association later. However, the stress on limiting hours of work was by itself quite self-defeating. The women and children interviewed by the Commission put the matter quite succinctly. Most of them favoured weekly holidays, and the children concurred in judging the hours of work too long. But when asked if they wanted a reduction, and being told that this also involved a reduction in their wages, they replied, 'What are we to eat?'[48] This was clearly a worry that did not resonate equally among all sections of the workforce. Those on monthly wages had less to lose from a reduction of working hours. But most millworkers, and certainly most women and children, were engaged primarily in piecework. For them, working in conditions of unstable and uncertain employment, a reduction of labour-time meant a reduction of crucial earnings.

Closely related to this was the question of the mode of wage-payment, something which the last two chapters of this volume will explore at length. Repeatedly, evidence appears in the Commission's proceedings to demonstrate that workers were paid their wages in the middle of a month for labour performed in the previous month. Given the absence of sufficient savings, they naturally turned to the services of money-lenders to tide them over in the intervening time.[49] For the moment, it is sufficient to remark that addressing the problems clustered around wages—the absence of regular times of payment, the inadequacy of pay for those at the bottom of the wage hierarchy, the persistence of piecework, and so on—was not something the Commission chose to do. Remarkably, it was not till well into the second quarter of the twentieth century that wages were addressed in *any* form by labour legislation for industrial workers (the Payment of Wages Act of 1936, which regulated modes and durations of wage-payment, was the first departure from laissez-faire in this domain). In this sphere, interestingly, plantation law was much in advance of factory law, formulating minimum wage commitments in the last part of the nineteenth century.

So the question of wages was raised continually by the Commission—but not, on its own terms, as a *problem*. It seems to have been taken for granted that this was one area the Commission—and, by extension, the state—had no right to intervene in. This is demonstrated by the pattern of the questions and their riders: Would you like shorter hours of work? If you would, you must remember you sacrifice your wages. Given this stark option, it is not surprising that most workers agreed to forego a limitation of work hours, an agreement that was read as 'contentment'. But the interviews do not reveal such a stable picture. The women at Manockjee Petit's mill who were interviewed stated that they found the hours of work too long.[50] The boys interviewed at the same mill complained that their wages were insufficient to maintain themselves and their families. When asked if they wanted a holiday a week, one of them replied: 'If I am to take four holidays, how am I to fill my belly?' Another said he would have liked to have attended school, but not at the cost of the wages he would end up losing for half-day.[51]

These appearances of the wage question were necessarily unsystematic. Wages were beyond the remit of factory legislation: this was never made explicit, but taken for granted as a condition of the Commission's duties. Childhood, by contrast, was very explicitly on the agenda of the Commissioners. Their one extended encounter with children, at the Girgaum spinning mill (where, incidentally, the operatives were not allowed drinking water), was significant as much for its tone as for its content. Among the children they interviewed, one was clearly so weak that they kept asking him if he was sick or had been sick recently. There is a particular poignancy to the following exchange:

> Q: What is your age?
> A: Ten years, though I am short in stature.
> Q: Are you sick?
> A: No, but I have been weak since childhood.
> Q: Does not your work fatigue you?
> A: Not now, I used to get fatigued earlier.[52]

Exchanges of this kind retain their pathos at more than a century's distance, but their significance is not limited to this. The evidence provided by workers—and most distressingly by working children—was to be pressed into service as rhetorical ballast for the cause of factory law. The emancipation of children, their release into a nebulously grasped world of working-class childhood, would become the prime plank of factory legislation. The social question introduced by Mary Carpenter—the vulnerabilities and dangers of working-class childhood—returned in encounters like the one just mentioned.

To conclude this account of the Factory Commission, let me engage in some risky but perhaps necessary abstraction and return to the general question of the relationship between state and capital. The key point here is that their modes of *appearance* were not always coextensive with their 'substantial' selves. The Commission was composed of designated experts who had very material stakes, as directors and shareholders of cotton mills, in the industry. It was also an institution that the state directly gave birth to: it was appointed by the state, answered to the state's deadlines, and produced knowledge so that the state could act. In other words, 'collective capital' *appeared in the form of the state itself.* Yet the reverse is equally, and simultaneously, true: the state, insofar as it carried out the function of gathering information on the cotton mill industry, appeared in the form of organized capital, of an association thoroughly dominated by some of the leading merchants and industrialists in Bombay. The self-separation of capital and state—their appearance in a form that was non-identical with their 'selves'—appears, in another determination, as the mirroring of each in the other.

The Campaign for Factory Law in Bombay, 1878–81

In 1878, the factory question reappeared in the field of legislative and political debate. This was due mainly to the efforts of Sorabji Shahpurji Bengali, a Parsi businessman and social activist who had become, by the mid-1870s, one of Bombay's major public figures. Bengali worked first as a banker and then as a guarantee broker for the British-owned cotton firm W.A. Graham and Co., eventually becoming the director of several mill companies. He was also one of the most prominent social reformers of the era, taking part in campaigns for female education and internal religious reform in the Parsi community. In the early 1870s, Bengali was a pivotal figure in the attack upon the profligacy of the Municipal Commissioner, Arthur Crawford. This developed into a campaign that engrossed large sections of Bombay's ratepayers and ended up producing a Municipal Commission based mainly on the electoral principle.[53] Bengali, as the *Indian Textile Journal* put it, 'improved his evening time' by writing for newspapers and journals, as well as running several of these.[54] He was part of the Young Bombay circle of progressive reformers who clustered around Dadabhai Naoroji, and in 1876 was elected to the Bombay Legislative Council.

Bengali's experiences as a social reformer led him into ambiguous relations, on certain issues, with the emerging capitalist bourgeoisie he was part of. For instance, he sharply criticized tariff reform in a long letter to Lytton in 1877, but explicitly dissociated himself from the accusations of commercial discrimination made by his more proto-nationalist colleagues and mill owners like Goculdas and Petit. He instead staked his argument purely on the grounds of financial stability and the crisis in Indian revenues.[55] A much more extreme and irreconcilable difference between Bengali and his fellow businessmen emerged over the factory question.

In the late 1870s, Bengali energetically took up the cause of factory reform. In April 1878, in his capacity as legislator, he drafted a Factory Bill which extended across Bombay Presidency, defining 'factories' as all places of work using steam power. It could be argued that in a certain sense this definition can be grasped as the founding moment of factory law, the necessary delimitation of a sphere of 'legitimate' interference in labour relations. It worked in two ways simultaneously. It precluded the incorporation of small industrial occupations, often involving hazardous work, which did not use mechanical power. But it was at the same time an expansive definition: it was not limited by the *number* of workers employed. The Factory Act which was eventually passed three years later would be considerably less generous.

Bengali's Bill, again in significant contrast to the Act it would reluctantly become the progenitor of, defined the 'occupier' of the mill in strict terms. The category engrossed the 'owner or owners of any Mill or Factory, whether such owner or owners be an individual or individuals or a company or association of persons either incorporated or not, and also any individual or individuals or company or association as aforesaid having on behalf of the owner ... the care or direction thereof ... employed therein'.[56] Bengali thus furnished a description of the mill employer that was both legally unambiguous and allowed for contextual specificity.

Bengali set out the operative distinction between adults and non-adults in an equally precise way by identifying a single, consolidated category of 'young persons' between eight and fourteen who were to be protected according to common rules. The hairline distinctions between 'child' and 'young person' that were to bedevil the future of factory legislation in India were thus precluded in his proposed enactment. 'Young persons' were to be employed no more than nine hours, adult women no more than ten, and adult males no more than eleven hours in a mill. Children below eight were not to be employed. Age was to be determined by 'certifying surgeons' without any material stakes or 'beneficial interest in any Mill or Factory'. Work was to be interrupted by a compulsory period, lasting at least an hour, for meals and rest. Violations of the Act were, upon conviction, to be punished by a hefty fine 'not exceeding Rs. 1000 for each day' that the factory worked in contravention of the rules. The law was to be enforced by the Chief Officer of Police, and obstruction was to be punished as a criminal offence under the Indian Penal Code.[57]

In September 1878, he proposed this Bill in the Bombay Legislative Council. He found, however, that

> the mill owners of Bombay had been too strong for me. They got information that I had sent in the draft Bill, and had sufficient influence to cause the draft to be forwarded to the Government of India (as required by existing arrangements, it seems) with a distinct opinion expressed by the Bombay Government that there is no necessity for an enactment even so limited in its scope as the one I proposed.[58]

After this rebuff, Bengali claimed, he had no option left but to 'try what can be done through English influence, which, as a matter of course, is so potent with our governing classes'.[59] This took the form of an appeal to the class in England which was most likely to back a demand for factory regulation—the Lancashire manufacturers. Bengali sent 100 copies of his draft Bill, by mail steamer, along with a copy of government correspondence on the matter, to John Croft, a Manchester industrialist, requesting him to 'distribute these copies to such people in England as are likely to take an interest in the matter'. Bengali had already sent six copies to Louis Mallet at the India Office, three to 'a Parsee friend in Manchester', and Croft was left to 'do what is required further'.[60] This, he suggested, could be done by forwarding the Bill to Shaftesbury. Bengali warned Croft of the force of opposition in Bombay: 'Mr. Maxwell (the "big boy" as you called him), Chairman of the Mill Owners' Association ... has expressed himself and is hard at work against any legislation whatsoever.'[61]

Croft wrote a letter to *The Times* in September, pressing Parliament to take on the responsibility of passing factory legislation for India.[62] Croft also wrote to Shaftesbury, who vowed in his reply 'to renew the struggle if no other will undertake it. But my shaft will be now, I fear, like Priam's "telum imbelle sine inctu".'[63] Priam's shaft was duly launched in the House of Lords in April 1879, when Shaftesbury made another impassioned plea for regulation, basing himself on the 1875 Factory Commission, which, he pointed out, contained much evidence contradicting its final judgment. He pointed to the absence of regularized holidays, the long hours that children had to work, the absence of any regulation of the work or the minimum age of working children, and dangers from machinery. He drew attention, again, to the 'injustice' done to Lancashire by the competitive advantage enjoyed by Bombay's mill owners. At the same time, he unprecedentedly widened the terms of debate beyond Bombay, observing the growth of jute factories in Bengal with conditions of labour similar to Bombay's.[64]

In the meantime, Bengali carried out a public campaign in the *Rast Goftar*, articulating the cause of factory legislation and, as is evident from the responses of other newspapers across the Presidency, making many enemies. In December, the newspaper published a letter from the Coroner, Thomas Blaney, who had served on the 1875 Commission, to the effect that mill labour was detrimental to the health and well-being of workers.[65] In early 1879, Bengali stressed the 4-anna fine workers incurred if they left work, and wrote critically of the system whereby agents were paid their commissions on the work turned out rather than the profits realized by a mill.[66] Rival newspapers, acting as mouthpieces for the Bombay Millowners' Association, accused him of twisting the facts to suit his case, pointing persistently to the Manchester interests that drove it forward.[67] The *Gujarat Mitra* went so far as to accuse him of conspiring to 'save Europeans from the odium of advocating it in Manchester's interests'.[68]

Bengali could not, in the end, be the author of the law he sought to bring into being. It was the combination of independent activist pressures, parliamentary influence, and the campaign by Lancashire that accomplished this between 1878 and 1881. In the process, Bengali was excluded from the process he had initiated. The objectives that had initially driven the proposal to regulate factories were inexorably eroded by the mediation of opposed and more powerful interests. Like Mary Carpenter and Sasipada Banerjee before him, Bengali needed state intervention to realize his reformist objectives. But the content of the intervention that eventually took place followed a logic determined by stronger pressures, exerted by the industrial bourgeoisie of both metropole and colony.

In October 1879, B.W. Colvin, a member of the Imperial Legislative Council, tabled a new Factory Bill. This received the meticulous and cheese-paring attentions of a Select Committee and several rounds of legislative deliberation before finally passing into law in March 1881. In his speech before the final tabling of the revised Bill, Colvin stated its purpose in terms which were extremely conciliatory:

> As regarded the scope of the Bill, its provisions would be limited strictly to those points for which legislation had been shown to be necessary. It was most important that nothing should be done which could

> check the development of manufacturing industries in India. From every point of view it was desirable that this field for capital and labour should be developed and extended to the utmost. ... The Bill, therefore, which he wished to introduce, would be carefully framed, so as to offer no obstacle to the free growth of manufacturing industries. It contemplated no interference with the due freedom of employers and employed. They would be left at liberty to make any arrangements which they might think most conducive to their own interests. It would provide only for the two objects of affording security to life and limb from accident, and of protecting children and young persons who had not attained to an age at which they would be considered free agents from being overtasked. It was not proposed to introduce into the Bill any of the other points for which legislation had been found necessary at home. The differences between England and India of climate, character and habits of life of the people were so great that much which was needed there would not only be inapplicable but perhaps actually injurious here.[69]

Colvin's anxious conciliation of mill-owning interests and his equally anxious reiteration of laissez-faire shibboleths, of course, stood in marked contrast to Bengali's vigorous labour reformism. Seen in this light, the development of the Factory Act between 1878 and 1881 embodies a series of displacements: from Bengali to Colvin, from reformist initiative to colonial state control, from a (relatively) generous proposal to a parsimonious and largely toothless statute. Viewed on its own terms, and its ability to ensure its stated object—the protection of factory workers at risk from exhausting and hazardous work processes—the Act accumulated successive layers of inefficacy. But there were other mutations in the meaning and scope of factory legislation which point in more ambiguous directions. To grasp this, it is necessary to engage in a closer reading of the Act and its principal interventions in factory structures and practices.

The simultaneous weakening and enlargement of the *scope* of factory legislation, as it moved from Bill to law, is a good place to start. Bengali's campaign had centred exclusively on Bombay. Croft's endorsement of Bengali's letter, too, dovetailed with Lancashire's specific demand for the control of the textile industry in Bombay. No reference was made to other industrial centres: in its initial phases, the battle over factory legislation was, in concrete terms, a very specific and localized conflict.

For factory regulation to come into existence *as law*, however, such a prior restriction of its terms of reference was not possible. It had to take the form of a universal principle and could not be reduced to a specific context. The regulation of Bombay's cotton industry was the question which directly gave rise to factory law, but the weight and influence of mill-owning interests, as had already been demonstrated by the Factory Commission, made such singling out politically untenable. Colvin's Bill accordingly applied to all of British India.[70] Provincial administrations were circularized on this point, with instructions to elicit local business opinion. A stream of hostile responses predictably flowed in. The most vehement objections to factory legislation came from Bengal, Madras, and the North-West Provinces. The Government of Bombay supported legislation, but, upon pressure from mill owners, insisted that such an enactment should be general, thus adding weight to Colvin's Bill. The force of the dissenting voices, however, initially forced Colvin to backtrack, and he suggested a compromise in the form of a 'permissive' enactment: 'The most convenient form for such a measure seemed to be that of a single uniform law, not extending to the whole of India, but applicable to any part of it, when needed.'[71]

A memo recorded by C. Bernard of the Judicial Department summed up what was at stake in what was on the one hand, a permissive enactment, and on the other, a 'positive' one: 'The proposed legislation is in the interests of a section of the population who do not know their own needs in this respect and could hardly make themselves heard if they did; also ... it is against the interests of most of the managers ... to ask for the application of the Act to themselves.'[72] At the same time, in theory, if all factory workers deserved protection equally, the Act needed to be made general. This was a position buttressed by the persistent pressure from the Bombay Millowners' Association, which sent a memorial to the Council claiming that, as originally proposed, the Act would have been 'a grave injustice to the Bombay factories, which would have been placed in a serious, if not ruinous, disability in their competition with other places in India, into which it was apparently the intention of the local governments not to introduce the proposed law'.[73] The Bill was eventually made compulsory, revealingly, on the ground that if the Act was permissive, it would be seen 'by the Indian public generally, as another instance of sacrificing the interests of India to the supposed interests of Manchester'.[74]

A communication from the Poona Sarvajanik Sabha, a nationalist organization which was a strong supporter of the mill industry, also argued in favour of the generalization of the Act, despite being adamantly opposed to its principles:

> Such permissive enactments … are always fraught with great disadvantages. … The necessity of protecting children from overwork is, if real, universal, and should be recognized and legislated as such. Even as it is, the law will not affect mills established in the Native states … and will thus favour these mills at the expense of those in British territory. … In the general interests of the country we submit the permissive character of the enactment must be expunged and the measure be made universally applicable to all provinces.[75]

The government eventually decided in favour of a 'positive' enactment. The Act which emerged from these debates, thus, faced in two directions. It placed a much greater range of enterprises under scrutiny than had initially been intended. However, it forestalled possible losses to Bombay mills from competition *within* British India and worked in the interests of the Presidency's textile lobby. It also ensured weaker provisions in factory law as a whole, since the government, at the time of legislation, had to take into account the interests of large and varied groups of employers across the country, rather than focus on a relatively small group of textile manufacturers in western India. Bengali's Bill had been much stronger, but the condition of its strength was its limitation to Bombay. The Factory Act, by contrast, extended across British India, but the condition for this was the weakness of its provisions.

The Factory Act defined a 'factory' as a workplace employing steam where over one hundred persons were employed simultaneously for at least four months of the year. This was far removed from Bengali's ambition to ensure the protection of all workplaces using steam power, and its effect, as factory inspectors were to find, was to exclude most forms of labour-intensive enterprise from the scope of legislation, rendering some of the most exploitative and brutal employers safe from 'interference'.[76] This definition of a factory was also considerably less generous to the worker than Colvin's Bill, which fixed the necessary number at fifty, had been. The work practices of Bombay's mills made evasion a relatively easy matter. It was a characteristic of the labour process in the early mills that there would frequently be occasions when 40 per cent of the workforce might be missing at a particular time in the day—which might, of course, happen to be the time that a factory inspector visited. A factory employing less than a hundred workers at work at the time an inspector visited could, technically, be excluded from the Act.[77]

The legal definition of a factory brought administrators face to face with the problems of categorizing forms of labour in India. The range of enterprises mobilizing collective labour for the purposes of manufacture of one kind or another were—and still are—so great in India that, depending on the lens one used, the term 'factory' could engross all establishments or practically none. Legislators and officials worried, when confronted with the original Bill, about a definition of 'factory' that would include 'every bazaar-brazier who would run a small brass casting ... every furniture workshop'.[78]

The size of factories was not, of course, the only controversial aspect of the definition. Shortly after the Factory Bill was tabled, the Revenue, Agriculture and Commerce Department sought opinions on its applicability to enterprises run by the government, including printing presses and jail manufactories. (The former were excluded, eventually, and the latter were not.) But these were not questions that were easy to resolve. As more than one official pointed out, what precisely was the principle on which government printing presses—to take just one instance—could be excluded from the purview of the Bill? Did children working in these establishments not need protection?[79] Similarly, there was extensive discussion in government circles about whether mines and collieries could be included within the Factory Act. It took until August 1879 to finally rule them out.[80]

The Act of 1881 unambiguously marked out the factory child as the major legitimate recipient of protective legislation. A 'child' was defined as less than twelve years of age; the hours of work for children between seven and twelve were restricted to nine a day, and children below seven were prohibited from working.[81] They were also to be protected from machinery in motion. These provisions substantially modified those in the Bill by erasing the category of 'young persons' that it had borrowed from UK's the 1844 Factory Act. Bengali's proposed enactment had gone much further: it had proposed varying degrees of protection for adult males, women, and young persons, excluding children below eight from employment altogether.

The protection of child labourers had a double function. It helped balance a certain commitment to the idea of protective legislation with a severe limitation of the scope of such legislation. Children were, as the evidence from the Commission shows, never the major part of the productive workforce. Looked at in the broader context of the specific pressures behind legislation, this demonstrates that, at the crucial moment when the Bill passed into law, Bombay's mill owners won their battle against the Lancashire and the reformist lobbies. By refusing to regulate the hours of work of adult labourers, the Bill ruled out the possibility of any genuine threat to the economic viability of the mills.

At the same time, the entitlements conferred upon children, while negligible, were real. An hour's interval was fixed for 'food and rest' for children during the day.[82] The exact times of these intervals were to be fixed by the local government.[83] The occupier of the factory was to set up printed or written notices in each factory, showing the times at which such intervals would be allowed.[84] Further, four compulsory holidays a month were fixed for working children, and notice of this had to be provided by employers to the local Inspector.[85]

How are we to read these provisions? To take the question of intervals for meals first, what this marked out was a fixed time for the child labourer—later to be extended to labourers in general—that the employer had no legal authority to interfere with. This did not necessarily suit the immediate interests of working children, who, it seems, were used to ad hoc and not very strictly regulated intervals. However, the Act contained no provision forbidding other irregular intervals to child workers. In addition to the breaks that they took daily, children were now *entitled* to an hour all to themselves. In the course of time, this would become a popular demand and be legally implemented for all workers. The provision for holidays for children, too, would eventually be universalized for all workers. Time, and consequently control, became potentially general fields of struggle as a result of processes that originated in the establishment of protective norms for child workers. The line between vulnerability and entitlement was slippery. Remarkably enough, a finite measure of protection for vulnerable children became the legal basis for claims mounted on behalf of adult workers. Precisely as a 'special category' of worker, the factory child was invested with rights which anticipated a more general entitlement.

The restriction of the Act to children did not go uncontested. A.O. Hume, at the time Secretary to the Department of Revenue, Agriculture and Commerce, wrote in August 1878 that women needed to be included within the proposed legislation.[86] Their labour, he argued, needed to be limited to ten hours a day. This repeated not only Bengali's old demand but also, in a condensed form, the ten-hours debate in Britain. In January 1879, the Surgeon-General of Madras wrote to the provincial government, demanding the protection of women, children, and young persons from night work, and also stating that pregnant women stood in need of special protection.[87]

There were pressures for the extension of legislation from other quarters as well. The Bombay Gazette of 23 November 1880 contained a report of the murder of a woman millworker, Nusseebehn, by a jealous former lover, on her way from her home in Grant Road to her workplace, the Colaba Spinning and Weaving Mills, at 4 in the morning. She needed to rush to the factory so early because it opened at dawn, and she stood to lose employment if she didn't leave on time.[88] This is a revealing glimpse of the pressures and tragedies of working-class life in Bombay in this period. What is equally revealing is a petition sent to the Government of India, deploying this incident as an argument for more comprehensive factory legislation.[89]

The signatories of this petition were organized by an ally of Bengali's, Janardhan Ramchandraji, who was Head Clerk at the Registrar's office at the University of Bombay. Ramchandraji had organized a memorial a year earlier on the subject of factory legislation, and would continue to memorialize the Bombay government in the early 1880s, asking for a 'local' Factory Act for Bombay with stringent provisions.[90] The signatories to the 1880 petition, a small but vocal minority among Bombay's intelligentsia, reiterated their plea in the light of Nusseebehn's murder, and their demand wove together an argument about the danger posed to women by existing factory conditions, with a plea for more comprehensive legislation for all classes of factory labour. Extrapolating from the murder, they drew attention to the insecurity of women who had to leave their homes in the dark of night and go to their workplaces singly or accompanied by other women. But they also extended this to a general argument about the lives of factory labourers, the insecurity of life—and the dangers to life—that they had to face daily because of the hours at which factories opened, the inhuman way they were forced out of their beds early in the morning, and so on.[91]

This is an interesting petition for several reasons. First, it offered evidence from a 'small' event in Bombay—which is unlikely to have made big headlines—to the Government of *India*, as an argument for a positive enactment to protect labour across India. Second, it interpreted the tragedy of the factory as the tragedy of the woman, thus implicitly arguing for an enactment whose scope would be greater than that of the Bill already in existence. Third, and simultaneously, the argument seamlessly breaks the boundaries between the protection of a particular category of labourer and the protection of labour in general. The danger faced by women going to work at dawn is read as emblematic of the existential insecurity and tragedy of a factory life, whether lived by man, woman, or child. It is a petition that articulates the experience of working-class suffering as universal.

This seems to have been the anxiety that dominated the minds of those hostile to legislation, both within and outside official circles. How was it possible to sustain a legal argument that protected only one category of labour? The extension of legislation to women, even as another 'special category' of labour, would raise the problem of controlling the boundaries of the law. This worry seems to have perhaps played a role in the eventual refusal to extend the Act to women. The correspondence between officials at this time anxiously harps on the need to stem the consequences of legislation, to make sure the enactment is as limited as possible, because extending the scope of the Act would eventually generate immense hostility from Indian mill owners.[92]

The Factory Act also made a tentative move towards accident regulation, which was necessarily more wide-ranging in its immediate implications than the child labour clauses. The employer was required to keep machinery fenced and protected, especially if there was the danger of children passing near it.[93] In case of accidents and injuries, he was expected to send 'such notice ... occurring to persons therein to such authorities and within such time as the local Government may from time to time by rule direct'.[94] If he neglected these responsibilities, he was liable to pay a fine of two hundred rupees.[95] There was also discussion of blending the principle of workmen's compensation into the Act, something much more significant in its implications than fines for unfenced machinery, since it potentially institutionalized demands voiced directly by workers.[96] The most radical suggestion in this vein came from Hume:

> In all cases where an accident has occurred ... found to have in no way resulted from the rashness ... of the sufferer ... he should be authorized to assess and propose for the acceptance of the mill or factory-owner a certain compensation, either in a lump sum or in the shape of a monthly allowance, or for a fixed period, or till death. That if the millowner accepted such award, he should sign his acquiescence of the same. The award thus signed to have the force of a decree of court. That if the millowner declined, the Inspector should be authorized to sue him in court for the same.[97]

So a feature of factory life—the constant danger of accidents—that could be naturalized and read off in terms of workers' negligence prior to the Act was made the basis for workers' claims and entitlements after legislation. What the *possibility* of enacting provisions like this did, in theory, was to turn the agreement between mill owner and worker, achieved through a 'free' bargain, into a relationship organized by the law. At the same time, the person invested with the agency to appeal to the law against transgression was not the employer—here the situation was dramatically different from plantations, public works, and mines—but the worker. Through a subtle and probably unintended loop, the relationship between mill owner and millworker was being gradually construed as agonistic or even antagonistic, vulnerable to the bad faith or exploitative tendency of the employer, and, thus, amenable to regulation by law. In the event, though, the only punishment spelt out by factory legislation was a limited fine.

But what was the mechanism for putting all these safeguards into place? The Factory Bill authorized the appointment, by local governments, of factory inspectors to examine working conditions. The status of these inspectors, however, was initially left unclear. It was stated that they 'may enter any Factory whenever any person is employed therein'.[98] But what was the penalty for not allowing them in? Neither this nor the precise functions of the inspectors were specified. Further, as correspondence within the Judicial Department took note of, it was unclear whether the decision to appoint inspectors was left to the discretion of the local government or whether it was binding upon them. It was decided, in the discussions that led up to the enactment of 1881, to make more stringent, compulsory rules for factory inspection.[99] It was made mandatory for local governments to appoint inspectors of factories, who were invested with the authority to enter the factory with their assistants when they chose, to examine the premises for any sign of violation of the Act, and to prevent the employment of any person considered below the minimum age prescribed by the Act.[100]

In practical terms, many obstacles stood in the way of effective inspection. First, though the Act compelled factory owners to keep registers recording the names and ages of children employed, this was difficult to impose in practice, for it was quite possible for children to shift from factory to factory. It was also possible for factory owners and managers to hustle children out of the factory at the time of inspection, so as to evade investigation.[101] Further, it was extremely difficult to ascertain the ages of children, despite the loose system of age certification by certifying surgeons marked out by the Act.[102] Initially, in fact, the onus was on the child to prove that he or she was of requisite age for employment—only later was it clearly spelt out that this was the manager's responsibility. With regard to accidents, the Act provided for the reporting of only 'serious injuries'. The Act also contained a clause making the fixing of notices on factory premises compulsory. Employers apparently had no particular difficulty complying with this rule.[103]

The production, by law, of these sites of investigation and protective legislation had complicated effects. It enabled a constellation of potential grievances and points of tension that could not be contained within the provisions of the first Factory Act. At the same time, the Act did produce certain key points of focus that made it more difficult to raise questions of another kind—about wages, benefits, and so on. Legislation thus acted as opening and closure simultaneously. A ladder of discursive steps was built *in potentia*, available for the enactment of new forms of protection—the regulation of women's labour, for instance, or the extension of protection to male adults. The limits of this were precise, but paradoxically this very precision made factory law a perpetually unresolved field.

There can be no question that early factory legislation in India was a process driven 'from above', in a much less complicated way than it had been in Britain. What makes it interesting, however, is the specific discursive logic that it produced. Factory legislation ushered in a small bureaucracy equipped with limited powers of protection, often ineffective and sometimes venal. At the same time, the raison d'etre of the factory inspectorate enjoined by the Act was the investigation of exploitation and the defence of workers' interests. This heralded a larger shift in the discourses of industrial relations: mill owners, for instance, had to change tack and move from a complete refusal of the idea of factory legislation to a grudging acceptance. More to the point, their very attack upon the regime of factory inspection had to rest upon a disavowal of exploitation—a tension which had already been rehearsed in the proceedings of the Factory Commission.

So as factory regulation gradually moved from idea to legal text to practice, it underwent several metamorphoses. The form of these changes was governed by the tense dialectic between the imperative to keep legislation as limited as possible on the one hand, and the propulsive character of the debates that crystallized around the factory question, on the other. Even as both state and capital worked to restrict the Factory Act to a cautious and parsimonious set of clauses, the logic through which the law unfolded produced new immunities and entitlements for workers, whose significance may have lain less in their practical effect than in the horizons of expectation they may have helped trigger.

Through all of this, it is possible to see the emergence of a specific *logic of administration*. In some of its forms this corresponded to what Bourdieu, in a more recent context, has described as 'the left hand of the state', and what Marx, in the context of the British Factory Acts, described as 'the first attempt to curb capital's drive towards a limitless draining away of labour-power by forcibly limiting the working day on the authority of the state'.[104] Both these statements, of course, deal in ideal types, but they are suggestive. They acknowledge that legislative/administrative logics of this sort represent counter-strains *within* 'the logic of capital and state', but retain the insight that such logics put the dominant structure of industrial and social relationships into tension with itself. In other words, despite its evident mildness, the logic of factory regulation perturbed some of the structures of industrial relations and acted as a tentative, reluctant ground for the institutionalized expression of workers' interests. The practice of law rendered its own frontiers unstable, and thereby rendered problematic social relations hitherto taken for granted.

Sowthoo's Letter

It should be clear from what has been stated earlier that factory regulation, in its initial incarnations as project and policy proposal, troubled both employers and the state, and disturbed their mutual relations. What, however, of the impact of these debates on workers' own lives? Here the evidence is slim and equivocal. In the 1870s, workers' dispositions towards protective legislation appear directly in the available sources only when their opinions were directly solicited by 'experts'. Such solicitations were weighted, and the manner in which questions to workers were framed effectively presupposed the answers which were given. Nor do 'worker witnesses' in the transcripts of the 1875 Factory Commission offer a particularly 'representative' sample of opinion. Workers' voices were mediated, then, at their very source. And they were ambiguous. Since both the mediation and the ambiguity were irreducible, it is more fruitful to posit them as starting points of, rather than blockages to, the question of the role played by workers' interests in these episodes. With this in place, a brief study of an intriguing episode in the early 1870s, well before factory regulation had achieved public presence in Bombay's debates, might cast some light on the deeper questions which legal restriction posed.

In May 1872, the *Times of India* received an unusual letter. Claiming to be a 'female rover in the old Manockjee Petit mills' named 'Sowthoo', the correspondent described her wages (Rs 15 to 16 a month), her expenses upon rent, clothing, and 'messing' or provisioning for three children and herself. Her husband, a sepoy, drank away his income (Rs 11 a month), and her elderly brother 'sleeps in a ruin, where he cooks his food and seems contented, on his so-called comforts, simply because our social situation is neither ameliorating nor improving'. In fact, observed the letter, 'we don't know what to wear, what to eat, and how to live'. In this context, a Factory Act, such as that recently recommended 'by a few Saheb Loke', would necessarily 'be maintained out of our poor selves'. The factory masters were certainly harsh, 'but, Editor saheb, we get paid for what we work'.[105] The writer, deploring the proposal 'to swell the Code of Laws', urged the city's notables, its 'Dasses and Jees', to provide, instead, 'a comfortable cheap lodging—next, wholesome food, and education for our young world'.[106] 'Therefore, Mr. Editor saheb,' concluded 'Sowthoo', 'let there be no *Factory Act till we want.*'[107]

The letter was marked with an 'X', indicating the services of a scribe, professional, or amateur. We have no way of tracing the chain of mediations that led from Sowthoo to the publication of the letter, nor can we rule out the possibility of a 'fake' letter, sent by a propagandist. Some of the prose—a clever allusion to 'an export of *code* and *coal* to India' in the last phrase of the letter, for instance—suggests, at the least, fairly pronounced intermediation. It was not uncommon for writers of letters to the *Times of India* and other newspapers and periodicals to assume pseudonyms. A random instance of this can be culled from letters to the *Indian Textile Journal*, designed in 1890 as the mill industry's public commentary upon its own affairs. In the 1890s, this journal printed letters by men who assigned themselves names such as 'Practical Experience', 'Economy', 'Textile Philosopher', 'Caution', 'On-Looker', and, memorably, 'One Who Knows'. A propagandist, then, a mill manager or one of the burgeoning professional middle classes in late nineteenth-century Bombay Presidency, may conceivably have composed the letter—an exercise in the extraction of some symbolic surplus value and its investment in the production of public opinion against factory legislation.

The force of the demands, coupled with the vivid description of Sowthoo's conditions of life (not to mention the precise accounting of her real wages), indicate the letter's authenticity. On the other hand, the principal vector of the argument, a separation of the conditions of social reproduction (food, clothing, housing, rent, education) from the province of the direct relations of production at the workplace, reflects the concern with 'the free negotiation between employer and worker' that characterized the public rhetoric of mill employers, their publicists, and their allies throughout the late nineteenth century. From the latter's perspective, this 'freedom' was embedded in the right of masters to decide the principles on which the mill was to be run; from the worker's perspective, as presented by the letter, it consisted in the right to a wage which would be grievously reduced by any form of legal regulation. And this wage, of course, was the foundation of the social reproduction of the workforce, which the writer of the letter identified as being pitched barely at the level of basic subsistence.

Even the demand that factory regulation be made contingent upon the active desires of workers proves more ambiguous than it might seem: this very argument was repeated and elaborated in the discourse of mill owners, managers, and upper middle-class public opinion in the Presidency through the next two decades. Indeed, the 'agency' of workers in the 1870s and 1880s was never transparent, in the sense that the connection between workers' actions and apparent 'concessions' to them by state and mill owners was never unmediated. Rather, in the increasingly bitter oppositions constructed around questions of factory legislation, the issue of 'what workers really want' increasingly became a central point of reference for *both* sides in a protracted rhetorical and political confrontation.

If, however, a woman worker named Sowthoo did dictate or otherwise authorize the letter, this indicates an unusual depth of social communication, enough to merit a separate research project. And while the letter's idiomatic English prose and its witticisms indicate that its 'mediator' intervened actively in the literary formulation of Sowthoo's thoughts, the precision of detail and the urgency of tone offer some support for its veracity. So does the 'X' in Sowthoo's name that appends the letter (it is signed 'The Mark "X" of Sowthoo')—if the letter was *not* authentic, we have to imagine an exceptionally committed work of fiction and dissimulation. And to what end? As mentioned earlier, we have no corroborative evidence, in 1872, for anything approaching a concerted campaign *against* factory legislation that might have enlisted or invented an aggrieved woman worker.

The matter of the letter's authenticity, then, is undecidable. Factory legislation as threat was either acutely felt by an eloquent woman especially effectively interpellated by her employers' discourses, or crafted by someone else as an imaginative (if cynical) exercise in ventriloquist propaganda, or achieved at an undefinable junction-point between worker and master, and/or worker and propagandist. If (as on balance seems more likely) the letter was an act of impersonation, the significance of its discursive form lies in the extent to which its writer made a brilliant and convincing attempt to imagine into existence a distressed woman worker upholding her right to employment in the face of state intervention. This was a powerful act of political imagination and an eloquent plea which, nevertheless, ultimately sought to reinforce the rights of employers in their laissez-faire modulation.

All these possibilities are encoded in the letter, and this suggests the plasticity and malleability of a discourse emerging around a set of problems beginning to take shape around the textile factory in Bombay—a physical and social form less than two decades old at the time. In other words, irrespective of the veracity of the letter itself, it serves analysis well to take the diegetic space enclosed by the letter seriously and speculate about the consequences of the arguments made in it.

Well before factory legislation had become a pressing concern either for the Government of India or that of Bombay, a radical ambiguity at the very heart of the project, as yet putative, was anticipated by Sowthoo's letter. Whose interests would, or should, a Factory Act limiting working hours and 'protecting' workers serve? Would it intensify exploitation, ameliorate it, or be of no practical use whatsoever? Would the Act confer a set of crucial entitlements upon a growing and impoverished population of millworkers or would it take away what little security they had, accentuating the problem of 'what to wear, what to eat, and how to live'? A decade before the first Indian Factory Act, this letter dramatized a set of problems, tightly knotted together, that the question of factory labour regulation posed for the emerging shape of industrial relations in late colonial Bombay. In this sense, the letter was a prescient intervention: its documentary value lies not so much in its expression of existing worker grievances, as in its *anticipation* of a set of tensions that was to both compose and perturb the structures of industrial relations in the textile mills of Bombay throughout the late nineteenth century.

It is, I believe, possible to thematize these problems more precisely.

1. *The problem of representation*: Who speaks for the worker? This is a problem indicated both by the aporia of the letter's 'authenticity' and in its direct, rather scornful reference to the well-intentioned publicists who were apparently voicing a public demand for factory legislation. Sowthoo 'herself' clearly critiqued the project of reducing working hours, but also stressed the necessity of public intervention in other domains—food, clothing, housing, and education. Regulation, then, could either be necessary or futile—this depended, as Sowthoo's final plea ('let there not be a Factory Act *till we want*') emphasized, on how truthfully the actual 'wants' of workers were represented. Thus, the question of social regulation to 'protect'

factory workers ineluctably led to the problem of an intervention, *on behalf of the workers*, to be carried out by 'legitimate' representatives. Who would these be? As factory legislation passed from idea to enactment to material practice to site of conflict, the position of 'true representative of labour' came to be urgently contested, with factory inspectors, Lancashire mill companies and their spokespersons, Bombay mill owners, and independent social activists competing for the right to speak for workers' interests.

2. *The impact of factory legislation upon the sphere of relations between employers and workers, in other words, the possibilities and blockages of law*: One of Sowthoo's misgivings about a potential project of legal regulation was that it would effectively be of no use to the worker: significantly, she cited the working of Bombay's Boiler Inspection Act in support of her argument, claiming that inspection had no effect upon the actual safety of machinery. The problem of the effectivity of factory law would crop up again and again, not only in the 1880s but all the way till the present day: employers have frequently been able to evade scrutiny of their transgressions of law; factory inspectors' punitive powers have always been limited to a minority of workplaces and circumscribed even within these. However, the intrusion of external, state-sponsored officials into the 'private realm' of workplace relations had consequences that were often far less tame than we might assume from these limitations. The entire sphere of 'industrial relations' is necessarily transformed when the 'free' negotiation between employers and workers (that is, the sovereignty of employers, the tyranny of managers, and the submission of workers within a regime of contractual 'equality') is subjected to external intervention. In the 1880s, no less than today and in some ways significantly more so, this new field-of-force contained multiple possibilities of confrontation, collusion, malpractice, and—even if occasionally—a reversal of, or at least a constraint upon, the freedoms of employers.
3. *The specific question of the consequences of regulation upon women workers*: Sowthoo's detailed inventory of her conditions of existence was geared towards a demonstration of her vulnerability, not just as a worker among many, but as a woman whose husband drank away his income, a woman who was burdened with the upkeep of a family with three children, a woman who, in other words, was

charged with the work of budgeting for the social reproduction of an entire household. In the delicate economic equilibrium in which this household's existence was maintained, any attempt to regulate hours of work would push real wages below survival levels. This was a problem workers faced in general, but evidence from the 1880s and more particularly the early 1890s suggests that women experienced this dilemma with particular force and immediacy.

4. *The connection between economic production (at the workplace) and the social reproduction of the working classes*: In Sowthoo's account, the constraints and insecurities of the latter made any regulation of the former undesirable; conversely, the privilege of a subsistence wage (note the pride in the exclamation, 'but, Editor saheb, we get paid for what we work') compensated for the privations and dangers of industrial labour. Factory law, set in a particular mould by its previous metropolitan incarnations (which more than partially determined the forms it could take in a colonial context), reversed the hierarchies of this equation: privileging workplace security (however minimal) over the exigencies of the wage, it effected a very precise separation between the domains of production and social reproduction, subordinating the latter to the former. Despite repeated demands, the makers of factory law never even considered any form of public wage regulation: in this sense, at least, laissez-faire was, as Amiya Bagchi noted in a related context, 'a policy rather than the absence of one'.[108]
5. *The spaces, within the social world of factory relations, where workers could actively intervene and change the coordinates of given situations*: This, once again, was presaged in Sowthoo's haunting last words, 'let there not be a Factory Act till we want'. Given the emergence, in the mid-1880s, of public campaigns both *for* and *against* factory legislation that *both* actively enlisted the support of workers, it is hard to avoid a familiarly teleological narrative that would describe factory regulation as a progressive movement from elite to plebeian domains of ideology, practice, and demand. This certainly has some force, but it is possible to argue, as I will do, that a very different kind of process of 'workers' agency' was in motion in the later 1880s and 1890s. This increasingly posed the torsion between the domains of legal regulation and social reproduction as a *problem*, expressed through a sequence of militant wage demands.

Sowthoo's letter, at one level, represented very little outside itself. Its provenance is impossible to determine, but it is quite likely that it originated in an impersonation, whereby an educated propagandist ventriloquized the voice of an at least partially imaginary woman worker on behalf of a laissez-faire agenda. However, the act in itself betrays small yet significant discursive tensions, not least in the need such an agenda clearly already had of a worker's voice for its own legitimation. As such, it was a letter which, read closely, can be seen to have anticipated certain key tensions within the emerging industrial landscape of Bombay, which would come to be dramatized by the events and processes of the next two decades. It is to these tensions that this book now turns.

Notes

1. A brief look at the *Times of India*, especially in the second half of the 1870s, confirms this.

2. *Administration Report of the Cotton Department for the Year 1872–73*, p. 5, IOR V/24/434, OIOC.

3. *Administration Report of the Cotton Department for the Year 1872–73*. See Peter Harnetty, *Imperialism and Free Trade: Lancashire and India in the Mid-Nineteenth Century* (Vancouver: University of British Columbia Press, 1972), pp. 101–23, for an account of the conflict between Lancashire and Bombay around the question of cotton frauds legislation.

4. *Statement of Moral and Material Progress and Condition of India, 1873–74*, in *British Parliamentary Papers 1875* (henceforth *PP*), p. 16.

5. K.N. Subramaniam, *Labour-Management Relations in India* (Bombay: Asia Publishing House, 1967), p. 11; Janet Kelman, *Labour in India: A Study of the Conditions of Indian Women in Modern Industry* (London: George Allen & Unwin, 1923).

6. *Times of India*, 22 June 1875.

7. *Times of India*, 22 June 1875.

8. Reports of Inspectors of Factories to Secretary of State for Home Dept, May–October 1874, *PP* 1875 (C. 1184), p. 30.

9. Home (Judicial) A, January 1880, nos 9–94 and K.W., National Archives of India, New Delhi (henceforth NAI).

10. Home (Judicial) A, January 1880, nos 9–94 and K.W., NAI, enclosure B: *Report and Proceedings of the Commissioners Appointed by the Governor of Bombay in Council to Inquire into the Condition of Operatives in Bombay Factories, and the Necessity or Otherwise for the Passing of a Factory Act* (henceforth *F.C.* 1875).

11. Jim Masselos, *The City in Action: Bombay Struggles for Power* (Delhi: Oxford University Press, 2007), pp. 46–81; Christine Dobbin, *Urban Leadership in Western India: Politics and Communities in Bombay City, 1840–1885* (Oxford, 1972).

12. 'Abstract of Report of the Health Officer of Bombay for 1874', in *Report on Sanitary Measures in India in 1874–75, PP* 1876 (C. 1615).

13. 'Abstract of Report of the Health Officer of Bombay for 1874', *PP* 1876 (C. 1615), pp. 123–5.

14. Two of them did: Blaney and Arbuthnot. It is not clear whether Moylan eventually voted or not. *F.C.*, 1875.

15. S.M. Rutnagar, *Bombay Industries: The Cotton Mills: A Review of the Progress of the Textile Industry in Bombay from 1850 to 1926 and the Present Constitution, Management and Financial Position of Spinning and Weaving Factories* (Bombay: The Indian Textile Association Ltd, 1927), p. 712.

16. Rutnagar, *Bombay Industries*, p. 712.

17. Rutnagar, *Bombay Industries*, p. 720.

18. *F.C.*, 1875, 1st meeting, 14 April.

19. There were hierarchies, too, implicit in the way the workers were questioned: jobbers and foremen at greater length, with more careful questions, the workers picked out from their work more casually. *F.C.* 1875, 7th meeting, 26 May; 9th meeting, 9 June.

20. *F.C.* 1875, 7th meeting, 26 May; 9th meeting, 9 June.

21. The minute argued that a Factory Act would constrain the 'healthy growth' of a burgeoning new industry; that workers' wages would fall and they would resent it; that the proposed measure did not affect the 'most injurious professions and trades'; and that overzealous officials might abuse their power. *F.C.* 1875, 10th meeting, 16 June.

22. *Akhbare Sowdagar*, 24 November 1875, *Report on Native Newspapers, Bombay* (henceforth *RNNP Bom.*), 24 November 1875.

23. *Jam-e-Jamshed*, 27 March 1875, *RNNP Bom.*

24. *Jam-e-Jamshed*, 27 March 1875, *RNNP Bom.*

25. *Yajdan Parast*, 28 March 1875, *RNNP Bom.*

26. See, for instance, *Satya Mitra*, 9 May 1875, *RNNP Bom.*

27. See *Bombay Samachar*, 18 May 1875 and *Jam-e-Jamshed*, 17 May 1875, *RNNP Bom.*

28. Evidence of Joseph Sharpe, *F.C.* 1875, 8th meeting, 2 June.

29. *Bombay Gazette*, 5 June 1875; *F.C.* 1875, 10th meeting, 16 June.

30. Letter from J.K. Bythell to Factory Commission, *F.C.* 1875, 8th meeting, 2 June.

31. Letter from J.K. Bythell to Factory Commission, *F.C.* 1875, 8th meeting, 2 June.

32. *F.C.* 1875, 7th meeting, 26 May.

33. *F.C.* 1875, 7th meeting, 26 May.
34. *F.C.* 1875, 7th meeting, 26 May.
35. *F.C.* 1875, 2nd meeting, 21 April.
36. *F.C.* 1875, 8th meeting, 2 June.
37. *F.C.* 1875, 4th meeting, 5 May.
38. Rutnagar, *Bombay Industries*, p. 698.
39. *F.C.* 1875, 5th meeting, 12 May.
40. This refers to the end of the American Civil War and the concomitant slump in the Indian raw cotton trade, which, among other consequences, eventually forced a number of capitalists—who had made and lost fortunes during the boom and then crisis of 1861–5—to once again start investing in the construction and operation of textile mills. The mill industry had come to a virtual standstill during the cotton boom.
41. *F.C.* 1875, 5th meeting, 12 May.
42. *F.C.* 1875, 7th Meeting, 26 May; 9th Meeting, 9 June.
43. See, in particular, Morris David Morris, *The Emergence of an Industrial Labour Force in India: A Study of the Bombay Cotton Mills, 1854–1947* (Berkeley: University of California Press, 1965); Rajnarayan Chandavarkar, *The Origins of Industrial Capitalism in India: Business Strategies and the Working Classes in Bombay, 1900–1940* (Cambridge: Cambridge University Press, 1994); Dick Kooiman, 'Jobbers and the Emergence of Trade Unions in Bombay City', *International Review of Social History* 22, no. 3 (1977): 313–28; and Richard Newman, *Workers and Unions in Bombay, 1918–1929: A Study of Organization in the Cotton Mills* (Canberra: Australian National University, 1981).
44. F.C. 1875, 7th Meeting, 26 May.
45. *F.C.* 1875, 7th Meeting, 26 May.
46. *F.C.* 1875, 9th meeting, 9 June.
47. *F.C.* 1875, 7th Meeting, 26 May.
48. *F.C.* 1875, 7th Meeting, 26 May.
49. *F.C.* 1875, 7th Meeting, 26 May.
50. *F.C.* 1875, 7th Meeting, 26 May.
51. *F.C.* 1875, 7th Meeting, 26 May.
52. *F. C.* 1875, 7th Meeting, 26 May.
53. N.S. Bengallee, *The Life of Sorabjee Shapoorjee Bengallee, C.I.E., (With illustrations, letters and a sketch in English)* (Bombay, n.d.), pp. 32–47.
54. *Indian Textile Journal*, 1892, no. 23, p. 228.
55. Bengallee, *Life*, pp. 328–40.
56. Draft Factory Bill, cited in Bengallee, *Life of Sorabjee Shapoorjee Bengallee*, p. 340.
57. Draft Factory Bill, cited in Bengallee, *Life of Sorabjee Shapoorjee Bengallee*, pp. 341–4.

58. Letter from S.S. Bengali to John Croft, 26 July 1878, quoted in a letter by John Croft to *The Times*, 13 September 1878, and in Bengallee, *Life of Sorabjee Shapoorjee Bengallee*, pp. 153–6.

59. Letter from S.S. Bengali to John Croft, 26 July 1878 quoted in a letter by John Croft to *The Times*, 13 September 1878, and in Bengallee, *Life of Sorabjee Shapoorjee Bengallee*, p. 153.

60. Letter from S.S. Bengali to John Croft, 26 July 1878 quoted in a letter by John Croft to *The Times*, 13 September 1878, and in Bengallee, *Life of Sorabjee Shapoorjee Bengallee*, p. 154.

61. Letter from S.S. Bengali to John Croft, 26 July 1878 quoted in a letter by John Croft to *The Times*, 13 September 1878, and in Bengallee, *Life of Sorabjee Shapoorjee Bengallee*, p. 156.

62. Letter from S.S. Bengali to John Croft, quoted in a letter by John Croft to *The Times*, 13 September 1878.

63. Letter from Shaftesbury to Croft, cited in Bengallee, *Life of Sorabjee Shapoorjee Bengallee*, p. 156.

64. Extract from the *Overland Mail*, Supplement, 11 April 1879, Home (Judicial) A, January 1880, nos 9–94 and K.W.

65. *Rast Goftar*, 29 December 1878, *RNNP Bom.*

66. *Rast Goftar*, 5 January 1879, *RNNP Bom.*

67. See *RNNP Bom.*, 1878–9: *Native Opinion*, 29 December 1878, 19 January 1879; *Gujarat Mitra*, 29 December 1878, 1 January 1879, 26 January 1879, 9 Feb 1879; *Jam-e-Jamshed*, 8 January 1879; *Jalgaon Samachar*, 19 January 1879.

68. *Gujarat Mitra*, 29 December 1878, *RNNP Bom.*

69. Abstract of the Proceedings of the Council of the Governor General of India, assembled for the purpose of making Laws and Regulations under the provisions of the Act of Parliament 24 and 25 Vic., cap. 67 (henceforth Legislative Council Proceedings), 11 March 1881, V/9/18–19, OIOC.

70. Home (Judicial) A, nos 23–5, February 1879; no. 1, 4 November 1878, NAI.

71. Legislative Council Proceedings, 7 November 1879, V/9/15–17, OIOC.

72. Home (Judicial) A, nos 23–5, February 1879; no. 1, 4 November 1878, NAI; memo from C.B, 6 August 1879.

73. Legislative Council Proceedings, 11 March 1881.

74. Memo from F.P.H, 21.8.1879, Home (Judicial) A, January 1880, nos 9–94 and K.W., NAI.

75. Quoted in J.C. Kydd, *A History of Factory Legislation in India* (Calcutta, 1920), pp. 17–18.

76. Kydd, *A History of Factory Legislation in India*, Appendix 1: Indian Factories Act (Act XV of 1881).

77. Report on the Working of the Factories Act, NAI, Home Judicial, October 1882, programmes 23–4.

78. Home (Judicial) A, nos 9–94 and K.W., January 1880, NAI.

79. Home (Judicial) A, nos 23–5, February 1879, including correspondence between C.B (19.11.1878), C.L.T (29.11.78), A.O.H (29.11.78), J.M.M (14.12.78), D.F.P (4.1.79), A.O.H (20.1.79), C.E.B (23.1.79), and C.B (24.1.79), NAI.

80. Home (Judicial) A, nos 9–94 and K.W., January 1880.

81. Home (Judicial) A, nos 9–94 and K.W., January 1880.

82. Indian Factories Act, 1881, in Kydd, *A History of Factory Legislation*, Appendix 1.

83. Indian Factories Act, 1881, in Kydd, *A History of Factory Legislation*, Appendix 1.

84. Indian Factories Act, 1881, in Kydd, *A History of Factory Legislation*, Appendix 1.

85. Indian Factories Act, 1881, in Kydd, *A History of Factory Legislation*, Appendix 1.

86. Note by A.O Hume, Home (Judicial) A, nos 9–94 and K.W., January 1880, NAI.

87. G. Smith, M.D, Surgeon-General, Indian Medical Department, Madras, to Chief Secretary, Govt of Madras, 20 January 1879, Home (Judicial) A, no. 25, January 1880, NAI.

88. Extract from *Bombay Gazette*, 23 November 1880, Home (Judicial) B, nos 103–4, February 1881, NAI.

89. Memorial to D. Fitzpatrick, Esquire, C.S, Secretary to Government of India, Legislative Department, Calcutta, 10 December 1880, in Papers Relative to the Factories Bill, Home (Judicial) B, nos 103–4, February 1881, NAI.

90. Dobbin, *Urban Leadership in Western India*, pp. 206–8.

91. Memorial to D. Fitzpatrick, Esquire, C.S., Secretary to Government of India, Legislative Department, Calcutta, 10 December 1880, in Papers Relative to the Factories Bill, Home (Judicial) B, nos 103–4, February 1881, NAI.

92. Home (Judicial) A, nos 9–94 and K.W, January 1880, NAI.

93. Home (Judicial) A, nos 23–5, February 1879; no. 1, 4 November 1878, NAI.

94. Home (Judicial) A, nos 23–5, February 1879; no. 1, 4 November 1878, NAI.

95. Home (Judicial) A, nos 23–5, February 1879; no. 1, 4 November 1878, NAI.

96. Home (Judicial) A, nos 9–94 and K.W, January 1880, NAI.

97. Memo from A.O. Hume, 7 August 1878, Home (Judicial) A, nos 9–94 and K.W, January 1880, NAI.

98. Home (Judicial) A, nos 23–5, February 1879, NAI.

99. Memo from L, 29 August 1879, Home (Judicial) A, nos 9–94 and K.W, January 1880, NAI.

100. Indian Factory Act, 1881, in Kydd, *A History of Factory Legislation*, Appendix 1.

101. Indian Factory Act, 1881, in Kydd, *A History of Factory Legislation*, Appendix 1.

102. Indian Factory Act, 1881, in Kydd, *A History of Factory Legislation*, Appendix 1.

103. Report on the Working of the Factories Act, Home Judicial, October 1882, programmes 23–4.

104. Pierre Bourdieu, *Acts of Resistance: Against the Tyranny of the Market* (New York: The New Press, 1998); K. Marx, *Capital: A Critique of Political Economy*, vol. 1 (Harmondsworth: Penguin, 1867), p. 416.

105. *Times of India*, 14 May 1872.

106. *Times of India*, 14 May 1872.

107. *Times of India*, 14 May 1872.

108. A.K. Bagchi, *Private Investment in India, 1900–1939* (Cambridge: Cambridge University Press, 1972), p. 117.

PART II

THE LIFE OF A LAW

3

The Work of Law

Factory Inspection in Bombay, 1881–7

In the first two chapters, I described the lines of force that led to the making of factory legislation in India between the late 1860s and 1881. I turn now to the operation of the law in Bombay. In this chapter, I consider the making of a regime of factory inspection, the mechanism through which law was enforced, between 1881 and 1887. I deepen this, in the next chapter, with an account of the internal dynamics of the principal thrust of the Factory Act, the regulation of child labour through the work of inspection, over roughly the same period. It was in these years that the administration of factory law was at its most experimental and least settled in its scope. During these formative years, when the scope of factory legislation was still a matter of strong debate, the frontiers of the law were insecure and shifting, with unexpected events and disclosures not infrequently pushing the regime of inspection beyond the limits designated for it, and disturbing the closures enjoined by the Act of 1881.

The Factory and the City

Through the 1880s, Bombay experienced unprecedented industrial buoyancy. The cotton mills of the city recovered from a slump at the end of the 1870s to register their fastest rate of growth yet over the course of the next decade.[1] At the beginning of 1875, there were fifteen cotton mills in Bombay city, employing a little over 5,000 workers. By the end of 1890, there were sixty-seven, employing over 70,000.[2]

Mill building, in common with the general tempo of industrial growth in the city, developed in sudden, dramatic bursts. Thus, of the forty-one new mills set up between 1874 and 1888, as many as thirty-four were constructed in three dramatic years—eleven in 1874, thirteen in 1883, and ten in 1888.[3] As early as 1891, millworkers constituted over 7.5 per cent of a (then) rapidly growing population; ten years later they would constitute over 10 per cent.[4]

This change was accompanied by a profound transformation of the social geography of Bombay, with particularly convulsive effects in the 1880s. It was in this period that the basic pattern of land use that was to characterize Bombay till well into the twentieth century was concretized. The city came to acquire precise socio-spatial divisions: an elite composed of Europeans and rich Indians in the south-west of the island, a 'native town' where busy local markets and shops twisted into narrow, crowded, and socially diverse residential alleys and streets, and a large industrial district ('Girangaon', or the 'mill village', as it was locally known) spreading north and east from the heart of the town. It was the spurt in mill building from the mid-1870s that set this pattern, quite literally, in stone.

In his nostalgic evocation of nineteenth-century Bombay, Dinshaw E. Wacha, a fairly representative member of Bombay's commercial elite, wrote of the radical transformation of Bombay in the 1880s:

> Industrialism came to stay in Bombay and vie with the spindles and looms of proud Lancashire. Suburbs which were dedicated to the ruling hierarchy of Governors, Members of Council, Judges and high State functionaries, for purposes of villa residences, were slowly appropriated by the new hierarchy devoted to the worship of King Cotton. … Industrial capitalism drove out Civilianism who, therefore, planted itself thickly on the breezy Malabar and Cumballa Hills. The suburbs were appropriated by the cotton mills and jerrybuilders of the day found chawls, now reduced to slums, for the accommodation of the growing industrial population.[5]

Wacha's memoir attests a very precise metamorphosis: prominent buildings, as Preeti Chopra observes, changed hands in these years. The Elphinstone College moved from Parel in the north to Fort in the south-west; the Parel Government House was eventually converted into a plague hospital in the late 1890s; access to the eastern foreshore of Bombay was blocked by trade and industry, forcing the city's propertied elites to virtually flee south-westwards. The north-eastern and south-western tips of the island, therefore, acquired utterly contrasting morphologies. Places like Byculla and Parel, formerly affluent and sparsely populated, were transformed into a continuous industrial landscape, characterized by massive horizontal factory buildings and towering chimneys.[6]

In May 1880, early in the city's industrial growth, the *Times of India* observed:

> Bombay has of late years witnessed the erection and starting of so many spinning and weaving mills, and other concerns of a similar nature, that it has come to be called the 'Manchester of India'. Tall chimney shafts show above the surrounding buildings on every side and give to the city, when viewed from a distance, an appearance of manufacturing activity which justifies the term which has been applied to it. This state of things must be a matter of congratulation to all those who have the progress and welfare of the Presidency city at heart; but private individuals, who are not directly interested in the mills, will come to look upon these concerns as unmitigated nuisances, if something is not done to prevent the nuisance arising from the smoke which issues from the chimneys. Those who have lived any time in Bombay must have noticed the thick black clouds of smoke which belch forth from the mill chimneys, and even to some extent darken the intense brightness of a tropical sky. The nuisance is most noticeable in early morning, when the mills are starting work, and when, presumably, fires are being stoked for the day's work.[7]

The article went on to express the need for a Smoke Prevention Act compelling mill owners to fit their boilers with smoke-preventing apparatuses, along the lines of large manufacturing towns in northern England. It also wistfully expressed the desire for an inspector modelled on similar precedents, someone who 'has the eye of an eagle and can tell amidst a forest of chimneys to whose mill any particular shaft belongs. He is no respecter of persons, and it is not an unusual thing to see a magistrate, or the mayor of a town, summoned for a smoke nuisance'.[8]

The complaints by 'private individuals' anticipated by the *Times of India* came soon enough, in 1881 and 1884.[9] A memorial to the Town Council from people living on Duncan Road, in the heart of the town, put the matter most eloquently. Writing of the deleterious effects upon the city of smaller enterprises, specifically corn-mills and wool-cleaning factories, the memorialists complained:

> Hitherto the authorities concerned—the guardians of the public health—who ought to move in the matter, have not as yet raised their voice against this nuisance, while the evil has been growing prodigiously … the chimney shafts of these Mills and Factories are considerably lower than the height provided for in the Smoke Nuisance Act, the smoke besides being dangerous to health, fills the houses of neighbours and gives their walls a smoky and dingy appearance, while the dust of the wool-cleaning factories is a much greater nuisance than anything the smoke may possibly do. The neighbours cannot open their windows without getting their houses filled with dust, dust on their furniture, dust on their clothes, papers and books, and wherever they turn, they seem to be moving in a poisonous atmosphere of dust. … Nor is this all. The sufferings to which the neighbours are subjected during the day are continued even at night. They are denied even the refreshment of sleep by the incessant whirl of the machinery which keeps working till that late hour, and the volumes of mingled smoke and dust entering their sleeping apartments.[10]

Blaney and V.N. Mandlik, both of whom had served on the 1875 Factory Commission, were members of the Town Council that received this memorial. The Factory Act itself came into force shortly afterwards. There is, of course, no direct causal relation between the two events. However, if the memorial is juxtaposed with the campaign for factory legislation stewarded by Bengali at the same time, it is possible to trace the outlines of a public middle-class concern about the effects of industrialization, a shared response to the ways factories were imprinting themselves upon the landscape and the imagination of the city.

Proto-ecological campaigns of this sort had a precise effect: they increasingly made the erection of new factories in the south of the city untenable. A suit brought against the Nicol Mill in Colaba in southern Bombay succeeded, for instance, in compelling the mill owner to 'keep the windows on the north side permanently closed so as to palliate as far as possible the noise of the machinery and the dust arising from the mill'.[11] In 1884, the Sanitary Commissioner of Bombay, Thomas Hewlett, observed: 'It is … satisfactory to notice that all the new mills are being erected on such open situations … where there is a free perflation of air and where plenty of space can be obtained for … the provision in the vicinity of each group of mills of proper habitations for the operatives.'[12]

Such paternalist optimism ran against the grain of Hewlett's own painstakingly collected evidence, which shows us an industrial buoyancy characterized, first and foremost, by competitive cost-cutting that ruthlessly levelled the conditions in which workers laboured downwards. At Tardeo, millworkers complained of having to work within a few yards from the privies of an adjoining mill. Another mill, at Agripada, was 'built alongside and within a few feet of the large open municipal drain … through which the sewage of Agripada is discharged'. Within the mill itself, there was little respite. Windows, as most observers noted, were almost always kept shut while machines were at work: budding collective psychologists among them attributed this to a pathological fear of fresh air among the natives, but more discerning (or truthful) investigators pointed out that the windows needed to be kept shut, at least in cotton mills, to prevent the breaking of the cotton thread.[13]

As Rajnarayan Chandavarkar and other historians of Bombay's textile industry have noted, mill owners were individually and collectively committed to keeping the cost both of their labour deployment and of mill upkeep as low as possible.[14] Given the inflexible costs of imported machinery and fuel, and in a context where migrant agriculturists and rural labourers from Ratnagiri and the Konkan coast flooded Bombay's labour market, such cost-cutting was not unsound economics. Its effects upon the bodies and lives of workers, unsurprisingly, were grim. In a meeting of the Bombay Millowners' Association (BMOA) called for the purpose of formulating a collective, anticipatory critique of the Factory Act shortly before its passage, a mill owner named John Hector burst out in a remarkable, eloquent act of self-criticism:

> Then as regards our own interests, how can we expect either men or machinery to last overworking them as we do? Exhausting labour is not economical labour. We have not yet felt the full effect of the system which we are now carrying on, but depend on it, we shall do so sooner or later and to our cost. … From the time they start in the morning the mills run on till 12 o'clock without stopping. The workmen take their food as best they can beside the machinery while it is working, but you know what sort of atmosphere they will then have to eat in, and I do not call that giving an opportunity for a meal … our manager told me that

> it was not at all an unusual thing for children to work on through the day without food.... I should like to propose that the present system of labour in Indian factories is injurious to the work-people and prejudicial to the interest of employers.[15]

Hector was an exception to the general rule among mill owners. He apparently granted his workers regular holidays, and had experimented with Sunday holidays in 1878 and 1879, long before this was mandated by the 1891 Factory Act.[16] However, this was a theme not uncommonly expressed by individual employers and managers: for the upkeep of machinery, for the replenishment of human energy, for the cause of greater stability in the exports of yarn and piece goods, some kind of collective restraint over working hours was necessary. But the structures of the mill industry ran up against professions of compassion such as Hector's. It was heavily dominated by agents whose commission was made off the production rather than the profits of the mills they managed. This was the result of a shift in the early 1860s. Mill agents had, in the early years of the industry, earned their commissions on the basis of the profits of the industry. The shift to commissions paid on production created a system of generalized overwork.[17]

The durability of this pattern of regularized overwork rested, as Chandavarkar has shown, upon the agency of the mill jobber, who was often effectively the supervisor of the production process, as well as the intermediary between management and labour.[18] In Bombay, the functional separation of proprietors and agents from the actual processes of production was very pronounced. If, as Chandavarkar has argued, the working classes of Bombay retained a remarkable degree of control over their own labour throughout the colonial period, this may have had something to do with this elaborate division between capital accumulation, profit-making, and factory-floor management.

These circumstances, in brief, composed the domain upon which factory law intruded in the 1880s, the last decade in Bombay's history marked by relative industrial peace. This 'peace', however, was a tense one, held in place by structures of exploitation and poverty on the one hand, and the emergent structures of a regime of factory inspection on the other. The latter force was pushed, through logics both intrinsic and extrinsic to it, against its own limits. Mill owners and the Bombay government, as I shall demonstrate in the remainder of this chapter and the bulk of the following one, circled uneasily around the introduction of a regularized system of (weak) state scrutiny into factories. Prior to legislation, industrial relations constituted a province marked, in theory and effectively in practice as well, by a thoroughgoing laissez-faire. The 'free' negotiation between employer and worker, along with the web of industrial relations that held this together, was both maintained and disturbed by the practice of the law, in the form of factory inspection.

The Work of Law: Factory Inspection in Bombay, 1881–7

Shortly after the Factory Act was passed, the Government of Bombay decided to ask for the services of a trained factory official from England to organize and supervise the early work of the factory department in Bombay.[19] The decision was taken in April but suffered a long gestation period. This took the shape, over the course of a year, of long discussions between Alexander Redgrave, Chief Inspector of Factories for the United Kingdom, the Governments of Bombay and India, and the India Office about the modalities of the appointment.[20] The first year of factory law was, therefore, administered by the Collector of Bombay, H.E. Jacomb, assisted by the Inspector of Boilers, William Moylan, neither of whom had experience of factory inspection.[21]

Eventually, in April 1882, William O. Meade-King, a Scottish mid-level factory inspector from Lancashire, arrived for a period of six months, on a salary of £780, a little more than what he was accustomed to in the course of a full year.[22] He appears to have responded to this incentive enthusiastically, peppering the Bombay government with information and advice, and, as I shall describe later, outlining the putative architecture of factory legislation in a manner sometimes radically at odds with the expectations and hopes of the mill owners and the Government alike. He was replaced by the first Indian factory inspector in the Presidency, Kharsedji N. Servai, a Parsi working in the Licence Tax Department.[23] In September 1883, however, Servai was replaced by another trained inspector from Lancashire, James Jones, who was deputed for a period extending up to five years, again on an enhanced salary. Jones served for four of these years, resigning finally in 1887. Significantly, the reason he cited was the stagnation of his salary at £600 a year in the face of a rising workload, given the rapid industrial growth of the city, and the annual increments his colleagues back in England were enjoying.[24]

This dispute over pay, while seemingly an insignificant administrative matter, is unexpectedly revealing. In the Bombay government's refusal to raise Jones' salary, and his consequent departure, we find a double closure. In the first place, the end of Jones' tenure also marks the end of explicit metropolitan intervention in the concrete administration of factory law in Bombay. While Manchester and Parliament were, between 1888 and 1892, to launch a far stronger campaign for the expansion of factory law than in the previous decade, and while their demands were to be partially met, the day-to-day administration of industrial relations became, less ambiguously than before, the province of the Bombay government.

In the second place, the refusal to increase Jones' salary also marked an upper limit, in a very precise financial sense, to how far and how deep factory law was to be allowed to extend. Thereafter, factory administration took its place as a fairly minor, moderately funded branch of government. The Government of Bombay, which during James Fergusson's tenure as Governor (1880–5) had been at the forefront of campaigns to extend the law, was now content to accept a situation where most industrial practices flourished untended by law, and the pace of industrial growth outstripped the reach of factory administration, despite periodic revisions of budgetary and staff allocation upwards.

This shift is bookended by two major inspectorial reports. The first was written by Meade-King for the Government of Bombay in 1882, and the second by Jones at Redgrave's behest. Meade-King's report functioned as fodder for the Government of Bombay, which, under James Fergusson, was actively pushing for the extension of factory law. Jones' report was addressed to Redgrave, who appended it to his general report on factories to Parliament for 1887. The former report, therefore, fed into a local drive for factory reform, and the latter fitted more imperial concerns: it was, for instance, eagerly picked up by some Manchester mill owners in their demand for the further regulation of Bombay's factories.

If the political climate that prevailed at the time of the two reports was subtly different, so was their tone. Meade-King's report amounted, as a whole, to a withering criticism of the mill industry. The insanitary conditions, child labour, overwork, and fatigue produced by factory work were placed under the microscope, and Meade-King's proposals embodied a desire for the thoroughgoing expansion of the powers of the inspectorate.[25] Jones' proposals were more modest, and the rhetoric, too, had changed: where Meade-King was aggressive, Jones was conciliatory, acknowledging at the outset that 'the English Factory Acts could not with fairness be put in force in India, the conditions of the country, climate, and people being so widely different'.[26] In a sense this shift discloses a precise administrative logic. Meade-King's intervention, unlike that of Jones, came at a time when the limits of factory law had not yet been mapped out. The former's reflections and recommendations, therefore, represent both a setting of these 'limits', as well as a more open and potentially expansive vision of factory regulation, which, of course, had to find its way through constant negotiations with employers. It is to these processes that I now turn.

Meade-King Investigates

Meade-King's visit came stamped with the authority of expertise and, of course, metropolitan mastery. This was not a prestige that officials swamped in the pressures and crises of actual governance could command, despite the much greater executive power at their disposal. Meade-King's legitimacy flowed from his location in metropolitan England.

There was another dimension to this authority: Meade-King represented a frontal assault on the principle of the sovereignty of mill owners in industry. If the state chose an external observer as arbitrator, then the ground of legitimate power was shifting from mill owners to the state.[27] The most interesting thing about this process is that mill owners seemed to realize it. Most mill owners went out of their way to please Meade-King: he spoke approvingly of their courtesy and helpfulness. Simultaneously, though, he embodied an emergent court of appeal, deployable by officials pressing for an extension of the Act, but also by mill owners who sought to limit its provisions and keep it within its current manageable limits.

Meade-King's visit was, of course, initially greeted with hostility. Upon receiving news that a British inspector was coming to inspect mills in Bombay, John Gordon, Secretary of the BMOA, sent a letter to the Bombay government asking for confirmation of this.[28] He received an affirmative response, with the reassurance that this inspector would only be appointed for a short period, and his purpose was to train officials for the job of inspection in India.[29]

Gordon, in his reply, raised strong objections: 'The Committee wish to protest … against a proposal which appears to them to be unnecessary, and likely, through prejudice and ignorance on the part of the officer employed, to lead to harsh and needless interference.'[30] The objection to outside interference was, then, particularly pronounced when it came to the possibility of scrutiny from the imperial centre, probably because of the far stricter regulations enjoined by English factory law. Further, a staple argument of the BMOA, since its inception, had been that conditions of factories in England and in India were fundamentally different and laws that applied in one situation could not apply in another. Therefore, Gordon reiterated, the employment of a British officer was unwelcome, given that the 'difference in climate, of the habits and customs of the operatives, and of their system of work are such as would render the employment of an officer of the Factory Department in England unsuitable to India, and would prove injurious to the legitimate operations of Indian manufacturing interests'.[31]

The lives and work of Indian factory operatives, it was argued in effect, were unintelligible in any terms that would make sense to alien observers. Codes that were axiomatic in England in the industrial relationship could not be applied here. The possibility of a trained inspector from England examining mill conditions seemed to cut the ground from beneath the BMOA's feet. If it was to emerge from the inspector's examination that factory workers in India were less content or enjoyed fewer human entitlements than English workers, the basis of the mill owners' legitimacy might be compromised.

For this reason, paradoxically enough, Meade-King's visit became all the more important. His brief was to set out durable principles for the functioning of factory law, and it was in the interests of both the mill owners and the officials who were to assist him that a mutually satisfactory balance be struck. This was dramatized early in Meade-King's visit in the form of a little dispute that centred on the relationship at the heart of the production process, between worker and machine.

Most textile machinery in Bombay came directly from England and was consequently expensive. Mill owners, faced with this structural constraint, as Chandavarkar has shown, deployed a range of strategies to economize on their costs. One of these was the use of old and partially or wholly unguarded machines. It was not unusual for capitalists to buy scrapped equipment or to simply run the plant they had inherited or bought without making any changes in the machinery used.[32] In a highly competitive environment, with a number of enterprises facing periodic capital shortages, short-run calculations were crucial, and major investments in new machinery were more often than not precluded. It was not uncommon, when such investments became unavoidable, for entrepreneurs to replace specific, damaged parts, rather than the whole machine.[33]

Under the Factory Act, it was mandatory to keep certain specified portions of the machinery securely fenced: 'Every fly-wheel directly connected with a steam-engine, water-wheel, or other mechanical or electrical power in any part of the factory ... every hoist or teagle ... near which any person is liable to pass or be employed ... any other part of machinery ... which may in the opinion of the inspector be dangerous'.[34] This was a definition both vague enough to be subverted and broad enough to be expanded. In September 1881, the Bombay government passed rules that defined safety standards more rigorously. However, this still fell short of a full technical definition of safety, and matters were largely left to the discretion of inspectors. It was specified, for instance, that each part of the mill-gearing 'shall be securely fenced in such manner as the Inspector considers sufficient or in such position or of such construction as to be equally safe to every person employed in the factory as it would if it were securely fenced'.[35] The inspector was equipped with the power to furnish occupiers of mills with orders stating what safety measures needed to be taken, and to initiate prosecution if these orders were flouted.[36] Accidents that were not of a 'trifling character' were to be reported within an hour of occurrence, and a notice was to be sent to the nearest police station.[37]

In October 1881, six months before Meade-King's arrival, the Collector of Bombay, H.E. Jacomb, set out in his new capacity as Inspector of Factories to investigate working conditions in mills in the town. He was accompanied by William Moylan who, as Inspector of Steam Boilers and Prime Movers since the Boiler Act of 1873, was one of the few officials in the city with extensive professional experience of factories. Jacomb's report stressed the need for prompt enquiry into accidents and the distinguishing of preventable from unpreventable cases.[38] It was Moylan's memorandum on the fencing of factory equipment, however, that was to be an immediate source of controversy.

Moylan's note focused on the distance, or lack of it, between machines. The carding rooms and the mule rooms were singled out for particular critical attention. He noted that mill owners preferred to place machines very closely together with a view to economizing space, in order to minimize expenses. Moylan acknowledged the legitimacy of this: 'It would entail a heavy expense upon mill owners to widen the open spaces by moving the machines, and some of them would necessarily have to be thrown out of use in each mill, entailing loss to business.' Workers, therefore, had to be extremely careful to avoid fatal contact with the driving straps and head gear in motion. He rounded his argument off with a stereotype: 'As a rule, native operatives are less cautious than English ones in avoiding dangerous contact with the gearing of the machinery, the superior intelligence of the latter enabling them at once to perceive and estimate real danger and to avoid it.'[39]

Moylan went on to suggest a compromise to the effect that the passages at one end of the machinery could be closed up by means of a rail or iron grating. These passages, he observed, were used by workpeople as short cuts from one side of the room to another. Given this practice, it made sense, he argued, to block entry and exit at one end of the machinery. Parenthetically, this practice may have something to tell us about the work-time economies practised by workers at the point of production, given the general prevalence of piece rates in factories.

In accordance with Moylan's suggestions, Jacomb sent out a circular of instructions to mill owners in the Presidency.[40] He was followed by the Inspector of Factories for Thana, the Collector of that district, who on 22 January 1882 circularized Thana mill owners, instructing them to, first, close up passages between carding engines with a moveable iron rail while machines were at work and second, to place a moveable guard of block tin on the headstocks of the mule. Rail and guard cost about Rs 2 each.[41] This order was to become the site of a revealing confrontation between officialdom and capital.

The manager of the New Dharamsi and Punjabhai Spinning and Weaving Mill, C.E. Wilkinson, appealed against this instruction to G.F. Sheppard, Commissioner of the Northern Division of the Bombay Presidency. The appeal was rejected, but Sheppard agreed to forward the documents of the case to Meade-King upon his arrival in India.

Wilkinson, along with other mill owners, seems to have seen this as a major opportunity to press the case against Moylan's instructions, for he went about assiduously collecting support for his viewpoint. In mid-May, he wrote to the Bombay government, enclosing a number of letters from prominent industrialists and managers and requesting that those be forwarded to Meade-King. Wilkinson marshalled his resources well; he could boast the support of the directors of the Framji Petit Company, the managers of the New Great Eastern Mills, the Hindustan Mills, the Sassoon Mills, and many other luminaries of Bombay's industrial landscape.[42] Within a week of the Bombay government's receipt of these appeals, Meade-King considered the case and pronounced judgment.

Meade-King upheld Wilkinson's appeal on the grounds that the spaces sealed off by the guards suggested by Moylan had never, in his experience, been the source of accidents, either in England or in India. He also, however, made a very revealing statement:

> We must not lose sight of the fact, nor should the operatives themselves for one moment forget that *all* machinery is dangerous, and to render it absolutely free from danger would, in many cases, have the effect of making it useless to its owner. The means therefore of protecting operatives from the dangers of machinery must of necessity be limited.[43]

Danger, then, is constitutive of the very experience of industrial labour, and is not something that can be wished away by regulation and efficient safety provisions. This disturbing admission lay at the heart of Meade-King's decision. Strictly speaking, it was not called for by the case since Meade-King went to great lengths to state the absence of danger either from the passages between carding machines or from unfenced headstocks. However, the unavoidability of danger was conceded, and conceded in no uncertain terms. Meade-King also went on to observe that it was no use placing a moveable rail 'in passages through which—to use Mr. Moylan's own words—operatives will, if they cannot walk, crawl and creep on their hands and knees'.[44] The physical space of the mill, then, was loaded with danger no matter what precautions were taken.

The trajectory of this case is revealing, both for what it tells us about Meade-King's status as privileged observer and arbiter, and for the light it throws on the evolution of the relationship between mill owners and inspectors. Clearly, Meade-King's arrival was seen not only as a threat, but also as an opportunity for mill owners to press the justice of their claims upon him. The presence of a super-inspector, as it were, became an opportunity for capitalists to strike a small but decisive blow against some of the intrusions on their sovereignty. Soon enough, the Commissioner of the Northern Division fell in line with this recommendation and the order issued by the Thana Inspector was revoked.[45] Several officials were relieved by this decision, which seemed to prove that mill owners and the state could work harmoniously together after all. Meade-King came in for a warm round of applause for having been able to 'ease the operation of the Act in the case of some mill-owners'.[46]

The dispute, nonetheless, had touched the nerve of a real anxiety that mill owners had to face—that factory regulation and legislation had not been closed off once and for all by the enactment of 1881. The provisions in it were open to change and extension and, at the very least, to constant reformulation, debate, and critical scrutiny with an eye to influencing further reform. Government officials and mill owners alike sought closure, a point where one could claim to have defined the 'basic' principles and coordinates of factory regulation, beyond which further legal enactment would be superfluous.

If Meade-King's intervention in this case affirmed one kind of closure, the general tenor of his reports pushed in the opposite direction. These reports were packed with uncomfortable details. Examining mills in Ahmedabad, he drew attention to the difficulty in making children conscious of their entitlements, a question other inspectors had not raised.

> A glance at the enclosed copy of children's hours of work ... will show the confusion which must exist in the minds of children who, it must be remembered, have no idea whatever of time, with regard to the hours at which they have to enter and leave the mill. The difficulty of finding out whether the hours of work have been exceeded or not will be no less apparent.[47]

Sanitation and ventilation also came in for criticism of the kind that they had been spared earlier since they were not a part of the Act. Meade-King wrote: 'The roof of one (mill) appeared to let in so much of the rain that the floors were in many places saturated. ... The atmosphere of one sizing room was almost intolerable'.[48] At Nadiad's sole factory (the subject of the concluding section of this chapter), he found that 'the inside walls of the mill were dirty and the reelers were working in miserable sheds with little light and less air: one of these sheds had no window.[49]

Meade-King's reports, in general, explicitly described appalling conditions, without, however, making an explicit judgment about mill owners. He frequently followed up his most damning observations with tributes to the goodwill of owners and statements to the effect that the provisions of the Act had been complied with. This is intriguing at first but, reading between the lines, there is no real contradiction. For Meade-King, the enforcement of the Act and the enforcement of humane factory conditions were not identical with each other. His amiability towards most individual mill owners was propelled by its own momentum towards much more damning indictments of the existing factory system. Other inspectors, Jacomb for instance, would fulminate over individual breaches of law. Meade-King, however, made the *general* statement that the law, as it stood, was not adequate.

Through careful and detailed description, Meade-King made visible to the official gaze facts about factories that were either unknown or could previously have been overlooked. Once inscribed in the records, however, observations of this kind had—have—a remarkable capacity to be deployed as ammunition in future exchanges and confrontations. They served as fodder for argumentation. And nowhere was this more evident than in Meade-King's final report to the Bombay government.

His arguments, in this remarkable document, articulated a thought which was ubiquitous in the rhetoric of colonial officials—that protection for factory operatives would not only deliver them from misery, but also be in the interests of employers, who had everything to gain from a secure and healthy workforce. Given Bombay's abundance of cheap labour, this was almost certainly not the case. This fiction, though, was powerfully entrenched in much reformist labour thinking in England, and was a useful tool to deploy in the Indian context. Meade-King wrote:

> The history of factory legislation in England will prove that judicious improvement of the condition of work-people will never injure the manufacturing interest. On the contrary, the surest guarantee of productiveness has been said to lie in proper conditions of labour. The English Legislature extended its protection to women and children gradually and steadily, in the face of a powerful opposition, but it cannot

> now be denied that the Factory Acts have conferred the greatest possible benefit on the operatives, while the employers are realizing the advantage to be derived from a superior set of work-people.[50]

This is an argument that, in various forms, has proved durable. It has regularly been deployed, strategically or unconsciously, as the founding argument for a justification of many kinds of industrial policy and employer practices, whether reformist or repressive. The argument collates various interests involved in industrial production and reifies them into the abstract interests of something called 'the industry'. If the interests of workers are promoted and protected, 'the industry' as a whole will benefit, as productivity and profitability will rise. All other kinds of calculations, of course, are occluded in this account: the social composition of the workforce, the abundance or scarcity of labour, the extent of employers' demand for skilled labour, the ability of employers to exhaust labourers and replace them readily—which seems to have been very high in Bombay.

The tensions *within* this regulative principle pervaded Meade-King's arguments for the protection of labour. Starting from the abstract principle that what is good for labour must also, at some level, be good for capital, that the interests of workers and employers *could* be harmonized, he went on to make recommendations for protection that would have made most mill owners' eyes bulge with horror. A picture of the mills appeared which did not in any sense correspond to the roseate representations in most mill owners' accounts. Meade-King, for instance, described 'the effluvia, arising from some latrines attached to a neighbouring mill', 'dust and fluff flying about', 'acrid steam' rising from sizing rooms.[51] 'I have endeavoured to ascertain', he further wrote, 'whether factory work is continued for 13 consecutive days without one whole hour's cessation in the daylight in any other country in the world.'[52] This statement grounded a plea for a lighter workload and the institution of weekly holidays for all women and children. 'Can the factory operatives of Bombay bear this continuous strain without injury either to themselves or to those who come after them?'[53]

Meade-King held back, however, from applying this judgment to adult male workers. This has something to tell us about the torsions at the heart of the principle of factory regulation, derived from British precedents, in a policy atmosphere still saturated with a laissez-faire ethic. On the one hand, the evidence frequently presented demonstrated the harshness of the current regime of time for *all* workers. On the other hand, most reformist arguments stopped short of extending the benefits of a holiday to *all* operatives. Children and, increasingly from the early 1880s, women were defined as the legitimate recipients of protection, and thus as 'special cases', necessary aberrations from the 'normal' worker, the adult male, who could look after his own interests.

Only by postulating this discontinuity between the interests and capacities of vulnerable and 'independent' workers was it possible to desist from formulating universal rules of protection—something that most official discourse sought to occlude. But this ineluctably ran into tensions of its own: it was not a stable point of rest for factory regulation because the field of modern industry was in itself not stable. Discursively, arguments for the extension of legislation to vulnerable workers could, in changed circumstances, supply ammunition for sharper articulations of workers' entitlements. 'Protection' was a discourse about vulnerability, but could also become a discourse about *right*: it was open to deployments which could reframe the former as the latter.

Such intimations of a more universalizing ethic of 'protection', importantly, did find their way into Meade-King's most telling intervention, which had to do with the very definition of a 'factory'. In England, the definition of factories had been widened over the decades through successive legal injunctions, culminating with the Act of 1878 that broke down the distinction between 'factories' and 'workshops', the latter referring to small enterprises employing less than fifty persons.[54] In England, investigative research and observation had uncovered several strategies followed by manufacturers to avoid factory regulation, many of which seem strangely familiar today. To circumvent the law, production could be dispersed and individual establishments could be kept deliberately modest. As the work of Maxine Berg, among others, on early industrialization in England has shown, employers had a wide and flexible range of options, and it was not necessarily more profitable to concentrate production physically, even for large manufacturers.[55]

In India, most workplaces *were* small, even in a Bombay rapidly on its way to becoming a major industrial centre. Large mills may have come to dominate the physical landscape of large parts of the city, with their smoking chimneys and their vast prison-like buildings. However, the 'small-scale sector', as it is now called, was expanding apace: wool and cotton-cleaning factories, bone-crushing units, ginning factories, cotton presses, and an array of seasonal occupations made up a growing world of informal industrial production. This very division of labour into two sectors, one marked by the world of law and regulation and the other left unregulated, was a creation of the state's choices.[56] One of the ways in which this choice was exercised was the way factories were defined. The Act ran:

> 'Factory' means any premises (other than indigo factories or … tea or coffee plantations) wherein is carried out, for not less than four months in the whole of any one year, any process for, or incidental to, making, altering, repairing, ornamenting, finishing, or otherwise adapting for use, transport or sale, any article or part of an article … wherein steam, water, or other mechanical power is used … wherein not less than one hundred persons are on any day simultaneously employed.[57]

Defined in this manner, most sites of industrial manufacture in Bombay, not to speak of other cities where large-scale industry had made fewer inroads, were exempt from the functioning of the Act. Many employers could change their production choices and exercise options that would exempt them from regulation. Most employers were, in any case, not subject to the law. But this remained a permanently unstable situation. Once the existence of factory regulation opened up a window into the working lives of labourers in mills, the excision of such an overwhelming majority of the workforce from protection became contentious.

Meade-King, at the behest of the Bombay government, visited fifteen small mills and factories in Bombay between 11 April and 9 June, 1882. He seems to have been deeply horrified by what he encountered there. This led him to what was effectively an extremely radical suggestion regarding the legal definition of factories. He argued that the number of workers employed should not be considered at all in the process of defining an establishment as a factory. The use of steam power alone would suffice. He pointed to English precedent: prior to the Act of 1878, which drew small workshops within the ambit of legislation, English law only addressed enterprises employing over fifty persons. This made it possible for manufacturers to evade the provisions of the Act by keeping down the number of their employees. In India, too, the dangers of this were real.[58] In these circumstances, using the number of employees working to define a factory was intrinsically a flawed idea, whether the minimum number was pegged at a hundred or fifty or twenty. The radical nature of this suggestion is borne out by the fact that to this day it is absent from the statute books in India—indeed, the contemporary drift is very much in the opposite direction.

The *potential* meaning of factory regulation, then, was transformed as a result of Meade-King's intervention. The Factory Act was initially conceived, within the legislative and commercial worlds of Bombay and India, as a limited and *singular* injunction which would accomplish the necessary standards of safety and security for workers. The finality of this injunction would secure industrial peace: at this juncture, prior to the emergence of a labour movement, this meant security in the relations between employers and state officials, rather than employers and workers. Such 'peace' rested on a prior limitation of the scope and meanings of legislation —and it can be argued that no enactment could be more limited, and parsimonious, than that of 1881.

However, the work of law cannot simply be reduced to the subjective inclinations of its makers. Investigative procedures were authorized by the law, and these uncovered practices and strategies of capitalists that seemed to discommode the efficient operation of protective regulation. Many of these practices occupied a shadowy line between legitimacy and illegitimacy, and the discourse of protection that had been set in motion by the debates around factory law found it difficult to sustain justifications for them. This led, in the medium term, both to actual legal revisions of the text of factory law and to pressures, arguments, polemics, and confrontations around the limits of such law. The former were constitutively finite and limited; the latter less so. It is this unstable dynamic which the events narrated in the following sections disclosed and made concrete.

A Small Death

Law can only *appear* final; events disturb the consensus that grounds it. But there is a tense dialectic here. Precisely because its founding myth of stability is so important to legal closure, the disturbing singularity—the event which cannot be absorbed within law's discursive frames—can break open and recast the terms of debate. Practices and situations the law cannot account for or anticipate acquire a propulsive character and exert pressures towards its revision.

Within the world of industrial law, accidents are uniquely positioned in this regard: they designate traumatic experiences that disturb illusions of stability, and—through the moral horror of industrial death or injury—force a reconsideration of existing safeguards. The factory is exposed by the accident as a space of danger, something that appears self-evident enough when a worker loses a limb or life, but has to be cloaked in a veil of unlikelihood in normal times of operation. Accidents operate within a particularly nervous dialectical field: they are by their nature freak, unexpected events. However, because of their periodic recurrence they generate a range of *structural* explanations: worker carelessness, industrial malpractice, faulty spatial arrangements among others. The individual accident is unexpected, but also immediately accounted for by a structure of expectations that explain it: if the light is bad, the worker is likely to suffer; if the worker has no rest, he is likely to be endangered; a careless labourer invites danger; and so on. Such explanatory narratives invariably operate upon an accident and produce an unruly chain of significations.

In the era before the great industrial strike, accidents had a particular significance. In the absence of industrial transparency, in a world where mills churned out smoke and commodities through an apparently invisible, mathematical juxtaposition of factors of production, where the labourer was rendered invisible by the walls and darkness of the workplace, the loss of a leg or a hand or life was effectively the only point at which the worker's relationship with the space of the mill could be rendered fully visible. Accidents could shed sudden light on work processes, relations in production, and forms of exploitation. And the trauma of this public revelation could generate debates about the protective measures necessary against the dangers of the workplace.

Seen in the round, factory legislation directly affected only two dimensions of mill experience—the labour of children and the dangers of machinery. But children were, as the next chapter explores, slippery in many ways. Their ages were a mystery much of the time; they were human and, therefore, mobile; they darted through doors and openings in mills and were difficult to pin down; and they could exchange certificates and fake their identities. Machinery, on the other hand, evaded nothing: there was nothing ambiguous about it. Inspectors' reports, therefore, tended to be much sounder on the issue of industrial safety than on concrete provisions for the protection of children. Further, the fencing and safety of machinery widened the horizons of the Factory Act, since it necessarily also engrossed the adult worker: the dangers from machinery were more universal in their scope than the vulnerability of children. At the same time, as the event narrated in the following section discloses, the two kinds of vulnerability could combine in meaningful ways in the unfolding of an accident.

In the middle of February 1882, a boy of fifteen named Radhoo Saitoo set out to work at his place of employment, a bone-crushing mill owned by a Mr John Stuart. It was five in the evening when he began his work, which consisted of gathering imperfectly crushed bones from under the crusher. The factory, employing as it did less than 100 workers, was not subject to the regulations of the Act. Even if it had been, Radhoo Saitoo would not have come under legislative protection, since at fifteen he was technically an adult. The law gave him no respite from work, and he was on night duty.

At seven in the morning, having apparently worked in the mill for fourteen continuous hours, the boy gave up the ghost. One end of his dhoti got caught in a cogwheel that was partially unguarded. The dhoti, as observers of factories had noticed, is not a garment that is conducive to work amidst fast-moving machinery. Radhoo Saitoo's body was carried over the wheel, and his bones, in an ironic twist, were crushed in a bone-crushing mill.

Thomas Blaney, the Coroner of Bombay, held an inquest on the boy's death on 24 February and sharply indicted the lack of fencing as culpable, though the factory owner faced no punitive action.[59] Blaney had, as mentioned earlier, been one of only two Factory Commissioners to support legislation in 1875. After the inquest, he got in touch with Jacomb, the Collector and Factory Inspector for Bombay, to plead for the extension of protection to small factories. Jacomb replied that his hands were tied since factory law did not apply to establishments employing less than a hundred workers. Blaney now wrote to the Judicial Department of the Bombay government directly. His letter is worth quoting at length.

> I think it my duty to represent to Government that in my opinion it is these smaller mills which stand most in need of having their prime movers efficiently protected—many, if not most of these mills, work

> by night as well as by day, and night labour must necessarily be more dangerous than day labour. As in the case of the death of the boy in the bone crushing factory now reported, the deceased was on duty for 14 hours, including the whole of the night. It is true also that the smaller factories in which less than 100 persons are employed are owned by men of small capital and this may reasonably be expected to lead to the use of inferior machinery and to carelessness or indifference in efficiently protecting such machinery. At the present time the number of these small mills and factories are rapidly being multiplied in Bombay, and unless they are brought under the provisions of the Factory Act, it is to be feared that many deaths, which the application of the provisions of that Act would prevent, will probably occur.
>
> On a previous occasion, about a year ago, I held a similar inquest on the body of a labourer in a small flour mill in Baboola Tank Road owned by a Mohammedan. In that case death resulted from the utter want of protection to the fly wheel at the engine.[60]

In this letter, Blaney made the connections that most of the officials associated with the administration of factory legislation were afraid of making, since they threatened the closures fixed by law. Most workplaces, after all, employed far fewer than a hundred workers. Blaney also made the causal connections that most explanations devised for accidents in factories steered clear of. The boy who was killed was working at night; he had been working fourteen hours at a stretch in bad light. It was not simply a technical fault in the machinery that caused Radhoo's death; the very conditions of his employment put his life at risk, and confirmed that risk by killing him.

Blaney also had his finger on the pulse of the times: he knew that he was living through a momentous period of industrial growth in Bombay. And while the most visible and impressive signifiers of this growth were the cotton mills, there were other and smaller establishments springing up all around, all the time. Flour mills, wool-cleaning mills, cotton-ginning and grinding mills, and bone-crushing mills were all inhabitants of a dense industrial landscape. And industry was not going to stand still and wait for legislation to catch up. Even as Blaney wrote, investors, both small and large, were planning the construction of new industries, new factories, new bone-crushers. Blaney understood the urgency of the need for law to address industrial labour in all its forms.

Jacomb, probably sensitized by his inspections of factories over several months in 1881 and 1882, lost little time in backing Blaney's appeal. On 24 March, he wrote to the General Department of the Bombay government, reiterating the need for more comprehensive protection of factory workers. He drew attention, in this memorandum, to a history of previous observations of working conditions in small factories.

> From a report by the Inspector of Steam Boilers and Prime Movers to the Municipal Commissioner of Bombay no. 55 dated 10 March 1877 on the condition of the small factories on Duncan Road, I find that ... some of the factories are erected in ill-lighted dwelling houses or in godowns situated in densely-populated parts of the native town in consequence of which the machinery is so very much crowded that the passages barely admit of the workpeople moving about, without considerable risk to themselves, and the danger would naturally be much greater at night. The danger is, moreover, enhanced when the passages are obstructed by heaps of cotton or wool or bags of grain and flour as they often are.[61]

Not for the first or last time, the physical organization of the workplace appears as a source of the worker's vulnerability. Jacomb also linked the dangers of accidents, as did Blaney, to the organization of work-time and argued that unless it was made mandatory for mill owners to work their labourers in shifts, the 'fatiguing exertion' of factory work would have debilitating consequences. Workers deprived of sleep would succumb to the dangers of machinery in the absence of regulations of either time or space in factories: 'Instances of severe mutilation have occurred by the attendants on machines in motion dropping upon them while in a sleepy state.'[62]

There was strength and eloquence to these demands, especially since they were being made by men with considerable influence in the city administration. Jacomb, Moylan, and Blaney were three of the most consistent advocates of the extension of legislation to smaller factories, and they were, respectively, the Collector, Inspector of Boilers, and Coroner of Bombay. The pressures they could exert were not negligible. In April 1882, the Government of Bombay resolved that 'it is most desirable that the provisions of the Act should be rendered applicable to the numerous small, ill-built, carelessly managed, and insufficiently equipped factories to be found in Bombay and other large towns'.[63] The resolution added that the central government should consider amending the Factory Act by making it applicable to establishments with twenty or even fewer workers.[64] It was also decided to forward this resolution to Meade-King, and this, more than anything else, probably accounts for the vehemence of his argument that *all* workplaces needed legislation.

Meade-King backed up Blaney's arguments, pointing out that the least investment in human security and well-guarded machinery was made in the small mills; further, the preponderance of night-work and excessive hours of labour in these factories was fatal, for these were 'the two conditions of labour in which so-called "accidents" are of the most frequent occurrence'.[65] The phrase 'so-called "accidents"' is revealing, signalling as it does an attempt to see accidental injury as structurally woven into the fabric of conditions of mill work in Bombay, or at least in its small factories.

Meade-King offered an even more damning indictment. He wrote that in two-thirds of the works he visited, he found unfenced flywheels and mill-gearing. His analysis of the dangers faced by workers, however, went beyond the threat of unguarded machinery. He pointed out that sudden injury to life or limb was usually public, but the most fatal and dangerous afflictions would be silent and invisible.[66] In England, some years before, several deaths had been traced to the effects upon work-people of sorting different classes of foreign wools. The primary cause for 'woolsorters' disease' was identified as fleeces that had been plucked carelessly from dead animals' carcasses, and to which particles of skin and flesh adhered. The two or three wool-cleaning factories in Bombay that Meade-King had visited alarmed him, for the dust coming from the wool was suffocating. The long-term effect of such working conditions on health could be fatal. Pointing to these cases and also stressing the tragedy of Radhoo Saitoo's death in the bone factory, Meade-King urged the government to reconsider the provisions of the Factory Act and extend them to small factories.[67]

There is evidence that suggests that apart from the unquestionable role of conscience in the campaign spearheaded by Blaney and Jacomb, there might have been other pressures at work, in particular, the pressure of a certain section of public opinion, mediated through the press. On 3 January, a month before Radhoo Saitoo's death, the *Bombay Samachar* had commented on the death of two labourers from 'the poisonous atmosphere of the deep hole in the Government distillery at Dadar' and also on the death of three sewage workers while cleaning the drain on Frere Road. In both these cases, the paper remarked, the Coroner's jury had entered a verdict that the deceased had 'died from poisonous atmosphere'. This wasn't enough, though, and the jury 'ought to have ascertained in each of these cases by whose negligence the unfortunate occurrences happened and what punishment the guilty parties deserved'.[68] Shortly after Blaney and Jacomb had begun their campaign to amend the Act, the *Yajdan Parast* made similar observations, reporting the loss of seven lives due to a roof of a cotton mill caving in, an accident it attributed to the negligence of the Engineering Department of the Municipality.[69]

What these reports point to is an incipient public discourse on accidents related to labour, and also the limits to the concern and intervention of public servants like Blaney, however genuine their humanitarianism may have been. The newspapers cited earlier were demanding justice in the form of the identification of guilty parties in accidents and their punishment—something, in other words, along the lines of employer liability. Blaney, at his angriest, did not contemplate this. For him, as for Jacomb, the point of considering cases like Radhoo Saitoo's was to urge the government to further humanize the law by preventing the worst abuses of workers' safety. There persisted, however, a deep-seated commitment to a certain notion of industrial peace, which could be ensured by amending statutes but not by holding employers accountable and punishable for the deaths and injuries of those who worked for them.

The effect of this was paradoxical. On the one hand, it disabled the possibility of naming a culprit in specific cases of accidental injury or death, even when the employer was clearly morally responsible. On the other hand, it enabled Blaney and like-minded people to make penetrating structural connections between conditions of mill work and the dangers faced by operatives, connections that went beyond the assignment of blame and concrete responsibility. The limits and possibilities of an emergent 'reforming' discourse were, thus, dialectically interwoven.

No immediate action was taken but the conditions of work inside small factories had clearly entered the concerns of the Bombay government. Subsequent to Meade-King's report, factory inspectors across the Presidency made a point of examining small enterprises and commenting on conditions of labour in them. This practice founded a new anxiety about the limits of existing legislation. The Government of India, when appealed to, refused to undertake legislation so soon after the initial enactment, but left a window open, saying that it was willing to reconsider the matter of amendment if reports from Bombay Presidency demonstrated the severity of the problem.[70] Matters came to a head in March 1884, when Jones, after taking over as Chief Inspector of Factories, submitted a report on small works using steam power in Bombay city. He noted the range of activities carried out in these small factories: bone crushing; flour grinding; wool and cotton cleaning; cotton spinning and pressing; engineering; and the manufacture of iron, brass, ice, rope, paper, surgical instruments, leather, soda water, and acids. All of these employed fast-moving, unprotected machinery. Accidents, wrote Jones, were rampant in enterprises of this sort, but were seldom made public. Legislation was urgently needed.[71] But this was not all.

> This, however, is not the greatest evil they have to put up with, for in the textile, bone crushing and flour mills, ventilation and efficient means for carrying off the dust and gases arising from the various processes of manufacture are conspicuous by their absence. I have passed through rooms so full of dust that I found it impossible to distinguish objects a few yards ahead and this dust is of such a vitiated nature that serious injury must ensue to the poor creatures who are obliged to breathe it the livelong day.[72]

These observations founded an urgent request for the reconsideration of factory law. The Bombay government responded by setting up another Commission of inquiry that would look into working conditions inside mills. The Commision was charged with the work of evaluating the need for an amendment to the Act of 1881. Blaney served on this Commission as he had on the last, and so did Sorabji Shahpurji Bengali. Probably, as a result of the initiative of these two, the Commission ended up recommending the extension of legislation when it made its final Report in early 1885. The Indian Factory Act, the Report argued, needed to be brought more in line with existing English factory provisions. Further regulation of the hours of work of working children was called for, the child was redefined as a person over nine, the regulation of women's labour was also suggested, holidays for women and children were suggested, and—most significantly for the purposes of this book—the Government was urged to extend legislation to all factories employing steam power and more than ten persons.[73]

As things turned out, the Government of India did not authorize further legislation on the grounds that it was too soon after the initial enactment and that any legislative interference would mean passing a general Act for the whole country. Its decision not to undertake factory reform was taken after consulting all the other provincial governments who emphatically refused further amendment.[74] The Bombay government was not forbidden to undertake special legislation for the Presidency, but even the officials most sympathetic to factory workers knew that the strength of the mill owners' lobby made such a move impossible. There the matter rested for the moment.

Several anxieties, then, crystallized around accidents such as Radhoo Saitoo's death: the hours of work inside factories, unprotected machinery, night work, the arbitrary definition of a factory in existing law. These anxieties were powerful enough to propel the Government of Bombay to repeatedly raise the matter of factory law amendment and request the extension of legislation to small factories. This was, in many ways, remarkable. After all, the death of a 'common' labourer was hardly a scandal in normal times. The drama propelled by this incident had to do with growing insecurities about the demonstrable weakness of factory law. This is in itself interesting. Factory law in India had, after all, been conceived with a view to interfering as little as possible with the working of industrial capital. However, the production of a system of administration around factory labour, centred around inspectors but also containing at its margins sympathetic public officials like Blaney, meant that the non-performance of the Act would always potentially be a source of worry and embarrassment.

A legal closure of sorts had apparently been achieved in 1881 with considerable difficulty. It could be sustained without much acrimony because it was weak and toothless, containing no real mechanism for implementation. What it did contain, however, was a mechanism that allowed inspectors—often far from unsympathetic to factory workers—to scrutinize and judge the space of the mill, a terrain hitherto considered inviolable. This capacity, conjoined with the actual weakness of legislative provisions, rendered the law extremely fragile. There were many forces arrayed against it, and some that wished to push it in more interventionist directions. The equilibrium between these forces was maintained, but not without anxiety. And given the tensions between state, capital, labour, and public opinion that existed, the capacity of individual, propulsive events to rupture the slender consensus and necessitate reconsiderations of the limits of law was significant.

Nadiad and Its Mill Owner

I now turn to another modality of the emerging relationship between industrial capital and factory law in Bombay Presidency. *Where* mills and factories subject to protective legislation were located, I suggest, had something to do with the reception and negotiation of factory law by mill owners. The tensions inherent in this process materialized, in the early history of factory legislation, in the life of one particular mill, notorious in its time for mismanagement and oppressive working conditions. This was a factory owned and managed by Sheth Manordas Harakchand in Nadiad, in the cotton-growing district of Kheda.

Two forms of capital investment predominated in late-nineteenth-century Bombay, one characterized by the socialization of risk, and the other characterized by private ownership. Most mills in western India in the last quarter of the nineteenth century were financed by shareholder capital.[75] After the initial incursions of pioneer capitalists into the terrain of cotton mill production in the 1850s, capital investment rapidly developed in highly socialized forms. As early as the 1870s, publicly subscribed shares accounted for a dominant proportion of the capital invested in mills, both in the island of Bombay and in up-country, 'mofussil' centres. Typically, shares were floated and the incoming capital administered by managing agents or directors. These agents determined levels of production, negotiated orders from the markets in the Far East, imposed a commission on each pound of mill production (and thereby generally guaranteed lucrative returns for themselves), and, not infrequently, speculated heavily on the share markets.[76]

As distinct from this, there persisted, through the late nineteenth century, a not insignificant minority of factories that were owned, administered, and often also managed by individual capitalists, men rich enough to furnish all or most of the capital needed to set up a mill. Nine out of the thirty-nine cotton mills in the Bombay Presidency in 1880, some of which boasted an impressive amount of paid-up capital, were run by individual entrepreneurs.[77] And while private ownership of mills that came under the Factory Act was the exception rather than the rule, this was not the case with smaller factories, which were generally marked by a preponderance of individual ownership.[78]

Administering the Factory Act in Bombay and regulating the mills' use of labour was, in one sense, facilitated by its industrial density: the offices of the relevant administrators were not far from any of the mills they had to survey. But on other counts the work of these administrators was made much harder. Labour in Bombay was mobile, sliding continually between different labour regimes. Capital, therefore, had flexible options. To avoid regulation, a mill owner could disperse his investment across small units or divide it between one large unit and several small units.[79] To add to all of this, the mill owners of the city could compose, when they wished, a coordinated and formidable body of organized capital, capable of effectively confronting the law.

Factories assembled in dispersed, provincial—and often rural—locations were different. They were usually linked to the same rhythms of global trade as their counterparts in Bombay city, but inhabited, in other significant respects, a very distinct world. Through the period between 1875 and 1880, there were only ten large cotton mills in non-Bombay locations within the Presidency. These were mainly scattered across cotton-growing rural districts and small towns in interior Maharashtra and Gujarat, and employed, by the end of 1880, 5,643 workers.[80] While these enterprises grew in number through the 1880s, this pattern of growth was dwarfed by the rapid progress of industrial concentration and consolidation in Bombay.

The patterns of industrial paternalism provide one kind of clue to the nature of such divergences. In locations where a small number of industrial capitalists—sometimes a single entrepreneur—could command most of the available pool of both capital and labour, experiments in factory paternalism were more feasible than in concentrated industrial centres. An interesting illustration of this was available in the testimony, before the 1875 Factory Commission, by Becherdas Ambaidas, one of the pioneer industrial capitalists in Ahmedabad. Asked how he had come to set up his enterprise, he replied that he had been a *rassalah* in the irregular force maintained by Government, which was dismissed in 1864. He had been, he said, 'struck by the want of employment' of his fellow-soldiers, and this was what spurred him to set up a mill for them.[81]

This potential for paternalism, however, was accompanied by its mirror reverse: the possibility of factory despotism. Industrial employers located outside concentrated industrial centres sometimes exerted near-monopolistic controls over local labour markets, and consequently enjoyed certain freedoms of initiative that a manufacturing industry such as Bombay's, which had certain weak but real self-regulatory constraints imposed by the immediacy of industrial competition, did not. This may well have produced a tighter circle of social relations around the workplace and, to some extent, closed the gap between entrepreneurship and factory management, functions that were rapidly divorced from one another in most Bombay mills. These relations may have corresponded, in certain cases, more to the intimacies—and intimate forms of exploitation—characteristic of small workshops than to the more sophisticated administrative mechanisms characteristic of expanding joint-stock concerns.

This was the terrain upon which factory law intruded. Confronted with the diversity of forms of mill ownership and control, and the separation of different forms of industrial control from one another, the Act chose to equivocate, and affixed responsibility for observance of labour regulations upon an undefined, shadowy figure, designated the 'occupier'.[82] This amounted, in effect, to a major gap within the law. One of its consequences was that private, individual mill owners, who exercised closer personal control over their employees than large companies which tended to delegate this responsibility, found it harder to evade factory law with impunity.[83] On the other hand, mills that were more or less governed by managing agents and directors could use this ambiguity within the law to their advantage and were much harder to prosecute for their transgressions.

This legal ambiguity points to an important tension: the Factory Act seemed to be designed for an industrial landscape constituted by individual, private employers (in whose case the blanket appellation 'occupier' made more sense). But while much industrial enterprise in the Presidency was actually organized along these lines, the limitation of the Act to larger factories meant that it operated in another landscape, where this personalized form of mill control was the exception. This partly explains one of the most persistent features of the Act: the relative rarity of actual prosecution. Through the 1880s, employers were constantly found napping when it came to carrying out the minimal protective measures enjoined by factory legislation. Major and minor violations of the law were routinely recorded by factory inspectors. Most of these violations, however, never reached the courts and were dealt with informally or were effectively ignored.[84] The administration of the Factory Acts, then, hardly ever led to litigation, which generally took place only after all other avenues of negotiation, settlement, and compromise had been exhausted.

It seems that the consequences of a regime of inspectorial scrutiny authorized by law could produce much greater ruptures in factories within the 'mofussil' than within the island of Bombay. One of the more immediate dimensions of this was that a battery of regulations suddenly pressed down upon employers who had hitherto enjoyed substantial internal and external sovereignty with regard to their mills. This was intensified by the fact that, unlike Bombay city, the forces of mofussil factory regulation were not administered by more or less middling government inspectors, but by other powerful forces in local politics. The tasks of provincial factory inspection devolved upon District and Assistant Magistrates and Collectors, up until the early 1890s, when the apparatus of inspection expanded for both city and mofussil.[85]

Inspectorial accounts from the 1880s reveal a complicated situation. Factory inspections in the mofussil were carried out by men with little practical instruction or experience in the craft of industrial scrutiny. Mill owners, who were often not members of the BMOA and were not bound by its rules, flouted the law with more impunity.[86] At the same time, their factories seem to have been *more* closely scrutinized: the reports on individual factories are more detailed and intrusive than their Bombay counterparts; they are also in many ways more careful, for lapses in reporting from a district with six or seven factories could be seized upon by bureaucratic superiors more easily than in a city with nearly a hundred large and small factories. Factory inspection could announce a new scheme of tensions in the relations between the state and the capitalist, one predicated on the abridgement of the latter's sovereignty as employer. A more extensive and frightening bureaucratic apparatus could bear down upon the industrialist. Mills which, prior to factory regulation, could have organized their practices with more or less total freedom from outside scrutiny felt the ground shift beneath their feet with the announcement of a protective regime, as they simultaneously suffered the scrutiny of several administrative regimes.

In all of Kheda district in central Gujarat in the early 1880s, there was only one factory. It was located in the town of Nadiad, which lay within the sub-division of the same name. This town had been, through the eighteenth and nineteenth century, an important commercial centre, reputed, as David Hardiman observes, more 'for its prosperity than for its beauty'.[87] In 1803, it had been handed over by the reigning Gaikwad ruler to the British Government. By the 1830s and 1840s, it had developed a considerable trade with Malwa and the Gujarat interior, importing grain, gums, and dye-stuffs, and exporting cotton, coarse cloth, calicoes, tobacco, and coarse sugar. In 1872, when the first census was taken, it was inhabited by 24,551 people and was the largest town in the district, its importance being enhanced by its status, from 1863, as a station on the Bombay, Baroda, and Central India (BB and CI) Railway.[88] In 1866, the town acquired a new civic organization, with the establishment of a municipality dominated by the Nadiad Desais, the major Patidar agriculturists of the area.[89]

Nadiad was a busy commercial town, its trade dominated by Banias and Brahmins. Cotton was grown in abundance in the district, and was, along with tobacco, the chief item in the town's export trade. The Gazetteer of 1879 noted that the opening of the railway had placed the finer piece goods produced by Manchester within easy reach of the richer sections of the population not only of the town, but also the surrounding villages.[90] The coarser piece goods from Manchester and the coarse cloth woven in local handlooms had come to be superseded by cloth produced in the mills of Bombay and Ahmedabad.[91]

In August 1876, a correspondent for the *Times of India* reported the opening of a mill in Nadiad, commenting perspicuously that while such an event was by now practically a weekly event in Bombay, it was much rarer in 'the country districts dependent on Bombay'. Mill building, organized by the new Nadiad Spinning and Weaving Company, a joint-stock concern, had apparently commenced in April 1875, but owing to 'the disasters of the sea', there had been several delays. This may have referred to the shipping over of machinery from Manchester and Bolton: Hetherington and Co. from the former city provided the spinning machinery, whereas Hick, Hargreaves and Co. from the latter supplied the two boilers for the mill, low and high pressure (16 HP and 30 HP) respectively. The new factory premises were situated about a mile from the station, and its lofty two-storeyed buildings 'make a good show, and serve very plainly to indicate that a new industrial era has arrived for this old-fashioned populous district of Guzerat'.[92]

The *Times of India* correspondent, to whom we owe the only detailed accounts available of the inauguration of the Nadiad Mill, went on to narrate an interesting legend associated with the enterprise. At the time of its inauguration, there was apparently a popularly narrated story about a Government Director of the railways, Mr Juland Danvers, who, on his way back from Ahmedabad, glimpsed the mill buildings dimly through a thicket of trees. Having just seen several mosques and temples in Ahmedabad, he apparently asked his companion, a railway agent, whether this was another temple. The agent facetiously replied in the affirmative—this was a temple of industry.[93] Such pleasant legends aside, the correspondent speculated, there may have been more than a grain of truth in the assertion, for 'our Hindu friends keep up their observance of religious ceremonial even in these sceptical times, and their ancient *shasters* are equal to meeting the exigencies of this secular age of mechanical triumphs'.[94] He expounded on this theme at length: mantra*s* had apparently been read at the mill by 'priestly men who invoked the blessings of Indra and Vishnu on this new application of their power and ingenuity with which the gods have endowed the men of the West, and from which the East is now to derive abundant benefit'. Rounding off his heavily orientalist but nonetheless telling fable, the correspondent spoke of the scented water thrown on the engines by 'young Hindu girls' prior to the mill's inauguration, and of the fact that the engines bore names from the Ramayana.[95]

The opening of the mill, in other words, was a major public event in the life of Nadiad. The formal inauguration took place on 17 August 1876 at a large empty godown adjoining the mill and was attended by a large number of public and commercial dignitaries from Bombay and Gujarat alike. These included the up-and-coming industrialist N.N. Wadia, established leaders of industry like Varjivandas Madhavdas (who chaired the inauguration ceremony), Nanabhai B. Jeejeebhoy, and Ardesir Furdonji, and featured a letter from the Collector of Kheda, G.F. Sheppard, which was read out on the occasion. The Chairman, in his address to the gathering, went on to explain the reasons for floating the mill:

> In fixing upon Neriad [Nadiad] as a place for a cotton mill, the promoters of this undertaking had in view the supply of a great want of this

population. From the first they were impressed with the desirability of selecting for the sphere of their operations a locality, which while removed from Bombay—where many mills are crowded together—combined the advantages of a good local demand for the productions of their mill on the one hand, and a much closer proximity to the cotton fields, as well as cheaper labour, on the other. (*Hear, hear.*) Looking to the central position of Neriad in the district, and its vicinity to the Baroda Railway line, which is but a few yards distant from where we stand, we trust that in planting our concern here, we have consulted the best interests of the company. The metal road from Neriad to Dholka, now in course of construction under the superintendence of Mr Little, the Executive Engineer of this district, will, when completed, connect this town with the anciently renowned district of Bhal, and open a new route of commercial intercourse. The bulk of the district population being agricultural, their character, habits and wants point to this kind of industry as one that will meet with prompt support, and its productions a near and ready market, having regard to the consumption of manufactured goods in the district, and the requirements of hand loom weavers and calico printers scattered throughout its different towns. Influenced by these considerations, our company was started about the latter half of the year 1874, when similar concerns were projected by the capitalists of Bombay. The company was duly registered on the 24 October, after which the directors proceeded at once to business. Negotiations were opened with private parties to secure an eligible site for mill buildings. This, however, did not succeed, and we had to apply to Government for the purpose. This took some time, but I have much pleasure in stating that the company is indebted to the liberality of Government for this convenient plot of land. On obtaining possession of it we set about procuring the designs of our mill buildings.[96]

So modern industry had arrived in a 'traditional' location. The proximity of the BB and CI railway line, the 'metal road' to Dholka and Bhal, the presence of a large rural population as a local labour catchment, the demand for both cloth and yarn in the district—all these spelt out great prospects for commercial prosperity. The mill boom of the mid-1870s, as we can see from this account, was beginning to spread well beyond Bombay city, igniting industrial and 'improving' imaginations on a large scale.

These hopes, however, were to prove abortive, and the subsequent history of the mill would be one of distress and disappointment. Within two months of the inauguration of the mill, the annual general meeting of the Nadiad Company's shareholders revealed serious tensions in the management of the mill, though at this stage these were suitably coated over by effusive sentiments of optimism. The work of training up local labour did not go as smoothly as anticipated, and a large number of skilled workers from Bombay and Ahmedabad had apparently been engaged in several mill departments—presumably at higher wages than earlier projected. Financial difficulties seem to have proceeded apace, and there was apparently a lawsuit against the company, decided to its detriment. There is an Aesopian mention, in the *Times of India*'s account of the shareholders' meeting, of mill secretaries having 'volunteered' to defray outstanding costs and debts, 'out of regard for the interests of the company'.[97] A year later, in December 1877, the third annual general meeting of shareholders bore witness to the durability of these problems. An irate shareholder named Hurrilal complained of extravagant expenses incurred by the mill, and hinted at insolvency. It also appeared that the labour problems faced by the mill had not yet been fully overcome.[98]

A year later, in November 1878, the joint-stock company came to a sorry end. Famine in western and southern India, a general depression in trade, heavy interest payments on borrowed capital for mill building, high cotton prices, and low demand for yarn combined to put the enterprise in serious trouble. The expenditure on mill machinery and construction alone exceeded the total paid-up capital by over Rs 200,000. Another irate shareholder, a Bhaskar Manockjee, asked the meeting why the mill had been started in the first place when there was insufficient capital—thus underlining the risks involved in the speculative investments which had been instrumental in floating the mill in the first place.[99]

Such vagaries were not uncommon in the volatile climate of early mill construction: indeed, Bombay's mills witnessed several closures, lawsuits, and angry shareholders' meetings at the same time that the Nadiad Company wound down. The enormous costs sunk into the Nadiad enterprise, however, combined with its evident centrality to the local economy to produce a potentially explosive situation. The company was formally liquidated in early 1879, but this still left a large mill with close to 10,000 spindles standing, as the largest employer of labour in the district. Capital shortages notwithstanding, it was risky to let such a concern vanish. One of the Nadiad Company's richest creditors, a local capitalist named Manordas Harakchand, thus bought the property and started it up again within a few months.[100] So by the middle of 1879, an enterprise which had begun as a large, optimistic joint-stock concern had narrowed into an individually owned factory, with all the attendant transformations which this implied.

An industrial capitalist operating in such circumstances must have stood out in Nadiad, and people would have taken note of him as one of his kind. Towards the end of 1881, the mill worked 9,744 spindles and employed 357 workers.[101] Manordas Harakchand reigned supreme over the administration of the mill, making profits from its functioning and managing its day-to-day administration.[102] His position was made secure by the fact that he was the largest employer of labour in the district.

These situational advantages conferred considerable authority and prestige upon Manordas Harakchand, but, after the passage of the Factory Act in 1881, these also became a source of anxiety and vulnerability. The administrative structure that loomed over him was formidable. There was, first and foremost, the Collector and District Magistrate of Kheda, who also acted after the 1881 Act as ex-officio Factory Inspector. The tier above this was occupied by the Commissioner of the Northern Division of the Bombay Presidency, a role now played by G.F. Sheppard, whom we have encountered as a key mover in the initial establishment of the mill as a joint-stock concern. If a major dispute was to break out, the authorities in Bombay could also intervene in the affairs of the mill. Matters were not helped by the fact that, through the 1880s, the mill owner and the municipal authorities frequently clashed over the mill, which was located just outside the boundaries of the municipality, and which the Collector—initially J.H. Grant and subsequently A.H. Spry—wanted to place within these boundaries. They achieved this, and also imposed an octroi tax upon goods going into the mill.

The additional responsibility of factory inspection that devolved upon the Collector gave him, as it were, an additional stick to beat the mill owner with. When, in November 1883, James Jones was appointed Inspector of Factories for the entire Presidency (the first time the post of Factory Inspector was separated from all other administrative posts), Spry suggested to the Commissioner that jurisdiction over the Nadiad Mill stay in his hands since Jones, despite his expertise in the matter of machinery, had insufficient time to examine each mill in the Presidency. This, at any rate, seems to have been an intrusion that the mill owner managed to block through successive, furious petitions to the Governor of Bombay where he claimed that Spry had 'never dreamed of losing his authority over the mill', and that he had been persecuting the mill owner ever since he was appointed Collector.[103] The conflicts over factory inspection which now ensued were thus caught up, from the beginning, within a circuit of local administrative tussles, which Manordas Harakchand was clearly in the process of losing.

Conditions of danger and vulnerability inside the mill alerted authorities to the possibility of violations of law. Official investigations began at the end of 1881, when the District Magistrate, Grant, and the Boiler Inspector, Moylan, inspected the Nadiad Mill. The fencing of machinery, wrote Grant, was defective both in the engine rooms and in other spaces within the mill. The factory floors were greasy with oil, and consequently very slippery. 'I do not think I would be able to walk about it for two days in boots or shoes without a fall.'[104] The care with which such details were collected and reported is worth remarking. The beginning of a practice of investigation and knowledge production about working conditions, of course, dominates the history of factory inspection everywhere. But in Nadiad the intensity of the official gaze was greater. None of the accounts of factory conditions in Bombay city, in the reports of inspectors, had contained such wealth of detail.

This detail reproduced itself persistently in the history of inspections of the mill. Accidents of workers and the illegal employment of children were reported every few months in the early 1880s. Machinery and accidents, typically, were a major source of tension, as Grant watched Manordas Harakchand's practices of management like a hawk. In August 1882, he found the machinery seriously defective: the guards for the headgear of the mule frames were off at the time of inspection, even though the mills were at work. The engines of the pulleys in the blowing room were insufficiently fixed. There was also a wrangle between the state and the employer over the organization of space in the carding room. Grant observed that the spaces between machines in the carding room varied greatly and that some machines were less than 20 inches apart. A 'servant of the proprietor' apparently then informed Grant that 'it was contemplated to introduce six more machines into the room, and reduce the spaces to twelve inches between each'.[105] Grant forbade this.[106]

Accidents were also relatively easier to track down if an inspector had the will to do so. Grant visited the hospital at Nadiad and took a list of accidents at the mill from the Hospital Assistant. These were relatively 'minor' accidents—a pulley grazed a boy's scalp and drew some blood, a leather belt caused an abrasion to a man's right forearm, and another man's forearm was incised by machinery.[107] Grant noted a cover-up when it came to reporting accidents. 'A report was submitted stating that a boy was injured in a fight with another, while it is correctly said that he was hurt by machinery.'[108] In a more detailed report that Grant submitted to Sheppard a few days later, he added: 'Two accidents were informally reported, but one did not clearly state the nature of the accident. The dispensary books show *three* accidents treated during the quarter, but, as the third person injured would, no doubt, deny that he was injured by machinery, it would be useless to follow this up.'[109] Grant also noted that the proprietor's proclivities towards a liberal interpretation of the truth did not stop with accidents: the proprietor had, among his other crimes, concealed the fact that his mill employed children. This litany of legal violation was noted by the Bombay government and Moylan was dispatched from Bombay to inspect the mill. Clearly a defiant man, Manordas Harakchand responded with a sullen refusal to fund the journey, a gesture hardly likely to endear him to his government interlocutors.[110]

In July 1882, Meade-King inspected factories in Gujarat. In a brief account of his visits to the Government, he made his displeasure with Manordas Harakchand felt. The mill, he wrote, was in a deeply unsatisfactory condition, despite the fact that the Collector of Kheda 'has evidently done all in his power to persuade the occupier to comply' with the Act.[111] 'The inside walls of the mill were dirty and the reelers were working in miserable sheds with little light and less air: one of these sheds had no window.'[112] The consequences of this kind of violation were spelt out in language that was terse and sharp.

> The Proprietor, who was present at the time, was given to understand that if he did not immediately proceed to carry out certain instructions which we felt it our duty to give him, legal proceedings would be taken against him for offences against the Factory Act. Mr Grant will doubtless pay another visit to the mill shortly and prosecute the occupier if he

then finds that no attention had been paid to the caution which has been given to him.[113]

Most importantly, perhaps, Manordas Harakchand's day-to-day dealings with his workforce thrust him into a new, antagonistic relationship with state authority in the long shadow cast by the Factory Act. In August 1883, Manordas Harakchand seems to have had a serious dispute with the workers he employed, who walked out of the factory. He instantly replaced his experienced workers with raw and inexperienced substitutes, making up in wage economies for what he lost in skill. The absence of skill had other consequences, though; in August and September, the number of accidents began to pick up again.[114] Most of these were minor, involving injuries to a finger or hand, and none of them, so far as can be told, leading to amputation. The records of the accidents show, however, that the proprietor had begun to staff his workforce with labour that was younger and more vulnerable. Between October 1882 and June 1883, six accidents were recorded. Three of the victims were twenty years and above, one was sixteen, another fourteen, and one was ten. Between August and the end of September there were no fewer than ten accidents. Most of these involved injuries to hand or finger; one saw a man fall and hurt his head and right leg, and another saw a boy of ten fall down the stairs of the mill. The ages of the victims between August and September, a time when the mill dispute had already transformed the workforce, are significant. The oldest victim was seventeen, one boy was fourteen, six were thirteen, one was eleven, and one was ten years old.[115]

On 20 September, the Collector paid a surprise visit to the mill. This was one of the few genuinely effective attack tactics an Inspector could deploy if he suspected mischief from a mill owner. Often, surprise visits lost their bite because word got around and mill owners had their mills in order before the inspector arrived. This was not one of those occasions. Four children who were certified by the Kheda surgeon as underage were found working in the mill. Upon further investigation, it transpired that this was not all. The proprietor had apparently not reported the last three accidents that had occurred in the mill. In the statute books after the passage of the Factory Act, these were the two most serious transgressions of law a mill owner could commit. Two cases were laid before Kennedy, the Sub-Divisional Magistrate, and Sheth Manordas Harakchand was found guilty and sentenced to a fine (or two months' imprisonment in default of this) in both. For employing underage children, he was fined Rs 80, and for not reporting accidents Rs 90.[116] It is not difficult to imagine the force of public shame that must have accompanied this conviction for a man who was the only large employer in a small town and thereby ipso facto an extremely 'prominent citizen'.

The precise effect of this humiliation upon Manordas Harakchand is not verifiable, but an incident towards the end of 1883 offers some clues. In the report that he wrote on the Nadiad Mill for Sheppard, Spry pointed out that severe administrative problems were being caused by the fact that the District Magistrate no longer had any locus standi in the matter of factory regulation after James Jones' appointment as sole Inspector of Factories for the Presidency.[117] Would it not be more advisable to leave these powers in the hands of the District Magistrate, namely Spry himself, since Jones, despite his expertise in the matter of machinery, had insufficient time to examine each mill in the Presidency?

Three months after this report reached the Government, news seems to have got around to Sheth Manordas Harakchand that his old adversary was pleading for the authority to resume his powers of inspection over the Nadiad Mill. The mill owner immediately wrote an irate letter to the Governor of Bombay. The rage of this text indicates the intense local tensions which could erupt over the regulation of factories, and also the capacity, at moments like this, for the 'restrictions' upon capital enjoined by law, usually so dilatory, to become momentarily and powerfully real:

> That your Excellency's petitioner has heard from a flying report that the Collector at Kaira has not been satisfied with the trouble he had given your Excellency's petitioner, while he was Inspector of the mill; but wants to regain the authority and thus to harass further your Excellency's humble petitioner.[118]

At an unspecified point in the course of 1884, the Chief Inspector of Factories, Jones, paid yet another surprise visit to the Nadiad Mill and its unfortunate proprietor. In his report to Redgrave in 1887, he described an unusual sight—a group of small boys, squatting some distance outside the mill, came up to him as he approached it, and handed him a piece of paper. The boys claimed that they had been employed beyond the hours stipulated by law for months, and that they had not been allowed the legal time for meals. Further, they claimed that their employer, whom Jones described as a 'well known rich miser', had slashed their wages by half on various pretexts and still owed them the remainder.[119]

A prosecution duly followed and Jones met the children and their employer again in court. He called them as witnesses to prove his case, they took the stand, and, one after the other, retracted their former statements, swearing that their master was 'a kind and good man who always treated them with the greatest consideration'.[120] Jones was able to prove one case of overtime employment and managed to squeeze a substantial fine out of the employer for it, but in the fourteen other cases that he had lodged against him there was no possibility of managing a conviction.[121]

Two contrary dynamics in the life of factories clashed in this encounter. Jones' intervention marked the outer limits of the new field of possibilities that may have been sensed by some labourers. Indeed, in this case, children, apparently the most powerless section of the workforce, had in the figure of the Factory Inspector a court of appeal they had lacked earlier. At the same time, the lines of power inside the mill, especially in a district where there was no other large employer of labour, ran against the possibility of achieving a settlement satisfactory either to the inspector or the appellants. What the encounter *did* bear witness to, as a halfway house between the entitlements of workers and the continuing prerogatives of masters, was a situation where the labour practices of the latter could, unprecedentedly, be made visible and public, and become a source of continuing and unresolved tensions. This was an encounter that would have been inconceivable for all the parties concerned before the passage of the Factory Act, and this demonstrates that, in Nadiad at least, factory law was not a dead letter.

Clearly, the world of factory regulation in Nadiad could tie up with civic tussles in a manner that, for someone such as Sheth Manordas Harakchand, was strange, new, and threatening. His world was suddenly transformed, and state authority, from different angles, seemed to be closing in on him. People with no knowledge of or sympathy for his work could come and inspect its fruits and pass humiliating judgment on it. A world where he had previously run his business and conducted his relationship with 'his' workers without outside interference had suddenly been rearranged and populated with new forces, crowded with new sources of danger. Each of his practices, earlier taken for granted, suddenly had meaning and legal significance, suddenly occupied a new relationship to legally inscribed ideas of permissible and impermissible. Worst of all, the children he was accustomed to employing, on the harsh terms he set, could turn against him and find succour in the state. This could not have been an easy world to live in.

It is possible, then, to track the emergence of certain legible relationships between labour, capital, and state along the trajectory of factory legislation. These relationships, I hope to have shown, were not monologic in character. Neither did they point in a single direction, nor were they set in stone. The Factory Acts themselves are best conceived as setting a particular field of force in motion, one that generated different sets of possibilities at different conjunctures in the life of the law, conjunctures where state and capital clashed, negotiated, compromised, or cooperated over the question of the entitlements and needs of labourers.

Notes

1. S.D. Mehta, *The Cotton Mills of India* (Bombay: Textile Association, 1954), pp. 40–3.
2. S.M. Rutnagar, *Bombay Industries: The Cotton Mills: A Review of the Progress of the Textile Industry in Bombay from 1850 to 1926 and the Present Constitution, Management and Financial Position of Spinning and Weaving Factories* (Bombay: The Indian Textile Association Ltd, 1927), pp. 9–24.
3. Rutnagar, *Bombay Industries*, pp. 9–24.
4. Morris David Morris, *The Emergence of an Industrial Labour Force in India: A Study of the Bombay Cotton Mills, 1854–1947* (Berkeley: University of California Press, 1965), p. 65.
5. D.E. Wacha, *Shells from the Sands of Bombay: Being My Recollections and Reminiscences—1860–1875* (Bombay: The Commercial Press, 1920), pp. 50–1.
6. Preeti Chopra, 'The City and Its Fragments: Colonial Bombay, 1854–1918', unpublished PhD dissertation (University of California, Berkeley, 2003), pp. 278–95.
7. *Times of India*, 25 May 1880.
8. *Times of India*, 25 May 1880.
9. No. 686, General Department (GD) 1881, vol. 5, Government of Bombay (GoB), Maharashtra State Archives, Bombay (MSA); Chopra, 'The City and Its Fragments', p. 292; *Gazetteer of Bombay City and Island*, vol. 2 (Bombay, 1909), pp. 188–9.

10. Memorial to Town Council, 15 January 1881, GD, vol. 5, no. 686, GoB, MSA.

11. Report on the Sanitary Condition of Mills, Factories, and Workshops in the City of Bombay, 1884, V/26/670/86, OIOC.

12. Report on the Sanitary Condition of Mills, Factories, and Workshops in the City of Bombay, 1884, V/26/670/86, OIOC.

13. Report on the Sanitary Condition of Mills, Factories, and Workshops in the City of Bombay, 1884, V/26/670/86, OIOC.

14. Rajnarayan Chandavarkar, *The Origins of Industrial Capitalism in India: Business Strategies and the Working Classes in Bombay, 1900–1940* (Cambridge: Cambridge University Press, 1994), p. 279.

15. Proceedings of Special General Meeting of Bombay Millowners' Association, 5 January 1879, L/P&J/6/10, no. 475, OIOC.

16. *Report and Proceedings of the Commission Appointed to Consider the Functioning of Factories in the Bombay Presidency*, Bombay, 1885 (henceforth *FC* 1884–5), 2nd meeting, 23 August 1884, pp. 17–18.

17. From Inspector of Steam Boilers and Prime Movers, to Collector, Bombay, no. 33, 23 February 1880, L/P&J/6/18, no. 1035, OIOC.

18. Chandavarkar, *The Origins of Industrial Capitalism in India*.

19. No. 1344, Bombay Castle, 26 April 1881, in GD 1881, compilation no. 328, part I, vol. 3, GoB, MSA.

20. No. 1344, Bombay Castle, 26 April 1881, in GD 1881, compilation no. 328, part 1, vol. 3, GoB, MSA; no. 2709, Secretary from GD, GoB, to Secretary, Home Department, Government of India (GoI), 18 August 1881.

21. No. 1344, Bombay Castle, 26 April 1881, GD 1881, compilation no. 328, part I, vol. 1, GoB, MSA.

22. No. 638, Bombay Castle, 21 February 1882, GD 1882, compilation no. 328, vol. 1, GoB, MSA.

23. No. 3165, 16 August 1882, GD 1882, compilation no. 328, part III, vol. 3, GoB, MSA.

24. No. 2170, Abstracts of Proceedings, GD (Misc.), GoB P/2683, OIOC.

25. W.O. Meade-King to GoB, 24 June 1882, 'Report on the Working of the Indian Factories Act', Home (Judicial) A, nos 23–4, October 1882, NAI.

26. Chief Inspector of Factories and Workshops' Report, October 1886–87, *Parliamentary Papers* 1888 (C. 5328), p. 114.

27. *Legitimate* power, it must be noted: in practical terms, of course, the power of mill owners remained very much greater, and was to remain so.

28. John Gordon, Secretary, BMOA, to Secretary to Govt of Bombay, GD, 25 May 1881, MSA.

29. John Gordon, Secretary, BMOA, to Secretary to Govt of Bombay, GD, 25 May 1881, MSA.

30. From John Gordon, Secretary, BMOA, to Under Secretary of Govt, GD, Bombay, 18 June 1881, MSA.

31. From Secretary, BMOA, to Under Secretary of Govt, GD, Bombay, 18 June 1881, MSA.

32. Chandavarkar, *The Origins of Industrial Capitalism in India*, pp. 279–80.

33. Chandavarkar, *The Origins of Industrial Capitalism in India*, pp. 279–80.

34. The Indian Factories Act, 1881 (Act XV of 1881), Appendix II, in J.C. Kydd: *A History of Factory Legislation in India*, Calcutta 1920.

35. No. 2972, GD, Bombay Castle, 10 September 1881, MSA.

36. No. 2972, GD, Bombay Castle, 10 September 1881, MSA.

37. No. 2972, GD, Bombay Castle, 10 September 1881, MSA.

38. No. 431, Bombay, 4 October 1881, GD, 1881, no. 328, MSA.

39. Memorandum regarding the fencing of machinery, submitted by Mr Moylan, GD, Bombay, 4 October 1881, MSA.

40. No. 4, 10 January 1882, Bombay, GD 1882, vol. 1, MSA.

41. No. 1492, 29 April 1882, Thana, GD 1882, vol. 2, MSA.

42. Letter from Manager, New Dharamsi and Punjabhai Spinning and Weaving Mills, 16 May 1882, GD 1882, vol. 2, MSA.

43. From W.O. Meade-King, no. 13, Bombay, 22 May 1882, GD 1882, vol. 3, MSA [emphasis in original].

44. From W.O. Meade-King, no. 13, Bombay, 22 May 1882, GD 1882, vol. 3, MSA.

45. Memorandum no. 2104 from Commissioner, Northern Division, 14 June 1882, MSA.

46. No. 2705, from J. Nugent, Esquire, C.S., Acting Secretary to GoB, to the Secretary to GoI, Home Dept., Bombay Castle, GD, 19 July 1882, MSA.

47. From W.O. Meade-King to Secretary to Govt., no. 21, Bombay, 14 August 1882, GD 1882, MSA.

48. From W.O. Meade-King to Secretary. to Govt., no. 21, Bombay, 14 August 1882, GD 1882, MSA.

49. From W.O. Meade-King to Secretary to Govt., no. 21, Bombay, 14 August 1882, GD 1882, MSA.

50. Report of Mr W.O. Meade-King on the Working of the Indian Factories Act, Poona, 24 June 1882, in GD 1882, vol. 3, no. 328, MSA.

51. From W.O. Meade-King to the Secretary to Government, GD, Poona, 24 June 1882, GD 1882, vol. 3, no. 328, MSA.

52. From W.O. Meade-King to the Secretary to Government, GD, Poona, 24 June 1882, GD 1882, vol. 3, no. 328, MSA.

53. From W.O. Meade-King to the Secretary to Government, GD, Poona, 24 June 1882, GD 1882, vol. 3, no. 328, MSA.

54. From W.O. Meade-King to the Secretary to Government, GD, Poona, 24 June 1882, GD 1882, vol. 3, no. 328, MSA.

55. See Maxine Berg, *The Age of Manufactures, 1700–1820: Industry, Innovation and Work* (London, 1994), pp. 48–65.

56. Prabhu P. Mohapatra, 'Regulating Informality: Legal Constructions of Labour Relations in Colonial India and the Caribbean' in 'Labour in the Public Arena: Representation and Marginality: An Anthology of Essays', presented in the 3rd International Conference of the Association of Indian Labour Historians, Noida, 2002, unpublished.

57. The Indian Factories Act (Act XV of 1881), in Kydd, *A History of Factory Legislation in India*.

58. From W.O. Meade-King to the Secretary to Government, GD, Poona, 24 June 1882, vol. 3, no. 328, MSA.

59. *Times of India*, 27 February 1882.

60. From the Coroner of Bombay to Secy of Govt., Judicial Dept, Bombay, 13 March 1882, MSA.

61. Memorandum from Collector to General Dept., no. 44, 24 March 1882, MSA.

62. Memorandum from Collector to General Dept., no. 44, 24 March 1882, MSA.

63. Resolution no. 1309, GD, Bombay Castle, 11 April 1882, MSA.

64. Resolution no. 1309, GD, Bombay Castle, 11 April 1882, MSA.

65. Resolution no. 1309, GD, Bombay Castle, 11 April 1882, MSA.

66. Meade-King to Secretary to Government, GD, Poona, 7 July 1882, Home (Judicial), October 1882, nos 23–4, NAI.

67. Meade-King to Secretary to Government, GD, Poona, 7 July 1882, Home (Judicial), October 1882, nos 23–4, NAI.

68. *Bombay Samachar*, 3 January 1882, *RNNP Bom*.

69. *Yajdan Parast*, 9 April 1882, *RNNP Bom*.

70. Memo, GD, 14 March 1884, GD 1884, vol. 2, no. 328, part 3, MSA.

71. No. 135, Secretariat, Bombay, 7 March 1884, GD 1884, vol. 2, no. 328, part 3, MSA.

72. No. 135, Secretariat, Bombay, 7 March 1884, GD 1884, vol. 2, no. 328, part 3, MSA.

73. No. 375, GD, Bombay Castle, 4 February 1885, in GD 1886, vol. 38, no. 592, MSA.

74. No. 765, Simla, Home (Judicial), 3 June 1885, NAI.

75. J.M. Maclean, *A Guide to Bombay* (Bombay, 1880), pp. 123–5; R.S. Rungta, *Business Corporations in India 1851–1900*, (Cambridge: Cambridge University Press, 1970), p. 153.

76. S.D. Mehta, *The Cotton Mills of India*, pp. 28–33.

77. Maclean, *A Guide to Bombay*, p. 123.

78. Maclean, *A Guide to Bombay*, p. 123.

79. W.O. Meade-King to GoB, 24 June 1882, 'Report on the Working of the Indian Factories Act', Home (Judicial) A, nos 23–4, October 1882, NAI.

80. *Annual Report of Bombay Millowners' Association*, 1895.

81. Home (Judicial) A, January 1880, nos 9–94 and K.W., NAI. At the time, it must be remembered, Ahmedabad was still a small industrial centre—its emergence as one of the biggest industrial cities in the country lay some considerable distance in the future.

82. Factory Act 1881, in Kydd, *A History of Factory Legislation*.

83. Reports on inspections of factories in Bombay Presidency, Abstracts of Proceedings of the Government of Bombay, GD (Misc.), IOR/P/2637, 1885; IOR/P/2683, 1886; IOR/P/3100, 1887, OIOC.

84. Reports on inspections of factories in Bombay Presidency, Abstracts of Proceedings of the Government of Bombay, GD (Misc.), IOR/P/2637, 1885; IOR/P/2683, 1886; IOR/P/3100, 1887, OIOC.

85. Reports on inspections of factories in Bombay Presidency, Abstracts of Proceedings of the Government of Bombay, GD (Misc.), IOR/P/2637, 1885; IOR/P/2683, 1886; IOR/P/3100, 1887, OIOC.

86. Reports on inspections of factories in Bombay Presidency, Abstracts of Proceedings of the Government of Bombay, GD (Misc.), IOR/P/2637, 1885; IOR/P/2683, 1886; IOR/P/3100, 1887, OIOC.

87. David Hardiman, *Peasant Nationalists of Gujarat: Kheda District 1917–1934* (Delhi: Methuen, 1981), pp. 70–9.

88. *Gazetteer of the Bombay Presidency*, vol. 3, no. 1673: *Kaira and Panch Mahals* (Bombay, 1879), pp. 175–7.

89. Hardiman, *Peasant Nationalists*, pp. 70–9.

90. *Gazetteer of Bombay Presidency*, vol. 3, p. 177.

91. *Gazetteer of Bombay Presidency*, vol. 3, p. 177.

92. *The Times of India*, 19 August 1876.

93. *Times of India*, 19 August 1876.

94. *Times of India*, 19 August 1876.

95. *Times of India*, 19 August 1876.

96. *Times of India*, 19 August 1876.

97. *Times of India*, 24 October 1876.

98. *Times of India*, 21 December 1877.

99. *Times of India*, 15 November 1878.

100. *Times of India*, 21 January 1879.

101. Quarterly Reports on the Working of the Indian Factories Act, no. 4, GD, Bombay, 10 January 1882, MSA.

102. Quarterly Reports on the Working of the Indian Factories Act, no. 4, GD, Bombay, 10 January 1882, MSA.

103. Petition from Sheth Manordas Harakchand to GoB, GD, 5 March 1884, MSA.

104. No. 4691, GD, Bombay, 12 December 1881, MSA.

105. No. 367, GD, Bombay, 14 August 1882, MSA.

106. No. 367, GD, Bombay, 14 August 1882, MSA.

107. No. 367, GD, Bombay, 14 August 1882, MSA, appended list of accidents at Nadiad Mill, 11 December 1881.

108. No. 367, GD, Bombay, 14 August 1882, MSA, appended list of accidents at Nadiad Mill, 11 December 1881.

109. No. 4, GD, Bombay, 10 January 1882, MSA [emphasis in original].

110. No. 58, GD, Bombay, 1882, MSA.

111. No. 21, GD, Bombay, 14 August 1882, MSA.

112. No. 21, GD, Bombay, 14 August 1882, MSA.

113. Meade-King to Secretary to Govt., GD, Bombay, 11 August 1882, MSA.

114. No. 4170, GD, Bombay, 6 December 1883, MSA.

115. No. 4170, GD, Bombay, 6 December 1883, MSA.

116. No. 4706, GD, Bombay Castle, 21 December 1883, MSA.

117. No. 4170, GD, Bombay Castle, 6 December 1883, MSA.

118. Petition from Sheth Manordas Harakchand to GoB, GD, 5 March 1884, MSA.

119. Report of James Jones, Appendix to Home (Judicial) A, April 1889, Progs. 223–78, NAI.

120. Report of James Jones, Appendix to Home (Judicial) A, April 1889, Progs. 223–78, NAI.

121. Report of James Jones, Appendix to Home (Judicial) A, April 1889, Progs. 223–78, NAI.

4

Law, Age, and the Factory Child

The preceding chapter ended with the strange tale of children petitioning a factory inspector against their employer. Child labour was, of course, the province most emphatically designated for the work of factory law. It is appropriate at this stage to thematize the entanglement of state, capitalists, and working-class interests over questions of child labour in the 1880s. To supply an adequate context to this, however, it is necessary to first briefly consider the social relations in which mill children were entangled.

Capitalists in Bombay drew principally upon pools of migrant male labour.[1] Children were and remained a minority of the mill workforces in India, in sharp contrast to their initial absorption into the industrial labour market in metropolitan Britain. There was always, however, a substantial number of cases where the male migrant either drew upon his own village connections, or upon the marriages and family networks he contracted within the city. Often, all that could be said with any certainty about the children investigated by outsiders to the mill (factory inspectors, doctors, journalists in the early twentieth century) is that they formed part of a family strategy, though it was hard to say whose. As the Chief Inspector of Factories in Bombay in 1908, P.B. Haigh, put it, 'If the child had no parents, he would have some other relation, for they all worked in families.'[2]

The subsumption of childhood into the logic of the mill not infrequently began with childbirth. As one of the witnesses before the 1875 Factory Commission testified, pregnant women were often 'confined to the mill' until the last months of their pregnancy.[3] In the absence of any regularized systems of childcare, infants frequently accompanied their mothers to work. In 1908, a former Factory Inspector told the Factory Commission that it was not uncommon for mills to allow mothers to 'sling the babies under the reeling machines'.[4] In other mills, very young children were apparently not allowed within the workrooms but allowed outside in the compound.[5]

When the children slung under mill machinery as infants grew a little older, but not old enough for work, they were still embedded within the life of the mill in a number of ways. On some occasions, they were found at school, in makeshift buildings erected by mill owners on the mill premises. On other occasions, they could be found within the mill itself, and the observer who chanced upon them, usually a Factory Inspector, could never quite decide whether they were there because there was nowhere else to keep them, or because they were a disavowed part of the workforce itself. Haigh elaborated this before the 1908 Factory Commission:

> At present large numbers of non-working children are to be found in every mill. This is most undesirable. The children themselves run considerable risk; and the work of the factory inspector is greatly hampered, as whenever a small child under nine years of age is found, apparently working, the manager or jobber at once says that the child had merely accompanied its mother.

He admitted, however, that it was 'most difficult to suggest any means of enforcing this prohibition without causing hardship to the children's parents employed in the mill'.[6]

Imperceptible to the official observer, almost like a law of nature, this state of matters passed over into one where the child emerged as a millhand. J. Gibbs, in a debate in the Legislative Council shortly before the passage of the Act of 1881, succinctly stated the problem:

> Little children … [were] carried with their parents to the mill. It was impossible for the people … to leave their little children at home; necessity made the women, if not the men, take their whole families with them, and the result of the children being taken to the mill involved their getting put to some light work which they would not otherwise have been put to.[7]

Kennedy, another member of the Council, referred to the 'natural imitative instinct' of children, and their 'restlessness', which made it difficult to prevent them, if permitted inside the mill, 'from doing something that might be called work'.[8] In gradual stages, then, the mill child made the successive transitions between infancy, childhood's 'idle' years, nominal work, unregistered and concealed work, and full-fledged adult wage-labour.

For a not negligible number of children, then, the line dividing work and life was blurred at the very inception of both—the mill was not merely a place of work, but something like a life-world. The implications of this were sensitively articulated in Janet Kelman's account of women in factory work, based on an investigation of mill labour in the 1920s, principally in Bombay and Calcutta. A passage from her book is worth quoting at length:

> One manager had the habit of giving each baby a small coin. In watching the reception it got, it was noticeable how soon the sense of the desirability of money was roused in the children. The gift seemed to be only for those who were still closely dependent upon their mothers, and who, if they could walk at all, had only just reached that stage of development. ... A tiny girl began to stretch out her hand, then, realizing that it was already full of fragments of sugar cane, and that somehow things would not work that way, spread the fingers wide, scattering the fibres on all sides, and grasped the coin. She had already showed a very clear perception of how to attain a desired end. When the manager, who had lifted her on his arm, tried to set her back on the iron ledge on which she had been sitting, her little body stiffened herself straight, in graphic protest, and it was only when her attention was distracted by the coin that she consented to be set down again. With all the kindliness, it is rather sad to think of the creation of so early a knowledge of the possibilities of money and, from another point of view, still more tragic to think that so small a sum should create the evident eagerness on the part of the mothers that their children should not be overlooked.[9]

Kelman's description alerts us to the quotidian gestures in the interior spaces of the mill that made up the lived experience of industrial childhood. At the most immediate level, it is important to acknowledge that the meanings of mill work for children were produced by practices that are mostly impossible to recover and tabulate. The passage, however, also points us towards lived experiences that can be understood more systematically. In particular, it tells us of the complicated circuits that connected the presence of children in the mill with the supervening structures of both family and wage-labour, structures that endowed vulnerabilities, capacities, responsibilities, and desires in equal measure. In a state of infant, pre-reflective being, the children in Kelman's account have their future laid out for them, as they are educated in a specific art of desire—the desire for a wage. They grab the coins as the manager and mother look on. This image serves as a metonym of a very specific circuit of authority, dependency, and subjecthood, producing at its conclusion the infant's nomination as future wage-labourer.

This field of experience, grinding and exploitative in its totality, was traversed by a series of ambiguous personal and institutional relationships. Contemporary accounts tell us that children in their early years were often habituated to the factory as a space of play as much as of work. The transfer of children's energies from one to the other could take various forms. Reports of children being 'detained' at work for an hour or two, as they brought food to their parents, jostle alongside reports of children playing with machinery in their free time, walking out regularly to smoke (as they often did from a very early age), and playing with each other in the factory yard.[10]

The diverse paths that led children into mill work were characterized by varying admixtures of coercion and consent. The testimonies of children before the 1890 Factory Commission are a good indication of this. Dhakia, a fourteen-year–old boy from Igatpura, the third of four brothers, was employed by the Bombay Cotton Mills at the time of his testimony before the 1890 Commission. He was described by his interlocutors as a 'dull, unhealthy, careworn lad, physically unfit to do more than half a day's labour'. Nevertheless, he had been working for six years at four mills in the city, supporting his mother, who 'lives in the house without work' (his father was dead). He left home for work at 4 in the morning and the mill stopped at a quarter to seven. Together, the four brothers brought home Rs 37 a month, contributed towards the sustenance of themselves and, in the case of two brothers, their wives. The two women, contributing Rs 6 each, brought the total monthly earnings of the family up to Rs 49 for seven people.[11] The two unmarried brothers were, at the time of the Commission's enquiries, both saving up for their own marriages, which would have represented a considerable investment for a family in these circumstances. Their family home in Igatpura had been sold when they were young, and they had been in debt till recently.[12] In the light of this testimony, Dhakia's final avowal that he 'goes of his own accord to work, and there is no pressure brought on him to work by his friends' simultaneously reveals and dissimulates the real relationship between choice and compulsion within labouring worlds.

Babaji Mahadoo, who followed Dhakia into the Council Room of the Bombay Secretariat, where the Commissioners interviewed him, seems to have come from less straitened circumstances. As a fifteen-year-old, and, therefore, technically outside the ambit of factory legislation, he was described by the Commissioners as 'rather overdressed for a boy in his class of life. Mr. Bengallee remarked "quite a masher". Has silver ornaments about him'.[13] His family apparently retained their own land in Ratnagiri, and Babaji had married earlier in the year. Apparently, his mother had given up work upon his marriage, and since then he had been 'maintaining her and his wife'. The wife, at seven, still living at home, was presumably also marked out for the mills, but the mother's premature retirement indicates that there may have been some money put by. Babaji had also attended school before joining the mill three years ago. Wages, in this case, seem to have been experienced more openly as emancipation of a kind, than in the testimonies of many workers his age: 'Looking back on his life', he observed, perhaps a touch wistfully, that he 'would have liked to have worked half day and had half day at school when he was under 12', and thus to have entered the wage-earning life earlier.[14]

Bhimi Luckha, a girl of ten or eleven, was at work at the Maneckji Petit Mill, one of the largest employers in the city with over 3,500 workers, when the Commission visited and interviewed her. She had been working there six months, and had apparently been compelled to come to work against her will (the notes of the Commission observe: 'this she says smiling'). She told the Commissioners that she was willing to work half the day for fewer wages, but that her overseer would beat her if she took time off, and her mother would beat her if she brought home reduced wages. The mill worked thirteen hours, and she worked the whole time, with half an hour off. She ate the meal she brought with her before starting work, so she went eleven hours without food daily.[15]

When Mary Carpenter and her associates campaigned for factory legislation in the 1870s, they discursively invested the factory with the responsibility of 'civilizing' children through education. This, they hoped, would replicate the metropolitan experience, where, over the course of half a century, factory legislation had come to be strictly wedded to education in the industrial districts. In Bombay, and in India at large, there were faded variants of this, mainly in the form of private initiatives, widely differing in scope and ambition, and of negligible effect in a context where state-supported education was largely absent. Narayan Meghaji Lokhande, whom we shall encounter in the next chapter as the spearhead of the first campaign that tried to articulate workers' demands in an organized manner, chaired a Night Schools Association in the late 1880s. He also told the Factory Commission in 1890 that there were several private night schools that had been opened by millhands and seven independently established night schools in Bombay.[16] At least one of the children interviewed by the Commission was at the time being educated in the night school set up by the Theistic Association.[17]

The early debates around factory legislation attest the survival of a discourse of enlightenment through factory education. The report of the Factory Commission of 1884–5 suggested that the minimum age of employment on restricted time be raised from seven to nine. It made a supplementary qualification, however, to the effect that children of eight who had 'passed a suitable and easy educational standard or put in a certain number of attendances at school' might be allowed to work. Correspondingly, it also suggested that while the legal age for adult work should be raised from twelve to fourteen, an exception could be made for children of thirteen who had 'satisfied a certain educational test'.[18]

James Fergusson, on the point of completing his tenure as Governor of Bombay, objected strongly to the first proviso, pointing out that schooling 'may educate the mind but it does not necessarily educate the body', and that since physical and intellectual development had no necessary connection, 'what is bad from a physical point of view for the uneducated must be equally bad for the comparatively educated child'.[19] Interestingly, though, Fergusson had no trouble endorsing the second of the Commission's recommendations—that the line separating childhood and formal adulthood for the purposes of mill work could partially be based on education. The implicit teleology of this is clear: at the initial stages of what was considered 'childhood', education, and the consequent enlargement of the child's capacities, could make no difference to the time she should be allowed to work, but the approach of adulthood could, within limits, be accelerated by the acquisition of education. Work here is implicitly constructed as an adult 'right', based on capacity and responsibility. Education endows such capacity and responsibility, and, thus, the uneducated child of fourteen and the educated child of thirteen are rendered equivalent.

Mill owners, by and large, disavowed pedagogic activity and responsibility. The District Deputy Collector of Surat, in 1875, had this to say:

> As for education, it would be a strange anomaly to insist upon it at the expense of the proprietors of the factories. ... These children would have been brought up in an equally, if not more, ignorant condition, if the factories had not existed; and certainly in much more indolent habits. People far above them in social position have yet to learn the benefits of education.[20]

So, besides the position—frequently reiterated—that mills were a sort of salvation for children, there was also a clear statement of the limits imposed upon the possible social needs of children because of the existing social order. Children of a certain class, in other words, did not need to be educated.

Some mill owners, however, *did* set up schools for children working for them, thus establishing pedagogic discipline as a supplement to industrial discipline. In 1907, before the Textile Factories Commission, Sir Sassoon David suggested that it would be best for half-timers (children between nine and fourteen, working restricted hours) to work only in one mill, where they 'work half in the morning and half in the afternoon. They must be kept in the Mill and either go to school or have recreation'. D.P. Sethna, agent of the Maneckji Petit Mills, present at the same meeting, offered as a possible model the school built in the compound of his mill, where children were taught between shifts.[21] In 1875, two mill owners told the Factory Commission that they had set up 'gratuitous schooling' for children in their mills.[22]

The first Indian inspector of factories, Kharsedji Servai, lauded the New Prince of Wales Mill, in 1882, for having started a school where children 'of the very poorest and low caste children are by this means taught to read and write and cast accounts'. The 'most advanced children', he wrote, were able to read Marathi satisfactorily and work simple sums. He wrote with particular approval of the role of the mill school in 'broadening the minds' of young girls, equipping them for a life outside traditional confines.[23]

Another possibility, however, is more voluminously represented in the available evidence. It is represented, for instance, in the testimony of L.W. Hartley, former Presidency Inspector of Factories, before the Commission of 1908. Schools, he argued, should not be built within the main walls of a mill building, 'as they are so very frequently used to cloak contraventions of the Act'.[24] Long experience as factory inspector had taught Hartley that 'a school in a mill was usually abused'. In other words, mill owners would use a school to tie child workers to the mill. In several cases the school was a convenient fiction, and the material structure that actually passed for a school was more a detention centre for young surplus labour. Education provided at the mill owners' expense could easily become a profit-maximizing tactic.

Meade-King, in the course of his investigations in 1882, also provided evidence of this. On one of his inspectorial visits, he took twelve children out of a mill at the close of a working day and questioned them separately about their periods of employment, finding, perhaps unsurprisingly, that their actual hours of work clashed violently with those formally prescribed by the mill authorities. The children in this mill apparently had to attend school for three hours in the day, but his respondents all said that they had been at work since 5.30 in the morning and had not attended school. 'I saw two children sitting on a form in the lodge, and was told that was the school,' wrote Meade-King, sardonically. 'It is needless to add that the school-master was abroad on that occasion.'[25]

Mill Children and Factory Legislation

Powerful rhetorical claims that factory legislation interfered with the freedom of the adult male worker structured debates around British factory legislation till the end of the nineteenth century. The distinction between 'free agents', who could negotiate their own interests, and categories of the vulnerable, deserving, and needy of legislative protection marked the very beginning of serious debates around factory law in the second decade of the nineteenth century.[26] The protection of children was posited as a permanent goal of factory inspection, and the 'freedom' of adult workers—to be used as their masters chose—was the other side of this. This dogma was amplified in the legislative debates that produced the Factory Act of 1881. The work of factory law was defined at the outset as the identification of vulnerability of 'children and young persons who had not attained to an age at which they would be considered free agents'.[27] The free agent, in the reasoning that grounded early factory law in India and Britain alike, was capable and responsible enough to shoulder the burdens of mill work without 'artificial' legal crutches.

The 1878 Factory Bill had set the minimum age of factory employment at eight, and the age of full-time, 'adult' employment at fourteen—the upper limit being identical to English law and, therefore, fairly predictably evoking a storm of protests mobilizing arguments about 'Indian difference'.[28] In deference to this, the Legislative Council unanimously agreed to reduce the minimum age of employment to seven and cut the legal definition of childhood off at twelve.[29] The Viceroy, Lord Ripon, later expressed his unhappiness at this change, which he attributed to massive pressures from the mill owners' lobby—a view echoed by Fergusson, the Governor of Bombay.[30]

The other major change—instituted by the Select Committee that mediated the Bill's passage into the Legislative Council—was the excision of the category of 'young persons' from law's ambit.[31] A radically simplified definition of childhood and vulnerability was thus authorized, apparently to bring it in line with Indian social realities. The stakes here were actually much higher than they were in the case of the definition of childhood proper: as Shashi Upadhyay has pointed out, the number of workers who fell into a grey zone between childhood and adulthood but were legally designated 'adult' workers was almost certainly a significant proportion of the workforce.[32] The question, however, haunted the subsequent history of factory legislation: as late as 1908, we find mill owners reacting with understandable horror when queried about their views on a possible, legally defined 'young persons' category.[33]

What happened when children working in mills made the passage to being subjects of factory law? In the first place, a large number of them lost their jobs. In the very first report on factory inspections in the Bombay Presidency, in October 1881, H.E. Jacomb, Collector of Bombay, wrote that over 600 children had been dismissed either in anticipation of or immediately following the passage of the Act.[34]

A year later, Servai reported that of the thirty-three mills in the city, seventeen had discharged their child employees.[35] A year later, 556 more children were dismissed.[36] Children were the most easily expendable section of the workforce, subject to dismissal whenever the immediate prospects looked bleak for the textile industry. For instance, in early 1885, when a rise in raw material prices and a slump in demand generated a brief recession and the first experiment by the Bombay Millowners' Association (BMOA) in short-time working, 124 children were excised from the mill lists in the course of three months.[37]

The proportion of children stabilized eventually with the steady and rapid mill expansion of the late 1880s. In 1891, 975 were recorded; this was around the time of the second Factory Act. After the passage of the Act, the number recorded jumped to around 3,000, in large part because the upper age limit for 'children' was raised from twelve to fourteen.[38] Indeed, till factory regulation tightened for both women and children in the 1920s and decisively recast the mill workforce as an overwhelmingly 'adult male' proletariat, the demographic balance of the mills remained remarkably stable. Through three Factory Acts and numerous reversals of economic fortunes, men constituted around three-fourths of the mill population, women consistently formed 20–25 per cent, and children, as legally defined, constituted a relatively negligible, if largely uncounted, proportion.

Nevertheless, as Emma Alexander suggests, the Factory Act was a major step in the ideation of the child as a being with a separate identity, independent of his or her imbrications in caste, community, and family ties.[39] The 'child' emerged as a being who could be defined and determined by law. At the same time, who exactly was a child? A system of certification, it was soon realized, needed to be devised to decide the age of children. This was operationally made difficult by the absence of birth certification and the difficulty of deducing the age of working children from physical appearance. The working child soon became the focus of investigation, as government departments and local administrations were asked to supply information about the children employed in enterprises.[40]

Putting this in practice, however, created paradoxes. Unsurprisingly, children grew up early: as contemporary observers noted, the factory child who was an object of tender legislative concern was also not infrequently a parent.[41] Kelman's description captures the strange grey zone inhabited by many children in the mills, where their empirically observable (if not always verifiable) childhood, and so often their sheer *littleness*, rubbed up against their incipient status as 'responsible' wage-earners. Another more precise way of putting it would be to say that mill children found themselves caught between two simultaneous but contradictory identifications—that of dependents within the family and that of breadwinners.

This tension runs through official considerations of children's wages. Consider the amendment to the Factory Bill of 1878 that was offered by J. Pitt Kennedy, member of the Imperial Legislative Council, during the debates of 1881. Kennedy proposed that 'no child, one or both of whose parents is or are employed in the factory, shall be deemed to be employed unless wages are paid for the work which he performs'.[42] This signals a persistent anxiety about the demarcation of childhood 'proper' from wage-labouring childhood. The Lieutenant-Governor of Bengal, supporting Kennedy's amendment, observed the persistence within mills of children 'too young to labour for wages and too young also to be left at home … undoubtedly employed in some slight and unimportant work in the factory,—helping their parents, holding baskets, and doing work as an amusement rather than as labour'.[43]

Colvin, who had proposed the Bill in the Legislative Council, countered this observation with one of his own: it was quite possible, he argued, for 'two or three rupees to be added to the wages of the mother or father on account of work done by a child'.[44] Lieutenant-General Donald Stewart, backing Colvin, related an anecdote: while inspecting a harness-factory, he had come across a father accompanied by children between six and twelve, all working by the piece. A consolidated wage was paid to the father, and 'the children got no wages at all'.[45] This was by no means an uncommon practice: the wages of children were frequently included within those of their parents, and these children were consequently not recorded as workers. These conceptual dichotomies could also characterize the work of children who were much less problematically 'wage-labourers'. The wages of children who *were* on mill payrolls were often pegged at levels not far below those of adult women, though both were paid far less than the adult male worker. Often, though, wages could be placed in a collective family fund. Sheoram Mahadoo, an eleven-year-old in 1890, said that he spent Re 1 on himself 'for sweetmeats' and gave the remaining five rupees to his parents.[46]

Two figures of the child were thus amplified in early legislative debates. In the first case, the child performs actions that may technically be described as 'work', without, however, 'really' working. In the second case, the child *is* really performing 'labour', participating in the economic rhythms of the mill and contributing tangibly to its output, but *technically* is not working, for she receives no wages. Now both these, quite undoubtedly, described real lived experiences within the life of the mill; further, these experiences were probably quite unexceptionable in the era prior to factory legislation. Legal debate, however, rendered them problematic by transmuting them, quite without intent, into figures of identification—'child inside the mill', 'working child', 'child wage-labourer'—that were often empirically undecidable and indistinguishable from one another.

Certification and Its Vicissitudes

The *Hindi Punch* carried, on 24 January 1892, a hilarious fable about the practice of factory law that is worth reproducing in its entirety.

> I am a poor boy earning my bare pittance in 'Girnipur'.[47] The *Mabap* Sarkar has recently passed a law to the effect that our tender constitution shall not be shattered by working in mills before a certain age. This is very kind of Government, but it sometimes involves a hardship. The doctor has to determine our ages—a somewhat difficult task. He first took to examining our teeth as they do those of a horse. He found it an unsavoury process, and grumbled that we exhaled foul breath and that there was an unpleasant odour about us. Some of us, I believe, tried to conciliate him by chewing highly spiced 'pan supari'. This must have annoyed him more, for, it is said, Englishmen regard such persons as 'walking red-ink bottles'. Others tried to propitiate him by rubbing a little 'ootna' or some scented oil over the body. These simple oriental scents often prove too strong for the olfactory senses of the occidentals, and the *Saheb* was probably stunned and would have no more of this, and changed the standard of the test from the teeth to the stature of the candidate for employment. We are now required to pass erect under a fixed horizontal bar, and those that strike their heads against the rod are selected, whilst those who, despite all attempts at elongating their bodies, pass free and unhurt, are rejected. Without

> the slightest effort to stretch myself upwards I hit my nose against the bar and triumphed. My mother followed me, but glided easily under the bar and was rejected as being under the legal age! We reasoned in vain against the decision; but there was the standard set up: it could not possibly err! Now, dear *Mr. Punch*, though the fair sex in the far West delight in understating their age and thus depreciating the value of census returns in that respect, an Indian mother will always feel indignant at being called younger than her own son! Cannot the new Factory Act be amended? What do you advise my poor mother to do? She does not only feel bitterly the sting of being thought younger than her boy, but is unable to earn her livelihood![48]

It is a fable that functions at several levels. In the first place, it satirizes the social and cultural distances that factory law, through the practices of inspection and medical scrutiny, had to traverse. The olfactory comedy attests this, as does the satire about the cultural differences between Indian and Western mothers. There are, quite clearly, proto-nationalist accents involved here, for instance, in the evocation of the '*Mabap* Sarkar', whose intentions, however kind, cannot but produce this sort of contemptible farce, fit to be mocked by its subjects. There is also a witty and subtle critique of 'standards' of 'objective' measurement that seek to subjugate experiences and selves that cannot be measured. The parable of the bar that is the 'standard' hitting the boy on the nose as it allows him his work and punishing the mother's evasion of the standard by excising her from factory work concretizes in a single image the dimensions of factory law stressed by its critics. The Factory Act, in this account, compares incommensurable human experiences and bludgeons them with a 'standard', producing palpably comic results.

There are also more precise polemical contexts to this fable. The amended Factory Act came into force at the beginning of January 1892—the same month in which the *Hindi Punch* entry was published. Besides raising the legal minimum age for employment to nine, the Act also limited the working hours of women to eleven, which upset the working routine of a number of factories. Particularly in Ahmedabad, several women working in mills, apprehensive that this would lead to expulsion (an apprehension that was often justified), sent a petition to the Government of India, pleading for exemption. This plea, which was eventually refused, flowed into the storm of ongoing debate about the need for and efficacy of factory legislation.[49] The entry in the *Hindi Punch* ends with the woman being denied work, and this has an added significance in the light of these ongoing debates.

Most importantly, though, the comedy of the piece is rooted directly in the frequent misrecognition of childhood that inspectorial scrutiny and medical examination involved. Such a dark comedy of misrecognition is one of the most important dimensions of the relationship between factory legislation and the children it 'protected'. Dilemmas surrounding the accurate identification of children rippled off in unexpected directions and raised wider questions about the texture of industrial relations addressed by the Act.

The Factory Act itself finally designated, as its principal legal subject, the child between seven and twelve who could be employed legitimately for nine hours in a working day. Following the passage of the Act in May 1881, the Government of Bombay instituted rules which filled out this broad regulation. 'Occupiers' of factories were compelled by these rules to keep registers of children certified to be of working age and show them to factory inspectors on demand. Certifying surgeons were appointed under the Act and given the work of granting certificates to children they examined.[50] The three Presidency Surgeons of Bombay, for the urban districts of Malabar Hill, Fort, and Byculla were to divide this work between them. In practice, since Byculla housed nearly all the mills, the third Presidency Surgeon, who covered that district, was saddled with most of the work.[51]

The work itself comprised, by the mid-1880s, three broad alternative routines, all performed in the certifying surgeon's office. The first was close to the situation that the *Hindi Punch* described. A group of children was sent with a foreman by the mill to the surgeon, who signed the register opposite their names after certifying them. In the second, individual children were accompanied by their relatives to the mill and given a certificate after their examination if found to be over twelve.[52] It appears that in many cases children below twelve evaded the injunction to procure medical authorization for mill work, 'as no one wants a certificate that he is between 7 and 12 or below 7'.[53] In such cases, they and their employers would have risked the possibility that they would be found of 'doubtful' age by the factory inspector and either prohibited from employment or sent up for certification. At regular intervals, then, inspectors randomly plucked out mill-children of dubious age and sent them to the certifying surgeon. This made up the third of the practices of certification.

As the *Hindi Punch* acknowledged in its mocking way, this was difficult work. Birth registration was only introduced in 1882, and the child yielded a very limited set of clues to the scrutiny of doctors. The formal identification of children as children was the biggest hurdle the Factory Act had to cross. The two classificatory separations that framed most of the content of the Act—the separation of childhood from adulthood, and of early from late childhood—were difficult to make. Precise distinctions were instituted by the Act, but medical knowledge had no corresponding precision to offer. The object of medical investigation was a childhood lived for the most part in abysmal housing conditions and vitiating conditions of industrial work, which depressed physical stature and strength to an egalitarian baseline of misery.

The rituals of certification produced an ontology of childhood that was self-contradictory, perplexing, and often evidently ludicrous. A report from 1887, when the procedures of examination were sufficiently fixed and stable, hesitates comically as it earnestly explores a range of physiological grounds for discrimination: the number of teeth in a child's mouth, the firmness of bone structure, height, weight, the shape of the chest, respiratory action, muscles, the rotundity of the body, mental intelligence, and genitals.[54] All these are considered at length, and new rules are prescribed for the test of teeth (the commonest test in contemporary medical practice)[55]: children with over twenty-eight teeth are to be classified as twelve and over, children with fewer than twenty-four teeth as below twelve, and developed anterior teeth indicate that the child is seven.[56] But while a desperate attempt at some kind of medico-analytic precision is made, each distinction seems to multiply the dilemmas. For a child with exactly twenty-four teeth, for instance, the doctor is invited to use his discretion to judge the probable age, presumably through a juxtaposition of the tests of teeth and general physique.[57]

The problem, as the Surgeon-General to the Bombay government (who composed the report in question) admitted, was that very little of this approached the objective 'standard', the measure of age that the law required (and the *Punch* parodied). Ultimately, despite some sketchy rule-of-thumb suggestions, the report circled round a grocery list of prescriptions and restated the premise of the whole problem as a solution: when judging a child's 'general configuration and appearance', the Surgeon-General wrote, 'no specific rules can be laid down and the facility of judging is a matter of experience and keenness of observation'.[58]

At this juncture, it might be fruitful to ask a parenthetical and apparently naive question: why age? Why was age, rather than some other measure of capacity, considered the optimal benchmark for factory work? Why was some other protocol of identification—general health, or strength, or weight—not considered a valid, 'objective' adjudicator of labouring capacity? Or, to put it differently, why did these variables need to be condensed into the ne plus ultra of *age* rather than furnishing independent justifications of children's work?

A full answer to this question would probably involve considerations of the emergence of 'objective' standards of measurement through the nineteenth century, the history of scientific procedures of identification. This would involve elaborating the ways in which ad hoc procedures of empirical investigation and judgment needed to be supplanted, or more precisely given shape, by universal designators of truth, fact, and value. Age, in an era of growing scientific expertise and codification, was one of the most important of such designators. It was, in theory at least, a measure of capacity that could be applied across barriers of space and culture. Its applications were always sought to be differentiated across such barriers, but such differentiations merely added the value of flexibility to that of 'objectivity'. Unlike health, it could be quantified; unlike strength, it could be measured.

These are speculations: what is incontrovertible, however, is that by the mid-Victorian era age *had* emerged as a putatively 'objective' measure that bathed other descriptive mechanisms with a new clarity. The very importance of age as a measure had certain significant intellectual/administrative implications that need to be registered.

To render this more precisely, it might help to dwell a little longer on the Surgeon-General's report in 1887, composed in the middle of a raging controversy over child certification that I shall consider at length in the last section of this chapter. The report speaks explicitly of the indeterminacy of age: diet and hygiene make children appear younger or older than they really are; children of the same age vary in height; average weight, likewise, is a matter of dispute; the shape of the chest is too general an indication to be of use; likewise respiration, genitals, pulse, and 'general configuration and appearance'.[59] The matter of real interest in this intervention is the *distribution* of different measuring standards and their mutual *articulation*. In an era that preceded effective techniques of birth registration, and in a context where it was freely admitted that age was concealed, dissimulated, and often not even known by its bearers, it was, nevertheless, implicitly assumed that the other 'standards' of judgment could be added up and juxtaposed, as contingent clues, to the overall 'truth' of age. Conversely, it was age that illuminated the other qualities and quantities enumerated by the Surgeon-General: height, weight, genital growth, teeth, and bone structure, for instance, acquired their own meaning only with reference to age as the ultimate arbiter. Age, as an 'objective' measure, in some sense, contextually rendered the other benchmarks in this case 'subjective', even if, in practical experience, the judgment of age (the Surgeon-General admitted this) was itself equally subjective.

The uncertainty at the heart of age certification was lucidly summed up by W. Doderet, who became Factory Inspector for Bombay in January 1888. Writing of an experience at a mill where he had identified children of doubtful age, only to find them certified as over twelve, he expressed 'considerable doubts' about the method of ascertaining age by the number of teeth. This was a common worry: Doderet went further, however, in asserting that 'it is a mistake to regulate the test of a child's capacity to work in these mills by age'. He plumped for weight as an adequate substitute: he argued that it could not only be measured more accurately, but it also provided a better index of physical capacity. This remarkable assertiveness seems to have stemmed from Doderet's inspection, where several of the boys—all certified 'adults'—weighed only 37 lbs.[60]

The government's response, however, was curt: even if the impossibility of deducing age from the number of teeth were granted, ran the relevant Resolution, weight offered no reliable index of physical capacity either. Since age had been made the criterion by law, there were no grounds for replacing it by weight.[61] The vehemence of the response is interesting, as is its 'law is law' argument: after all, the Government of Bombay could legitimately have appended a weight test, and the question of age-certification had by this time come to vex it sorely. If, despite these fairly compelling reasons, the government chose not to even consider Doderet's arguments seriously, this indicates a generalized commitment to the principle of age-certification that goes well beyond the bounds of rational expediency.

This accent upon age as the sole criterion of capacity was not limited to factory legislation, and this fact contains an important clue. It is a remarkable coincidence (if a coincidence at all) that the other great fin de siècle piece of age-related legislation, the Age of Consent Bill, which marked the culmination of a long debate about *sexual* capacity, was passed at the same session of the Imperial Legislative Council as was the Factory Act of 1891. The apparently iron grip of the age criterion upon the question of capacity is at least partly clarified by the existing precedents: metropolitan law, and law in most parts of the world, had by now come to accept age as the only valid identifier of an able body. Setting to one side the large, global question of how age came to stand in for capacity across a range of legislative and moral spheres, it is at least possible, in the light of this congruence, to *re-describe* the ethico-legal function of age.

To put it telegraphically, the legal primacy of age against all other contending signifiers of capacity created a certain moral baseline within the field of what were essentially relations of force and domination. That moral baseline, for children working in factories, as for pre-pubertal girls, was childhood. The legally enshrined immunity of small, 'immature' bodies from violation—by husbands, by employers—demarcated a certain zone of entitlement. It was within this zone—a shifting, furiously contested space—that childhood came to acquire its legal coordinates.

This field of negative entitlement, generated by law, significantly complicates the question of 'maturity' and the 'free agent'—the working man who is the subject of his employer rather than law (or, analogously, the wife who is the subject of her husband). There is, I would suggest, a speculative identity between the two major pieces of age-related legislation that were signed into law in 1891. The aggressive rhetorical claims that factory legislation threatened the interests of the worker and his employment relations—claims emblazoned upon several polemical masts in both Britain and India—were roughly analogous to conservative claims, in the late nineteenth century, to the effect that age-of-consent legislation intruded upon the domain of conjugal relations between husband and wife.[62]

In both cases, the argument only became operative upon a certain transformation within the field of discourse, which came to be—rhetorically at least—structured dominantly by what I term 'figures of consent': the child who was willing to work independently of regulation, the girl who consented to early sexual relations. These figures of consent are interesting because, in the first place, they do not correspond to what a range of public discourses designated as 'free agents'—law defined them in terms of their vulnerability, and the question of their willing consent (to work in the mills, to enter early conjugal relations) was raised in the context of long debates around their forms of subjection. As 'willing' workers and wives, they were mobilized to a particular end by the opponents of legislation in both cases—an end which amounted to their effective abandonment to the possibility of extra-legal forms of coercion.

If one turns to the 'figures of consent' *actually* produced by debates around legal regulation, however, there is a catch, or rather a shift, in both imagined and material terms. For in both cases, legislative protection did eventually take wing to a (very) limited extent. The factory child, like the girl below twelve, *did* legally come to be invested with certain immunities. In this process of dialogue between law and its opponents, in both cases the consenting figure came to be re-signified. In the case of age-of-consent legislation, the girl above twelve, 'free' of the shackles of legislative restriction, was effectively abandoned to a conjugality that was by no means necessarily 'consensual'. Similarly, the adult male worker, 'free' of the 'restriction' of legislation, defined as an unshackled, agentive subject, was effectively abandoned to unprotected conditions of work by virtue of his distinction from 'weaker' categories of worker—this lasted till the dramatic changes between 1905 and 1911, which universalized protective factory legislation across the divides of demography and gender. In both cases, there was an obverse to the creation of subjects who enjoyed substantive legal protection, which was the creation of an ironically 'free' subjecthood, with all the ambiguities that this naming entailed.

All this has another important dimension: the objective character of the standard marked by age was *putative* in its character. Scientific knowledge having advanced to a stage where it was apparently possible to deduce age from external signifiers, however imperfectly, it was possible, in theory, to postulate a time when the measurement of age would acquire perfection. As the Surgeon-General frankly confessed, that time lay in the future and not in the present. However, the anticipation that the time *would* come short-circuited, in a sense, the existing reality of indeterminacy and elevated age into an 'objective' principle of adjudication. To put it differently, a certain discourse centred around age-measurement *anticipated its own fullness* even as it acknowledged its present limitation, and this had, among other things, the effect of grounding and defining a specific field of expertise. It was, therefore, at the point of age-measurement that the expert knowledge of surgeons was primarily elicited by factory legislation. It was also at this point that the dilemma began.

What kind of dilemma, precisely, was this? The constitutive confusion about the lines marking off childhood from adulthood and sub-dividing childhood itself was, within its own terms, a problem for designated 'expert' knowledge, experience, and insight. These were the necessary terms in which factory legislation formally conceived its objects—the factory, the child, the requisite standards by which capacities, vulnerabilities, and entitlements could be measured. These were problems which expert opinion, informed by experience and tact, would handle. At the bottom of this, it is important to realize, lay an assumption inherent to the ideology of 'industry'—that enlightened ideas and practices generated by expert knowledge harnessed to the ends of the state and employers alike could resolve dilemmas like this; that these were, essentially, problems of knowledge.

In the actual situation in which the various actors on the stage of the Factory Act found themselves, however, the question of certification was an irreducibly *political* one, a conflict—and negotiation—between differently positioned and balanced forces over the practical meaning of factory legislation. There is a Foucauldian sense, of course, in which this is immediately, almost axiomatically true: the practices of inspection, certification, and measurement instituted by legislation produced new forms of effective power. But I mean the description in another (though not incompatible) sense: the ambiguities of medical certification for children generated a politics around the factory, principally played out *within* the domain of the state, most directly between factory inspectors and surgeons. This was a struggle over the letter of the law that spilled into the way industrial relations in Bombay were conceptualized. It generated profound, if implicit, anxieties about the future of these relations.

There was a major gap that structured the politics of child certification: the gap between the definite, invariable kinds of age classification demanded by factory law and the indeterminacy of medical procedures for the investigation (and ascription) of childhood. The paradox implicit in this gap was that the very weakness of medical knowledge became a source of immense localized authority for the individual certifying surgeon.

Since there was no scientific principle endorsing a radical physiognomic difference between the ages six and seven, or twelve and thirteen, there was also no generalized scientific common sense a factory inspector had access to. A particular circuit of exchanges between the factory inspector, the mill, and the certifying surgeon sprang up as a consequence. The inspector would frequently find children working in mills to be of 'doubtful' age, and, not being able to trust his own authority on the subject, he would refer them to the doctor for certification. The certifying surgeon emerged as an intermediary figure in the industrial relations of the time, for he held the power to authorize or disallow mill employment for children.

Presidency surgeons, as middle-level figures in the Indian Medical Service, partook of the unrest over pay levels that suffused their ranks in the early and mid-1880s.[63] The certification of factory children was an addition to their normal workload, without additional compensation. It did not take long for this to spark sharp exchanges between the doctors and the Bombay government. In late July 1881, Surgeon-Major Arnott, the Presidency Surgeon for the Fort district of Bombay, wrote an irate letter to the Surgeon-General of the Bombay government, complaining of having lost a whole morning examining 120 children sent by the manager of Chanda Ramji Mills. There was no legal provision for the payment of certifying surgeons at this stage, but the manager had apparently agreed to pay Re 1 per child examined.[64] There existed, however, no official rule about the remuneration of surgeons for the examination of factory children.

This was a matter that was discussed within government circles in July and August. Would surgeons have to gratuitously examine all children who were sent for examination to them? If examination was to be remunerated, how was this to be achieved? Officials were clearly anxious that this should involve no extra burdens upon the state exchequer, beyond the salaries already drawn by the Presidency surgeons for their other duties. But how then to ensure the workability of certification, which—given that the Factory Act protected only child labour—was at the heart of protective legislation?

Arnott's complaint signalled an incipient discontent that could only grow, given the lack of remuneration for the work of certification performed by surgeons. At the same time, the idea that a fee should be slapped upon mill owners by law potentially expressed an intrusion upon the mill owners' right to run their factories as they pleased, a worry powerfully articulated in arguments around the issue of factory legislation since the mid-1870s. But if a regularized system of certification was not instituted, the very basis of protective legislation for children would be undermined.

To tackle this, officials chose to institute a fiction of free choice. The Government of Bombay expressed the opinion that the Chanda Ramji Mills' manager had, in paying an agreed fee, acted 'in the spirit of the Act, and is not to be discouraged'.[65] It admitted that granting certificates under the Factory Act was a heavy burden. However, instead of making legal provision for the payment of a regular fee by mill owners—which would logically have extended the provisions contained in the Act—it chose, instead, to legally validate a laissez-faire arrangement for payment between surgeons and mill owners. The payment of fees was made contingent upon the mill owner's wishes, and there was no legal injunction that made it compulsory for mill owners to subject each child they chose to employ to medical scrutiny. However, if the inspector detected a transgression of the age restrictions and confirmed his suspicions through medical examination of the child, the mill owner's infraction was punishable. For the capitalist, certification of his employees was an option, since only children of doubtful age needed certificates.[66] But the decision not to submit children for certification was obviously fraught with danger.

Even more critically, the resolution wavered deliberately between the institution of a compulsory fee and the recognition of free negotiation between surgeon and mill owner. If the mill owner wished to pay a fee, he was free to do so. And this choice was regulated. A sliding scale of payment—Re 1 for ten children at a time, 8 annas for more—was established, in all probability, to ensure that surgeons could not extort any amount they liked from mill owners. If fees were to be paid, they would be paid only according to this scale.[67] But the formulation that fees were purely contingent upon the mill owners' wishes did not square well with this. Did this mean, correspondingly, that medical examination and certification were also contingent upon the surgeon's wishes? If a mill owner was not willing to pay—and why would he want to pay?—did the surgeon, too, have the right to withhold his services? The ambiguous and incomplete wording of the resolution left this unclear and a loophole emerged in the text of the law.

The 'choice' offered to mill owners was, in effect, a fiction, for the ambiguity of the law produced a practice of fee-payment for certification that was de facto compulsory. But like many fictions, this had material force, for it defined a convoluted sub-structure of industrial relations. From the perspective of the certifying surgeon, the self-contradictory injunctions of the government implied a fair amount of effectively unpaid labour. He circumvented this by pirouetting between the self-contradictory injunctions of the law and demanding fees from mill owners and child workers in return for certification. Mill owners, for their part, generally seem to have complied with the demand for payment, but also to have battened upon the wages of the children they employed (and their families) to make good the minor financial losses that resulted. Children and their families, finally, seem to have resigned themselves to the transaction that secured them the right to work in exchange for a fee that represented a not negligible proportion of their earnings.

To elucidate the operations of this structure of relations, I now consider two small events in the history of factory law administration in the 1880s, which operated at the intersection of factory inspection, medical examination, and employment practices. Together, these constitute one of the more coherent 'internal histories' of the Act as it moved between norm and practice. Both these incidents flowed (in the first place) from the legal ambiguity inscribed in the state-authorized practice of fee-payment, and (in the second place) from the 'malpractices' of certifying surgeons under the Act, who extorted fees from mill owners and children against the letter of the law. Such extortions generated anxieties within the circuits of government, and these anxieties, as acted upon by the factory inspectorate, came to re-signify some of the material and conceptual dimensions of industrial relations.

Extortion and Anxiety I: The Case of Dr Partridge

On 3 September 1881, H.E. Jacomb, the Collector of Bombay, found on his desk a letter from a J.W. Latimer, who was the Secretary of the Anglo-Indian Spinning and Manufacturing Company.[68] Latimer was worried by a note he had received from W.P. Partridge, third Presidency Surgeon, in charge of certifying mill children in the Byculla district. He enclosed a copy of the surgeon's letter for Jacomb's perusal.

Partridge, the letter stated, was willing to examine the children employed in Latimer's mill, and to grant them certificates of age, upon the payment of a fee. A fine of Rs 500, warned the doctor, could be imposed if any child under twelve was found working full-time, or if anyone under seven was found working at all. 'It will be doubtless clear to you,' wrote Partridge, 'that it will be a decided advantage for each millowner to be furnished with certificates.'[69] He, therefore, asked the mill owner to agree to send all his boys for examination in batches of not more than ten at a time, and to pay Re 1 per examination. 'It would save much trouble if the fees could be brought at each examination.' The proposal to pay a fee for each child, Partridge wrote, had already been approved by the manager of another mill, the Chanda Ramji Mills.[70]

Partridge's demands contained a number of misreadings of the Act. First, the fine prescribed for employing children under the minimum age was Rs 200 and not Rs 500. Second, the Act did not make it compulsory for mill owners to present all their children for examination, but only those whose age was ambiguous. This ambiguity, however, as I have explained, was fairly pervasive among child millworkers. Partridge clearly sensed the capacity this circumstance had to generate anxieties among mill owners, and so turned on the heat. If *all* the children in the mill had to be paid for at the rate prescribed by Partridge, he potentially stood to make financial gain that would not be negligible. He did not explicitly state that payment was compulsory, but strongly implied that he would not agree to certify children without payment. And the clause in his demand that made it necessary to send children up in batches of ten and not more represented, of course, a brilliant deployment of the provision that surgeons could charge Re 1 per head for groups of up to ten children. The law, then, was being turned to good pecuniary advantage.

Latimer's letter to Jacomb suggested that if examination fees were to be enjoined upon him, he would be forced to deduct the amount from the wages of the children employed in his mill.[71] Mill owners, then, had a strategy ready to circumvent impositions of this kind, and in sheer practical terms the issue was not so very bothersome. What the correspondence reveals, though, is anxiety that operates at another level and one that cannot be reduced to the practical difficulties of working the Act. Rather, these difficulties constitute both the stage upon which the drama of the developing relationship between mill owners and the state was enacted, and the ways in which the future of this relationship was envisaged.

What was the texture of these emerging worries? An indication is offered in a letter Jacomb wrote to the Government of Bombay on 6 September, three days after he received Latimer's worrying communication. He stated he had visited several factories to ascertain the ages of children, spoke glowingly of 'the spirit in which the provisions of the Act have been received by millowners, the uniform courtesy shewn me by themselves … as also their prompt and cheerful compliance with all my requirements'.[72] He went on to add that the Act had worked smoothly, and wrote:

> I think therefore that it is much to be regretted that Dr Partridge should have seen fit to address a letter to Mr. Latimer who has good standing in the mercantile community and possesses considerable influence among millowners, calculated not only to be misleading … but also productive of some degree of irritation, inasmuch as his proposals are opposed to the letter and intention of the Act, and are moreover ungraciously premised by an allusion to the liability of the millowners to a penalty … which, at least, has the appearance of a desire to enforce upon Mr. Latimer's acceptance the proposals as to fees submitted to him for approval.[73]

This opens a window upon the way the Factory Act was imagined by its executors at its inception. The knowledge of factory labour conditions that had been produced by the Commission of 1875 contained a dangerous surplus of information, which was potentially damaging to the myth of the relative prosperity and happiness of millworkers. In mill owners' representations, and the reports of newspapers sympathetic to mill owners, rhetorical strategies were being constantly devised to contain this volatile knowledge through an invocation of the virtues of the factory system. This form of rhetoric found its way into the documents and correspondence of state officials as well. Men like Jacomb were in an uncomfortable position. On the one hand, the formulation of the Act as a piece of protective legislation wedded them, independent of their will, to the implementation of a law that ran against the idea of the capitalist's autonomy in the workplace. This placed government officials in a potentially tense relationship with the industrial capitalists who made up an increasingly important and vocal section of the city elite. So official documents of the time are replete with protestations that the Factory Act was actually in the interests of the harmonious working of industry, and the smallest sign of approval of its provisions on the part of mill owners was trumpeted as a victory for the idea of the Act.

Partridge's transgression destabilized this consensus. This happened not through active resistance to the idea of state–mill owner cooperation, but through something much more routine—the corruption and distortion of the Act in the work of putting it into practice, such distortion as could accompany the implementation of any law. Minor loopholes in administrative discourse produced the possibility of Partridge's extortionate claims, but this in itself betokened a wider threat. The very existence of an administrative setup—doctors, inspectors, civil servants—that would scrutinize the practices of mill owners posed a structural obstacle to their freedom to run their mills as they chose.

For the mill owners, then, Partridge was potential nuisance value in his embodiment of some of the possibilities of the Act's perversion. For the Bombay government, he represented the danger of corruption, but also something more. He served as a reminder that, unless carefully controlled, the Factory Act could end up articulating hostility rather than harmony within the textile industry. Partridge's action could be explained away on the grounds of individual dishonesty. But what if it actually expressed a wider problem? What if, in the future, legitimate enforcements of the letter of the law carried similar threats to the interests of capitalists? Jacomb's letter to the Bombay government articulates all these worries. He is at pains to emphasize the courtesy and understanding shown to him by the owners of mills and to celebrate the friendship between state and capital that it represents. He takes note of Latimer's importance within 'the mercantile community'. A small irritant like this evokes the fear of an incipient breakdown in this cordiality. Mill owners must not be compelled to pay fees, this must remain optional, and this freedom is something the state has to guard.

Partridge responded to the government's demand for explanation in what officials considered a 'grasping' and inexcusable manner. He enclosed, in a letter to the Collector, support from the employers' community for his enterprise, in the form of a note from the secretary and manager of Greaves Cotton Ltd, saying he would be happy to comply with Partridge's 'very reasonable instructions'.[74] The surgeon admitted that he had 'made a mistake' in citing a fine of Rs 500 and attributed it to not having a copy of the Act. He made mention, however, of correspondence with other mill owners who had acceded to his request.[75] On his terms, as he presented them, the demand for the payment of fees was perfectly within his rights as compensation for the work of certification. Was this claim genuine or was he simply trying to mask his own corruption? The answer is irrelevant. What mattered was that he reformulated the letter of the law in practice. And this had disturbing implications.

Members of the Bombay Legislative Council clearly saw red. 'Dr Partridge's greedy letter is most improper and discreditable to him. He also interferes and blunders in matters with which he has nothing to do.'[76] On an even stronger note: 'Dr Partridge's conduct seems so grasping that I would, unless his explanation places his conduct in a more favourable light, remove him from his post and place his services at the disposal of His Excellency the Commander in Chief for military duty.'[77] The footnote to this memo is terser, but equally revealing: 'NB: An answer should at once be sent to Mr. Latimer.'[78] Damage control involved, above all, pacifying and reassuring the injured mill owner.

While all this righteous indignation was being aired in the correspondence of the General Department, the doctor dropped another bombshell, writing again to Jacomb on 20 September 1881.[79] In this letter, he spoke of three exchanges with mill owners since his request for the mandatory payment of fees. The owners of the National Spinning and Weaving Co. and of the Jadhavji Raghuvji Spinning Mill had, he said, already sent boys up for examination. He also mentioned a letter from the secretary of the BMOA, who expressed his willingness to recommend children to him for examination, but protested that Re 1 per head was excessive, and wanted to pay no more than 8 annas per head.

The secretary also wished only to arrange for the examination of boys newly employed in the mill, and among these, only those who were considered to be of doubtful age by the Inspector.

Partridge offered, in his letter, an account of his response to this suggestion: 'In reply I have told them, that of course, they can do what they like about sending or not sending the new hands, but that with regard to the new boys, I think that if I consent to the fee of 8 annas they ought to send up all the new boys.'[80] He went on to add: 'I think that they will consent to this my very moderate proposal. Otherwise, if they neglect to have the new boys examined, and should boys be found when the Inspector goes to the mill, below the age of 12 working fulltime, the fine should be inflicted.'[81] So, at one level, Partridge was haggling with the mill owner over the practice of certification. At the same time, he was extending another threat: if mill owners did not employ his services for all the children they employed, things would not go well with them. If the Bombay government wanted the whole process of factory regulation and inspection to represent harmonious relations between mill owners and the state, Partridge's invocation of the factory inspector in his letter subverted this promise.

This was clearly the last straw. A departmental submission declared that the new letter from Partridge was, 'in its nature, more objectionable than the first one'.[82] Two departmental resolutions were drafted to put an immediate end to the doctor's extortions. The Collector was instructed to conciliate Latimer without delay, to assure him of the following:

> Mr. Partridge had no authority to address to him the letter … that millowners are not bound to do anything not required of them by the Act and Rules under the Act, that the payment by them of any fees for certificates is entirely optional, and that the mention of such fees in a Resolution of Government was simply a suggestion thrown out for the convenience of millowners who may desire … to take larger precautions to ascertain the age of children.[83]

Anxiously, the resolution repeated time and again that Partridge's demands were entirely opposed to the spirit of the Act, and condemned the language of his letters, which 'appear to be carefully calculated to constrain mill owners to pay him systematically the highest possible amount of fees'.[84] Partridge was instructed to state his monetary gains from these transactions he had devised and to immediately withdraw the letters he had sent to mill owners in his district. Another resolution, a week later, repeated the government's discomfiture with the surgeon's 'solicitation' and invoked again the spirit of the Act, condemning his violation of it.[85]

It was only now that the doctor fell into line and admitted the error of his ways. In a letter addressed to the Surgeon-General with the Government of Bombay, he apologized for his mistake in prescribing a fine of Rs 500, stating, however, his 'trust that it will not, for a moment, be imagined that the error was intentional'.[86] He protested, contrary to the evidence from his previous letters, that he had no intention of making mill owners think that the payment of fees was compulsory and that he had explained this to them in person frequently. Addressing finally the government's main worry, he wrote there was no reason to suppose any annoyance on the part of mill owners except, of course, in the case of Latimer. Mill owners had been uniformly courteous to him. 'I have met with nothing but courtesy and good feeling from everyone with whom I have had anything to do as yet.'[87] Partridge was rebuked in strong terms. A final resolution from the General Department, penned in obvious relief, stated that the doctor's explanation 'cannot be deemed satisfactory', but agreed to shelve the matter. 'Government trust, however, that their views on the subject are now understood.'[88]

Partridge's own 'corruption' is really a red herring. His 'extortions' disclose another, more important story, that of the tensions of a Factory Act confronting its own postulates and principles. If his own financial motives are subtracted from analysis, Partridge's demands simply represent the attempt to assemble protective legislation for the factory worker into some sort of coherent administrative form, to give substance to the Act's demand for certification by setting up a structure of medical inspection and the certification of age. This was routine administration, and that is the whole point. For these tensions and worries burst precisely from a routine, everyday administrative practice. While the Act operated, it was impossible to be fully secure about the relationship between state and mill owner. Leaving the letter of the law as it was afforded no comfort, for a minor state official, a surgeon, could radically recompose its meaning without intending to. What was to prevent other kinds of challenges to the desired harmony of interests within industry? Thus, the government had to continually step in with resolutions and proclamations to work the Act away from its deployment against the interests of mill owners.

The rebukes administered to the errant doctor can be read as a strategy of containment. By reducing the case to a matter of individual corruption and deviance, some of the wider tensions produced by the existence of the Factory Act could be discursively occluded. But this was not, even at this stage, a complete closure. The body of official discourse also contains another fracture, one that derives from the position of the labourer—the child—within it. The child labourer, the central focus not only of certification but, at this point, of all factory regulation, is tucked away in the margins of the departmental correspondence I have examined. However, at certain moments of pressure, the child moves centre stage. The first of these is Partridge's initial letter to Latimer where he addresses the possibility that the amount payable by the mill owner to him may well be deducted from the wages of working children, or from their parents, rather than paid from Latimer's own pocket. 'All I ask is that if it be decided that the parents are to pay the fee, the amount will be paid by you, and afterwards deducted from the boy's wages.'[89] Latimer mentioned this in his letter to Jacomb, also adding that this imposed a heavy financial burden upon the children concerned.[90]

Subsequently, when he wrote to the General Department, Jacomb indicated his awareness of this possibility. He wrote:

> [I] fully shared the opinion of Mr. Latimer as to its hardship upon the young workers many of whom have had to submit to a reduction of wages through being put on short time consequent upon the introduction of the Act. ... I would beg to submit that, on every account, the Government may be moved to reconsider the question of fees chargeable to these poor little creatures, in view to these fees being placed in abeyance until definite arrangements are made.[91]

The Secretary of the General Department, in his letter to the Undersecretary, added on to this another worry, 'The fees, though they may be paid by the manager in the first place, will be recovered from the pay of the children, which does not amount to more than Rs. 3 or Rs. 4 per mensem…'.[92]

The moral legitimacy of the official attack upon Partridge, then, could not derive solely from an invocation of the rights of mill owners. I would tentatively suggest that the trajectory of official response to infringements of the Act had to move in two directions at once, given the government's new identity as the protector of factory labour. The interests of the mill owners' community were supreme, but it also had to be demonstrated that, simultaneously, Partridge's demands constituted an unwarrantable attack upon the livelihood of child workers. And discursively, then, the two—capitalist and labouring interests—were conjoined. An attack upon the interests of mill owners was equally an attack upon the interests of workers, for what hurt the industry hurt both equally. This replicated, interestingly enough, both the structure of argument used by mill owners when they opposed factory legislation in the first place (legislation would hurt employment prospects) and that used by upholders of legislation (protection was actually in the interests of capitalists, since it delivered a content and efficient workforce into their supervision). A fiction of harmony was thus produced and continually restaged within official discourse.

This was, however, an uncomfortable fiction to sustain, for it was consistently subverted by the way the actual practices of medical certification proceeded. While Partridge was censured in strong terms, the Bombay government, unwilling to either compel mill owners to pay for certification or to pay certifying surgeons out of state revenues, tacitly continued to reproduce the legal ambiguity that grounded these practices. The matter imploded again, within the circuit of state anxieties and industrial relations, in the course of 1887, when a remarkably similar case of 'malpractice' in medical certification was uncovered by W.W. Drew, the fourth Inspector of Factories under the Act.

Extortion and Anxiety II: The Case of Dr Hunter

At the beginning of June 1887, Drew, who appears to have been one of the more interventionist inspectors in the early history of the Factory Act, sent three boys to G. Yeates Hunter, who had replaced Partridge as the Presidency Surgeon for the Byculla district.[93] Hunter wrote back stating that he intended to withhold certificates for the time being, and would grant them 'on the fees being sent out'.[94] An angry correspondence, uncannily reminiscent of the Partridge controversy, ensued. The arguments rehearsed in the earlier case reproduced themselves here. Drew reiterated, in a series of increasingly hostile letters to the doctor, that mill owners and the children they employed were entitled to certificates free of charge and the payment of fees was entirely optional.[95] Hunter, for his part, stuck to his guns and continued to demand fees from the children he certified.[96] He claimed that the payment of fees was customary and accepted as such by both mill owners and factory children, and that 'non-payment is an entirely new departure ... so far as my experience (of some years) goes'.[97]

Drew discovered concrete evidence of further 'malpractice' on 8 June, when it transpired that Hunter had given a boy a certificate confirming his fitness for full-time work, upon receipt of Re 1 as fee. 'The boy was not sent by any mill owner, but simply went with a relation to get a certificate prior to seeking employment.'[98] Hunter's response emphasized a practice that the earlier debate around Partridge's extortion of fees had dimly registered but then elided. 'I was not aware,' he wrote, 'who sent the boy in question or by whom he was sent—a boy simply presented himself for examination, obtained a certificate of age, and the person who paid him brought Rs. 1.'[99] In contrast to the usual practice followed by mills—where a foreman or a mill official brought a batch of children to the doctor for certification, along with the prescribed printed form where their ages and names were registered—here the negotiation between doctor and child worker seemed to bypass this rule-bound system in favour of a more laissez-faire practice.

Following his discovery that Hunter was extracting fees for certification directly from the children themselves, Drew issued a circular to the mill owners of Bombay, forwarding them the Government resolutions on the subject of fee payment and stressing (much as Jacomb had six years ago) its optional character, 'as the examination of children is part of the Presidency Surgeon's regular duty'.[100] The principal point stressed by Drew, however, differed significantly from that of his predecessor, and gives us a clue to the transformation of the nebulous state anxieties that undergirded the theory and practice of medical certification: 'If however you prefer to pay a fee, *you must pay it yourself, and neither take it from the child or its parents, nor deduct it from the wages*.'[101]

The apprehension that working children and their families were being made to bear the financial burden of certification drove Drew, between July and October, towards a fuller, more aggressive investigation of the actual practices of fee-payment by mills and millworkers. On 13 July, he inspected the City of Bombay Mill and marked out ten 'doubtful' cases of boys whose ages ambiguously straddled the dividing line between 'protected' and 'adult' work. He issued instructions that none of them was to be employed as full-timers until they produced certificates demonstrating they were over twelve. On the 21st, he reinspected the mill and found the same boys at work, still without certificates. The manager told him that Hunter had verified their ages as above twelve, but had, once again, refused to certify them without the payment of fees.[102]

This led Drew to write to the proprietor of the mill, informing him that an offence had been committed under the terms of the Act, but that he was at the same time aware that 'it is partly the fault of the Presidency Surgeon who illegally refuses to give certificates without fees'.[103] This was an allegation that incensed Hunter, who reported it to the Surgeon-General with the Government of Bombay the following day as 'defamation'. Hunter was clearly made extremely anxious by the 'verbal directions' issued by Drew to the mill owners to the effect that no fees were to be paid to the doctor at all—an aggressive extension of the statement in the earlier circular which stressed the optional character of fee-payment. Against this, stressing the ambiguity of the government resolutions on the subject, Hunter argued (not unreasonably):

> The millowners recognize that though Government could scarcely order payment of fees, such payment was allowable, and even looked for, otherwise Government would never have issued Resolutions on the subject.
>
> Granting that it was the intention of Government that millowners engaged in private enterprise should pay a small fee to the Government certifying surgeon, I am at a loss to understand why years after such fees have been *willingly* paid the Inspector should take upon himself to issue a circular laying stress upon the fact that such payment is voluntary, when it was meant to be all along. For pointing this out could only lead to the impression that he did not wish mill managers to pay, at least so they understand it, though I am glad to say several do not act upon it.[104]

The Bombay government's response was characteristically ambivalent, reproducing the concern over the rules and ethics of fee-payment that had been produced in the first place by its own resolutions. Drew's complaints about Hunter were registered, and the doctor was sharply rebuked. Hunter's complaint that Drew had violated the spirit of the law by going behind the government's back and issuing instructions to mill owners not to pay fees, however, was also taken note of, and both the inspector and the doctor were censured (the latter more sharply).[105]

The matter might have rested there, but Drew pushed it further. This might have been because he was stung by the departmental censure passed against him or it might have been because, as a departmental submission of 16 August observed, the Inspector, not being 'afraid to face the responsibilities of his own position, will not allow factory inspection to be a smooth but useless routine matter, and has exerted himself to find out abuses'.[106] Drew initiated an extensive investigation into the actual practice of fee-payment for certification in September 1887. He wrote a letter to the thirty-seven cotton mills in the Byculla district, asking their proprietors whether (*a*) they knew the payment of fees was optional, (*b*) they had paid fees out of mill funds, and what these payments amounted to if they had, (*c*) how many children they had sent for certification since the circular he had issued in June, (*d*) how many boys had received certificates gratis, and (*e*) whether the certificates that had not been received free of charge had been paid for by the mill owners or the children themselves.[107]

The mills' responses, while perhaps not surprising, had a consistency that is worth exploring at length. Virtually none of the mills claimed knowledge of the nuances of the successive government resolutions that had instituted the principle of free choice in fee-payment. Most of the responses on this count were cursory: 'Did not know fees optional',[108] 'Did not know',[109] 'Believed fees compulsory',[110] and 'Not aware'.[111] The Alexandra and E.D. Sassoon Mills ventured a more cogent explanation, which can more or less be safely extrapolated to the industry at large: 'As the Factory Act of 1881 was silent as to who should pay the fee for the examination of children as to their age, the fee charged by the Presidency Surgeon was considered compulsory and not optional until the receipt of your circular.'[112]

It transpired that 238 children had been sent to Hunter for examination since Drew's circular.[113] Of these, only twenty-nine had received certificates free of charge, fourteen of these, significantly, being from the Dinshaw Petit Mill, the largest in the city, and one that could perhaps impose its terms upon the surgeon more readily than others could.[114] At the same time, the practice of fee-payment does not seem to have generated very much anxiety and unrest among mill owners or, as far as one can deduce from the scanty evidence, millworkers either. As Hunter continued to argue, and as the responses of the mills demonstrate, in the six years between the controversies surrounding Partridge and Hunter, the payment of fees for medical certification had become an established customary practice, a moral economy of sorts, centred around the certifying surgeon's right to compensation. The agents of the Alexandra and E.D. Sassoon Mills told Drew that 192 children had been examined by the successive certifying surgeons under the Act since the post had been established in 1881, of which 147 had paid Re 1 each and the remainder had paid 8 annas each.[115] Similarly, the Gordon Mill had sent up 209 children for examination since its foundation in 1884 and Rs 205.5 had been paid over the three years.[116] The manager of the Mahalakshmi Mills, Joseph Hadwin, was alone among his fraternity in claiming knowledge of the optional nature of fee-payment, 'because the Factory Act does not say that the fee is compulsory'.[117] Significantly, however, he does not seem to have exercised this choice and fees were paid as usual.[118]

The modes of compensation varied at the point of payment, but eventually always drew upon the earnings of wage-labouring families. In some cases, fees were paid out of mill funds, but subsequently deducted from the wages of the certificated children. In others, the fees were paid directly by the children sent up for certification, or by family members who accompanied them to the doctor's office. Only in three cases—in the Sunderdas, Great Eastern, and People of India Mills—were fees, at some point between 1881 and 1887, paid out of mill funds without recourse to the earnings of working families.[119]

The response of the manager of the Ripon Mill to Drew's circular seems to have spelt out the principal mode of operation: 'The children were told the day previous to being sent to bring the money, and they all brought one rupee each and paid it to the surgeon themselves.'[120] Drew responded to this with a demand for clarification: why, when he had issued a circular stating that children were not to pay the fees themselves, had they been told to do so anyway?[121] The manager replied that 'the children were sent without money, as your circular informed us they were to be passed without payment of fee. They were sent back again and told they must bring Re 1 each before they could be passed, so they brought money with them the next day and I sent them again to be passed'.[122]

All this followed, at one level, the procedures enjoined by factory law: in the cases just mentioned, the mills rounded up children who sought employment, or whose ages were suspect and required medical 'confirmation', and sent them to Hunter for certification. There was, however, a substantial grey zone of mostly undocumented practice that lay beyond this, which consisted of children—and their families—seeking and obtaining (or failing to obtain) certificates before applying for employment. It appears from many of these testimonies that children sought certificates from the surgeon *before* applying for employment in the mills—which is to say that they bypassed the legally sanctioned relationship of mill and doctor, and forged their own, independent of their employers-to-be.

The agents of the David Sassoon Mill, for instance, vaguely stated, 'We think the fees for certificates of age were taken from the children.'[123] Drew, ever vigilant, pressed them for a clearer answer.[124] They replied that they did not know how the fees for children were paid, 'and have no means of making this enquiry now, as all such hands have left the mill service'.[125] Kharsedji Pandey, manager of the Alexandra and E.D. Sassoon Mills, more forthcoming in his responses than most, told Drew that 125 children between 1881 and 1887 had brought certificates with them prior to their employment.[126]

All this attests a certain hierarchical structure of displacement that authorized the employment of children and delimited its terms in the 1880s. Drew reported to the Bombay government in July that 'the mill owners take no interest in the matter at all. It is left entirely to the managers, who almost all thought that the fee was compulsory and to be paid for by the *children*'.[127] But if the responsibility of mill owners was—in this as in many other cases—displaced on to mill managements, it was almost immediately displaced again and came to rest upon the backs of mill-working families.

This yields an insight into how factory law operated in actual practice when it came to the 'protection' of mill-working children. The processes of age certification and registration, conceived as a measure to separate the legal from the illegal, and define the legitimate employment of small children in factories, were given their substance by a labyrinthine set of negotiations around some sort of incipient 'right to work' for children. In order to secure this right, children and their parents had to pay a fee that was strictly speaking illegal, and in most cases, undocumented: an extensive structure of informality, thus, sustained the 'formal' reality of child-employment. There are multiple levels of displacement that operate here: from the mill owner to the manager, from the manager to the working-class family, from the legal to the illegal, from the formally defined and delimited to the informal and the contingent. These displacements did not merely subvert, but also, in a very real sense, *constituted* the structure of practices and negotiations that led children seeking employment into the mills, drove them out, or concealed their 'illegal', undocumented, unregistered work.

Law and illegality, then, sustained each other. The law of certification was made operative through a series of dubious, informal practices, which, in a circular motion, drew their efficacy from the letter of the law itself, which was deeply ambiguous. Drew's intervention changed this, and examining it closely we find an important difference between the Partridge and Hunter affairs. In the first case, as I have shown, the anxiety that governed official response was the incipient breakdown in relations between factory law administrators and mill owners. This theme continued to play a part in the discursive network generated around the Hunter case, but the prime worry seems to have shifted, and the source of anxiety was no longer the mill owner victimized by a grasping doctor, but the working child and his family, forced to pay a significant proportion of their wages for certification. The now routine character of fee-payment—it is significant that no mill owners between 1882 and 1887 seem to have registered a protest against the practice—was clearly sustained by the extractive pressures exerted by mill owners or doctors upon the child seeking work, and, therefore, certification.

For Drew, this represented a major violation of the Act, and he made this clear in his correspondence with mill owners. If his circular in June apprised them that they were not obliged to pay fees, his investigations in September were accompanied by polite but firm instructions to them not to cut the fees from the wages of their child-workers. J. Dunkerley, manager of the James Greaves Mill, for instance, wrote in his response to Drew's circular in September that he had advanced the boys in his mill the fees for certification 'but have not yet decided whether to cut them from their wages'.[128] Drew responded by telling him not to do so, 'as they were entitled to certificates free'.[129] After a series of letters back and forth, the manager agreed.[130] A similar negotiation took place around the payment of fees for children at the Connaught Mill, where, again, Dunkerley was manager.[131] Other mills had similar stories to tell, and Drew doggedly pursued them with questions, increasingly aggressive, asking why the parents or children had been made to pay for something that was theirs by right. The manager of the Ripon Mill added an interesting caveat: 'I have held out a promise to the children to give them their rupees back again if they continue on in my service.'[132] In the absence of supporting evidence, it is impossible to tell whether this was instituted to deal with a specific labour shortage or as a response to the pressures exerted by the Factory Inspector. From the context in which it happened, the latter seems likelier.

Attending closely to the internal trajectory of this case furnishes important insights into what had changed, in the realm of industrial relations conceived in a broad sense, between the Partridge and Hunter controversies. Superficially, the two cases seem almost identical. In both, the interventions of the factory inspection regime disclosed a grey zone of informal practice that the state perceived as malpractice and corruption. The doctors in both cases, by contrast, mounted spirited and unashamed defences of their procedure. Hunter, for instance, wrote that 'a great deal of extra work' had been thrown upon him on account of the difficulties in certifying age.[133] He complained that the practice, enforced dogmatically by Drew, of certifying without payment, had robbed him of legitimate fees for nearly fifty certifications.[134] The Surgeon-General to the Government of Bombay offered some sympathy with this point of view: 'Mill owners are ordinarily a wealthy class, and they are well able to pay fees, and in my humble opinion they ought to do so. If medical officers are to perform contentedly and satisfactorily the duty of examining numerous dirty children, they must be remunerated from some source. Matter needs to be reconsidered.'[135]

In the Hunter case as in its predecessor, the Government of Bombay responded with alarm and anxiety to the intimation of a coercive relationship of fee-payment between surgeon and mill owner. In the former case, Partridge had evoked considerable ire from various officials; in the latter, both doctor and inspector earned censures, though of differing weight. What was different in the Hunter case was the inspector's determined, persistent activism on behalf of the mill children and their right to free certificates. This recast the terms of the game.

At one level, it is possible to view this through the prism of law and custom: law impinged upon and repressed a particular customary practice, and conversely law was subverted by the operations of a moral economy that flowed from custom. The picture, however, has greater complexity than this: there was certainly a conflict between the economy of certification enjoined by law and the moral economy of fee-payment for doctors' services, but the point is that both—legally enjoined practice and moral economy—were produced directly by law itself, through the ambivalence inscribed in its text.

The moral economy in question was produced by the new, unremunerated duties thrust upon already overworked surgeons (the claim to a payment that they had the right to extract informally from mill owners), and the specific relationship this produced within the mill (mill owners sending children up for certificates that the latter eventually had to pay for) and outside (children and their parents negotiating directly with surgeons for certificates, and paying the requisite fees). Against this, Drew's exertions on behalf of young millworkers posited an alternative moral economy, based on the protected figure of the mill child, who could not legitimately be asked to pay fees for a certificate that was his by right. Read in conjunction with the earlier controversy around Dr Partridge, we can glimpse a movement within the enclosed world of factory law, from a situation where the rights of the employer were paramount to one in which the immunities of the mill child were beginning to acquire new depth and substance.

Notes

1. Rajnarayan Chandavarkar, *The Origins of Industrial Capitalism in India: Business Strategies and the Working Classes in Bombay, 1900–1940* (Cambridge: Cambridge University Press, 1994), pp. 94–9.

2. *Report of Indian Factory Commission*, 1908 (Simla, 1908; henceforth *FC* 1908), vol. 2: Proceedings, p. 49.

3. Proceedings of Bombay Factory Commission, 1875 (henceforth *FC* 1875) 5th meeting, in Home (Judicial) A, 9–94 and K.W., NAI.

4. *FC* 1908, Proceedings, p. 47.

5. *FC* 1908, Proceedings, p. 47.

6. *FC* 1908, Proceedings, p. 49.

7. Legislative Council Proceedings, 11 March 1881, IOR V/9/18–19, p. 103, OIOC.

8. Legislative Council Proceedings, 11 March 1881, IOR V/9/18–19, p. 105, OIOC.

9. Janet Harvey Kelman, *Labour in India: A Study of the Conditions of Indian Women in Modern Industry* (London: George Allen & Unwin, 1923), pp. 103–4.

10. Legislative Council Proceedings, 11 March 1881, IOR/V/9/18–19, OIOC.

11. *Report of the Indian Factory Commission* (Calcutta 1890; henceforth *FC* 1890), 6 October 1890, pp. 23–4.

12. *FC* 1890, 6 October 1890.

13. Proceedings, *FC* 1890, 6 October 1890, p. 24.

14. Proceedings, *FC* 1890, 6 October 1890.

15. Proceedings of 7th Meeting of Factory Commission, 10 October 1890.

16. *FC* 1890, p. 43.

17. *FC* 1890, p. 37.

18. *Report of Bombay Factory Commission*, 1885.

19. No. 375, Bombay Castle, 4 February 1885, GD, 1886, vol. 38, no. 592, MSA.

20. Report of Mr M.C. Entee, District Deputy Collector, Surat, to Government of Bombay, 20 November 1875, cited in J. C. Kydd, *A History of Indian Factory Legislation* (Calcutta: Calcutta University Press, 1920).

21. *Evidence Recorded by and Written Statements Recorded by the Textile Factories Labour Committee, 1907*, Evidence of members of the Bombay Millowners' Association, taken on 8, 10, and 11 March 1907, pp. 12–13.

22. Report of Factory Commission, 1875; Kydd, *History of Indian Factory Legislation*, p. 9.

23. No. 28, GD, Bombay, 11 October 1882, MSA.

24. *FC* 1908, p. 47.

25. From W.O. Meade-King to Secretary to Government, GD, Bombay, 24 October 1882, Home (Judicial), NAI, nos 23–4, October 1882.

26. See Neil Smelser, *Social Change in the Industrial Revolution: An Application of Theory to the British Cotton Industry*, p. 267 and *passim*, (London, 1959).

27. Legislative Council Proceedings, 17 October 1879, IOR V/9/15–17, p. 241, OIOC.

28. Kydd, *History of Indian Factory Legislation*, Appendix I.

29. IOR, V/9/18–19, OIOC.

30. See A.K. Gupta, *Between a Tory and a Liberal: Bombay under Sir James Fergusson, 1880–85* (Calcutta, 1978).

31. IOR, V/9/18–19, p. 241, OIOC.

32. S.B. Upadhyay, *Existence, Identity and Mobilization: The Cotton Millworkers of Bombay 1890–1919* (Delhi: Manohar, 2004), p. 101.

33. *FC* 1908, p. 49.

34. No. 431, GD, Bombay, 4 October 1881, MSA.

35. No. 28, Secretariat, GD, Bombay, 11 October 1882, MSA.

36. Report on Inspection of Factories in the Bombay Presidency, quarter ending 30 September 1883, GD, vol. 3, MSA.

37. Reports on Inspection of Factories in the Bombay Presidency for the quarter ending 31 March 1885, no. 2278, 19 June, IOR/P/2637, OIOC.

38. Upadhyay, *Existence, Identity and Mobilization*, p. 102.

39. Emma Alexander, 'Labour Regulation or Protection for the Factory Child', in *Labour Matters: Towards Global Histories*, edited by Prabhu Mohapatra and Marcel van der Linden (Delhi, 2009).

40. Home (Judicial) A, nos 9–94 and K.W., January 1880, NAI.

41. Textile Factories Labour Commission, p. 13.

42. Legislative Council Proceedings, 11 March 1881, IOR V/9/18–19, p. 105, OIOC.

43. Legislative Council Proceedings, 11 March 1881, IOR V/9/18–19, p. 106, OIOC.

44. Legislative Council Proceedings, 11 March 1881, IOR V/9/18–19, p. 107, OIOC.

45. Legislative Council Proceedings, 11 March 1881, IOR V/9/18–19, p. 108, OIOC.

46. 7th meeting of Factory Commission, 1890.

47. Literally 'the mill town'. This was interchangeably used, through the twentieth century, with the name 'Girangaon', or 'the mill village'.

48. *Hindi Punch*, 24 January 1892, *Report on Native Newspapers, Bombay*.

49. See Chapter 5 with heading 'The Antinomies of Industrial Relations, 1884–95' for fuller discussion of this controversy.

50. Rules under Factory Act, no. 2972, GD, Bombay Castle, 10 September 1881, in GD 1881, no. 328, part 1, vol. 3, MSA.

51. Circular from J.M. Campbell, Acting Collector of Bombay, to factory owners, July 1881, cited in Collector's letter to GD, Bombay., MSA.

52. W.W. Drew, Inspector of Factories, to D. Mackenzie, Secretary to Govt, 25 June 1887, no. 144, GD 1887, vol. 3, no. 328, part 3 (A), MSA.

53. Drew, Inspector of Factories, to D. Mackenzie, Secretary to Govt, General Department, 25 June 1887, no. 144, GD 1887, vol. 3, no. 328, part 3 (A), MSA.

54. From Surgeon-General with the Government of Bombay to General Department, no. 4351, 24 August 1887, GD, Bombay, MSA.

55. The standard medical reference seems to have been William B. Carpenter's *Principles of Human Physiology*, published initially in 1839 and reprinted in 1851 and 1876.

56. No. 4351, GD, Bombay, 24 August 1887, MSA.
57. No. 4351, GD, Bombay, 24 August 1887, MSA.
58. No. 4351, GD, Bombay, 24 August 1887, MSA.
59. No. 4351, GD, Bombay, 24 August 1887, MSA.
60. From W. Doderet, Inspector of Factories, Bombay, to the Chief Secretary to Govt, GD, Bombay, no. 3, 2 April 1888, MSA.
61. Resolution no. 2320-A, Abstracts of Proceedings, GD (Misc.), Govt. of Bombay, 4 July 1888, IOR, P/3336.
62. See Tanika Sarkar, *Hindu Wife, Hindu Nation: Community, Religion and Cultural Nationalism* (Ranikhet: Permanent Black, 2001).
63. D.G. Crawford, *A History of the Indian Medical Service* (London: W. Thacker, 1914).
64. Letter from Surgeon-General with Govt of Bombay, GD, no. 3299, 28 July 1881, MSA.
65. Resolution no. 2729, Bombay Castle, GD, 18 August 1881, MSA.
66. Resolution no. 2729, Bombay Castle, GD, 18 August 1881, MSA.
67. Resolution no. 2729, Bombay Castle, GD, 18 August 1881, MSA.
68. Letter from J.W Latimer to the Collector of Bombay, enclosed in Collector's letter to Secretary to Govt, GD, Bombay, 6 September 1881, in GD 1881, no. 328, part 2, MSA.
69. Letter from W.P. Partridge to J.W. Latimer, 1 September 1881, in GD 1881, no. 328, part 2, MSA.
70. Letter from W.P. Partridge to J.W. Latimer, 1 September 1881 in GD 1881, no. 328, part 2, MSA.
71. Letter from J.W Latimer to the Collector of Bombay, enclosed in Collector's letter to Secretary to Govt, GD, Bombay, 3 September 1881, in GD 1881, no. 328, part 2, MSA.
72. No. 310, GD, Bombay, 6 September 1881, MSA.
73. No. 310, GD, Bombay, 6 September 1881, MSA.
74. Letter from Secretary and Manager, Greaves Cotton Ltd., to Dr Partridge, 8 September 1881, MSA.
75. Letter from Dr Partridge to the Collector of Bombay, 10 September 1881, MSA.
76. Memo from 'Hon'ble Member', 12 September 1881, MSA.
77. Note in GD files, 17 September 1881, MSA.
78. Note in GD files, 17 September 1881, MSA.
79. No. 385, GD, Bombay, 20 September 1881, Bombay, MSA.
80. Letter from Dr Partridge to the Collector, 15 September 1881, MSA.
81. Letter from Dr Partridge to the Collector, 15 September 1881, MSA.
82. Memo in GD, Bombay, 21 Sept 1881, MSA.
83. Resolution no. 3122, GD, Bombay Castle, 21 September 1881, MSA.

84. Resolution no. 3122, GD, Bombay Castle, 21 September 1881, MSA.

85. Resolution no. 3223, GD, Bombay Castle, 28 September 1881, MSA.

86. Letter from Dr Partridge to the Secretary to the Surgeon-General with the Government of Bombay, 24 September 1881, MSA.

87. Letter from Dr Partridge to the Secretary to the Surgeon-General with the Government of Bombay, 24 Sept 1881, MSA. Such statements of cordiality seem to have been a necessary addendum to almost any official correspondence regarding mill owner–state relations at this time, and such repetitions are redolent of anxiety that things might be otherwise.

88. No. 3366, GD, Bombay Castle, 8 October 1881, MSA.

89. Letter from Dr Partridge to Secretary of the Anglo-Indian Spinning and Manufacturing Company, Bombay, 1 Sept 1881, GD, MSA.

90. Letter from Mr Latimer to the Collector of Bombay, enclosed in Collector's letter to Secretary to Govt, Bombay, in GD 1881, no. 328, part 2, MSA.

91. Collector's letter to General Department, no. 310, GD, Bombay, 6 Sept 1881, MSA.

92. Secretary to Under Secretary, 9 Sept 1881, MSA.

93. No. 144, GD, Bombay, 2 June 1887, MSA.

94. No. 144, GD, Bombay, 3 June 1887, MSA.

95. No. 138, GD, Bombay, 18 June 1887, MSA.

96. No. 139, GD, Bombay, 18 June 1887, MSA.

97. Letter from G.Y. Hunter, Presidency Surgeon, to W.W. Drew, no. 21, GD, 6 June 1887, MSA.

98. No. 139, GD, Bombay, 18 June 1887, MSA.

99. Hunter to Drew, no. 25, GD, 20 June 1887, MSA.

100. Circular no. 136, Secretariat, GD, 15 June 1887, MSA.

101. Circular no. 136, Secretariat, GD [emphasis mine].

102. No. 227, GD, 14 October 1887, MSA.

103. Letter no. 155, from W.W. Drew to City of Bombay Manufacturing Company, GD, Bombay, 21 July 1887, MSA.

104. From G.Y. Hunter to the Secretary to the Surgeon-General, GD, no. 29, 22 July 1887, MSA [emphasis in original].

105. Government Resolution no. 2688.

106. Departmental submission, GD, 16 August 1887, MSA.

107. Letter from W.W. Drew to the 37 cotton mills in the 3rd District, GD, no. 197, 14 September 1887, MSA.

108. From Leopold Mill to Drew, GD, Bombay, 19 September 1887, MSA.

109. James Greaves Mill to Drew, GD, Bombay, 19 September 1887 MSA; Connaught Mill, GD, Bombay, 19 September 1887, MSA; Khatau Makanji Mill, GD, Bombay, 20 September 1887, MSA.

110. Obkeda Khepsey Mill to Drew, GD, Bombay, 20 September 1887, MSA.

111. Morarji Goculdas Mill to Drew, GD, Bombay, 20 September 1887, MSA.

112. Alexandra and E.D. Sassoon Mill to Drew, GD, Bombay, 27 September 1887, MSA.

113. Calculated from mill owners' responses to Drew, GD, Bombay, MSA.

114. Dinshaw Petit Mill to Drew, 21 September 1887, GD, MSA.

115. Alexandra and E.D. Sassoon Mill to Drew, 27 September 1887, MSA.

116. Gordon Mill to Drew, 17 September 1887, MSA.

117. Joseph Hadwin, Manager, Mahalakshmi Mills, to Drew, 4 October 1887, GD, MSA.

118. Joseph Hadwin, Manager, Mahalakshmi Mills, to Drew, 27 September 1887. Hadwin also stated that fees were paid out of mill funds, and this is the only testimony where there is no mention of the children's families paying the fees. This, however, does not necessarily mean that the usual practice was not followed.

119. No. 227, 22 July 1887, GD, MSA.

120. J. Enturst, Manager, Ripon Mill, to Drew, 20 September 1887, GD, MSA.

121. Drew to Enturst, 21 September 1887, GD, MSA.

122. Enturst to Drew, 23 September 1887, GD, MSA. The manager seems, however, to have been sufficiently impressed by Drew's admonitions to have promised 'to give them their rupees back again if they continue on in my service', a mark of the small but real ways in which the factory inspector's intervention shifted the terms of the practice of certification and child-employment.

123. Agents, David Sassoon and Co., to Drew, 22 September 1887, GD, MSA.

124. Drew to Agents, David Sassoon and Co., 22 September 1887, GD, MSA.

125. Agents, Sassoon and Co., to Drew, 5 October 1887, GD, MSA.

126. Kharsedji Pandey, Manager, Alexandra and E.D. Sassoon Mills, to Drew, 27 September 1887, GD, MSA.

127. No. 29, 22 July 1887, GD, MSA.

128. From J. Dunkerley, Manager, James Greaves Mill, to Drew, 19 September 1887, GD, MSA.

129. From Drew to Dunkerley, James Greaves Mill, 21 September 1887, GD, MSA.

130. From Dunkerley to Drew, 11 October 1887, GD, MSA.

131. Drew to Dunkerley, 21 September 1887, 10 October 1887, GD MSA; Dunkerley to Drew, 27 September 1887, 11 October 1887, GD, MSA.

132. J. Enturst, Manager, Ripon Mill, to Drew, 23 September 1887, GD, MSA.

133. From G.Y. Hunter to the Secretary to the Surgeon-General, no. 27, 24 June 1887, GD, MSA.

134. From the Presidency Surgeon to the Secretary to the Surgeon-General, no. 29, 22 July 1887, GD, MSA.

135. From the Surgeon-General to the Secretary to Government, no. 3467, 4 July 1887, GD, MSA.

PART III

FACTORY LAW AND INDUSTRIAL POLITICS

5

The Antinomies of Industrial Relations, 1884–95

The feeble legal regulation mandated by the Factory Act was pushed to its limits in the 1880s, before encountering a decisive crisis in the following decade. This crisis substantially transformed the relations between state, capital, and industrial labour. The contexts for this change involved both the peculiarities of the system of production prevalent in Bombay's mills, and wider international regulative and commercial currents.

They also involved the growth of a new kind of industrial politics around the 'factory question', which can be traced in two linked domains. First, the emergence of political debates over factory regulation between those who claimed to best represent workers' interests. Between the mid-1880s and the early 1890s, working conditions and workers' needs turned into an identifiable field of political conflict and polarization. Second, the growth of a more fractious, combative culture of industrial relations, which emerged from the elaboration of this 'field of conflict', but also rapidly transcended it, with the visible emergence of something resembling a labour movement, or at least an organized and militant culture of protest, by the later 1890s. Wage questions—which I described in the Introduction as the 'great unthought' of factory labour regulation—were at the centre of this transformation. Retrospectively, then, we can see the 1890s as a period that ushered in patterns of industrial confrontation and working-class action which were to pervade the future of Bombay's textile industry, till its demise in the 1980s.

International Regulation, Factory Legislation, and the Tensions of Capital

By the mid-1880s, the cotton-mill industry in Bombay was apparently characterized by unstoppable growth. Thirty-eight new mills were built in the course of the 1880s. By 1890, seventy mills operated in Bombay city, employing over 59,000 people.[1] Frenetic mill-building, which characterized the early years of the textile industry, slowed down subsequently, as Bombay's mill owners focused more on extending existing plants, making technological improvements, and swelling individual units. The number of workers, however, continued to rise.[2]

To a substantial extent, the growth of the mill industry was based on Bombay's growing influence in the markets for yarn and piece goods in China and Japan. By the end of the 1880s, Bombay had largely displaced the UK in Far Eastern yarn markets, and the growth of composite spinning and weaving units promised future ascendancy in the piece goods markets as well.[3] Periods of turbulence and uncertainty, however, punctuated this growth, necessitating new, if temporary, capitalist and managerial strategies. In long-term historical retrospect, these appear little more than ripples on the surface of continuous growth. However, these crises had tangible, if ambivalent, consequences for the texture and trajectory of industrial relations in Bombay.

China, which generated most of the demand for Bombay yarn, was a buoyant market but, often, less than reliable. In 1878–9, according to Moylan, the Boiler Inspector, the market was overstocked, and this induced some mills to reduce working hours and others to suspend production entirely.[4] In 1883, which the annual meeting of the Bombay Millowners' Association (BMOA) for that year characterized as the worst since the founding of the industry, the export of yarn fell from 312,000 to 298,000 bales. For the first time since the period of mill expansion that had commenced at the end of the 1870s, mill owners were compelled to collectively discuss the possibility of closing mills regularly on a weekly basis. They resolved not to work their mills on Sundays, a decision which was rescinded early in 1884.[5] The question of a weekly holiday for Bombay's millworkers, already on the anvil of legislative debate, briefly came to the forefront. James Jones, Factory Inspector for Bombay, optimistically observed in a report to the Bombay government that 'in a very short time, owners and agents will see it to their advantage, from a monetary point of view, to give their hands one day's rest in seven and I hope they will take the initiative and ask for legislation in this direction'.[6]

In early 1885, as a consequence of the Sino-French war, Bombay's exports suffered yet again. The closing of several ports, including Hong Kong, as a result of diplomatic pressure exerted upon Britain by China, coupled with a sharp spike in the prices of raw cotton, hurt the cotton trade, as stocks of yarn and cloth piled up in the mills. Once again, following an emergency meeting convened in March, mill owners decided to close their mills one day in seven between April and December. In another letter to the government, Jones expressed the hope, once more, that, at the expiration of the period decided upon, mill owners would 'see it in their interest to institute a weekly holiday'.[7] Yet again, the resolution fell through in a matter of months because the end of the war restored the China market's former buoyancy.

Consider, also, the exports of piece goods to China and Japan between 1877 and 1891 as an index of the micro-convulsions that shook the textile industry in its earliest years of growth and prosperity:

TABLE 5.1 Exports of piece goods to China and Japan, 1877–1891

Year	Exports to China and Japan (in yards)
1877	14,400
1878	1,612,862
1879	374,040
1880	2,022,685
1881	173,389
1882	749,951
1883	2,754,723
1884	1,795,849
1885	3,717,649
1886	2,988,890
1887	2,589,240
1888	15,892,009
1889	2,017,197
1890	3,684,374
1891	6,102,250

Source: Figures adapted from *Annual Report of BMOA*, 1891.

The fits and starts of the piece goods market in the Far East echoed the uneven and jagged development of the weaving units of mills till the end of the nineteenth century: the early Bombay mills, between 1854 and the early 1870s, tended to be composite spinning and weaving units, but the imbalance in the demand levels for yarn and piece goods in Bombay's principal markets, and the rivalry between the handloom sector and the mill sector of textile production, subsequently produced a preponderance of units that only spun cotton. Nevertheless, it is possible to mark a very precise shift in the fortunes of the cotton industry from 1888, the year in which piece goods (and yarn) from Bombay glutted the China market, leading to a plunge in demand levels, which could perhaps have been remedied in the coming years, but was intensified, in the 1890s, with a currency crisis that drove the Bombay mill industry into the doldrums.

In June 1893, the Government of India, as a step away from the silver standard, closed the Indian mints to the free coinage of gold and silver, stripping Indian mills of their major source of protection against Lancashire, the depreciating price of metal.[8] This intensified the depression the textile industry was already facing with the volatility of the Chinese market. Exchange rates collapsed in the wake of the currency regulations and yarn exports fell again in 1893.

The crisis that began in 1888 marked another round of collective strategy-making from the mill owners, and the Committee of the Bombay Millowners' Association made much more concerted attempts to enforce short-time working. A regular stoppage of work—earlier the subject of experiment and debate—began to appear irresistible if a full-fledged crisis of production was to be avoided. In 1889, 1890, and 1891, the BMOA formulated stricter and more binding rules, eventually achieving general—though by no means universal—acquiescence from its individual members.[9] In some ways, the Factory Act of 1891 amounted to a legal recognition of the conjuncture within the industry. Factory inspectors and reformer-activists like Bengali and Lokhande seized upon this moment to press a demand that had been brewing since the early 1880s: a legally binding weekly holiday for all workers. For a brief period, then, the 'objective' needs of the textile industry and the desires of those who sought more far-reaching factory legislation converged.

It is significant, though, that it was not till 1891, its fifth sustained attempt at enforcing some kind of collective regulation of working hours, that the Committee of the BMOA could pronounce itself satisfied with the results of the 'short-time movement' which it had enjoined upon its members. Fifty-nine out of the sixty-six mill owners and agents of Bombay voted for a measure which, in accordance with similar experiments the preceding two years, enforced two days of rest a week. The yarn markets in China were 'exceptionally depressed', and the Association found it 'gratifying to observe how strictly these terms were adhered to, quite unprecedentedly'.[10]

Working mills short-time, and perhaps even regularizing a weekly holiday, may seem perfectly logical choices within the frameworks of capitalist rationality, but the structures of control in Bombay's mills were geared against such choices, at least by individual mills. This was, as most contemporary observers noticed, at least partly the result of the commissions that mill agents enjoyed on the production, rather than the profits, of the concerns they managed. It was the direct relationship between labour-time and commissions, rather than profitability, which dictated managerial decisions for the most part. In the early history of Bombay's cotton textile industry, therefore, we find a near-ceaseless tussle between organized 'collective' capital, in the form of the BMOA, and the decisions made by most individual mills.

Factory legislation was the terrain upon which this dilemma found (temporary) resolution. In the late 1880s, the case for extending the scope of Indian factory legislation was reopened. In the first place, this was fed by James Jones' farewell report on Bombay's mills, which I have alluded to in the third chapter. Jones, in his report, referred to the long hours and the absence of regularized holidays in factories; the dangers from machinery confronting workers and the 'incompetency of mill managers'; the ill-ventilated and insanitary condition of many workrooms; and the withholding of wages from millhands.[11] This triggered off a fresh round of debate: questions were raised in the House of Commons about working hours in Indian factories in 1888, and the India Office, upon Parliamentary pressure, requisitioned full reports on the working of the Factories Act from the Government of India.[12] After prolonged correspondence over the next three years, a new Factory Act was passed in 1891, restricting the labour of women to eleven hours, redefining the legal limits of childhood (workers between nine and fourteen, rather than twelve, were to be considered 'children'), and abolishing Sunday labour.[13]

Two principal lines of force fed into this enactment. The first was a pan-European move towards the standardization of labour codes. This took the form of an International Labour Conference at Berlin in the second half of March 1890. 'Plenipotentiaries'—ministers, administrators, factory inspectors, and prominent businessmen—were appointed by the governments of Great Britain, Germany, Austria-Hungary, France, Denmark, Italy, Luxembourg, the Netherlands, Portugal, Switzerland, Sweden, and Norway. Separate commissions of enquiry were set up over these two weeks to consider the formulation of a common code of rules.[14] The implicit contexts of such an internationalization—or at least Europeanization—of the 'labour question' were spelt out lucidly by the President of the Conference, Baron von Berlepsch (the German Minister of Commerce and Industry):

> The labour question calls for the attention of all civilized nations, since the peace of the different classes appears to be threatened by strife resulting from industrial competition.... All European states, in face of this question, are in a similar or identical situation, and this analogy alone seems to justify the experiment of bringing about an agreement among the various Governments to obviate the common dangers by the adoption of general measures of prevention.[15]

The conference succeeded in drawing up the first systematized international principles of labour regulation: compulsory Sunday closing; the regulation of mining labour; the restriction of the work of women and young persons' (between fourteen and sixteen); and the prohibition of work for those below twelve years of age.[16] This raised two problems for the British delegation. The first worry flowed from the durable fiction that grounded the tradition of British factory regulation, the 'liberty of adult male workmen to work as long as they please', as James Fergusson, writing to a British delegate on behalf of Salisbury (then Prime Minister) put it.[17] British officials were clearly, at this stage (and later) far more reluctant to impose rules upon the use of adult male labour than their counterparts in other European countries.

The second worry involved the generalization of these principles in an imperial context, principally in India. It is perhaps no coincidence that the head of the British delegation to Berlin was Sir John Gorst, Under-secretary of State for India.[18] As a telegram from the India Office to the Viceroy put it, in February 1891, the resolutions of the Berlin Conference 'have great weight with Her Majesty's Government', and—in contrast to the 1881 Act—imperial pressure behind the revision of Indian factory law was persistent and decisive.[19] Unlike 1881, again, the BMOA, beset with the problem of controlling working hours in a time of over-production, did not oppose the *fact* of legislation. The Association's worry was expressed in more Aesopian terms: the Factory Act, 'it is to be hoped, in the interests of employers and employed alike, will prove the termination of legislative interference with the manufacturing industry for many years to come'.[20] The precise contours of this worry had already been expressed by the Madras Chamber of Commerce in 1888:

> The Chamber does not deprecate legislation on the subject; but it submits that such legislation should be guided, not by the desire to procure uniformity with similar legislation in England, so much as by an enlightened perception of what is conducive to the welfare of this country irrespective of the demands of competing interests.[21]

This referred, of course, to Lancashire. In November 1888, the Manchester Chamber of Commerce had passed a resolution to the effect that the British Factory Acts should be explicitly extended to cover India.[22] In 1890, the Blackburn Chamber of Commerce took up the battle, pointing to the discrepancies between factory conditions in India and England, and calling for an equalization enforced by law: 'There should not be one law for England and another for India, but ... the Indian operatives should receive in full the same protection which is granted to their fellow-operatives in England.'[23] To buttress this claim, the Blackburn Chamber furnished a table describing these discrepancies, as they compared the hours worked by factory labourers in England and India. They pointed out glaring gaps: adult women worked an average of ten hours in the former as compared to eleven in the latter; the same discrepancy characterized the working hours of 'young persons' between fourteen and eighteen; twelve- to fourteen--year-olds worked eleven hours in India and only five in Britain; children between ten and twelve worked nine and five hours respectively; and children between nine and ten worked nine hours in India, whereas their labour was prohibited in Britain.[24]

Lancashire's tender solicitude for Indian workers was, of course, self-serving. Nevertheless, the consequences it triggered cannot be reduced to the 'selfishness' of its motivations. Most dramatic, perhaps, was the Blackburn Chamber's demand, made in 1890, that workers should be systematically quizzed about their views on the hours they worked.[25] Richard Assheton Cross, the Secretary of State for India (and also, significantly, the person responsible for the revision of labour legislation in Britain in the 1870s), subsequently wrote to the Viceroy, Lansdowne, asking that the views of factory operatives be taken into account before enacting fresh legislation for them.[26] A new Factory Commission was set up, based *entirely* on interviews with millhands, and it was from the ruminations of this body, which I consider later in this chapter, that a new enactment sprang. The elevation of the worker's voice to a position of authority in matters concerning his well-being, then, was at least in part an ironic outcome of inter-capitalist competition within an imperial frame.

In 1892, as it became clear that the Government of India was not prepared to consider yet another revision of the Factory Act, Lancashire's mill owners conceded defeat. The terms in which they phrased this are revealing: at the annual meeting of the Blackburn Chamber of Commerce, they regretfully admitted that the 'indifference of the public and general apathy of working-class leaders in Lancashire, Cheshire and Yorkshire' had blocked the campaign for further factory legislation in India.[27] This admission discloses the principal purpose of Lancashire's agitations—the construction of a stable Other, in the form of the competition from Bombay's mills, that workers and employers in Britain would have to contend with in alliance, setting aside their own industrial disputes. This explanatory displacement of an emerging terrain of class conflict on to inter-capitalist competition failed, and this failure, perhaps, was of some consequence for the fractious relations that were to characterize British industry at the end of the century.

Such a trajectory, however, was not confined to Britain. A very similar relationship—between industrial confrontation and discursive strategies that construed 'industry' as a place of harmonious relations disrupted only by external machinations—was emerging in Bombay at the same time. Much as in Britain, though in the context of an emergent rather than well-established industrial capitalism, Bombay witnessed significant shifts in industrial politics in the late 1880s and early 1890s. It is necessary to avoid an over-schematic rendering of these politics, and in the following section I shall trace their dynamics through a narration of two sequences through which the lineaments of a 'labour question' were made visible. One of these flowed directly from the decision to extend factory legislation in 1891 and took the form of a polemical confrontation over the theme of regulation, centrally involving the exertions of K.N. Bahadhurji, a uniquely talented campaigner who set himself at the service of the mill industry and its employers. The second, which involved the emergence of a specific *style* of labour advocacy ('agitation', to use the parlance of the times), had its roots in developments in the 1880s and was marked by the ascendancy of N.M. Lokhande, often seen—reductively if not entirely wrongly—as the 'father' of the labour movement in Bombay.

Struggles over Representation

K.N. Bahadhurji and the Mill Women of Ahmedabad

By the end of the 1880s in Bombay, the principle of factory legislation itself had won more generalized acceptance, but its limits were more than ever a matter of contestation and anxiety. A new, or at least substantially modified, political terrain emerged. Berlin had placed the necessity for comprehensive factory legislation across national borders squarely on the agenda, and Lancashire's capitalists responded, in a strategically intelligent move, by raising the stakes of the debate: they presented themselves as the legitimate spokesmen for Indian workers, who 'have no idea as yet of combining to further their own interests'.[28] The response to this, from Bombay's mill owners, was a shrill, anxious reiteration of the impossibility of a common standard and the unfairness of such universality, the brunt of which would have to be borne by the Indian worker. The spokesmen of Lancashire and Bombay both, therefore, had to clamber on to the ground of workers' interests to sustain their programmes.

None of these themes were new in themselves; the form of their articulation, however, was. In July 1891, Lancashire and Bombay confronted each other in London at the International Congress of Hygiene and Demography, where there was a special session on Indian factory labour. The propagandist for further legislation was Holt S. Hallett, formerly an official of the Public Works Department in Burma.[29] Hallett was in the process of constructing, in alliance with Lancashire's spokesmen, a vigorous campaign for the extension of British factory law to India. This took the form of a series of articles in the *Times*, which reached a crescendo in a long presentation at the conference in July.

Hallett's speech was filled with details of the abominable conditions in Indian factories: dark unventilated workrooms where the windows were blocked by bags, unguarded machinery that snapped up lives and limbs, the ubiquity of disease and the wasting of working bodies, and working days beginning with a trek to the mill at 3 a.m. All this detail grounded a plea for the immediate marriage of Indian factory legislation to British precedent, in a much more thoroughgoing manner than the Act of 1881 had achieved.[30] An objectively accurate picture of working conditions, based upon the copious evidence produced by factory inspectors and medical men in Bombay, was pressed into the service of the imperial generalization of factory law, and of a struggling metropolitan industry.

Hallett's enemy was K.N. Bahadhurji, a brilliant young physician practising in Bombay, who took up cudgels on behalf of Bombay's mill owners. Bahadhurji was the first Indian to obtain the degree of Doctor of Medicine at London in 1884 and was subsequently associated with the Indian National Congress.[31] These details suggest the growing importance of professional, especially medical, expertise in the adjudication of factory relations. They also provide an early instance of the association of mill owner–friendly discourses with incipient nationalism.

Bahadhurji was initially deputed to the conference by the Government of India, but the deputation was withdrawn at the last minute, following which he accepted an invitation from the BMOA to counter the allegations Hallett was expected to make. He performed this task skilfully, contemptuously dismissing Hallett's accusations of overwork and his dramatic depictions of Bombay's dark satanic mills. Indian workers, he argued, worked 'according to their customs and natural inclinations', and it was 'fruitless to go against the traditional ways of the Indian'. A cultural explanation of this was forthcoming: the Indian worker was not 'habituated' to continuous work within limited hours on the English model; his interminable working day sufficed, rather, as a pleasantly organized life-world where relaxed and intermittent work was interspersed with rest, leisure, and enjoyment. 'To expect the mind and muscle of the Indian operative to work like those of the English mill-hand,' declaimed Bahadhurji sententiously, 'would be to go against natural laws for the purposes of factory legislation. One might as well think of exacting from a hack buggy horse the spirit, the speed, and the work, of a race-horse.'[32]

In other words, the Indian millhand more or less did everything but work. Bahadhurji told a Panglossian tale of Bombay factory work, and his horse metaphor perhaps reveals more than his patently disingenuous narrative. At the same time, his description contained a moment of truth: observers of Bombay's mills often remarked, with perplexity, the apparent control workers could exercise over their own time. This was, to a substantial extent, the effect of the structure of relations inside the mill, where a relatively flexible pattern of work partly compensated for long hours. Bahadhurji's stratagem was to render all this in cultural and racial terms.

Bahadhurji basked in the adulation of Bombay's mill owners, addressing a special meeting held in his honour after his return where he recounted his triumphant rebuttal of Hallett's propaganda.[33] A Factory Act was looming, though, and the ideological and practical battles were far from over. Bahadhurji now turned his attention more concretely to the conditions of mill work, and attempted to build a plausible campaign that would limit the effects of factory legislation and would be more concerned with genuine grievances felt by millworkers. His opportunity came towards the end of the year.

At the margins of the Act's operation, the limitation of working hours was received with suspicion and open hostility. Events in late 1891 and early 1892 illustrated the Act's less-than-welcome consequences for certain categories of women involved in mill work. Historically, as Chandavarkar has pointed out, the effect of factory legislation was to first limit, and then, from the 1920s, drastically reduce the numbers and proportion of women working in the factories notified under the Act.[34] At the same time, as Upadhyay has observed, it was not until the 1920s that the proportion of women employed in the textile industry began to decline perceptibly. This can be connected to attempts to realize in practice normative ideas of a male breadwinner and the massive extension of protective labour legislation.[35]

In Bombay itself, as in several other parts of the Presidency, women inhabited separate enclaves of employment, their work being mostly confined to reeling and winding, which conversely were domains of work entirely filled by female labour.[36] While factory inspectors and other observers expressed apprehensions of a general excision of women from the industrial labour market, this does not seem to have been the result in most places. Women occupied an ambivalent position within the labour market for the cotton mills. Their wages were low, their proportion always limited to around a quarter of the total working population, and their commitments lighter than those of the male operatives employed at the machines, though this relative lightness was more than counterbalanced by domestic commitments. They usually left work earlier than men, and, for the most part, fell comfortably short of the upper work limit—eleven hours a day—prescribed by the Factory Act of 1891.[37]

At Ahmedabad, however, which was one of the fastest-growing cotton manufacturing towns in the Presidency, conditions of employment were significantly different. Here, a third of the workforce consisted of women. Workers in Ahmedabad, more than in Bombay, were wholly reliant on mill work for an income. Women in the Ahmedabad mills worked on the same machinery as men, in the spinning rooms; they inhabited the same labour market as men and could be replaced by them.[38] Here, the Factory Commissioners had been told by managers that women would be dismissed from their work if a Factory Act limiting their hours of work were to be enforced.[39] One of the mill managers, a Parsi named Sorabji Dinshaw Karaka, had written pieces in the local press about the suffering inflicted on the women by the threat of unemployment.[40] The women interviewed at the mills gave ambivalent answers, indicating that they felt overworked and would like shorter hours, but that they felt that the choice was between work and starvation.

The Commission took note of the circumstances of the Ahmedabad mill industry in its report, where it noted that 'the law supposed to be passed for their benefit will inflict serious permanent injury on these skilled mill hands and deprive them of the chances of earning a living in these factories, as they will be replaced by men, the difference in the wages between male and female operatives being very small'.[41]

It was a group of women working in the Ahmedabad mills who most articulately attacked the consequences of legislation. They organized a campaign against the eleven-hour rule and enlisted the services of Bahadhurji.[42] The *Times of India* noted: 'Dr Bahadhurjee has certainly recently scored, for the female mill-hands of Ahmedabad made a direct appeal to him to try and obtain for them exemption of the eleven-hour rule.'[43] At the end of December 1891, Bahadhurji forwarded a petition signed by the women to the Government of India.[44] It is not possible to ascertain the extent of Bahadhurji's actual involvement with the making of the petition. However, there was, certainly, a temporary convergence of interests, which Bahadhurji was quick to capitalize on.

Bahadhurji's own concern with the effects of the Factory Act in Ahmedabad dated back at least till September, when he had written a letter to the *Times* describing the perils of women's unemployment, deploring the effects that factory legislation would have upon them.[45] In December, writing to the Government of Bombay, he amplified his arguments: the Berlin conference had laid down rules that allowed exemptions from its principles; a special exception should be made, therefore, for the mill women of Ahmedabad.[46]

In their petition to the government, received a month before the Factory Act was due to come into force, the women mobilized by Bahadhurji testified that 'protection' would, indeed, throw them out of employment. They all worked, they said, on machines run by steam power: the drawing, slubbing, intermediate and roving frames in the card room, and the winding frames in the weaving department. Further, 'the production of the spinning machines and of looms depends on the regular working of the frames in charge of your Lordship's petitioners'.[47] Faced, therefore, with a choice between working the whole mill for shorter hours because of the stopped frames, and dismissing the women to replace them with male workers who were not bound by an eleven-hour rule, mill owners would naturally choose the latter option.

This would happen, the petition pointed out, to women 'who have learnt the art of working the machinery with a great deal of trouble and lapse of time, and some of them know no other profession, and if they were turned out of the mill, they will be actually starved to death'.[48] The price of grain, especially wheat and bajra, said the signatories, was three or four times more expensive 'than what it was in former years', but they were 'very thankful to God that mill industry is introduced here by which thousands of poor people are able to earn their bread with comparative ease'. They assured the government that 'they are not overworked and they don't feel unhappy as they are', and the choice for them, starkly, was between 'happy livelihood or bitter starvation'.[49]

The government, however, was unbending. On 1 January, the day the Act came into force, the Government of India wrote to Bombay, stating the impossibility of exemption. The *Indian Textile Journal* noted the consequences of this: a large number of women were dismissed;

others were either employed on less remunerative work (such as reeling) or converted into half-timers at halved wages; many took to begging. Some hired themselves out as labourers at wages approximating a third of what they made at mill work, and some, noted the journal with delicate disdain, 'have fallen into a state of immorality which cannot be touched on in a publication'.[50]

The episode of the exclusion of the Ahmedabad mill women speaks with force of the tensions and ambiguities within the operations of factory law, and also within the emerging politics of labour, mediated by spokesmen who derived their authority both from workers and from official recognition. It made visible some of the polarities of interest that ran through the industrial working class of the Presidency, constituted as a unit by law in an uneasy and artificial way that concealed widely divergent priorities and needs. Gender and place combined: the unique and isolated position of the Ahmedabad mill women rendered them vulnerable to the exclusionary possibilities of the Act, materialized in this episode. It also laid the ground for Bahadhurji's remarkable campaign, which demonstrated the fluid significations that 'the cause of labour' could acquire in the political battleground of factory legislation.

Lokhande

Nevertheless, a campaign for enhanced legislative protection *had* emerged with force in the mid-1880s, and it had managed, to a substantial extent, to dominate the field. At the centre of this was the Satyashodhak reformer Narayan Meghaji Lokhande. Bahadhurji, in a banquet organized in his honour by the BMOA in 1892, accused Lokhande of being in cahoots with Holt Hallett in a conspiracy against the industry.[51] In a negative way, this attests to Lokhande's importance in the incipient field of industrial politics in the 1880s.

In the 1880s and early 1890s, Lokhande became an increasingly vocal representative of the interests of mill labour before the colonial state. He was the unelected leader of the Bombay millhands, the editor of the one paper professing commitment to their interests, and organizer of the one association bearing their name. Lokhande's rise indicates certain subtle and important political shifts in the course of the 1880s and 1890s. Who could legitimately claim the authority to speak for a new class of labouring people, for a new form of social life? How was this legitimacy to be tested? This was the polemical battleground upon which Lokhande intervened.

Born in 1848 to a poor *phulmali* family that lived in Thane on the outskirts of Bombay, selling vegetables, fruits, and flowers, Lokhande rose to intermediate positions in the mill industry.[52] Between 1875 and 1884, according to his testimony before the 1884 Factory Commission, he worked at the Morarji Goculdas, the Hindustan, and the Mandvi Mills. He served as a store supervisor at the first two and rose to the position of manager's assistant in the third.[53]

At the age of twenty-six, around the same time that he entered the mill industry, Lokhande also entered the world of Bombay's lower-caste social agitation, joining Jyotirao Phule's Satyashodhak Samaj. In 1880, he became the editor of its popular and widely circulated weekly newspaper, the *Din Bandhu*. He edited the paper for seventeen years, till his death in the plague epidemic of 1897. As Gail Omvedt has observed, Bombay, despite boasting one of the earliest Satyashodhak branches and the newspaper office, had a relatively slack and weak non-Brahmin movement.[54] This weakness, while detrimental to the overall cause of egalitarian social mobilization, may well have spurred Lokhande and his associates into deeper involvements with the labour question than would otherwise have been possible.

These circumstances allowed Lokhande to reshape *Din Bandhu* into a 'Journal in the Interests of the Working Classes'. The *Din Bandhu*'s intransigent attacks upon the practices of Bombay's factory employers set the paper and Lokhande, quite early, against the tide of the nationalism that was beginning to grow within vernacular journalism.[55] Lokhande's principal social commitments to the cause of lower-class uplift through the Satyashodak Samaj also set his politics against the incipient (upper-class and higher-caste) nationalism of the time.

This objective opposition of interests may have been politically significant: it may have attracted the attention of government authorities and factory inspectors looking for possible allies in the campaign to extend factory legislation. Whatever the truth of the matter, Lokhande managed, in a short period of time, to simultaneously claim the leadership of a campaign that involved mass mobilization among millworkers, and to endear himself enough to the colonial state to become a specially appointed expert in 1890.

Lokhande's rise to an influential position as public advocate, however, was grounded in a decade-long experience which it might be appropriate to briefly survey here. This experience was inextricably linked with the development of debates around factory legislation. In 1881, just a few months after the passage of the first Factory Act, Lokhande, still employed in the mill industry, seems to have made a concerted attempt to set himself up as an intermediary between employers and workers, speaking for the latter's interests. Drawing attention to the indebtedness and economic insecurity faced by millworkers, he set out a scheme for lending money to them at low rates of interest, thereby reducing their dependence on 'Marwaree' moneylenders.[56] He also suggested a scheme for the supply of cheap foodgrains to workers. Both these schemes, however, foundered upon the same rock—they required not only the willingness but also the active participation of mill owners: Lokhande suggested that they supervise these initiatives and take responsibility for their functioning. He himself would carry out the necessary work, but under their aegis. As with all schemes aimed to secure the social reproduction of the workforce before the late 1890s, this fell through, since employers were not at this stage willing to invest any attention and, more to the point, money in such matters. It is not unreasonable to speculate that this early disappointment may have deepened and radicalized Lokhande's critique of mill employers and the cotton industry.

As early as 1884, he was given considerable time and space to air his views before the Factory Commission. Here we find Lokhande rehearsing a role he would play repeatedly over the next decade, as one of the Bombay government's chosen interlocutors on the question of factory regulation. In this respect, his 'agitation' resembled that of S.S. Bengali's over the preceding decade. However, unlike his predecessor's meliorism, Lokhande's activism had teeth, since it drew upon active mobilization among workers. In 1884, Lokhande set up a Millhands' Association, the first quasi-formal organization set up in the Presidency that claimed to directly represent the interests of industrial workers.[57] The Association organized two mass meetings of millhands, on 23 and 26 September 1884, each attended by over 5,000 workers.[58] These were the first public meetings ever held by Bombay's millworkers. They evoked some consternation in business circles, and the *Jam-e-Jamshed* warned direly of the influence of 'interested parties', and threatened dire consequences for millworkers should they carry their agitation 'beyond legitimate bounds'.[59] A petition to the Factory Commission resulted from this initiative, and this was far from accidental. The three mill jobbers interviewed by the Commission—all of them involved in Lokhande's movement—made this clear. While the Millhands' Association had been meeting monthly over the previous year, they told the Commissioners, the giant public meetings in September were designed chiefly to pressurize the Commission into recommending legislative intervention. The chief burden of this agitation was the restriction of the hours of work for all workers by the institution of a compulsory weekly holiday, clearly spelt out opening and closing times for each mill, and a general working day between 6.30 a.m. and sunset.[60]

The petition also made direct reference to the burdens shared by workers as a class—the staggered payment of wages and the resultant chronic indebtedness, long working hours preventing them from 'attending to their household duties', physical enfeeblement as a consequence of incessant labour, abandonment to the consequences of sickness and accident. It sought, in a sense, to universalize the intimations of weakness and vulnerability that law had already recognized and named in the figures of working children. The 'agitation'—as the mass meetings and petition were designated by the Factory Commissioners—reveals, at this juncture, something like a virtuous circle between discussions over the amendment of factory legislation on the one hand, and Lokhande's mobilizations among workers on the other. The former provided the rationale for the latter; the latter extended the potential horizons of the former.

Lokhande's ascendancy marked an important shift: the authority he claimed as millworkers' spokesperson was substantially different from the authority sought by meliorist-activists from the 1870s like Bengali. These men spoke as 'concerned citizens'; in other words, as respectable, elite men speaking as public figures, but in their capacity as private, concerned individuals. Lokhande came from a subaltern background: at the same time, his enthusiasm for social intervention by the state outstripped that of Bengali and the *Rast Goftar*. The latter retained certain proto-nationalist preoccupations (Bengali himself was also one of the most articulate critics of imperial tariff policy) and, thus, retained a certain scepticism about colonial diktat.[61] Lokhande straddled two worlds: the world of mass political activism, a new phenomenon upon the urban stage of Bombay, and the world of political gradualism, supplication, and petitioning. Throughout his campaigns in the 1880s, he managed to inhabit both worlds successfully, and led a campaign that enjoyed material success in the form of a shortened working week.

The form of his campaigns—mass meetings, petitions, letters to the government, charters of demands, press reportage—indicates a key shift in political mobilization around workers' questions. Older traditions and techniques of agitation were forced, as a result of the growing visibility of millworkers upon the urban scene, to accommodate mass demands, to speak for large collectivities of people who were not ratepayers or, formally speaking, citizens. New strains, therefore, entered what was essentially a formal civic politics dominated by the propertied, by merchants, manufacturers, and professionals.[62]

Lokhande boasted a personal experience of mill work that gave his claim to 'expertise' a value that outstripped other opinions. Since this was an expertise that claimed direct and intimate experience of the conditions of working-class employment and life, it supplemented the investigations of factory inspectors. If Bengali, in the public life of Bombay, frequently assumed the authority of a legislator, of one whose decisions made things happen, Lokhande played a role akin to that of the investigator, the inspector, bringing the concealed and dirty truth to light. He used the limited public sphere that was open to him skilfully, publicizing and amplifying the opinions offered by workers, mobilizing his knowledge of workers' conditions to make coherent demands for finite measures of amelioration. At the same time, he adhered to formal and ritualized modes of dispute, using legitimate, recognized techniques to press for concrete and modest ends.

The year 1884 was a relatively turbulent one in a torpid half-decade. In June, three months prior to the formation of the Association and the mass meetings of millworkers, a mill strike broke out in Kurla, principally over Sunday work, which I investigate at length in the next section of this chapter. S.S. Bengali seized upon this in his campaign to extend factory law. Bengali placed a copy of a report of the strike in his *Rast Goftar* before the Factory Commission in August 1884.[63] The Commission eventually recommended a weekly holiday on Sundays for women and children, but refused to recommend direct intervention in the working hours of adult men.[64] Bengali and Blaney, who were the only dissenting voices on the Commission, argued in vain that Bombay's industrialization, based on the preponderance of migrant male labour, was significantly different from that which operated in Britain's factory districts and towns, where women constituted a much larger proportion of the factory workforce. Given this national difference in the composition of the workforce, they argued, men ought to be engrossed within a general law that instituted a compulsory weekly holiday.[65]

The renewed campaign for factory legislation in 1884 failed. In a public sphere where Lokhande was a major force, however, these demands were amplified, and they gathered force. The *Din Bandhu*, through the course of the 1880s, stood at a sharp angle to the rest of the press in Bombay, replacing the *Rast Goftar* as the principal organ for the expression of demands made on behalf of industrial workers. It also boasted a considerable circulation, turning over more than a thousand copies a month on a regular basis.[66]

Between 1889 and 1890, Lokhande constructed another astute political campaign, blending public meetings, petitioning, statements to official investigatory bodies, intermediation between workers and state officials who sought their opinions, and negotiations with mill owners into a coherent set of regulatory demands. The campaign began in the aftermath of the crisis in the Far Eastern markets in 1889, when mill owners instituted, across a large number of mills, a compulsory eight-day break in the month, an unprecedented move that amounted to a strike by capital. Lokhande appears to have marshalled his resources carefully in preparation for a repetition of the same strategy from the mill owners the following year. The result was a petition from the Millhands' Association in October 1889, which did not directly raise the issue of the mill closures and the hardships they caused, but, instead, demanded a permanent weekly holiday enshrined by law.[67]

The effects of the sudden plunge in demand continued to make themselves felt; mill owners responded in 1890 with another sustained recourse to the eight-day stoppage, and the Millhands' Association confronted this with a huge demonstration, of over 10,000, on the Mahalakshmi Race Course, a central location.[68] Lokhande followed this up with a letter to the Secretary of the Millowners' Association, asking that the BMOA concede the millhands' demand for a weekly holiday and that they discontinue the mill closures since they were cutting into the workers' incomes and producing economic hardship.[69]

John Marshall, the Secretary, wrote back telling Lokhande that the stoppages would continue. The millworkers' demonstration and the indication of their emergence as an organized political formation, however, seem to have impressed the mill owners, who tacitly conceded the principle of a compulsory weekly day of rest by committing themselves to giving their workers Sunday off and allocating two hours on Saturday for the cleaning of machinery—precisely, as it happens, the demands made by the Kurla strikers six years back.[70]

By the end of 1890, the reform of factory law was imminent. A sketchy code of universally applicable rules of work and rest had been formulated at Berlin, the cotton manufacturers of Lancashire had raised the demand for further restriction of working hours in Indian factories, questions had been raised in Parliament in 1888 and 1889, and the testimony of successive factory inspectors seemed to support the case for further legislation. Two shifts consequently took place: first, the Government of India belatedly reconsidered, with favour, the request for the extension of factory law made by the Bombay government in 1885. Second, Lokhande and his fledgling movement were elevated to the privileged position of 'official spokespersons of labour'.

Imperial pressure from above and activist pressure from below pressed into being, in October 1890, a Factory Commission presided over by a medical man, Surgeon-Major Lethbridge. Bengali sat on this Commission, and so did Lokhande, as an associate member for Bombay.[71] Lokhande's appointment was made possible, even necessary, by the terms under which the Commission was set up. These terms required the permanent Commissioners—Lethbridge, Bengali, and the Director of Land Records for the North-Western Provinces (NWP) and Oudh, Mir Mohammed Hussain—to consult the expertise of figures closely associated with mill labourers. Lokhande, thereby, reached the pinnacle of his influence. He supplied twelve witnesses, who were, we can infer from fragmentary traces, members of his Millhands' Association.[72]

Lokhande thus established himself as a crucial mediator between the government and the millworking population. Workers' testimonies were sought assiduously by the Factory Commission in 1890, a new departure in itself. The Factory Commissions of 1875 and 1884 had, quite openly, endorsed the primacy of the perspective of the mill business, the Commissioners largely being businessmen, and the perspectives of managers and businessmen quite clearly predominating over those of workers. The Commission of 1890 reversed the emphasis: all its ninety-six witnesses, interviewed across a whirlwind tour of Bombay, Ahmedabad, Kanpur, and Bengal in a month's time, were mill operatives, drawn from different wage and skill levels. Further, not one of the members of the Commission spoke for the interests of the mill industry.[73]

Lokhande was, then, in a situation strategically equivalent to that of a mill jobber, supplying labourers to the Commission to produce official knowledge. He was an industrious member, attending all but one of the eighteen meetings held by the Commission in Bombay and Ahmedabad. He used the Commission as a public space in which to elaborate the demands that his campaign, as crystallized in the Millhands' Association, had put forth in 1884 and 1889.[74] With this intervention, in a sense, Lokhande cemented his official position as public spokesperson on behalf of mill labour.

In a separate Opinion which he appended, as associate member, to the proceedings of the Factory Commission, Lokhande observed that, despite their assurance that mills would be closed every Sunday, the Millowners' Association had not enforced this, 'not a single mill-owner has acted up to it'.[75] These statements played a crucial role in plotting the trajectory of shortened working hours for all, including adult males, from the charters of workers' demands drawn up in public meetings and petitions to the statute books.

These testimonies (and Lokhande's gloss on them), in combination with the continued polemic in the *Din Bandhu*, made public a range of concealed and half-concealed practices of exploitation: the snatching of time from the half-hour allocated for daily rest in the mills, the physical deterioration induced by continuous, fatiguing work, and the absence of a weekly holiday. It was in the public statements made by the Millhands' Association that the industrial working class was politically constituted for the first time, as for the first time a collectively organized body of millworkers put forth demands as a unit.

The demands of 1889 repeated and elaborated those of 1884, and revolved essentially around the limitation of working hours. This consisted, in the first place, of the demand for a full day away from work, a holiday uninterrupted by the need to clean mill machinery, an unpaid duty which most mills forced on their workers.[76] Sunday, argued the petition, an argument followed up by Lokhande, was the day that most workers in other enterprises across British India were free from work, and so millworkers could meet their friends on Sunday if it was legally defined as a holiday.[77] A regular day of rest, the petition assured employers, 'would derive benefit by securing a body of healthier operatives'. It would also allow workers 'the much-needed opportunity of attending to their household duties for which they have no time at present, notably for making purchases in the market'.[78] The petition claimed that a glance at the muster rolls of most mills would confirm that a day's absence from work led to the docking of a day's pay, something confirmed later by most witnesses before the Factory Commission.[79]

One of the rhetorical claims sometimes made by advocates of factory regulation was that, given the current distress in the market, mill owners were closing their mills on Sunday in any case, and, in other cases, a legislative enactment would merely confirm what a number of mills practised in reality: weekly holidays. Lokhande made this argument in his replies to the Royal Commission on Labour in 1892, but it was disingenuous. Lokhande himself knew better. In his note to the Factory Commission, he accurately described the relations of power inside mills that such regulation as he called for would inevitably hurt: a situation in which employers were free to curtail and extend production at will, and workers were thereby abandoned to the vagaries of market demand and employer strategy. If the strike in the Kurla mills—and, as I shall show later, the testimonies of factory workers themselves—indicated anything, it was the existence of a discernible demand, from below, for regulation that was *not* achieved by the 'free negotiations of employers and employed', that was externally mediated, enforced by the public authority of a state, however unrepresentative. Such intervention was needed, argued the petition of 1889, to make public the voice of workers 'who are ill able to make themselves heard against the influential voice of their employers'.[80]

In addition, the petition demanded a universally applicable definition of the limits of daily mill work, suggesting the hours between 6.30 a.m. and sunset.[81] Half an hour's recess should also be made compulsory, argued the petition, the mills at present 'grudgingly' granting a recess that effectively consisted of no more than fifteen or twenty minutes, the remaining time being taken up by noon-day attendance verification, the timekeeper checking the workers' tickets.[82]

Lokhande made these demands the centre of his campaign for further factory regulation and expressed them articulately in his separate note to the Commission.[83] The Commission's own investigations disclosed the extent, but also the limit, of the grievances built around experiences of time-discipline in the mills. I briefly turn, now, to testimonies by individual workers that dramatized these experiences.

Ganesh Narayan Dewal was a weaver and spare jobber who was evidently higher placed socially than his fellow workers. Dewal knew English and was 'evidently qualifying to fill the higher posts in a cotton mill'.[84] Speaking from his experience in Jalgaon (in the district of Khandesh), a town where millworkers appear to have held monopolies over their positions and their wages, he said he believed that the wages of millworkers would not suffer if they were granted a weekly holiday.

> Our mill is not stopped even once a fortnight. The mill stops at 2 on Saturday for cleaning, and the operatives go at 3 or 4. On Sundays they work full-time. When they had much yarn lying in the factory, for two months the mill-owners of Jalgaon closed the mill of their own accord. During this time the millhands did not earn less wages, and they were very pleased with the holidays.[85]

The relations of employer and employed in a corner of the mill industry where there was no immediate threat to jobs seem to have been characterized, then, by customary wage rates not hurt by weekly holidays. At this end of the spectrum, the support for a weekly holiday was unqualified.

At the other end of the spectrum stood Tukaram Laximan, a piecer in the mule department at the Imperial Cotton Mill, who appears to have frustrated the Commissioners, who described him as 'dull and heavy-witted'.[86] He wanted his mill entirely shut on holidays, he said. At the same time, 'If it came to a distinction between wages and comfort, I want wages.' One of the questions the Commissioners asked all adult operatives was whether they would rather work in a mill that gave its workers regular holidays or none. Laximan answered that workers would prefer the latter, but then contradicted himself: 'How can I work all the year around without holidays?'[87]

These fumbling answers illustrate the difficulty of the choice most workers felt themselves confronted with, implicitly, when asked to consider the effects of a more inclusive regime of factory regulation upon their own conditions of work and life. The responses of many of those who testified before the Commission indicate, with a kind of rhetorical starkness, the bleak choices posed. A fifteen-year-old doffer at the New Great Eastern Mills said: 'I would prefer to work less hours and thus prolong my life.'[88] A young man working at the roving department of the Bombay United Mills said: 'We want it for our comfort, never mind the less pay.'[89] A worker at the Ahmedabad Spinning and Weaving Mills, anticipating the consequences of the legislative restriction of women's working hours by factory legislation, said: 'If the hours for women are shortened, the mill-owners will turn the women out and they will starve.'[90]

The ambiguities of this choice should not, however, obscure the fact that the workers interviewed by the Commission seem to have, by and large, accepted the premises and postulates of the campaign led by Lokhande, as also the proposal to institute fresh legal protection. Manawar, a warper at the Sassoon and Alliance Silk Mill, hesitated when he was asked to choose between more pay and a weekly holiday, and then chose the holiday.[91] Paroo Bai, a silk-winder at the same mill, was more assertive: she wanted to be able to leave work an hour before the men, like women in the cotton mills did, even if it meant a sacrifice of wages.[92] Despite the double threat posed to their earnings by the weekly holiday and the special legislation envisaged restricting their hours of work, most women interrogated by the Commissioners seem to have welcomed the prospect of a weekly holiday, as did most men. Sunday, they universally testified, was the day most convenient for making purchases in the market, as also to meet friends and relatives working in other occupations where a Sunday holiday was in force.[93]

Most workers also wanted a legislative definition of a general working day, applicable across mills, with fixed hours of work and fixed intervals of at least half an hour. As several workers observed, the half-hour nominally given by many mills was often consumed in attendance verification, and mill owners could vary the opening and closing of the mills at their will, send their workers away because of an early closure, or work them longer. A general working day, then, was conceived by workers as a form of protection against the arbitrariness of their employers.

There was a productivist strain that occasionally joined this line of argument: fixed and regulated hours of work, claimed the millhands' petition of 1889, would generate better and more productive labour for employers, besides renewing the physical energies of the workers.[94]

The testimonies of most individual workers, however, seem to have signalled a different horizon of needs: time away from work, respect for which was to be legally binding; time for renewal and recreation, a day of leisure they could claim as their own; and a working day that was slightly easier to negotiate, to feel a little less overwhelmed by because it obeyed fixed rules. Most of the workers testified that they wanted to spend the end of their Saturdays cleaning the machines so that they could have Sunday off. Against this, the rule in force in the majority of mills was unpaid machinery and mill-cleaning on Sundays.[95]

Through the medium of the Factory Commission, and with the mediation of Lokhande, workers were able to publicly articulate their demands. Their views became part of the rhetorical and real struggle over conditions of work. Lokhande and the Millhands' Association led the first organized campaign that both drew its arguments from the lived experiences of workers and rested upon active workers' support, something Lokhande courted also through his Chairmanship of a Night Schools' Association.

The Act of 1891 was, in content if not in form, shaped by the junction between social reform and workers' organization crystallized in the Millhands' Association. The campaign was, in its essence, an uneasy alliance between a workers' politics that was slowly acquiring its outlines and a philanthropic meliorism that the government drew upon as a source of expert opinion, embodied by activist figures and clusters. Lokhande's historical significance as a labour activist lies not in his actual influence, though this may not have been negligible, but in the fact that he fulfilled *both* roles—that of an often radical labour representative and that of a 'constructive' advisor to the government. In the 1890 Commission, we find him submitting chosen labourers and their testimonies to the scrutiny of the state and pressing, through the force of their testimonies, for the legislative intervention he and his organization had in mind. In 1892, in a remarkable testimony to the Royal Commission on Labour, he performed the same role, but this time in accents that were distinctly more radical.

This is an episode that displays Lokhande at his most politically creative, as a labour spokesman determined to 'speak truth to power', and also as a canny strategist. At the beginning of the year, Parliament set up a Royal Commission on Labour, the first of its kind, to conduct a general survey of labour conditions in Britain and across its Empire.

The bulk of the testimonies received by the Commission came from employers and government officials; Lokhande submitted written testimony that the government initially refused to forward. Lokhande, much like Bengali in 1878, deployed metropolitan assistance, in the form of Holt Hallett, clearly Lancashire's preferred spokesperson on the subject of Indian factory legislation. In November, upon imperial instruction, the Government of Bombay reluctantly submitted his replies to the Commission's questions, enclosing along with them two dissenting opinions, one from the Collector, James Campbell, and the other from A.M.T. Jackson, the Chief Inspector of Factories.

The terms of Campbell's discomfort with Lokhande's initiative are revealing. Lokhande could have, he complained, used the questionnaire directed at 'trades' unions' to furnish his opinion. Instead, he had chosen to fill in the form addressed to employers. Campbell's worry can be explained by the fact that it was the questions addressed to employers that touched most directly upon workplace relations. Lokhande, inserting his own—and the Millhands' Association's—opinion into this space, cleverly introduced a rift within the description of industrial and class relations furnished so far principally by employers and officials.[96] His opening remarks, deplored by Campbell as 'somewhat unsuitable', ran thus:

> The Association I represent is workers composed solely of poor millhands. The day seems distant when from among these poor operatives any 'employers' are likely to arise and found establishments for the class to which they owe their opulence. Many millhands are unwilling to be known as connected with our association for fear of losing their employment, so jealous are the employers of labour here of any combination among them for their mutual benefit.[97]

This was, in its very disavowal of effective authority, a claim to authentic representation. Mill owners' 'jealousy' was posited as the obstacle to a meaningful collectivity of workers, and the ironic comment about capitalists' relations with 'the class to which they owe their opulence' could not have failed to strike a radically discordant note within what had been originally a compilation of testimonies circling around questions of industrial control from a perspective dominated by employers. As against this, Lokhande produced an alternate truth about industrial relations by effecting an imperceptible twist in the terms of discourse.

Lokhande's evocations of the threatening spectre of industrial discontent were barely disguised. Mill owners unanimously denied the presence of strife, perhaps in order to forestall further imperial interference, but also in order to maintain a collective fiction of control in times that were increasingly fractious. Most of them denied that strikes were common; Lokhande, against this, submitted his opinion that 'the strikes are of frequent occurrence in every one of the mills in this city', lasting up to four days, usually on account of arbitrary wage reductions without prior notice.[98] Campbell's explanation was that Lokhande was referring to temporary, 'trivial' stoppages of work among 'a section of operatives', and that this practice 'does not affect the accuracy of the statement that any general stoppage ... is of very rare occurrence'.[99] Campbell was, indeed, more 'accurate' in his description, but Lokhande, in accentuating the centrality of class struggle at the heart of the industrial relationship in Bombay, expressed, as the strikes later in the year were to show, a deeper truth.

Lokhande offended on several other counts. He made the 'insinuation', as Jackson angrily termed it, that factory inspectors gave prior intimation of their visits to employers, a possibility that official archives never admit, but seems well within the institutional logic of factory legislation. He accused employers of neglecting the safety of their factories, argued that workers died early or aged and tired soon (attested, he claimed, by the rarity of elderly men working in the mills), proposed a uniform working day of eleven hours for all workers, and suggested that employers fired their workers at will.[100] Campbell and Jackson indignantly denied all of this.

Against this bleak picture of industrial relations, Lokhande sought to institute, in the form of binding rules, a structural paternalism within industrial relations. Fines levied on workers could be used for the purposes of a mill fund. Pension and insurance schemes could be worked out, as could 'cheap lodgings, shops, dispensaries and schools'. To which Campbell responded that 'arrangements of this class cannot either wisely or fairly be demanded by all the owners of mills', and that 'a beginning in such matters must be left to wealthy and independent mill owners'.[101] Campbell's model for such a figure was J.N. Tata, who had emerged through the 1880s as one of the more visionary of Bombay's mill owners, turning bankrupt mills into successful ventures and combining this with a dash of paternalist welfare.

Lokhande, then, simultaneously mounted a strong claim for representative authority on behalf of Bombay's millworkers, and for the construction of a new system of industrial relations. This was well within the digits of a putatively paternalist and mildly welfarist capitalism, but in the Bombay context it marked a demand for a radical break. Worried by Lokhande's rise, mill owners tried to mount an alternative claim to represent workers, explicitly directed against Lokhande and his politics. Bahadhurji frequently made contemptuous references to the *Din Bandhu*'s 'misguided' campaigns.[102] A more sustained campaign was launched by one of Bombay's most powerful industrialists, N.N. Wadia. Between 1889 and 1893, Wadia seems to have set himself up as a sort of shadow Lokhande. At the beginning of 1890, shortly after the Millhands' Association had delivered their petition to the Government asking for shortened working hours, Wadia mediated the passage of another petition to official attention. This was signed by over 17,000 operatives and contained the suggestion that, to avoid 'needless hardship on employers and employed alike', the Sunday following a 'native holiday' might be legally allowed to be a working day.[103] The polemical claim underlying this was clear: workers, in their thousands, sought not the further limitation of their working day but recognition of their right to maintain their earnings by working Sundays if necessary.

Lokhande, clearly sensitive to this challenge to his authority as public spokesperson, wrote to the Government, indignantly claiming that 'certain individuals interested in the Mill Industry at Bombay are endeavouring to obtain the Mill operatives' consent to a petition which from its tenor you will find does not represent their real wants and grievances in their entirety'.[104] He expressed, also, his fear that the mill owners would 'succeed by using coercion'. 'These interested individuals,' he went on, 'did not even succeed in calling a public meeting, and I am aware that the millhands have up to this time refused to give their signatures to the petition.'[105]

Taking note of the *rapprochement* between the campaigns mounted by Lancashire and those mounted on behalf of factory labourers by Lokhande, the business-friendly *Jam-e-Jamshed* launched an attack on Lokhande's credibility in November:

> Mr. Lokhande is said to be the President of the Textile Operatives' Association, but little is known in Bombay about the constitution of this Association, how many operatives have joined it, when the periodical

> and other meetings of this association are held.... There are in Bombay more than sixty thousand textile operatives, and if the Association is formed of so many as these it is undoubtedly an influential body, of which, however, little is heard except the assertion that Mr. Lokhande is its President.[106]

In a neat, probably unintended, riposte to Lokhande's claim that the mill owners had not succeeded in getting up a meeting against him, the paper asked, 'Was a meeting of the mill-hands convened to state their complaints?'[107]

Mill owners and their supporters in the press, then, questioned Lokhande's credentials on the basis of the shadowy, vague nature of his organization. This is a complaint that the historian of these years must repeat because the Millhands' Association *is* a shadowy figure in the archives, appearing as it does with a mass meeting and petition, then fading into a period of apparently total silence, and then reappearing—with another mass meeting and petition. Lokhande could clearly mobilize men and signatures at very short notice, which attests a real base, however limited, of collective support and organization. But what permanent, empirical strength could he demonstrate?

If we turn back to the Millhands' Association's earlier campaign in 1884, we may find some indications of the structural limits of Lokhande's activism. The fusion of mass mobilization and finite demands upon that Commission by the Association is best expressed in the selection of worker witnesses. Three workers who testified were involved in the agitation for factory reform, had attended Lokhande's meetings, and were perhaps chosen for the Commission by Lokhande himself. These three—Raghoo Bhikaji, Genoo Babaji, and Narayan Surkoji—were all employed as jobbers. As such, they occupied a relatively privileged position within their mills: they received more generous wages (ranging from Rs 60 to Rs 85 a month). Two of them were paid fixed monthly salaries, in contrast to the men who worked under them, who were mainly employed on piece-rates.[108] Their function as jobbers placed them in an intermediary position: they recruited and supervised labour as well as worked on the machines themselves.

However, at other levels their everyday experience did overlap with that of their subordinates. Genoo Babajee, mule jobber in the Empress Mills, for instance, observed, 'We have to start for the mill in the dark and sometimes we break our hands and legs.' He went on to show the

Commissioners his right hand, 'the first finger of which was cut off', and said, 'I lost this finger in the dark'.[109] It is clear from his testimony that, to a substantial degree, his twenty-eight years of mill experience trumped his present position as a jobber. 'I was 10 or 11 years of age when I commenced working in mills. I am all sick and all my limbs are aching. I am altogether broken to pieces and I shall soon die.' (This from a man in his late thirties.)[110] Narayan Surkoji, head jobber in the Anglo-Indian Mills, was (unlike Genoo Babaji) employed on a fixed monthly salary (Rs 85) rather than on piece work. He, too, however, complained of having to start work in the dark, of waking up at three in the morning to get to the mill. Outlining a grievance which would have explosive consequences in the following decade, he spoke of receiving his pay on the '26th, 27th, 28th, and even on the 1st of the second month after my wages are due'. This, as we shall see in detail in the following section and the last chapter of this book, produced an intractable experience of permanent indebtedness. For his part, Narayan Surkoji, who otherwise easily qualifies as part of Bombay's 'labour aristocracy' in this period, was in debt to the tune of Rs 200.[111]

Gender and caste, arguably, posed more durable barriers to organizational unity among millworkers than the fact of wage differentials, or even the division between jobbers and ordinary workers. The testimony of Sakoo (objectified in the Commission as 'the widow of the late Mahadoo'—clearly her most salient identification for the men interviewing her) provides some evidence of this. Sakoo was, at the time of the Commission's enquiries, working as overseer in the reeling department of the Colaba Mill on monthly wages of Rs 30–3 (about half the amount earned by her counterparts among male jobbers). Asked about her involvement in the September 1884 'agitation', she replied, 'I know there was a meeting of the operatives for the purpose of petitioning Government. We will do according to the wishes of those operatives who attended the meeting.... The women have not joined the agitation: they were not asked. If they had been, they would not have gone; they did not wish to go.'[112]

Gender hierarchies and separations at the workplace were clearly one part of the story here: Sakoo also spoke of her own unwillingness—and that of the women working under her supervision—to work alongside men. 'If I could not get employment in reeling I would not work with men; I would do needle-work.' Evidence as fragmentary as this is hard to generalize; however, it seems a reasonable speculation that such dispositions and constraints were part of the context for the monopoly of reeling and winding employment by women workers across the cotton industry. Sakoo went on to suggest that these constraints did not necessarily originate *within* the workplace, but were also framed by domestic determinations: 'Our husbands would prefer us working in the reeling rooms of a mill to working outside. Our husbands prefer to see us working in mills with other women.'[113]

Sakoo's testimony also highlighted another key social division. 'There are Moochees, Mohammedans and other castes, and if any of them touched our food we should be defiled.' Upon being asked if this was truly intractable, she responded: 'What is caste made for, if it is not to be maintained?'[114] Maya, 'a girl of 14' also employed in the Colaba Mill, confirmed this. As a 'Moochee', one of the 'lowest' castes employed in the cotton industry, she worked in the throstle department, for wages (Rs 6–7) much lower than that of the women in the reeling department. She went on to say that if she sought work in the reeling department, the reeling jobber (perhaps Sakoo herself) would no doubt give her work. But: 'I belong to the Moochee caste, consequently I cannot mix with the higher castes in the reeling room.' Caste, gender, and sociality were clearly mixed together in ways which framed durable structures of exclusion and hierarchy.

These divisions would continue to play a key role in the subsequent history of the Bombay cotton industry in the twentieth century, despite its impressive history of left-wing militancy. If we turn back to Lokhande and the accusations levelled at him by mill owners, we can perhaps adduce an additional context from this evidence. Mill employers, as outlined earlier, accused Lokhande of being unrepresentative, of representing a tiny fraction of the workers he claimed to speak for. In the face of such evident differences and hierarchies within the workforce, the shaft must, at some level, have hit home. Yet at the same time, the volatility of the overall industrial situation meant that such divisions did not necessarily negate the possibility of sustained collective action—something Bombay's capitalist development would prove time and again. So the situation was irreducibly mixed and ambiguous. Lokhande's most durable base was, as pointed out by his opponents, clearly confined to 'leading men' within the workforce. But this did not mean that his 'agitations' were confined to them: the grievances he and his Association drew upon went deeper, in ways which ironically both gave him the basis to rebut mill employers' claims that he represented falsely, and which ultimately undercut his own authority as 'agitation' moved in more militant directions in the 1890s.

In the event, quite clearly their jibes taunted him enough to spur him to organize an 'annual meeting', widely publicized, of the Millhands' Association at a vacant site in Byculla owned by fellow Phulmalis in late December. Two thousand millhands were reported to have been present at the meeting, which appears to have consisted largely of Lokhande denying that he had abetted recent strikes, and also denying, angrily, that he derived personal benefit from his activism.[115]

The *Bombay Samachar* responded scornfully. The 'flashy' denomination of an 'association' had been assumed, it said, 'but all that it amounted to was that a few Marathas made speeches'.[116] The *Samachar* upbraided Lokhande for falsely claiming the authority to represent millworkers, but at the same time expressed alarm about the possible success of the campaign they attributed to him. 'The attempt made by Mr. Lokhande, through the instrumentality of the Millhands' Association, to teach the mill-operatives how to make demands on their employers to increase their wages and to make other concessions ought to be frustrated by the mill-owners and the discreet portion of the public conjointly.' The *Samachar* expressed alarm at the 'false and injurious ideas' that the Millhands' Association would doubtless instil in the minds of the workers, leading them to 'harass their employers'. It spelt out an alternative code of workers' mobilization by employers against agitators: an association needed to be formed 'for the purpose of delivering addresses to mill hands, which should explain to them that looking to the condition of the country there is much need of poor people like them being satisfied with their present condition instead of allowing themselves to be carried away by false notions'.[117] Mill owners, the newspaper went on, should get new workers ready to replace anyone who joined the Millhands' Association, and set up a new association of millworkers to counter Lokhande's machinations.

Lokhande's real strength and influence among millworkers is hard to judge, but the anxieties of mill owners do indicate that he commanded a popularity that was far from negligible. When the workers of the Sassoon Mill went on strike in October 1892, the Committee of the Millowners' Association instantly accused Lokhande of instigating and abetting the dispute. N.N. Wadia carried on his campaign to set himself up as a workers' leader, getting up another petition in early 1893, from millhands, to the effect that they considered him 'a right and proper person' to represent their interests in the Legislative Council.[118] An alternative, conservative politics of workers' representation was being chalked out in these manouevres, resting on the myth of harmonious relations between employers and employed, on the paternalist, proto-Gandhian idea of employers as protectors and guardians of their workers.

Two things need to be noted about this contest over representation. First, the ground of argument, of discursive opposition, had shifted between the mid-1880s and the early 1890s. In large part as a result of Lokhande's early attempts at mobilization, and also in part as a result of the kinds of governmental initiative that dominated the late 1880s, millworkers had to be recognized as, at least in part, adjudicators of their own fortunes and sufferings. Lokhande occupied a unique position for a while: more so than any other public figure in Bombay, he spoke to two worlds simultaneously, one marked by the accumulation of workers' grievances and industrial dispute, characterized by relations of control that were beginning to look fractious; and one a world of ritualized, coded meliorist protest, pushing through minimally reformist designs.

Second, Lokhande's campaigns and techniques of mobilization, too, rested upon ground that was beginning to shift under his feet. Lokhande may have radically changed the terms of discourse, but his campaigns remained transfixed within the idiom and practice of legislative amelioration, which meant, among other things, identifying the terrain of intervention marked out by law as the terrain for collective action. He was, no less than Bahadhurji or Wadia, dependent upon a fairly stable system of industrial relations, marked generally by the absence of open, violent conflict. Despite numerous localized disputes and tensions, something akin to industrial peace characterized the internal relations of the textile business till the 1890s. A politics of amelioration, blending the mass campaign and the petition, but eschewing the militancy of the street, was appropriate to an industry where strikes were confined to single mills or departments, and where legislative protection was conceived of as a benefaction from on high. In the early 1890s, this world started to come apart, as workers increasingly resorted to direct forms of action that upset their implicit social contract with their employers.

The Wage Question: Strikes and the Limits of Factory Regulation

It is now time to turn to the basic structural tension in the relations between employers and employed, which exploded into militant workers' protest in the 1890s. This is best read as the conflictual relationship, sustained by mill capitalism and extended by law, between the *social regulation of the factory* and the *social reproduction of factory labour*. Sowthoo's letter (which I analysed at the end of Chapter 2) separated these domains by stressing the urgency of public intervention into the latter, while tacitly accepting the privations of the former in the shape of the tyranny of employers and managers. In the two subsequent decades of deliberation and contest over factory regulation, the terms of this separation were reversed: factory legislation emerged as a field constituted by purely workplace considerations. Yet, there was a very obvious and precise mechanism that held these two domains together, so that any proposed intervention could not but link them even as they separated them. This was the mechanism of the *wage*—it is this that allows us to think of the worlds of factory production and social reproduction as a bounded unity. Closer consideration of this is thus necessary. What was the 'wage question' that emerged as a political *problem* in late nineteenth-century Bombay, and how did it affect the politics of labour regulation?

First and foremost, the question of wages has to be understood as an *absence*, but of a peculiar kind. It was not an *empty* absence, a deficiency: rather, it functioned as an absent *cause* which limited, structured, and threw into tension the entire field of regulatory interventions into workers' lives and made the pattern of industrial relations established by factory law inherently unstable. To put it telegraphically, 'laissez-faire' should here be understood as a form of social regulation in itself. The persistent, *real* fiction (which structured lived social experiences) of the 'free relation between employers and workers' precluded the direct public regulation of wages in any form. It also negated the possibility of wage-agreements on a formalized basis between employers.

There are three features of this absence and its consequences that need to be noted here. First, the *isolation* of the problem of wages by explicit legal intervention: by excluding the wage from their domain, the Factory Acts may well have dramatized it and contributed to its rapid politicization at the end of the century. Second, the *threat* to wages that was noted by Sowthoo, by propagandists against factory law, and by workers in the 1880s and 1890s, which flowed from the move to legislate hours and conditions of work. Third, the elaboration of forms of *non-wage compensation through social regulation* that acquired propulsive force in the 1890s. The debates of that decade over workers' housing, the need to supply alternative sources of credit and cheap grain, and the need for employers to establish controlled patterns of labour migration into Bombay, coupled with welfare policies (a project proposed by Tata as early as 1888), all exemplify this.

Second, the wage-question has to be understood in its specificity, in terms of what it was *not*. It was not a sustained demand for higher wages coordinated across the industry: forms of labour organization adequate to this purpose did not exist in the nineteenth century. It was not a demand for the legal regulation of wage-scales in a manner beneficial to workers: this, too, was strictly beyond the bounds of what was imagined as possible. The fiction of free employer–worker negotiation at the point of production, in this sense, exercised real force across the field of political oppositions around factory legislation. The wage question was, instead, increasingly posed as an insistent demand by workers and their 'representatives' for the institution of a standard regulating *wage-payment*. The weekly, fortnightly, or at any rate regularized payment of workers' wages was what workers struck for, signed petitions for, or went to court for. And yet, the 'politics of labour' promoted by Lokhande and the Millhands' Association in the 1880s and 1890s consistently foregrounded a Factory Act principally based on the regulation of working *time* as its horizon. To understand how this worked, it is necessary to schematize the structures of industrial control that characterized Bombay's textile capitalism. Having examined these structures, it will then be possible to return, circuitously, to the question of 'workers' agency' that was foregrounded in Sowthoo's letter in 1872, and to understand the tensions that emerged between working-class mobilization and industrial regulation in 1890s Bombay.

At the apex of the mill industry's structures of control were managing agents, whose commission was made off the production rather than the profits of the mills they managed. In the early 1860s, the agents of Bombay mills had shifted from a system of commissions paid on profits to a quarter anna paid on every pound of mill out-turn. W.O. Moylan, who as Boiler Inspector was the official with the greatest continuous experience of Bombay's factories, argued that it was this shift that led the mills to eschew an older system of slightly gentler work, based on weekly holidays and working hours between 8 a.m. and 5 p.m. Workers accepted longer working hours, since this produced a spike in wages, which were in the early 1860s still paid largely according to time. The shift to piece work as the dominant mode of payment followed about six months after the shift to commissions based on output.[119] Working hours, as a result, were raised from eight to thirteen and sometimes fourteen hours in the mills, a single company apparently formulating the scheme and all the others following in its path.[120]

Moylan anatomized this situation cogently: the commission-system, he wrote in 1880, 'is universally adopted. It forces operatives to forfeit a part of their wages—in the shape of fines for work spoiled through inferior cotton being used, and for absence from work'. He mentioned cases where commissions either ate into profits or swelled losses, and one case where the commission in a profit-and-loss account came to Rs 43,000 while the mill made a loss of nearly Rs 23,000. The total profits made by mills that paid commissions in 1879 amounted to Rs 721,248, while the commissions added up to Rs 546,732, or over three-fourths of the profits.[121] Mill companies, added Moylan, citing several individual instances from the 1870s, floated their mills without sufficient capital, and so their expenses often far outstripped the subscribed capital. They consequently borrowed large sums and ran up large debts, failed to repay dividends, and responded to these pressures by working their mills 'from the earliest dawn till nightfall, their sole object being to derive as much benefit from the labour of their operatives as possible'.[122] The power of mill agents within company structures and the separation of their incomes from the profits made by their concerns, as Moylan noticed, combined to press down conditions of work and render workers vulnerable to fatigue, accident, and heightened exploitation.

Wage controls constituted the other principal mechanism whereby exploitation in the cotton mill industry was sustained. Part of the structure of wage repression was embedded within the workplace itself, in the form of fines upon faulty or damaged work, late attendance, and other minor infractions. The major part, however, consisted in the delicate way in which the structures of wage-payment were attached to the structures of social reproduction among Bombay's millworkers, and the ways in which this connection gave birth to a vicious cycle of arrears and debt. In order to offset the possibility of workers 'decamping' with their wages to other workplaces (a perpetual possibility in a time of industrial expansion and concomitantly intense wage competition between different enterprises), mill managements routinely retained workers' wages for well over a month, and sometimes over three months. In other words, wages due in October would not be paid till mid-to-late November, and often as late as December or even January. This delay in wage-payment forced workers upon neighbourhood-based structures of credit, sourced from bania or Pathan moneylenders at exorbitant rates of interest, which kept workers and working families afloat. The repayment of loans necessarily came from workers' belated wage receipts, and, as more than one observer noted, the Court of Small Causes in Bombay was always busy adjudicating moneylenders' claims upon workers' earnings, often in the form of the 'attachment of wages'. This meant that mills were frequently compelled to hand over their workers' incomes to moneylenders as repayments of debts—a classic case of double alienation, where the structures of neighbourhood life and social reproduction overlapped with the structures of workplace exploitation, generating perpetual penury.

The mutually constitutive theft of workers' time and money thus locked them into the quotidian forms of subjection and submission that characterized both mill and neighbourhood life. When factory legislation, in its combined avatars of legal form, material practice, and site of discursive and political contest, arrived in the 1880s, it not only systematically foregrounded the issue of workers' time (the hours worked by women and children and the absence of regularized holidays), but also *equally systematically* excluded the wage question in its entirety, as a province in which law, or any form of external 'interference', was impermissible. In effect, then, law clarified and extended the separation of spheres upon which the effectiveness of factory control was premised: the realm of the social reproduction of the workforce was sustained by the 'free' play of market forces and contract, while conditions at the workplace emerged as a site of public debate and intervention. This would have profound consequences for the structure of industrial relations in the mill industry, and for the disputes that broke out in the early 1890s in what employers and their allies excoriated as 'strike mania' or 'strike fever'.[123]

Before examining the strikes of the early 1890s, which marked a significant shift in patterns of industrial disputes in the mill industry, I would like to construct a speculative genealogy of disputes that foregrounded the links between production and social reproduction. I will do this chronologically, in order to demonstrate the gathering pressures that worked upon the structure of industrial relations at the point of their virtual implosion during the protracted crisis of the 1890s.

In December 1877, we find perhaps the first recorded instance of the entire workforce of a mill taking recourse to strike action. At the Remington Spinning and Weaving Mills, an attempt by the mill management to reduce the piece work rates from '6 pies to 5 pies' per pound of production was countered by a stoppage of work. This episode, recounted in a very brief passage in the *Times of India*, signals a tension initiated by the 'the theft of wages' practised by mill agents in their attempt to bolster the commissions they received on production. This was a time when shareholders and mill companies frequently clashed over agents' commissions, and wage reductions may have been a way of resolving this conflict, though specific evidence in this case is hard to come by. Interestingly, the *Times of India* reports that 'the men state that (out of Bombay) they can earn one rupee daily, and that the only inducement which makes them stay in Bombay is to be among their relatives'.[124]

In February 1879, we find the wage question cropping up again, in a slightly different form. At the time, the tensions *within* mill capital had reached a point of implosion and several enterprises had to go into liquidation as a result of financial fiddling by one of the city's managing agencies, Nursey Kessowjee and Company. One of the consequences of this was the inability, by the affected mills, to pay their workers' wages. On 3 February, a crowd of around 500 workers of the Colaba Spinning and Weaving Company gathered outside the mill manager's house, demanding immediate payment of their wages. Upon the manager's reply that the company was going into liquidation and therefore wages could not be paid until the accounts had been adjusted, the workers retorted that their immediate dismissal and unemployment was his (the manager's) fault and threatened him with physical injury. The crowd was dispersed, and a probable riot prevented, by police action, but the incident illustrates the vulnerabilities of the late 1870s well: the constant speculation by mill agents and the instability of companies' future prospects frequently led to mill closures in this decade, and coupled with the fluctuations in demand in Bombay's export market, this would have produced a generalized insecurity of remuneration and life for thousands of workers.[125]

A month later, the workers of the four companies whose assets were seized by their creditors, approached the latter asking 'in a humble and temperate manner' for the payment of their wage-arrears. This was, predictably, in vain. However, the mill creditors expressed warm sympathy for the workers' plight, they reasoned that 'British law' prevented them from acceding to their demand. The same meeting was interrupted a few hours later, when 'some of the women and children employed on the mills came back into the room to represent their case but were speedily sent back. Apollo Street was crowded by the mill employees during the whole of the afternoon'.[126] This episode, then, engrossed the threat of militant violence, the spectacle of workers' self-abnegation, and the pressure of what appears to have been a peaceful demonstration—all to no avail.

The year 1884 witnessed, as has already been noted, the emergence of Lokhande's Millhands' Association. The Association's first campaign was directed at the Factory Commission that was set up in this year. This was significant in itself: it effected a junction point between law and labour activism. Equally, though, the rapid elaboration of demands and staging-posts for conflict in 1884 drew upon the emergent industrial politics of factory workers.

In June 1884, a strike broke out at the Kurla Cotton Spinning and Weaving Mills, a large concern in a suburb on the northern border of Bombay. The conflict broke out after the workers refused to clean their machines on a designated holiday, which happened to be a Sunday. Among their grievances, interestingly, was the claim that workers at a neighbouring mill were allowed this 'custom'. When the workers returned to work on Monday, the presumed 'instigator' of the strike was dismissed. The workers immediately left their posts, and the mill's weaving department lay idle for a week.[127]

The weavers at the Kurla Mill, then, transmuted a contingent practice, a management choice made at another mill, into a right to be claimed by workers at other mills, and by themselves as workers. They also sketched out a very precise image of the right or 'custom' that they claimed—a fortnightly exemption from work, including the work of cleaning machinery, that paralleled the 'custom' at a neighbouring mill, where, perhaps, their own family members and friends worked. Millworkers could, then, derive their sense of right and entitlement from more liberal relationships of employment that were visible to but not enjoyed by them. In this way, the plurality of working arrangements in a spatially concentrated mill industry, driven by the choppy rhythms of cooperation, competition, and crisis served to open up fleeting spaces for the elaboration of workers' demands.

The shareholders of the mill used two kinds of threats to quell the strike. First, the labourers who were on strike were to lose their wage-arrears due to their misconduct. Second, if they wished to rejoin employment their names were to be entered afresh—they were to start over again, as newcomers.[128] Employers, then, had immediate recourse to wage-arrears as a form of discipline: they sought to circumvent the demand for a regular holiday by deploying their control over the system of wage-payments. The threat of being forced to begin employment again also implied, of course, the further accretion of arrears, since new workers forfeited their early payments. While the strike itself was not built on a wage dispute, it nonetheless revolved, at a central moment, on the wage-controls employers commanded.

So, at one level, the strike articulated the kind of purely workplace grievance, namely excessive working time, which could be most effectively mobilized in the campaign for protective legislation. However, investigation by the *Rast Goftar* disclosed another grievance, one that was harder to fit into the established pattern of workers' demands. The workers complained of having to pay rent on behalf of their employers, a circumstance that reveals the beginnings of what was later to be a persistent concern of mill owners—intensified control of the structures of their workers' spatial and social relationships. The mill company, anticipating the twentieth-century spatial integration of mills and working-class neighbourhoods in Girangaon, had rented a large chawl beside the mill. Much of the chawl, however, remained unoccupied, and the rent actually payable did not match the compulsory Rs 250 payment demanded from the Company. A certain monthly sum, therefore, was extracted from the workers to make up the deficit, irrespective of the actual number of tenement rooms occupied. The grievances based at the point of production in the mill were, thus, compounded by problems of social reproduction.

The strike at the Kurla Mill was not unusual or against the grain of the times in itself. Large and sustained industrial strikes were virtually unknown in Bombay in the 1880s, but small disputes in a single mill, or more commonly, as in this case, a department of a mill, broke out with reasonable regularity. Between 1881 and 1887, there was on average a strike a year at the Kurla Mill.[129] These strikes, however, were almost invariably wage disputes, according to the agents of the mill in their testimony before the Royal Commission on Labour in 1892.[130] This is an interesting detail: the predominance, in the Kurla strike, of the issue of working time indicates the triggering force of law, with its specific exclusions, in moulding workers' demands. The Kurla strikers may well have been part of the groundswell behind Lokhande's campaign for reduced working hours and a weekly holiday. Nevertheless, the problem of working time and 'leisure' dramatized the question of workers' social reproduction in a manner related to the surrounding tensions around wage-payment.

In its petition of 1884 to the Factory Commission, the Millhands' Association clarified the links between production and social reproduction in a systematic manner, in the form of five distinct demands. First, complete Sunday rest for all workers. Second, a strictly observed half-hour recess at noon every working day. Third, the limitation of mill work between 6.30 a.m. and sunset. Fourth, and crucially, the payment of wages no later than the 15th of the month following that they had been earned for. Fifth, the payment of full wages to injured workmen till their recovery, and compensation and sustenance in the case of permanent disabilities contracted at work. These demands were further explained in the petition through an account of the physical needs and financial insecurities of workers. These concessions, explained the petition, would deliver a healthier workforce to its masters, since the entitlements to reasonable breaks in work would help renew workers' bodies. The uncertainty of working time was a source of great inconvenience for workers: there were no clearly defined opening and closing hours, and this cut into the time workers had to sustain their energies outside the workplace.

There are indications, though, that the demand for the payment of wages on the 15th of each month occupied a very central place in the initial articulation of workers' demands in 1884. Lokhande seems to have played on this theme eloquently in his address to the mass meeting on 24 September. He spoke, according to the *Times of India*, of the 'rather sorry scenes invariably enacted' at mill-gates on paydays, when moneylenders 'pounced upon their victims the moment they left the premises, depriving them in several cases of their entire hard-earned monthly wages'.[131] The Millhands' Association's petition to the Factory Commission argued that the debt problem universally faced by mill-workers would largely be resolved if wage-arrears were restricted, by law, to a fortnight's earnings.

In the same meeting, Lokhande further urged critics of the workers' demands to examine the records of the Small Causes Court and visit the local Debtors' Jail, 'where they would find that the mill-hands predominated over the other debtors'.[132] This theme would be further elaborated in the second major campaign mounted by the Millhands' Association, in 1889–90, as another Factory Commission appeared on the horizon, offering fresh hope. In their petition of 1889, the Millhands' Association spelt out the consequences of workers' entrapment within the circuit of wage-arrears and debt:

> Speaking about wages, your petitioners feel constrained to remark passingly that cases in which the employers illegally withhold the hard-earned pay of the poor are so frequent that a reference to the Court of Small Causes will convince Government that wages are in many cases recovered only by recourse to the Courts. But hundreds of operatives forego their wages on account of the trouble involved in appealing to the Judges. The many strikes in the Mills will, on enquiry, be found to be attributable either to the withholding of wages in this manner, or to threatened reductions in them.[133]

There had been a typical illustration of this late in 1885, in a dispute at the Dinshaw Petit Mill, the largest in Bombay. The proprietors of the mill had effected a reduction in wage-rates in April and May, and the workers had agreed to this on condition that the old wage-rates would be restored at the end of Diwali. They repeatedly petitioned Dinshaw Petit, without reply. In September, about 600 workers 'waited upon' Petit, notifying him that they would strike if the old rates were not restored. They once again received no response and struck work, and subsequently sent the mill a lawyer's letter demanding their arrears. Simultaneously, they petitioned the Government of Bombay, pleading that the latter intervene in this case. They were informed, curtly, that 'the matter of their complaint is not one in which Government can intervene'.[134] The matter ended in litigation, and the Court of Small Causes ruled against the workers on the ground that they had not given the required fifteen days' notice before quitting work. At both ends of the workers' pendulum of choices, in this case, wage subtraction was effected: if a reduction was not acceptable, the workers would have to part with or, at the very least, continue to be estranged from earnings due to them.

In 1890, after the mass meetings of millworkers organized by Lokhande as a protest against the mills' decision to close twice in the week, the Millowners' Association appears to have considered the question of wage-payment with more care. The Committee of the BMOA sent out instructions to the mills asking them to fix regular monthly times for the payment of wages, but the consent of most mill owners, unsurprisingly, was withheld from this scheme.[135]

A related dimension is disclosed by an episode in 1895. The agents of the Morarji Goculdas Mills complained to the Millowners' Association that they were being flooded with orders for the attachment of wages by moneylenders who had prosecuted indebted workers for unpaid loans in the Court of Small Causes.[136] The Association employed solicitors to look into the matter of whether the attachment of millhands' wages was legal, and whether it was possible to legally prevent creditors from compelling attachment through court orders.[137] In March, the Bombay United Spinning and Weaving Company succeeded in convincing the court to cancel an order for attachment.[138] Since this only decided the individual case and neither confirmed nor delegitimized the principle of wage-attachment, the Association asked for legal opinion. It was told that such orders could not be prevented. The case demonstrates that some of Bombay's mill owners were cognizant of the explosive potential of technical questions surrounding wages and their payment.

In each of the cases described earlier, the drive to institute some kind of regularity in wage-payments and wage-receipts encountered an abrupt blockage. In the dispute between workers and the Petit Mill, the government refused to intervene in a matter which it pronounced to be outside its domain. The BMOA's drive to regulate the payment of wages foundered upon the apparently permanent resolve of its members to act against decisions made by the Committee. A legal action taken by mill owners that sought to de-legalize attachment by court orders and thereby make sure that workers at least had the wages to take home failed. Attempts by the BMOA to control the incidence of late wage-payments and limit arrears to six weeks—hard as this too was on workers—also failed.[139]

J.M. Campbell, the Collector of Bombay, noted the prevalence of this practice by mill owners, and added that 'in spite of difficulties and inconvenience to the employers a month's delay should become an extreme concession, and that the principle should be accepted and gradually introduced that delays in excess of a fortnight are an unjust burden from which the Bombay millworkers should by degrees be set free'.[140] However, he stopped short of calling for legislation on the subject and noted that this was one point on which the government could 'fairly call for help from the public spirit of the better class of millowners'.[141] This, however, was the limit: to go any further, and to actually legislate upon the matter, as Lokhande and the Millhands' Association had wanted the government to do, would be to tread upon the most sovereign province within industrial relations, the domain classically characterized by complete laissez-faire.

The pattern is clear: within the existing structures of industrial relations, any attempt at a workable, permanent regulation of wage-payment was out of the question. The state considered this a matter of free negotiation between employer and worker, and refused to intervene at any stage in the making and working of the contractual agreement between them. Mill owners could not enforce a collective rule; their interests were too disparate and conflictual. Besides, the present wage-arrears system, which often ended up stuffing mill owners' purses permanently with two months' back pay, was both lucrative and a reliable weapon of discipline. It was security against both desertion and insubordination. For millworkers, though, it was a burden and a source of insecurity.

Through the course of the economic difficulties of the early 1890s, factory inspectors, other administrators, mill owners, and managers apprehensively watched the storm clouds gather over the normal relations of authority in the factory. There are moments in the record when profound tensions break through to the surface. For instance, G.T. Whittle, mill owner at Viramgam in the northern division of the Presidency, responded to the queries of the Royal Commission with an intemperate outburst:

> The questions above propounded are unsuited to the condition of the people and the country, and are extremely mischievous. India is a country that is yet blessed with a large amount of honest simplicity, and still retains an uncorrupted civilization. It is, therefore, hard to comprehend

> how or in what way it is proposed to benefit this people by the introduction of questions on the relation of capital and labour, strikes, agitations, and combinations. Those are the excrescence of an over-hasty civilization, and are as far from a good purpose in this country, or a kindness to its people, as the east is from the west.[142]

The desire to preserve the myth that modern industrial conflict was somehow artificially transplanted onto a purer, gentler oriental civilization was a powerful one. The questions Whittle objected to so violently were not asked of millhands, but, for the most part, employers like himself. The very naming of certain themes—strikes, combinations, agitations—made him anxious, as though they somehow signalled the dread events themselves, as though voicing them could render them real. The very act of asking such questions, to use Whittle's idiom, was 'extremely mischievous'.

There were, as numerous observers attested, no organizations in Bombay that could be properly described as trade unions, and so the organization necessary for sustained industrial action was apparently missing. James Campbell, Collector of Bombay, however, observed that several rules of solidarity practised by Bombay textile workers actually corresponded quite closely to the principles of trade unionism. Individual workers, for instance, were threatened with a boycott if they agreed to work for wages 'lower than what that form of labour has hitherto commanded'.[143] The principle of solidarity, while not extended to collective action around wages, could be impressive at the level of neighbourhood and community, as meetings were organized quickly and subscriptions raised 'to repair a rest-house, dig a well or re-shrine a god in some up-country village'.[144]

Campbell, in common with other administrators and factory inspectors, felt that the absence of sustained workers' solidarity over explicitly industrial issues was determined by a stability in wage-rates that was unique to Bombay. Over thirty years between the 1860s and the 1890s, the monopoly wage-rates which the first generation of millworkers had commanded had remained in force through most of the Presidency. Through all the swings in the cotton trade, wage-rates had remained more or less constant, even at times of crisis. The Chief Inspector of Factories in 1892, Jackson, concurred. Wages had been kept at levels that 'in the eyes of the workers received the sanction of … the custom of more than a generation'.[145] This, and nothing else, accounted for the relative stability of industrial relations: no substantial interference with wage-rates had ever been contemplated generally across a number of mills.[146]

The same evidence, of course, could be interpreted in radically different ways. N.A. Moos, a schoolmaster who had briefly served as factory inspector in the late 1880s, also furnished answers to the Royal Commission. He interpreted 'wage stability' as stagnation and as a source of intense distress at a time when 'the purchasing power of money ... has steadily and considerably decreased'.[147] Summing up the state of industrial relations, he wrote:

> The relation between the employers and the employed is said to be cordial. True, they do get on smoothly and well, but good feelings arising from equality of give and take do not form the basis of the understanding. Power on one side and ignorance and mildness on the other are the basis on which the present relations, and the relations are quiet, rest.
>
> In case of difference, the weaker side gives in; there is nothing like specified modes of settling differences, & c. How could there be when the employers are able enough to dictate their own terms?[148]

Read in relation to each other, these contradictory accounts convey a relatively equilibrated experience of industrial relations. The 'stability' of wage-rates certainly demonstrated the stability of the 'hold' employers had on their workers: at the same time, it seems to have been a compromise hammered out in open and covert class struggle. For instance, workers rarely went on strike demanding higher wages, but, as the 1880s wore on, they seem to have responded militantly and often violently when wage rates were reduced or when increases that were promised were not delivered. 'Concessions' made by mill owners were rapidly transmuted into rights. On the other hand, given the rapid and unstable growth of the mill industry in the 1880s, and the insecurities that bedevilled workers' lives, what seems most remarkable is the relatively 'peaceful' nature of industrial relations in that decade. Conflicts rarely spilled beyond individual mill departments, and the segmentation of labour conditions—differential wages paid by different mills, the hierarchies *within* the workplace, and, related to this, the wage competition between mills—sustained this structure of quiescence.

This quiescence broke down in the crisis-ridden industrial climate of the early 1890s. Profits on production had been falling steadily for two decades, from 15 pies in the pound in 1872 to 4 pies in the pound in 1892. This was largely the consequence of the commissions commanded by mill agents, which lay at the base of the constant investment in mill expansion, the setting up of new mills, and, most consequently, the constant stress on high levels of production, irrespective of price or profit levels. Mills continued to expand production even when demand levels dropped or prices sank, and the sustained and rapid expansion of the industry in the 1880s was accompanied, counter-intuitively, by constant crisis and cycles of mini-recession.

All this had happened without a corresponding decline in wage rates, and eventually mill owners and mill agents found it imperative to press down wages—more to the point, they were able to combine forces to that end. This took place in the summer and autumn of 1892, and marked the first coordinated, industry-wide attempt to regulate workers' remuneration. This provoked the first strike wave Bombay had seen, as the workers of several mills struck work, one after the other, at the beginning of November.[149] Such intensity of industrial action had never been seen before, and the *Indian Textile Journal* spoke of a 'strike mania' that seemed to have overcome workers.[150]

The most protracted battle was at the Sassoon Mills, where the agents enforced a reduction in the wages paid per pound of production in July. The workers accepted the change, but protested when they learned that the mill owners were planning to introduce new machinery that would increase the out-turn of the mill, unaccompanied by a wage rise. After negotiations over wages broke down, several men went on strike on 31 October, followed by about five hundred men—the entire weaving department—on 2 November.[151] Several other mills followed suit immediately afterwards, and strikes crippled the mill industry in the first half of November.[152] Mill owners discussed the possibility of a common strategy against strikes, based on preventing mills from employing men who had left work at other mills and holding jobbers personally responsible for the strikes in their departments and mills.[153]

In December one of the strike leaders at the Sassoon Mills, Ganpat Sewram, filed a case against the Sassoon Spinning and Weaving Company for the recovery of the wages due to him for October. These amounted to Rs 15. The case was dismissed. The *Indian Textile Journal* contains a vivid description of what happened next:

> About four hundred hands of the Sassoon Mill, who were on strike, collected in the precincts of the Court, anxiously waiting to know the results of the aforementioned suit, which was brought as a test case, and when they were informed of the result of the proceedings the strikers apparently got irritated. On the mill manager, Mr Perozshaw Bomanjee Jeejeebhoy, who was accompanied by Mr J. Heap, the weaving master, and the timekeeper of the mill-hands, named Ardesheer, leaving the premises of the Court, the whole gang of men pounced upon the manager while getting into his carriage, and demanded the immediate payment of their wages, and threatened to molest him if he did not comply. The manager made an attempt to pacify the men, but they became very furious, and some of the gang assaulted Mr. Perozshaw with sticks inflicting a nasty cut on his forehead and dragged him about, and his turban fell off.

The police intervened at this point, in the form of two convoys of sepoys, escorting the battered manager to safety and arresting five men, who were later sentenced to five months' imprisonment with hard labour.[154] Here again, then, we see the system of wage-arrears and (we may assume) the privations of debt cracking open the shell of industrial relations, now on a larger scale than ever before. The very 'hold' employers exercised over workforces became, in the 1890s, a source of irreparable tension and workers' militancy. The propulsive effect of arrears and debt manifested itself in industrial locations elsewhere in the Presidency as well, most notably in Ahmedabad. Here, towards the end of June 1895, the mills took a collective decision to institute fortnightly rather than weekly payment of wages (which, in contrast to Bombay, was actually the norm). On the 28th, the workers employed by the Ahmedabad Spinning and Weaving Company (managed by Ranchhodlal Chhotalal, who had established the mill industry in the city) struck work, followed immediately by the rest of the mills. The strike escalated into a riot in early July, and Ranchhodlal Chhotalal 'barely escaped with his life'.[155]

The mounting antagonisms between workers and employers in the 1890s are best understood, then, as a structural crisis rising from the exigencies of the wage-arrears system. This was not always the *overt* focus of conflict, but acted as a structuring force. Wage levels were difficult to force down not only because workers had experienced their 'stable' wages as an inviolable entitlement—a common enough feature in industrial relations—but also because the combination of delayed wage-payments, debt at high interest rates, and stagnant earnings had created a potentially explosive situation. Any wage depression in this context could unleash disproportionately intense levels of insecurity and immiserization, because the intricacy with which wage-arrears and debt cycles were interlocked must have necessitated survival strategies that were inflexible. Precisely *because* the world of mill earnings was structured by excessive dependence on predatory forms of local credit, there was very little room for flexibility and manoeuvre when it came to wages. If millworkers were locked into a perpetually reproduced dependency on moneylenders, mill owners were, beyond a point, unable to intensify their levels of exploitation without suffering a violent backlash. It was this point of no return that was reached in the 1890s.

Notes

1. S.M. Rutnagar, *Bombay Industries: The Cotton Mills—A Review of the Progress of the Textile Industry in Bombay from 1850 to 1926 and the Present Constitution, Management and Financial Position of Spinning and Weaving Factories* (Bombay: The Indian Textile Association Ltd, 1927), pp. 386–7.

2. Rutnagar, *Bombay Industries*. While fewer than twenty new mills were constructed between 1890 and the war, the number of workers listed in 1914 was 111,000, nearly doubling.

3. Rutnagar, *Bombay Industries*, pp. 386–7.

4. From Inspector of Steam Boilers and Prime Movers, to Collector, Bombay, no. 33, 23 February 1880, L/P&J/6/18, no. 1035, 1880, OIOC.

5. S.D. Mehta, *The Cotton Mills of India, 1854–1954* (Bombay: Textile Association, 1954), p. 42.

6. No. 101, 19 January 1884, GD 1884, vol. 2, Maharashtra State Archives (MSA).

7. No. 15, 2 May 1885, GD 1885, vol. 3, MSA.

8. Mehta, *The Cotton Mills of India*, pp. 43–4.

9. *Annual Report of Bombay Millowners' Association*, 1891.

10. *Annual Report of Bombay Millowners' Association*, 1891.

11. Chief Inspector of Factories and Workshops' Report, October 1886–87, *PP* 1888 (C. 5328), pp. 112–23.

12. J.C. Kydd, *A History of Factory Legislation in India* (Calcutta, 1920), pp. 41–3.

13. Act XI, 1891, of Governor-General in Council to amend Indian Factories Act, 1881, *PP* 1890–1891, C. 194 (henceforth *IFA* 1891), in Kydd, *History of Factory Legislation in India*.

14. Correspondence Respecting the International Labour Conference at Berlin, Commercial no. 8 (1890), *PP* 1890 (C. 5914).

15. International Labour Conference, Sitting of 15 March 1890, Commercial no. 16 (1890), *PP* 1890 (C. 6042).

16. International Labour Conference, Sitting of 15 March 1890, Commercial no. 16 (1890), *PP* 1890 (C. 6042).

17. Correspondence Respecting the International Labour Conference at Berlin, Commercial no. 8 (1890), *PP* 1890 (C. 5914).

18. Correspondence Respecting the International Labour Conference at Berlin, Commercial no. 8 (1890), *PP* 1890 (C. 5914).

19. Telegram to Viceroy, 17 February 1891, *PP* 1890–91 (C. 224).

20. *Annual Report of Bombay Millowners' Association*, 1891, p. 2.

21. Kydd, *Factory Legislation*, p. 47.

22. Kydd, *Factory Legislation*, p. 47.

23. From Henry Harrison, President, Blackburn and District Incorporated Chamber of Commerce, 5 April 1890, cited in *Labour Movement in India: Documents 1891–1917* (henceforth *LMI*), edited by S.D. Punekar and R. Varickayil (Delhi, 1990), p. 353.

24. From Henry Harrison, President, Blackburn and District Incorporated Chamber of Commerce, 5 April 1890, p. 350.

25. Diary, no. 76, Home Judicial (A), July 1890.

26. No. 44 (Statistics), India Office, London, 15 May 1890, From Cross to Lansdowne, no. 95, Home Judicial (A), July 1890.

27. *Times of India*, 19 March 1892.

28. Punekar and Varickayil, *LMI*, p. 353.

29. Letter from John Marshall, Secretary, BMOA, to Dr K.N. Bahadhurji, 29 June 1891, *Annual Report of Bombay Millowners' Association*, 1891, p. 30.

30. 'India Factory Legislation', paper read by Holt S. Hallett, at International Congress of Hygiene and Demography, reproduced in *Annual Report of Bombay Millowners' Association*, 1891, pp. 34–43.

31. Rutnagar, *Bombay Industries*, p. 698.

32. 'Factory Labour in the Indian Spinning and Weaving Mills', paper read by Dr. K.N. Bahadhurji, *Annual Report of Bombay Millowners' Association*, 1891, pp. 44–51.

33. 'Factory Labour in the Indian Spinning and Weaving Mills', pp. 52–4, 95–6.

34. R. Chandavarkar, *The Origins of Industrial Capitalism in India: Business Strategies and the Working Classes in Bombay, 1900–1940* (Cambridge: Cambridge University Press, 1994).

35. S.B. Upadhyay, *Existence, Identity and Mobilization: The Cotton Millworkers of Bombay 1890–1919* (Delhi: Manohar, 2004), pp. 97–111.

36. Report on working of Indian Factories Act, GD 1889, MSA.

37. Report on working of Indian Factories Act, GD 1889, MSA.

38. In Bombay, by contrast, most women were employed on hand reeling and winding; both tasks were generally performed entirely by women, and the labour market was, therefore, more segmented.

39. *Report of the Indian Factory Commission, Appointed in September 1890, under the Orders of His Excellency, the Governor-General in Council, with Proceedings and Appendices. Calcutta, 1890)*, 1890, p. 65.

40. *FC* 1890, p. 65.

41. *FC* 1890.

42. Demi-official from Ahmedabad mill women to Dr K.N. Bahadhurji, 1 December 1891, no. 7, Home (Judicial) A, January 1892, NAI.

43. *Times of India*, 23 March 1892.

44. From Dr K.N. Bahadhurji to Secretary to the Government of India, 26 December 1891, no. 6, Home Judicial A, January 1892, NAI.

45. *Times*, 28 September 1891.

46. From K.N. Bahadhurji to the Chief Secretary to the Government of Bombay, GD, Cumballa Hill, Bombay, 18 December 1891, MSA.

47. Petition from female operatives employed in the spinning and weaving mills in Ahmedabad to Lord Harris, Governor of Bombay, Home (Judicial) A, January 1892, NAI.

48. Petition from female operatives employed in the spinning and weaving mills in Ahmedabad to Lord Harris, Governor of Bombay, Home (Judicial) A, January 1892, NAI.

49. Petition from female operatives employed in the spinning and weaving mills in Ahmedabad to Lord Harris, Governor of Bombay, Home (Judicial) A, January 1892, NAI.

50. *Indian Textile Journal*, March 1892, quoted in *Times of India*, 26 March 1892.

51. *Times of India*, 24 February 1892.

52. Nalini Pandit, 'Narayan Meghaji Lokhande: The Father of Trade Union Movement in India', *Economic and Political Weekly* 32, no. 7 (1997): 327–9.

53. *Report and Proceedings of the Commission Appointed to Consider the Working of Factories in the Bombay Presidency, 1884–85*. Bombay, 1888, p. 111.

54. Gail Omvedt, 'Non-Brahmans and Communists in Bombay', *Economic and Political Weekly*, vol. 8, nos 16–17 (1973): 749–59, 800–5.

55. Uma Das Gupta, 'The Indian Press 1870–1880: A Small World of Journalism', *Modern Asian Studies* 11, no. 2 (1977): 213–35.

56. *FC* 1884–85, pp. 122–3.

57. Pandit, 'Narayan Meghaji Lokhande', p. 328.

58. *Times of India*, 25 September 1884.

59. *Times of India*, 27 September 1884.

60. *FC* 1884–85, 15th meeting, 4 October 1884.

61. The *Rast Goftar*'s interventions of the early 1890s disclose a growing discomfort about the consequences of the factory legislation it once endorsed so vocally, especially after the strikes of 1892. *Rast Goftar*, *RNNP Bom.*, October and November 1892.

62. Jim Masselos, *The City in Action: Bombay Struggles for Power* (New Delhi: Oxford University Press, 2007), pp. 46–81.

63. *FC* 1884–85, 16 August 1884.

64. *FC* 1884–85, 16 August 1884.

65. *FC* 1884–85, 16 August 1884.

66. See figures of monthly circulation, *RNNP Bom.*, 1882–90.

67. Home (Judicial) A, October 1890, nos 235–74, NAI.

68. Pandit, 'Narayan Meghaji Lokhande', p. 328.

69. Lokhande to BMOA, 23 April 1890, *Annual Report of the Bombay Millowners' Association*, 1891.

70. Lokhande to BMOA, 23 April 1890, *Annual Report of the Bombay Millowners' Association*, 1891.

71. Home (Judicial) A, October 1890, nos 235–74, NAI.

72. The other five witnesses who were interviewed in the Commission's office were produced by S.P. Kelkar, a Brahmo reformer whose witnesses, state the minutes, 'were not the members of the Millhands' Association'. Seventeen witnesses were produced by such mediation, and the other thirty who were interviewed in Bombay and Ahmedabad were picked out, at random, from among workers at mills that the Commissioners visited without prior notice (*FC* 1890).

73. Home (Judicial) A, October 1890, nos 235–74, NAI.

74. The public nature of the Commission is attested by the fact that all the newspapers of Bombay sent reporters to collect a copy of the evidence (*FC* 1890, p. 30).

75. Appendix to *FC* 1890, Lokhande's Opinion, 8 November 1890.

76. Petition of operatives employed in the Spinning and Weaving Mills in the City of Bombay, FC 1890, pp. 91–2; Punekar and Varickayil, *LMI*, pp. 303–6.

77. *FC* 1890, pp. 91–2.

78. *FC* 1890, pp. 91–2.

79. *FC* 1890, pp. 91–2.

80. *FC* 1890, pp. 91–2.

81. *FC* 1890, pp. 91–2.

82. *FC* 1890, pp. 91–2.

83. Lokhande also mentioned the other demands made by the millworkers in their public meetings and petitions for the introduction of accident

compensation, and for a fixed time for the payment of wages, the arrears only being recovered by difficult and uncertain litigation in the Small Causes court at the present time. In addition, he appended in his note to the Commission two demands that had never been expressed in the public statements by the Association: the limitation of the working hours of women and the raising of the legal age for adulthood to fifteen. Here, perhaps, it is possible to find two forces at work within Lokhande—one drawing upon the issues that stirred workers to agitate, petition, and occasionally strike, and the other responding to the issues that flowed logically from the legal trajectory of factory regulation, where questions of childhood, the work of women, and questions of safety predominated. As this chapter later demonstrates, there emerged, by the late 1890s, a divergence and potential tension between the meliorist trajectories of official intervention in mill conditions and the questions urged upon official consideration by the collective action of workers themselves.

84. *FC* 1890, 5th meeting.

85. *FC* 1890, 5th meeting.

86. *FC* 1890, 4th meeting.

87. *FC* 1890, 4th meeting.

88. *FC* 1890, 2nd meeting.

89. *FC* 1890, 5th meeting.

90. *FC* 1890.

91. *FC* 1890, 12th meeting.

92. *FC* 1890, 12th meeting.

93. Home (Judicial) A, no. 42, 20 November 1889, NAI.

94. Punekar and Varickayil, *LMI*, pp. 303–4.

95. Home (Judicial) A, no. 42, 20 November 1889, NAI.

96. *Royal Commission on Labour, PP* 1892, C.6795-XI (henceforth *RCL* 1892)), p. 173.

97. *RCL* 1892, p. 168.

98. *RCL* 1892, p. 169.

99. *RCL* 1892, p. 174.

100. *RCL* 1892.

101. *RCL* 1892.

102. See, for instance, *Times of India*, 24 February 1892.

103. Home (Legislative) A, April 1891, 74–312, NAI.

104. Lokhande to GoI, 20 November 1889, Home (Judicial) A, no. 42, February 1890, NAI.

105. Lokhande to GoI, 20 November 1889, Home (Judicial) A, no. 42, February 1890, NAI.

106. *Jam-e-Jamshed*, 24 November 1892, *RNNP Bom*.

107. *Jam-e-Jamshed*, 24 November 1892, *RNNP Bom*.

108. *FC* 1884–85, 15th meeting, 4 October 1884.

109. *FC* 1884–85, 15th meeting, 4 October 1884, p. 100.

110. *FC* 1884–85, 15th meeting, 4 October 1884, p. 100.

111. *FC* 1884–85, 16th Meeting, 6 October 1884, p. 105.

112. *FC* 1884–85, 19th Meeting, 25 October 1884, p. 143.

113. *FC* 1884–85, 19th Meeting, 25 October 1884, p. 142.

114. *FC* 1884–85, 19th Meeting, 25 October 1884, p. 144.

115. *Bombay Samachar,* 27 December 1892, *RNNP Bom.*

116. *Bombay Samachar*, 28 December 1892, *RNNP Bom.*

117. *Bombay Samachar*, 28 December 1892, *RNNP Bom.*

118. *Indian Textile Journal* III, no. 34 (July 1893).

119. From Inspector of Steam Boilers and Prime Movers, to Collector, Bombay, no. 33, 23 February 1880. L/P&J/6/18, no. 1035, 1880, OIOC.

120. From Inspector of Steam Boilers and Prime Movers, to Collector, Bombay, no. 33, 23 February 1880. L/P&J/6/18, no. 1035, 1880, OIOC.

121. From Inspector of Steam Boilers and Prime Movers, to Collector, Bombay, no. 33, 23 February 1880. L/P&J/6/18, no. 1035, 1880, OIOC.

122. From Inspector of Steam Boilers and Prime Movers, to Collector, Bombay, no. 33, 23 February 1880. L/P&J/6/18, no. 1035, 1880, OIOC.

123. *Indian Textile Journal* III, no. 36 (September 1893).

124. *Times of India*, 3 December 1877.

125. *Times of India,* 4 February 1879.

126. *Times of India*, 6 March 1879.

127. Investigation by the *Rast Goftar* disclosed other motives for the strike. Of the fifty to seventy-five workers employed in each department in the Kurla Mill, only one person at a time was allowed to go out to relieve himself (or, as the newspaper put it, 'for passing water, & c.'), and so 'a great deal of pain is caused to the man whose turn it is to go last'. *Rast Goftar,* 15 June 1884, *RNNP Bom.*

128. *Rast Goftar,* 15 June 1884, *RNNP Bom.*

129. Replies from Morarji Goculdas and Co., Agents, Kurla Spinning and Weaving Mill, *RCL* 1892.

130. *RCL* 1892

131. *Times of India,* 25 September 1884.

132. *Times of India*, 25 September, 1894.

133. No. 43, Home (Judicial) A, February 1890, NAI.

134. No. 4761, 14 December 1885, Government of Bombay, GD (Misc.), P/2637, OIOC.

135. *Annual Report of Bombay Millowners' Association*, 1891.

136. Goculdas and Wacha to John Marshall, Secretary, BMOA, 3 January 1895, *Annual Report of Bombay Millowners' Association*, 1895.

137. John Marshall to members of BMOA, December 1895, *Annual Report of Bombay Millowners' Association*, 1895.

138. John Marshall to members of BMOA, December 1895, *Annual Report of Bombay Millowners' Association*, 1895.

139. *RCL* 1892, p. 134.

140. No. F.I – 4, GD, 26 July 1892, no. 52, MSA.

141. No. F.I – 4, GD, 26 July 1892, no. 52, MSA.

142. *RCL*, 1892, p. 119.

143. GD, 26 July 1892, MSA.

144. GD, 26 July 1892, MSA.

145. *RCL*, 1892, p. 128.

146. *RCL*, 1892, p. 128.

147. *RCL*, 1892, p. 134.

148. *RCL*, 1892, p. 136.

149. *Jam-e-Jamshed*, 4 November 1892, *RNNP Bom*.

150. *Indian Textile Journal* III, no. 26 (November 1892).

151. *Indian Textile Journal* III, no. 26 (November 1892); *Annual Report of Bombay Millowners' Association* 1892; *Jam-e-Jamshed*, 4 November 1892, *RNNP Bom*.

152. *Times of India*, October–November 1892.

153. *Annual Report of Bombay Millowners' Association*, 1892.

154. *Indian Textile Journal*, December 1892.

155. *Bombay Gazette*, 8 July 1895.

6

Snapping the Tie

Chronicles of the Plague Years, 1896–8

In September 1896, Bombay's municipal administration declared the presence of bubonic plague in the city.[1] Within weeks, a series of ramshackle medical and sanitary fortifications against the epidemic had been erected, but these proved ineffective. In the winter of that year, the plague toll rose dramatically, and by March 1897 over 10,000 lives had been lost, despite an array of draconian measures of plague control.[2]

Correspondingly, a 'popular panic' gripped the city, as much in response to the administration's attempts to survey, control, and attack the bodies and congested neighbourhoods of the city's working poor as to the fact of the epidemic itself. By January, a little under half of Bombay's population had fled to a countryside which itself was ravaged by famine. It was, indeed, the grimly Malthusian balance between famine and plague that lay at the root of Bombay's survival as a city, as flight to the countryside was balanced, in the medium term, by flight *from* the countryside.

Plague mortality peaked in March and receded over the spring and summer. People started drifting back to the city in the summer months, but the flow was reversed as the toll began to rise again during and after the monsoon.[3] This, broadly, was the pattern for several years to come: ferocious epidemic attacks at the end of the year, a slackening of virulence over the spring and summer. The popular panic of the first year and a half, however, was never quite replicated, and plague gradually took its place as one of many killers that stalked a city racked by many crises.

A claim that resonated in these years tells us something a little more precise about the new social relations that may have emerged at the confluence of death, flight, and urban devastation. 'The year 1897 witnessed ... the shattering of the tie hitherto binding the employer and employed', wrote S.M. Edwardes, successively Factory Inspector, Census Commissioner, and Police Commissioner for Bombay, in 1902.[4] This apprehension was one commonly voiced during the plague years. The nostalgic invocation of a past harmony, of course, describes no concrete reality that Bombay had ever experienced. Nevertheless, Edwardes was on to something, as was the Chief Inspector of Factories for Bombay in 1897 when he wrote of the emergence, for the first time, 'of a Labour Question comparable to those of Europe'.[5] An epidemic crisis that was most intensely felt by Bombay's labouring poor simultaneously seems to have become the source from which unprecedented assertions of effective working-class strength flowed.

Millworkers, as one of the major, collectively identifiable social fractions within the city, and as the bedrock of its trade, played a major role in the making of this crisis, and it is their actions that I seek to elucidate in this chapter. I begin by considering millworkers within the urban context in which their actions were conceived, executed, and received their meaning. The first section of my chapter, therefore, begins by locating millworkers within the economy of popular unrest and state anxiety that marked the first year and a half of the plague, between late 1896 and early 1898. I try to explain the ways in which millworkers partook of and responded to the perennial urban unrest that accompanied the epidemic. In the process, I also demarcate the contours of state concerns about the emergence of millhands as a disruptive force in the micropolitics of the city.

I move from this to a close reading of the crisis of political authority that convulsed the life of Bombay's mills, as millworkers asserted and sustained new claims and entitlements in their daily work. This shift towards labour in the pendulum of industrial relations was grounded in larger economic and political forces in the 1890s, but reached a dramatic intensity in 1897, one that would not be replicated in over two decades. This new bargaining power the workers commanded flowed, paradoxically, from their mortal vulnerability. I try to explain the ways in which this precarious, temporary structure of industrial relations worked, and how it eventually produced a fresh compromise between the interests of workers and employers.

Plague and Associated Panics, 1896–8

Plague began to lay claim to Bombay as early as August 1896, but it was only in winter that a genuine popular panic began to emerge. By the end of the year, there had been 2,544 plague cases reported, and 1,936 deaths, of which 1,271 happened in December alone. In January, the number of deaths outstripped the total plague mortality of the preceding year, the toll for the month being 2,110. February claimed 3,349 and March 2,424. It was not till the summer months that the toll slipped significantly.[6]

By the spring of 1897 Bombay was visibly a city near collapse. The contagion of plague appeared to travel the streets hand in hand with the contagion of urban breakdown. The most visible signifier of this was the devastating flight from the city. People began to escape Bombay in droves in the winter of 1896. In October, an estimated 20,000 people fled the city. In November and December, 171,500 were added to that number.[7] By the end of January roughly 400,000 people had fled, which amounted to a little less than half the city's total population.

A verse account from 1899, by B.F. Patell, a teacher at Elphinstone High School, evokes the sense of colossal calamity that was produced by the plague. The verse is less than inspired, but Patell's description of a deserted, crumbling city is nonetheless eloquent:

> Now, silent as the grave these streets
> A straggler here and there one meets.
> And where is gone the surging crowd
> That made the city look so proud?
> A part unto that dismal bourne
> From which no traveller may return:
> But most have fled to distant parts,
> Sad fugitives with bleeding hearts.[8]

The epidemic seemed to bear mortal consequences not only for the individuals who encountered it, but for the city as a whole. Shortly after the outbreak of plague, Bombay was threatened with an international trading embargo. While the British kept their ports open throughout the decades of the global pandemic, their trading partners were quick to impose regimes of surveillance and regulation upon all ships from India. The French, for instance, intimated the possibility of riots in Marseilles, the site of Europe's last major plague attack in 1721, barred

South Asian passengers from their Mediterranean ports, and issued tight controls on Indian trade, including a ban on raw hide imports.[9] Such threats were seen as portents of economic death for Bombay, a future which contemporary observers ranging from officials to visitors held all too possible. Global pressures, then, also drove British responses to plague, formalized in the Epidemic Diseases Act of 1897, which gave the Municipal Commissioner wide-ranging powers of regulation, without reference to a magistrate.[10]

This sense of helplessness was accentuated by the fact that the aetiology of bubonic plague was only very dimly understood in the late nineteenth century.[11] Miasmatic schemes of explanation, linking plague to 'emanations' from stores of decaying grain, described one vector of understanding, which associated the epidemic with local sanitary conditions. Officials and experts repeated, over the months, their apprehension that the plague was 'in the soil', and the ground itself needed to be broken up and disinfected. A telegram from the Secretary of State to the Governor on 22 January 1897 attests the urgency of this apprehension: 'Experts lay stress on importance, in addition to general disinfection, of casting away and burning earth of floors to depth of four inches.'[12]

'Pythogenetic' explanatory schemes, on the other hand, identified the cramped and insanitary living conditions of the city as a sort of meta-vector of the disease, while contagionist understandings targeted the human body as the prime vector.[13] These schemes provided the prime scientific bedrock for state-imposed measures of plague control. In the absence of a reliable consensus, and given the relative newness of voluntary inoculation and vaccination as a solution, the measures initiated by the city's municipality and, subsequently, government-appointed Plague Committees necessarily bore the marks of other anxieties, namely those about the industrial transformation of the city and its social consequences. Health officials' reports and medical testimonies from the 1860s and the 1870s had warned, though very intermittently, of the possible consequences of such uncontrolled urban expansion: population overload; overburdened drainage and sewage networks; insanitary concentrations of poverty behind fortresses of dirt and disease.[14]

To colonial and municipal legislators, corporators, and officials the plague represented both a nightmare of death for Bombay and a ground where fantasies of social control could be enacted. The hotly contested debates over the explanation of the plague and the most efficient methods to combat it meant that plague control had of necessity to be experimental. The programme of the Bombay Municipality, and subsequently a government-appointed expert body, a Plague Committee (installed in February 1897, with General Gatacre at its head), in the period between 1896 and 1898 rested, successively or simultaneously, on the following measures: compulsory hospitalization and segregation of plague 'suspects'; disinfection and, if necessary, destruction of homes and buildings labelled 'Unfit for Human Habitation' or 'U.H.H.'; compulsory medical examination; forced entry into homes; projects of sanitation and conservancy.[15]

These were the principal regulatory choices the administration saw before it, and the path described by plague policy travelled, nervously, between them. Plague policy was in one sense triggered by the immediate crisis, but in another sense it immediately signalled a long-term project aimed at controlling the consequences of industrialization and crowding in a growing metropolis, exposing it to the disciplines of sanitation, inspection, and medicine.

These experiments both rested on and accentuated a double crisis: of urban flight and of the unravelling of the fragile social compact that governed relations of authority and subordination in Bombay. Patell's poem describes, in some detail, the dominant form taken by the threat of Bombay's devastation—the flight, specifically, of the networks of labour that sustained the city:

> [M]enial servants of all grades,
> And votaries of the humbler trades,
> Hamal, masal, cook, ayah, syce,
> Each one with bag and baggage flies;
> The dhobie, gavlai, butcher, baker,
> The barber, tailor and shoe-maker
> A motley crowd, all fleeing fast,
> They think the town redemption past.[16]

The flight of the city's labour force, then, was clearly one of the most visible effects of the epidemic crisis. Each instance of labour flight touched on in Patell's poem suggests a breakdown of the normal configuration of class and labour relations in the city: no one left to cook for those who employed cooks; to clean the houses and look after the children of the rich; to wash other people's clothes; to deliver milk, meat, or bread; to cut their hair, tailor their clothes, mend their shoes. The channels of authority and subordination that sustained everyday social relationships in Bombay had been ripped to shreds by flight. The forms of labour upon which the city was built were now aggregated into a 'motley crowd', not organized for the purposes of civil unrest, but, perhaps even more damagingly, for the purposes of mass desertion.

The 'snapping' of the 'tie' that bound employer and worker, to use the words of the Factory Inspector, constituted and sustained a challenge to designated and accepted forms of social and political authority. The chaos intensified the value placed upon labour in the work of keeping the crumbling city functioning. Paradoxically—but only apparently so—two dynamics intensified simultaneously in fin de siècle Bombay: the extension of, but also the popular attack upon, the sources of 'legitimate' political authority. Consider the path of plague policy itself. The measures of control outlined earlier were shaken, and not infrequently reversed, by fierce resistance on the streets of Bombay from the city's working classes. There were three dramatic events between 1896 and 1898 where the dynamics of plague control policy and popular assertion clashed, and attending to these more closely may help elucidate certain broad patterns established in these months.

The first of these was a millworkers' demonstration and riot at the end of October 1896, at a time when the epidemic had moved rapidly through the southern district of Mandvi and had begun to threaten the clustered working-class neighbourhoods to its north and east. The Municipal Commissioner, P.C.H. Snow, put together a plague control policy that involved the forcible isolation and 'segregation' of suspected victims, and their removal to the Infectious Diseases Hospital at Arthur Road, a ramshackle building with few doctors and underpaid, overworked hospital assistants and nurses in the heart of the city's mill district.[17] The high rates of mortality in the hospital and the cries of pain that could be heard from its interiors on the crowded streets outside produced rumours that plague policy was effectively an instrument to isolate and kill the poor.[18]

On 29 October, following a month of murmurs of discontent, matters reached a head when a hapless Goan cook, going from mill to mill in search of employment, was accused of being an agent of the Municipal Health Department, who had allegedly gone to inspect the factories with the ulterior motive of carrying away workers. Millhands congregated before the hospital during their lunch break, threw stones, broke into the compound, and threatened hospital employees. The riot lasted a short time, and when lunch break ended, most workers came back to their posts.[19]

The brief incident spiralled, however, into wider anxieties as the sanitary staff of the city, reported by Snow to be in 'almost open sympathy with the millhands', threatened to leave Bombay.[20] This threat bore terrible portents. The work of the untouchable sanitary workers, *halalkhores* and *bigarris*, in cleaning and desilting municipal drains, overhauling water connections to houses, disinfecting and lime-washing godowns and rooms, and so on was labour that constituted the backbone of plague control. Their discontent had deeper roots: a long wage freeze and a situation where their sources of ready credit—the banias and shroffs of south Bombay—had already fled.

The threat of the withdrawal of their labour, in a city whose masters had suddenly woken up to the long history of sanitary neglect coupled with frenetic economic growth and construction, heralded a potential situation where 'Bombay would have in a few days become uninhabitable'.[21] Municipal and health officials anticipated a situation where the turbulence initiated by the millhands would spread to sanitary workers, and thus to other low-caste employees of different municipal departments. The Municipality backtracked on its plague policy instantly and issued proclamations withdrawing the clauses on forcible segregation and hospitalization. Simultaneously, railway and steamer companies were instructed not to issue tickets to scavengers and sweepers trying to leave the city.[22] An uneasy mixture of conciliation and coercion, then, characterized the first major shift in plague policy.

In February, the municipal administration's control over plague policy had been transferred into the hands of General Gatacre's Plague Committee, which intensified the authoritarianism of earlier strategies. The escalation of plague over the winter had reversed the state's temporary retreat from draconian measures in the wake of the October crisis, and Plague Committee employees were instructed to carry out house-to-house searches, isolate victims and dwellings suspected of plague, and were given the power to mark buildings 'U.H.H.', a condemnation that came to be scrawled liberally across the walls and doors of working-class chawls and huts.[23]

On 6 and 7 April, there were two enormous strikes in the southern part of the city, near the docks. In the first instance, over three thousand casual workers, mainly cartmen employed in transporting goods to and from the docks, and coolies employed by the Municipality went on strike against the destruction of their dwellings. This was after repeated requests and a petition had failed to move the authorities.[24] The Colaba Causeway and Cotton Green were filled with large numbers of workers mobilized to prevent other cartmen and coolies from infringing the strike. It took a large contingent of police, merchants concerned about the disruption of their business by the cartmen's cessation of their labour, and carting agents and contractors to quell the strike.[25]

The very next day the discontent rippled further south, and the docks stood empty as over eight thousand dockworkers went on a day-long strike against house-to-house visitation and the destruction of their dwellings. Ironically, many of the cartmen who had been on strike the previous day over the same issue and had now returned to work found themselves blocked by striking dockers when they tried to transport and unload goods for the docks. The strike lasted till afternoon, when an agreement was reached clarifying that the gratuitous destruction of workers' possessions would be restrained.[26]

The third, and most explosive, of the urban crises of these months happened in March 1898. By now, the scholar-administrator J.M. Campbell had taken over from Gatacre as head of the Plague Committee, and, after the slight thawing of plague measures with the decline of the epidemic over the previous spring, controls were tightened again. This time, the functions of the Committee were militarized, and soldiers were introduced into the work of segregation and inspection. On the morning of 9 March, the day after Holi, a search party gathered at the house of a Muslim weaver in Madanpura to take his twelve-year-old daughter away to hospital on (as it was later proved) unfounded suspicions of plague. The girl's parents resisted, and a large crowd rapidly gathered on the clustered and winding streets outside.[27]

When a hastily assembled party of policemen opened fire, the crowds scattered, but recouped, hydra-like, as they ran through the alleys, their numbers swelled by a large number of Hindu millworkers.[28] These workers would normally have been back in their Konkan homes for Holi, but were locked into the island by quarantine measures and had celebrated the festival in the city. Riot fanned riot, and symbols of state authority were systematically attacked: plague hospitals were invaded, and, in a symbolically insurrectionary gesture, the gallows-screen outside the Arthur Road Jail was burned down. Police reinforcements, drawn from scattered outposts across the island, were late, and through most of the afternoon pitched street battles were fought.[29] The violence rapidly spread and the police lagged behind, chasing people through alleys, twisting streets, and neighbourhoods that they never really controlled. At key moments, the coercive apparatus could be just as vulnerable as its targets and victims.

The riot amplified old tensions and left the city scarred with new ones, but it assumed a particular, retroactive force in the minds of city officials and administrators because of what followed it—a huge general strike, perhaps the first example of a bandh in Bombay, when the forms of labour and trade the city rested on ceased: small traders in grain and cloth shut their shops; bullock-cart drivers went out on strike; butchers, dockers, municipal employees, and railway workers did likewise.[30] The strike was finally halted, after prolonged and conciliatory negotiations by the state with traders and foremen, after nearly a week, on 15 March.[31]

Major concessions had to be granted. Sandhurst, the Governor, effected wide-ranging changes in plague administration, withdrawing soldiers from plague work, declaring arbitrary house inspections illegitimate, and prohibiting the forcible removal of people to hospital. Campbell, the head of the Plague Committee, was asked to go on leave, and he never returned to India: a powerful career in colonial administration was ingloriously terminated as a direct consequence of popular agitation. This coincided, as Catanach has pointed out, with a decisive reconsideration of plague policy at the national level, and a move towards the institutionalization of voluntary inoculation, rather than forcible hospitalization or house destruction, as the basis of plague policy. This had only partly to do with advances in medical knowledge, for it was still not widely understood that plague could not be easily transmitted through bodily contagion. Nor did it have to do with a slackening of the epidemic itself: 1899, 1901, and 1903 all claimed more lives than 1897 or 1898 had.[32] Nevertheless, the plague crisis as a crisis of authority reached its real terminus in mid-1898, as the most coercive forms of epidemic control were rolled back in response to popular rioting.

How can we read the trajectories of these events? In the first place, a dramatic, if temporary, shift in the political life of Bombay seems to have been triggered by the plague. At its heart lies the assertive, and simultaneous, mobilization of different segments of Bombay's labouring poor. The state's authority rested on chains of command that were suddenly laid bare during the interwoven crises of epidemic disease and death, panic, and flight. As measures of plague control intensified, so too did forms of resistance, some of them violent.

In the early years of the plague, two forms of contagion were dreaded by the colonial and municipal authorities in charge of Bombay. The first was the contagion of human contact, which was supposed to be the chief vector of the epidemic. The second apprehension, more abstract but equally potent, was the contagion of social disorder. The incidents I have described seem to bear out—and were seen to bear out—the second of these threats. Popular resistance to plague measures that originated in particular localities and spaces of work seemed, within moments, to escalate and infect other places and labouring locales. The effect was to draw different segments of the city's working classes into a common, active, and frequently violent opposition to plague administration, and this was a domino effect that was particularly hard to control, since it spread through streets, alleys, houses, neighbourhoods, factories and workplaces, and railways—in other words, through every channel of communication imaginable. The riot of 1898 exemplified this: a very specific, local issue became generalized and came to pose urgent dangers to civic peace within minutes of the initial confrontation.

Second, the plague seems to have catalysed several kinds of connection between the different segments of the urban labour market. It is clear from the official records that the major threat that moments of urban unrest were seen to pose was their capacity to spill beyond their 'normal' frontiers. A strike could become a riot, a riot could spill over into a strike, and the discontent of different labouring groups—millworkers, sweepers, cartmen, dockworkers, casual labourers—came to be articulated with one another in complex ways.

These articulations could be organized along the axes of solidarity: for instance, the support of untouchable sanitary workers for rioting, largely caste-Hindu millworkers, in 1896, or the unexpected solidarity between Muslim weavers and Hindu millworkers in the riot of 1898 (it was these very two sections that had clashed so violently in the communal riots of 1893). On the other hand, the cartmen and dockers who went on strike in 1897 complained bitterly that low-caste municipal workers were allowed to enter and disinfect their homes, and they simmered down once they were assured that their caste boundaries would not be violated. The railway strike at the beginning of 1897 was chiefly a mobilization of European and Eurasian engine-workers and guards, partly in protection of entitlements (bonuses) they had enjoyed as racially privileged workers. The introduction of Indian staff by the railway companies in the 1890s triggered an attempt to level earnings downwards, and the removal of bonuses for enginemen and guards seems to have been on the anvil. Some popular suspicion seems to have attached to the striking workers, and the *Indian Spectator* reported rumours that this was a conspiracy between the government and the railway companies to keep the city's population from fleeing the plague.[33]

There was no generalized structure of sustained solidarity across occupational lines among the labouring poor, but in certain ways this might even have accentuated the threats such actions posed. The working class emerged not as an empirical unit, but in spectral form, dispersed across various locations. It emerged at the intersection of urban turbulence and state anxieties, spread across diverse work regimes and experiences, but always confronting the same enemy: arbitrary, draconian plague control.

Third, the cessation of labour, or the threat of cessation, played a pivotal role in each of the three incidents just described. Labourers involved in municipal sanitation, local trade across the city's roads, the unloading and loading of goods at the docks, waste disposal and sweeping, and the railways threatened to, and at various points did, go on strike. At a time when the state was seized with a sudden awareness of the centrality of their labour in the functioning of the city, such cessations of labour carried dangers they never had before. In 1896, the millhands were feared not so much for their own turbulence as their capacity to cause similar discontent amongst the city's sweepers and scavengers. In 1897, on successive days, workers involved in transporting goods, clearing roads, and dock labour went on strike. In 1898, a riot in a working-class neighbourhood was followed by a cessation of all the arterial forms of trade and labour that kept the city running. These moments lay at the heart of the tensions provoked by public mobilizations of the labouring poor. It was this, I believe, more than anything else, that underpinned the shifting, nervous nature of the state's plague policy between 1896 and 1898: invasive advances followed by rapid backtracking, conciliation, and negotiation.

The Crisis in the Mills

Millhands, the largest distinct occupational group in the city, frequently partook of, and were always witnesses to, such street mobilization. They lived in clustered working-class neighbourhoods marked by complex and intricate networks of exchange, credit, dependency, and solidarity, and felt the brunt when the state intruded. The violence of the intrusion was sometimes matched by the violence of mobilized resistance, and millhands were the first to take the lead in this, in October 1896, in the wake of the suspicions and rumours that had coagulated around the high-handed policy of arbitrary removal to hospital. They shared chawls with other labourers and were among the first to protest against the state's policy of 'condemnation' in April 1897 in the form of a petition to the government that they drafted with other chawl residents just before the successive strikes in Colaba. The Police Commissioner, R.E. Vincent, and other contemporary observers marked them out as enthusiastic participants in the Madanpura riots of 1898. Contemporary accounts do not, by and large, elucidate the particular ways in which millworkers were mobilized, or their specific actions. But there are intriguing hints: newspapers, for instance, reported a violent attack on Jacob Sassoon, one of the biggest mill owners in the city, during the riot on 9 March, quite possibly authored by workers at his mills.[34]

In the course of the experiences of street unrest between 1896 and 1898, then, millworkers stamped themselves indelibly upon the official gaze as a potential source of grievance and violence. The growing frequency of industrial strikes since the early 1890s had in some measure contributed to this, as had the communal riot of 1893, where Hindu millhands had played a major role. This was in significant contrast to the images of millworkers that had previously predominated in the discourses of officials and mill owners. Millhands were clearly coming together more frequently as a body to press collective demands, something dimly in evidence during the deliberations on factory regulation, and more violently expressed in riots and strikes. It was the crisis of

1897, however, that put the seal upon the official identification of millworkers as a potential threat to the peace of the city and the stability of its economy.

The world internal to mill work, too, was undergoing convulsions through 1896 and 1897, and it is to these convulsions, which both corresponded to and differed from the challenges faced by the state, that my narrative now turns.

Patell's poem describes the everyday reality of Bombay's cotton mills in 1897 in a few lines:

> Mill-hands, foregoing work and pay,
> By thousands pour out every day;
> ....
> The mills stop work for want of hands,
> Mill labour now high price commands.[35]

By the late 1890s, workers in the cotton mills numbered near 80,000, roughly a tenth of the city's population. The plague crisis, as we have seen, galvanized them into militant action in October, but it was only in December that plague began sweeping the working-class neighbourhoods clustered in the north and east of the city and triggering a massive exodus. Millworkers were slower to leave the city than other labourers, but the last weeks of the year and the first weeks of the next saw their flight attain, in the words of one of their employers, 'the dimensions of a stampede'.[36] As a consequence, the supply of labour to the mills—at a time when the demand for Bombay yarn in China and Japan was still high—dwindled to a fraction of its former volume.[37] To keep the mills working, mill owners offered the remaining able-bodied labourers substantial concessions. The attempt made by millworkers to retain these concessions, as a matter of perceived right, led to industrial conflict of an intensity that had hitherto not been seen in Bombay.

This is a theme whose absence from the bulk of research published on the labour history of Bombay has been surprising. In the most important historical account of industrial relations and working-class politics that we have, by Raj Chandavarkar, a detailed description of popular politics and the plague omits all analysis of the industrial disharmony experienced during the epidemic.[38] He is not alone in this omission.

Of late, this missing link has been skilfully restored by Prashant Kidambi in the first major historical consideration of the theme.

Kidambi takes as his point of departure the debate that once raged among interpreters of South Asian labour and industrial relations on the question of labour scarcity in colonial Bombay. In 1955, challenging established wisdom, Morris had argued that large industrial employers experienced little difficulty procuring labour for their mills in the colonial era.[39] Chandavarkar had complicated this debate by suggesting that historians turn their attention to the demand side of the equation and consider the context of fluctuating demand for industrial labour that the question of 'labour supply' was actually situated in.[40]

Kidambi argues that Chandavarkar's account of industrial relations in Bombay, in common with most others, draws most of its material and argument from the interwar years, where indeed there was no real crisis of labour supply. The period between 1893 and 1918, however, he demonstrates, saw conjunctural forces combine to produce a genuine crisis in the labour market and unprecedented patterns of industrial strife as relations at the workplace threatened to implode.[41]

Kidambi identifies four agents at work. First, the intermittent nature of demand for cotton exports in the Far Eastern markets that composed the major trading destination for Bombay's mills. This unreliability of demand, which developed through the 1890s and 1900s, was underpinned by the periodic saturation of the market, the rapid growth of a cotton manufacturing industry in Japan, and the impressive beginnings of another in China. Second, the monetary policy of the Government of British India, which removed India from the protections of the silver standard and caused a fall in exchange rates that greatly devalued textile exports. Third, the fiscal policy of the 1890s, which instituted tariff barriers against exports of yarn and cotton piece goods woven in India and, thus, hurt both the spinning and weaving units in Bombay. Fourth, the coupled devastations of plague and famine in western India in the late 1890s and early 1900s. Mortality levels rose dramatically after 1896 in both the city and the countryside, which were also both rocked by flight, as peasants and landless labourers tried to escape the famine and working-class inhabitants of Bombay fled the city upon the annual recrudescence of plague.[42]

All this created a hitherto unprecedented shift in the pendulum of industrial relations, as Kidambi argues, away from capital and towards labour. The bargaining power of workers reached unprecedented levels between 1893 and the end of the First World War, years that also saw a significant intensification of strikes and urban social conflicts of various kinds that featured the industrial working class.[43]

The plague crisis of 1896–7 was a pivotal moment in this transformation. Kidambi persuasively reconstructs the importance of the *conjuncture* (of 1893–1918) in the making of patterns that characterized industrial relations in Bombay. His account is also suggestive because of its shift away from Chandavarkar's framework. Chandavarkar had offered, to put it telegraphically, an account of the *structure* within which Bombay's cotton mills functioned between the late nineteenth century and the 1940s: the constitution of the labour market, its relations with capitalist strategies, and the politics of work relations are elucidated within a long-term framework of regularities. Kidambi, reversing, as it were, Fernand Braudel's prescriptions about the hierarchy of structure, conjuncture and event, seeks to deepen our understanding of Bombay's labour market by moving from structure to conjuncture.[44] His focus is temporally narrower, but this is an advantage rather than a limitation since it helps isolate a specific and unusual period in Bombay's social history where long-run structures and immediate contingencies can be shown to overlap.

My purpose, in a sense, is to complete this reverse-Braudelian Movement by restoring to the *event* (here the plague pandemic) its full historical efficiency. It is of course necessary to understand the larger structures of class, geography, ecology, and economy that gave form to the plague's social effects in order to demystify the apparent suddenness with which the epidemic burst upon Bombay. However, I would like to argue, perhaps controversially, that such demystification, stretched beyond a point, can actually produce a reverse mystification by rendering the new and traumatic intrusions of a social crisis in overly familiar terms. The 'surface' strangeness of the plague cannot be exhausted or cut down to size by carefully historicizing its conditions of emergence. Indeed, to draw upon an argument philosopher Slavoj Žižek has made in a number of contexts, sometimes there may be more truth in the illusion of a sudden traumatic rupture than in contextualizations that rob it of its mystery. To argue this is not to cleave to a romantic conception of sudden and irreversible breaks and ruptures. But if one believes in different scales of historical temporality working in simultaneity, following Braudel (against the letter), it is necessary to not reduce these scales to each other. In other words, reducing the plague to its 'conditions of emergence'—whether understood in structural or conjunctural terms—is to refuse to understand what constitutes its 'event-ness', what gives it the quality of a dramatic, unique eventuation that properly *exceeds* its conditions, and what makes it possible—up to a point—to isolate it as an object of historical enquiry.[45]

I shall return to these conceptual considerations in the conclusion to this chapter. For the moment, it is sufficient to register that the plague was a significant moment in 'the life of labour' in more ways than one. Most obviously, it produced new sources of vulnerability and mortality and exacerbated old ones. It also, however, produced new forms of collective organization among workers. For a while, millworkers who were in many cases days away from death nourished, through the persistence of their desperate demands and the force of their solidarity, a radically new form of industrial relations.

Snapping the Tie

Bombay's mills had suffered a turbulent decade beginning in 1890, as their main export market—China—was periodically glutted, and mini-periods of buoyancy were regularly followed by recessions in the trade in yarn and goods. The crisis of the plague years, however, was qualitatively different and could not be reduced to a temporary market fluctuation that would correct itself through the requisite market mechanisms. The flight of labourers, beginning in the winter of 1896, produced the tightest labour market the city had ever known, and the industry stood poised on the brink of collapse. In March 1897, at the height of the crisis, the weaving sheds had been completely shut down and mills worked 65,000 spindles of a total of over two million.[46] The biggest employers of labour in the city employed between a tenth and a third of their machinery and hands.[47] Bombay's mill owners were haunted by the spectre of a city where their commercial interests would simply have no place, for there would be no one left to make their commodities and their profits for them.

When we turn to the experiences of millworkers in this time, we find, predictably enough, desperate vulnerability. Millhands consistently numbered 12 per cent of the plague mortality figures.[48] The credit mechanisms that ensured their subsistence collapsed, as the bania and shroff moneylenders were amongst the first to flee the city, and workers were consequently either poised on the point of death or the point of flight. Flight, even when unavoidable, offered no real answers, since famine raged in the countryside and the prospect of going home and finding neither work nor food was a real one. Millworkers were, thus, squeezed between an urban epidemic and rural scarcity, caught, as it were, between rival ways of dying.

The 'tie' snapped, in the first instance, on the streets, in the context of the crunch in the labour market. Accounts from the 1870s and 1880s tell us of workers sleeping before the gates of mills at early dawn in order to make it to work on time, of casual labourers thronging outside through the day, hopeful of work as *badlis* or substitutes. By contrast, the most resonant image of 1897 is rival jobbers scouring the streets of the mill districts, bidding up their mills' wages desperately in order to attract labourers at high daily rates. Consequently, workers would often leave their posts in the middle of their work and join casual labourers on the streets to ascertain the prices offered by other mills and walk off with the highest wage-bidder in the bazaar.[49] A letter by a mill manager to the press in January 1897 speaks of 'mills that actually post men at the mill-gate to cry out "Ready cash paid daily in this mill; come as many as want eight annas a day"'.[50]

The practice of paying millhands daily was an entirely new improvisation, and it reversed a long-established procedure, that of keeping workers' wages in arrears for weeks, sometimes months, as security against desertion and as a form of industrial control. Assuming an arrears period of a month, a worker would traditionally be paid his November wages in January, his December wages in February, and so on, and would have to copiously borrow from moneylenders to make up the lag. An intricate interlocking of wages and credit constituted the prime mechanism of industrial control: this, rather than the mutual reciprocity contemporary observers wrote so nostalgically of, constituted the 'tie' that bound workers to employers.

Bania and shroff moneylenders, who controlled a substantial proportion of Bombay's credit, had been among the first casualties of the plague in Bombay city. 'The pressing need of the poor of Bombay at the time was food,' wrote A.L. Wood, Chief Inspector of Factories, 'that is to say ready money wherewith to buy it; for the mass of *Banias* had fled and petty credit had well-nigh ceased.'[51] Wage-arrears, in such a situation, quite literally spelt starvation and death.

The old form of industrial control collapsed with the flight of both moneylenders and large numbers of workers from the city. Initially, most mill owners tried to use the policy of wage detention to keep their workers in the city, refusing, at the beginning of 1897, to pay them the wages for November.[52] This proved unsustainable since the panic that accompanied the journey of the plague forced workers out of the city regardless of whether they had been paid what they were owed. In the first week of January, the workers of the Indian Manufacturing Company at Ripon Road launched the first millworkers' strike of the plague years, protesting against the detention of their November wages.[53] Two weeks after this, on 22 January, a meeting of mill jobbers drafted a petition asking employers to pay up for December.[54]

By this time, with the competition for labour between mills produced by the plague exodus, many employers had already begun to switch to a form of daily wage-payment. The competitive logic of this led to a significant increase in the rates of wages. In late January, the Committee of the Bombay Millowners' Association (BMOA) made ineffectual attempts to forge a consensus on wage-rates between different mills, and prescribed liberal maximum limits to day wages. In order to facilitate a return to fixed monthly wages without endangering the mills' chances to keep procuring labour, the BMOA also fixed daily rates of bonus to be paid over and above the fixed monthly wage for workers not employed on day wages.[55] As a mill manager, writing to the press in March, pointed out, this effectively legitimized wages that, at both daily and bonus rates, ranged between 40 and 90 per cent more than previous levels.[56] Comparing levels of wage payment in 1896 and 1897, he found that drawers' wages had jumped from Rs 9-7-0 to Rs 16-4-0, slubbers' wages from Rs 12-13-0 to Rs 22-12-0, and rovers' earnings from Rs 12-4-0 to Rs 19-8-0.[57] The mills, prophesied this gentleman bitterly, 'will go to the dogs'.[58]

It was not till the end of April that the BMOA, caught as it was between the desire of the Committee to enforce standard rates of payment and the wage competition practised by its individual members, was able to officially call a halt to the system of daily wages.[59] Even at this stage, though, with impoverished millhands streaming back into the mills, it was seen to be necessary to fix a scale of daily bonuses to offset the possibility of unrest rising from the change. In practice, it proved much more difficult to impose a return to monthly wages, and the daily wage system began to enter a terminal decline only from October onwards.[60]

The collapse of the wage-arrears system facilitated the corresponding collapse of many of the anchors of authority and subordination within the mills. Mill owners and managers complained, persistently, of broken machines, the confusion of functions ('A drawing room tenter is given in charge of a roving frame,' exclaimed a mill manager), and the extent of wastage.[61] The average out-turn per head was reported to have been reduced and labour was seen to be suffering from serious inefficiency, which caused worries about the 'disrepute' Indian yarn might be saddled with in the global export trade.[62] Comments of this kind continued well into the autumn of 1897, long after most of the mill-hands who had fled Bombay at the beginning of the year had returned, and 'inefficiency' could no longer be blamed on the unskilled, untrained 'loafers' who had filled their places the previous winter.

The millworkers who returned, pushed out of the countryside by famine and attracted back to Bombay by the decline of plague and the increase in mill wages, found themselves in a completely different working environment, marked by much less industrial control and discipline. Instead of heading straight into for jobs held in place for them, they found themselves, all of a sudden, in a new, fluid labour market—but, for perhaps the first time, fluid on *their* terms. With jobbers still crying out for labour at street corners, old forms of discipline and control seemed to have cracked, and employers seemed to be having a hard time reinforcing them.

Wood, the Factory Inspector, summed up the anxieties of mill owners:

> And all this extra remuneration, it must not be forgotten, was paid for less work per head; less in time by late attendance and haggling at the gates of mornings and by early stoppage for payment of evenings; less in quantity through slackness of discipline in all departments and, in those commonly paid by piece, not only through the loss of that incitement but through the failure of the attempt to impose even a minimum daily task.[63]

J.N. Tata expressed the matter with even more felicity: for him, daily wages 'had at the present moment placed the employers of labour in the unenviable position of employees'.[64]

If these words express an anxiety about declining standards of industrial efficiency, they communicate an equal worry about the forced loosening of authority. Many of the material ties that bound workers to the particular modalities of their work had now disappeared. To quote the Factory Inspector again,

> A man would stand before a mill-gate in the morning, knowing little or nothing of the work that went on inside, but sure of a welcome and of half a rupee if he stayed there till evening. Next day he would walk the streets spending his half rupee, and would hear that another mill was going to pay nine annas. On the third morning he and his likes would beset the gates of the second mill, and the first would run so many spindles shorter.[65]

Dismissals, which mill owners had easy recourse to in ordinary times, must have been harder to effect or even to contemplate at a time when any labour available would have seemed evanescent, its availability threatened either by death or by flight.

If hitherto reliable modes of coercion vanished, with employers as desperate for labour as they were, so did the structures of incentive that sustained the long hours traditionally worked in Bombay's mills. Piece work, which kept workers working longer and often overtime in search of a higher wage, had by now largely been replaced by fixed day wages or bonuses and could no longer be an instrument of industrial control.[66]

Workers, thus, had more control over their work time, and instead of beginning their work at sunrise, as they had for decades, they now found it possible to stay away from the mill till 7 or 8 in the morning.[67] The withholding of wages in arrears had, for the moment, been put to an end. It was possible for a worker to walk from street to street freely looking for an employer who would give him a high wage; it was no longer necessary to be tied down to the routines and petty frustrations of a fixed job that had to be eked out day by day, and work requirements, in a situation where simply keeping the machinery running was the stated priority of mill owners, were slack.

Street-corner bidding for labour, increased wages paid at the end of each day, bonuses, and intimations of industrial sloth and insubordination: these practices and apprehensions were knitted into a common framework of working-class bargaining power in the early months of the plague. Such inversions of the normal pattern of industrial relations were bound to provoke strong responses. In early February, A.L. Whittell, engineer and manager of the Union Mills in Parel, wrote bitterly of the way workers 'decamped' to other mills paying high daily wages the moment they received their arrears. Mills, despite paying daily wages and offering free rice, were short of men, 'and the majority of those that come are schemers and doggers, ruining the machinery and turning out bad work. They will work for a day or two, and then hearing of another mill offering an anna or two more daily, will be off there'.[68] The regular monthly workers, observed Whittell, took advantage of this situation, and despite the blandishments and sops held out by their old masters—free rice, *dal*, and so on—regularly walked off to other mills without a word of notice.[69]

> My experience of seven and a half years has taught me ... that, taken in the majority, he (the millworker) is a fraud, and that the only way to manage him ... is in the first place to owe him a substantial amount of his wages, and in the second place to 'rule' him with a rod of iron, to be firm, and very sparing, with kindness where due.[70]

Rumblings of the sort just quoted had little purchase in February, with the mills still working at less than half their capacity and labour being a scarce commodity. But as the first wave of plague passed and workers began to flock back to the city in April, complaints in this vein began to gain in urgency and force. The BMOA began to take a harder line on daily payments. Hesitantly and half-heartedly, with very little coordination among themselves, some mill owners began attempts to roll back day wages and restore the older system of monthly payments.

This sparked off a series of confrontations between employers and workers. If the flight of workers and the expansion of the bargaining power and entitlements of those who remained had marked the winter and spring of 1897, the summer was characterized by a series of strikes, big and small, in defence of these now threatened entitlements. At the beginning of June, the mill owners made their first serious attempt to collectively confront the crisis of authority they were faced with, and announced a return to monthly wages in a number of factories in Mazagaon, Byculla, Kamathipura, Tarwadi, and New Nagpada and, further north, in Mahim, Worli, and Parel .[71] They were instantly faced with a general strike of mammoth proportions. Labourers working in over thirty mills came out on the streets and assembled in front of their workplaces early in the morning of 1 June and continued to withhold their labour, obdurately, for over a week.[72]

In contrast to the images of riotousness and disorder that pervaded contemporary accounts of collective millworkers' action, and which had been given some force by the riot in October, this was a disciplined and peaceful strike, but the message was clear: they would not countenance a return to the earlier system of monthly wages with a month's arrears as deposit.[73] Shareholders and mill owners, writing to the press, urged that the time had come for decisive action against the blackmail workers were subjecting their employers to. 'Who are to be the masters of the situation, the work-people or the mill-agents?' wrote an irate shareholder. 'The work-people had it all their own way for some months, and are not likely to give way at once.'[74] He suggested an escalation of hostilities—a withdrawal of the bonus as well as the daily payments to which workers had become accustomed.

The strike lasted nearly ten days, waxing and waning as some of the mill workforces capitulated and new ones joined the ranks of the insurgents. An uneasy compromise was reached after 9 June, whereby the workers of several mills tacitly conceded a return to monthly wages, but claimed, as their pound of flesh, all their previous arrears and enhanced rates of bonus.[75] The strikes, in the Factory Inspector's words, 'were summarily terminated by the arrival from the Agents' offices of the silver earned half a year before',[76] and, in addition, daily advances equivalent to the bonus were given to workers, which constituted, in effect, a disguised form of daily wages.[77] The mill owners' offensive in June, then, produced less than satisfactory results.

At the beginning of July, fresh crises broke out, dispersed across several mills in central and north Bombay. Workers in some factories protested attempts to discontinue their daily advances; in others, they struck against the reduction of their bonuses. The prime agents in many of the strikes in July, however, were Muslim *Julaha* weavers, who, while better-paid than most of their counterparts in other mill departments, had often been laid off through the year as mill owners chose to temporarily close down their weaving shed and concentrate on spinning, the demand for yarn outstripping that for woven goods. With the cotton export trade improving over the summer, the weavers came back to work, but were denied the bonus and advances granted to other workers. Violent strikes broke out in several mills, involving clashes between weavers and blacklegs hired by their employers. The mill owners climbed down again and the weavers got their bonus.[78]

Strikes continued, with diminishing frequency, till September. The main points of contention continued to be attempts by mill owners to withdraw daily wages and bonuses, though in one instance, in August, there was a small but violent strike against the withdrawal of grain compensation as well.[79] There are teasing suggestions here: If workers could demand grain compensation from their employers by right, do we have in this the intimations of new moral economies born at the point of a crisis?

By October, mill owners were effectively masters of the situation again as the city's workforce finally returned to its normal levels and it became feasible to restore some of the old practices of industrial control. However, those who commented on the mills noticed a new spirit of sustained tension. 'There remains in the chawls of Byculla and Parel,' observed Wood, 'a spirit of independence, not to say unrest, which was unknown before. The immemorial trades-unionism of caste and kinship and country has for the first time asserted itself, and not without a measure of success: it will make itself felt again should need arise.'[80]

Reconstructing Industrial Relations

This strange yoking of death and power, which founded the successful defence by millworkers of their new rights, lasted till the summer of 1897, when it began to crack under the pressures of the re-stabilization of the city's labour force, a slow but real process. The terminus of this process, not surprisingly, was the reconstitution of the power of mill owners within the industry. However, the effects of the plague were serious enough to make it clear that the forms of employer power would themselves have to be reimagined. They could not be precisely the same as they were before. In this section, I offer a brief consideration of the two major streams of thought that emerged among mill owners in their attempts, in 1897, to reconceptualize the ordering of industrial relations.

The first of these schemes was a strategy devised by J.N. Tata, who was fast emerging, by the late 1890s, as the prime organic intellectual among Bombay's industrialists. As early as 1888, Tata had written to the Government of Bombay and the BMOA, urging them to facilitate the importation of landless agrarian labourers from the North-West Provinces to work in Bombay's mills, on the grounds that labour was getting dearer in the city, and workers from the north, accustomed to lower standards of living, would work for lower wages. He was turned down unequivocally on that occasion by the Government of Bombay, which held that assisting privately owned mills to procure labour through what would effectively be a process of impressment was not part of its remit.[81] The BMOA felt that this was a policy that would impose artificial patterns upon the natural relations of the supply and demand of labour, which adjust to produce the optimal results and the optimal labour force. Undeterred, Tata repeated his plea to the BMOA in 1892 and was turned down again on the same grounds.[82]

The plague provided Tata with the perfect opportunity to push his pet project forcefully. In a series of letters and statements addressed to the Committee of the BMOA in 1897, he argued that the relative cheapness of northern labour, especially at a time when famine was ravaging agrarian society in the north, would provide a needed antidote to the indiscipline and inefficiency of the 'Konkani', who would 'wake up to a sense of his own worthlessness and incompetency, and return fair value for the wages paid to him'.[83] Saddled with an undue sense of his own importance and his temporary position as 'master of the situation owing to his enjoying a monopoly', the Konkani labourer was likely to 'hamper the legitimate growth of the industry in Bombay'.[84] The labourer from upper India, on the other hand, was ideally suited to mill work in Bombay since, owing to his landlessness, he had no material ties to cultivation, which always constituted an alternate pole of attraction for the Bombay labourer. The northern labourer would be transported along with his family and would, unlike his Konkani counterpart, entirely lose his ties with the land and become dependent upon the mills for his livelihood.[85]

At a time when the Konkani workers castigated by Tata were undermining the bases upon which authority in Bombay's textile mills functioned, this was clearly an idea whose time had come. In what appears to have been a cleverly timed piece of public relations strategy, Tata gave a press interview in May where he spoke disparagingly of the workers he currently employed and the 'dilatory and easy-going manner in which these men worked' and publicized his strategy.[86] The strike in June spurred the BMOA into action: Tata's scheme, in the light of the current labour unrest in the city, was applauded as a potential solution to the dangerous deadlock in which mill owners found themselves, and a way to contain the cycle of escalating strikes and militant demands. On the day the strike broke out, immediately after the mills had reverted to monthly payments, the BMOA unanimously passed a resolution agreeing to facilitate the importation of labour from the north.[87]

The subsequent fortunes of the scheme, however, belied the hope with which it was launched. An Agent, a Mr Moolla, was appointed with a budget of Rs 3,000 to travel to Nagpur, Kanpur, and other parts of the Central and North-Western Provinces to procure labour. He met, however, with fairly humiliating refusals. The wages offered by the BMOA (which were considerably below what the Bombay millhands were being paid in the summer of 1897) were rejected by most of the people he approached. He found only 114 people willing to accept the rates offered by the BMOA, and a few mills did manage to procure labour from the north, and this proved an even more unsavoury experience, 'as the men had, in many cases, refused to work at the wages laid down in the agreement and left their employment'.[88] By the close of 1897, Tata's vision, an ambitious drive to utterly reconstitute the labour market as well a geographically extended strategy of strike-breaking, was finally given up.

The other scheme imagined by mill owners was also more welfarist in its orientation, responding in a different way to the challenges posed by the labour situation in Bombay. We have already encountered N.N. Wadia, the chief architect of this scheme, in the last chapter, as a would-be 'representative' of millworkers from among the employers, a move designed to blunt Lokhande's popularity. Wadia was one of the richest mill owners in the city and came from a family which had made fortunes in shipping, trade, and finance. His family, in common with the Petits, the Sassoons and a few other of the large commercial family concerns of the time had major investments in philanthropic projects in Bombay.[89]

During the strikes of the summer, he was one of the few employers who supported the continuation of bonuses for workers, at a time when there were many who were angry enough to call for the cessation of all concessions to employees.[90] Wadia consistently foregrounded an ethic of reciprocity and care in his public pronouncements. His main intervention, which dovetailed with the preoccupations of the Bombay government, was an argument for the provision of cheap housing for millworkers. Each mill, argued Wadia, should house its own workers.[91]

The alternative he offered, then, was a systematic paternalism, which had some material foundation in the practices of some mills, such as the setting up of shops to provide grain to workers on mill premises and the construction of makeshift dwellings on mill land for them.[92] As one of the bigger landlords in the city, Wadia had both the will and the wherewithal to launch such housing schemes. The intention, according to the Factory Inspector in one of his more maudlin moments, was 'to bind employer and employed together by a more humane tie than mere rupees.... Perhaps this is a dream, but it is a good dream, and I may therefore be pardoned for indulging in it'.[93]

Wadia's scheme, as it turned out, proved to be one of the foundations of the Bombay City Improvement Trust, a collaboration between state and private business geared towards the radical reshaping of city space and re-housing of the urban poor. Wadia's ideas for the reconstitution of capitalist authority pointed in a direction that was significantly different from Tata's, and reflected the emergence, for the first time, of a major welfarist thrust in the strategies of control formulated by private business. Wood noted the following:

> [The plan, if accomplished,] should lead to the supplying to the work-people of the necessaries of life—not excepting that all-pervading necessary credit—and even of some of its comforts; to the substitution of competition in the provision of good dwelling-rooms, and of facilities for obtaining necessaries and comforts, for competition in mere money-wages; and to the creation of clans of men who will hold to the same mill from father to son, as they hold to their forefather's fields.[94]

In other words, the purpose of the plan was to institute a form of employer control that was *founded* on welfare, on the necessity of taking steps to ensure the reproduction of the labour force.

Tata and Wadia's strategies may have been conceived with slightly different ends in mind: the former explicitly addressed the question of labour control, whereas the latter claimed a more principled and meliorist basis. But they pointed in the same directions. In the first place, they contended with a new world of industrial relations where the practices of employers and employed bore the stark imprint of a war of position, where victories rested on the formulation of new, sometimes radical, strategies. In the second place, employers were directly affected by the form that their workers' vulnerabilities now took. The disappearance of credit mechanisms that had sustained workers' daily needs, after the flight of a large portion of the city's moneylenders, produced a situation where a more directly negotiated relationship between capitalist and worker seemed unavoidable. For the workers, daily wages received in cash were the solution. Tata and Wadia's visions were predicated on the same need: employers needed to find a way to bind labour to their mills, and subsidized immigration and housing were momentarily plausible solutions. The social reproduction of the workforce, both Wadia and Tata realized, could not, at this moment of crisis, be left to itself.

The moment, however, passed. Once the plague crisis had lost its immediacy, the thick dust of multiple mediations accumulated upon the structure of housing welfare suggested by Wadia. The Bombay Improvement Trust was a project undertaken jointly by the state and private commercial and landowning interests in Bombay, in that sense a classic, broad alliance of the city's elites. It fell prey soon enough to the pressures of cost-cutting minimalism, which generated unsatisfactory and often delayed housing for workers in the vicinity of their workplaces. Welfarist impulses like Wadia's were twisted into a parsimonious, shoddy rehabilitative project in the actual work executed by the Improvement Trust (and, to a significant extent, by its successor, the Bombay Development Department, set up in 1920).[95] It was difficult, until major reforms in workers' housing enacted by the Congress ministry of 1937–9, to persuade tenants to settle in their new tenements, which lacked adequate water facilities, sanitation, and living space.[96] The expropriation of the city's poor from their homes and neighbourhoods ran far ahead of their rehousing and resettlement, thus establishing and extending a pattern in Bombay's growth that lasts to this day.

Consequences and Conclusions

Through the 1870s and 1880s, millworkers had appeared in the discourses of employers and state in various guises, most of which reduced them to passive beneficiaries/victims of industrialization, grateful recipients of protection from a benevolent state or charity from kind employers. In the twentieth century, by sharp contrast, they were to appear alternately as riotous mobs or, later, as militant class warriors corrupted by Bolshevism. The 1890s provide a semantic as well as a temporal bridge, and I would suggest that the plague years, in some ways, constitute the critical bridging period when the working classes emerged as a persistent force of disruption, their demands and collective mobilizations imposing a heavy burden upon the coercive and regulatory apparatuses of state and employer alike.

It would be tempting, but far too facile, to conceptualize the labour unrest that hit the mills between 1896 and 1898 through the optic of an all-pervasive chaos, as a sort of historical aberration. Superficially, the evidence sometimes seems to point strongly in that direction: workers milled about on the streets at a time when their employers could not work out how to keep them working; they rioted and went on strike; mills closed or worked with half their workforce; and the industrial base of the city was nearly shattered. It was, by any standards, a time of catastrophe and disorganization.

If this is the whole story, then we are left with a neat, if absorbing, narrative, fully decipherable within the digits of orthodox economic history. Plague depopulated the city, workers fled in droves, and those that remained gained ascendancy in industrial relations momentarily, as a consequence of their relative scarcity in the labour market. However, as they returned through the summer, history began to readjust itself to more 'normal' patterns of industrial relations, and the plague crisis remained just that, a crisis, a ripple upon the surface of an unfolding narrative of industrial growth and prosperity. Morris David Morris offers a classic formulation of this in *The Cambridge Economic History of India*: wages, he writes, suffered temporary fluctuations, but the 'unstabilizing effects' of this were 'worked out' by mid-1898.[97] It appears to me, though, that something else was happening as well: even as old patterns of industrial relations were torn apart, they were simultaneously being reconstituted, in complex and contested ways.

What precisely were factory labourers *doing* in the most dramatic months of 1897? The answer is that they were demanding reconstituted terms of employment and sustaining them through powerful demonstrations of collective force. Concessions that were, from their masters' point of view, strategic gambits to keep them working or acts of charity to save them from utter destitution and despair were, for workers, *rights* to be defended at all costs. Charity was translated into right.

Through 1897, workers made successful demands that threatened the structure of industrial relations that had persisted through the preceding decades. Despite admonitions from the BMOA, the majority of individual employers felt that surrendering to these demands was the only strategy that could secure labour for them. From the point of view of the industry as a whole, the payment of 'irrationally' high wages and the granting of 'excessive' concessions may well have been suicidal. But paradoxically, this flirtation with economic suicide kept the mills alive.

The point is that in the months under discussion, the relationship between employer and employed achieved its own micro-historical *stability*, through the setting of new standards and practices of wage-payment. The daily wage and the bonus were, in their initial form, concessions born of pragmatic choices made by mill owners. But once granted, they became claims that structured, for almost a year, the forms of industrial relations in the city. This was not pure chaos born of a desperate situation. To reverse this and restabilize an older structure of employer control required protracted conflict and the defeat of at least one major strike. All this points towards a slice of historical time where a particular form of *regulation* was achieved, one which we might describe as 'regulation from below', sustained through the conjoined threats of death, workers' flight, and industrial protest. It was a time of militant, far from unorganized, industrial conflict, something that could no longer be viewed as an 'instinctual' response to industrial conditions that would disappear as the industry gained a firmer footing.

The year 1897, then, was not simply one of industrial chaos, but a year when a new, contingent, and fleeting *structure* of industrial relations was devised through the capitulations of mill owners and the assertions of workers. What makes this paradoxical, of course, is that these assertions were made, sustained, and defended literally at the point of death. The temporary gains made by workers at the height of the plague crisis and the strength of their agitations suggest a far more classically 'mature' working class, the kind that is supposed to grow into a corporate, unionized, stable identity with the expansion and development of industrial capitalism. The strangeness of this historical moment lies in the fact that such gains were made not at a moment of strength, but of constitutive, defining weakness and vulnerability, both for capitalists and for workers. Instead of the (partly) virtuous cycle of industrial growth and working-class ascendancy that has been seen to characterize the 'normal' trajectory of industrial relations, this structure of workers' strength was sustained by a backward spiral, which threatened both the cotton industry and its workers with death. These were workers who often enough did not even know if they were likely to be alive at the end of the day. What they *could* be assured of at the end of the day, however, was a daily wage.

It is possible to identify a closer relationship developing between state and capital, as labour came to acquire the status of a major *political* problem for both. The scale of the millworkers' assertion in 1896–8 was unprecedented in the prior history of the city's mills, and the increasing demographic preponderance of millworkers within the city's population was beginning to crystallize in more active, 'agentive' forms. In response to this, common or compatible structures of control needed to be devised by both the state, to ensure civic stability and the reproduction of the power relations that sustained the city, and by employers, to reinstitute their authority over an increasingly fractious workforce.

If the attempt to overhaul the structure of working-class housing was an agenda executed by an alliance of the state, private business, and landowning interests, the problem of civic order was faced most directly by the state. The reorganization of the city police, along with the consequent intensification of coercive police controls, was a marked feature of early twentieth-century Bombay.[98] Edwardes' attempts, as Police Commissioner, to control the Moharrum processions more tightly betrayed traces of an anxiety borne over from the 1890s about the opacity of the plebeian and proletarian fractions of the Muslim community to state scrutiny and the perceived potential for riot and rebellion that the Muslims, Julahas predominantly, had displayed, in 1893 and equally strikingly in 1897.[99]

The changing texture of relations between state, employer, and worker can perhaps be best elucidated by closing the circle of this book, as it were, and returning, very briefly, to the question of factory regulation. The anxieties about industrial control that I have described were prefigured, at the time of the plague, in the peregrinations of the Factory Department, where the new potential in the city for industrial discontent seems to have cast a long shadow on the 'protective' functions of inspectors. The report for 1897 by the Chief Inspector of Factories, A.L. Wood, bears this out. He wrote:

> During the first half of the year, in deference to the disorganization of industry, the Act was administered with studied leniency, particularly in the matter of children and holidays. When a child would often not be in the same mill for more than a few days together, it was impossible to insist on the production of certificates; and two or three offences in this and other respects were condoned which might well in ordinary times have been taken into Court.[100]

This was evidently a temporary strategy driven by crisis: the latter, more stable half of the year did indeed witness three prosecutions.[101] But there are glimmerings of a wider political and discursive shift here, which can be buttressed by a brief reference to the Factory Department's changing attitude to the question of wage-arrears. I have written, in the last chapter, of the reluctance of the state to obtrude upon the domain of wage-payment and the 'free' negotiation between employer and worker. At the same time, the holding of wages in arrears was, in the 1880s and early 1890s, a source of worry for factory officials, who were, after all, designated protectors of millworkers and who had received complaints mediated by Lokhande on the practice of late wage-payment prevalent in Bombay's mills. In late 1896, the Government of India belatedly responded to the worries expressed by factory inspectors to the Royal Commission and asked for information on wage-practices from the Bombay government.[102] The convulsions of the plague crisis seem to have slowed down correspondence on this issue, and a comprehensive reply only arrived in February 1898, in the form of a letter from R.M. Kennedy, the Collector, and an appended report by Wood.

The mill industry, wrote Kennedy, 'is now passing through a convulsion in which the mill owners have by no means the most advantageous position, and it appears to me wisest to see how the relations between employer and employed will stand at the conclusion before interfering with circumstances'.[103] Wood was less circumspect:

> The masters have for many years professed to be in combination, but this is now proved to have been a fair-weather combination. No doubt they will try—and have tried—to secure better cohesion, but their elements are various and discordant. The men are a homogeneous mass who have

> now for the first time combined—by accident, it is true, but with conspicuous success. What they have done by accident they will know how to do by design. *In my humble opinion, the Bombay mill-hand can now look after himself.*[104]

Something has changed here, and changed palpably and dramatically. The millhands of Bombay, in the eyes of their designated protectors, are no longer the helpless, needy figures they had once putatively been, subjects of law and objects of protection. They are, instead, more than vaguely frightening, a 'homogenous mass' who are not to be trifled with. 'The men have learnt their power', writes Wood, and this statement announces a new phase in Bombay's industrial relations.[105]

To grasp the plague as an event in the history of Bombay's labour relations is a conscious interpretative choice, rather than something transparently offered up by the available historical sources. In contrast to the general appreciation of the plague's significance for Bombay's larger *social* history, its remarkable effects on the city's labour relations have received only muted recognition. My hypothesis is that by restoring the 'evental' significance of the plague, we might achieve a significantly new narrative of labour relations in the medium and long term as well.

First of all, the plague crisis *clarified* the social relations of authority and subordination upon which Bombay's urban order rested. Paradoxically, though, these relations achieved this crystalline clarity—as visible to contemporary observers as to future scholars—only at the point of their possible extinction. With millworkers, as well as with other classes of urban labour, it was the very rupture of employment relations that revealed the structural patterns of social power in their starkest form. In the mills, the wage-arrears system, prior to the intrusion of the plague, had been grasped as merely one element of many that made up the relations between employers and workers. The collapse of wage-arrears, however, ruptured the hierarchies of the employment relationship so massively that a new and 'objective' historical truth was produced at the moment of this collapse, one in which the cycle of arrears and debt was revealed as the very heart of the social relations upon which the city's reproduction rested, without which the employment form—and the urban form—simply could not be sustained in their 'normal' state.

Simultaneously, however, the plague crisis *reconstituted* relations of capitalist authority in the mills (as well as other work sites and regimes) in a new key. As employers subsumed many of the functions of social reproduction by moving to control labour supply, credit, housing, and food provisioning (functions that had hitherto been nested in the 'informal' relations of neighbourhood and community), new images and practices of industrial relations were momentarily forged. In the short term, these proved evanescent: as the initial crisis of the labour market faded and workers returned to the mills, older structures of control could be restored—but only up to a point. Since the plague crisis introduced a hitherto unimaginable structure of workplace relations—which I have characterized as 'regulation from below'—the existing instruments of employer domination could no longer be taken for granted. Much of the subsequent history of Bombay's mills was to consist of the elaboration of forms of social welfare and reproduction, of labour supply and control, which were far more tightly and consciously regulated by both employers and the state.

Moreover, the new constellations of relations of production and social reproduction emergent in the early twentieth century were also, especially after the First World War, to be punctuated by enormous episodes of strike action and workers' collective resistance. Wage-arrears as an instrument of control would eventually disappear, in mill after mill. Bonuses, initially conceived as an emergency concession, would become regularized as a right workers commanded. Mills would come to provide canteens, grain shops, housing, provident funds, and the like on a far more general scale than before. In other words, temporary concessions made during the plague towards workers—and also towards a more direct, unmediated employer–employee relationship—would stabilize, in subsequent decades, as dominant forms.

This might appear as a simple point about the 'consequences' of the plague crisis, but there is a twist. In the first place, to speak of 'consequences' is perhaps to deploy the wrong model of causality for the plague-as-event, given that many of these modifications of the institutions of social reproduction happened decades after the epidemic and cannot be traced back to it in any linear fashion. (In the case of the reforms effected by the Bombay Improvement Trust, especially with regard to housing, the causal links are clearer.) However, the plague crisis *foreshadowed* many of the future social compromises that were to be hammered out between employers, state, and workers over decades of intense class struggle and negotiation. As such, the event *anticipated* the shape of much of the future, without in any direct way *producing* it.

The *crystallization*, *shattering*, *reconstitution*, and *foreshadowing* of urban social structures and relations: these, then, were the modalities of the plague crisis as a historical event. Absolutely immanent to a very specific and bounded historical situation, it exceeded it both in its immediacy and in its legacies. As such, the brief period between 1896 and 1898 occupies a strange and disjointed relationship to its conditions of emergence. Materially and ideologically embedded in its time, the event, nevertheless, was its own creature, in peculiar and paradoxical ways. It constituted a point where the past (of the city and its labour relations), the present (of absolute social crisis), and the future (of new and emergent social structures) met. It is the *simultaneity* of these different logical 'moments' which gives the plague crisis its character as historical event.

Notes

1. *Abstract of Report of the Sanitary Commissioner with the Government of India for 1896*, in *Report on Sanitary Measures in India* (henceforth *RSM*) *1896–97*, vol. 30, p. 105.

2. *Abstract of Report of the Sanitary Commissioner with the Government of India for 1897*, in *RSM 1897–98*, vol. 31, p. 120.

3. *Abstract of the Report of the Health Officer of Bombay City for 1897*, in *RSM 1897–98*, vol. 31, p. 228.

4. S.M. Edwardes, *The Rise of Bombay: A Retrospect* (Bombay: Times of India Press, 1902), p. 330.

5. Annual Factory Report, 1897, no. F.I.–421, Home (Judicial) A, March 1899, NAI (henceforth *Factory Report*, Bombay, 1897).

6. *Abstract of the Report of the Sanitary Commissioner with the Government of India for 1897*, p. 120.

7. *Abstract of the Report of the Sanitary Commissioner with the Government of India for 1896*, p. 106.

8. B.F. Patell, *History of the Plague in Bombay* (Bombay, c. late 1890s), p. 32.

9. Myron Echenberg, *Plague Ports: The Global Urban Impact of Bubonic Plague, 1894–1901* (New York and London: New York University Press, 2007), pp. 55–6.

10. From Governor, Bombay, to Secretary of State for India, 14 February 1897, Papers relating to the outbreak of bubonic plague in India, *PP* 1897 (C. 8386).

11. Indeed, it continues to be a contested question today. Where did the oceanically transmitted bubonic plague that hit China, Bombay, and various

other parts of the world really originate? Was the origin in Hong Kong, or did the disease travel in flea-infested bales of Egyptian cotton? Were there, perhaps, mutations within the genetic structure of *Y. Pestis* (the bacterium that produced the plague, borne on the vector *X. Cheopis*, or the rat flea): did the plague, in other words, arise where it occurred? This would mean that miasmatic theories of the origins of plague, such as those put forward in Bombay in 1896 by Lieutenant Colonel George Waters of the Indian Medical Service, accidentally had a certain purchase upon the realities of the epidemic. See George Waters, *Plague in Bombay: A Lecture Delivered at the Sassoon Mechanics' Institute, Bombay* (Bombay, 1897).

12. From Secretary of State to Governor, 23 January 1897, *Papers Relating to Outbreak of Bubonic Plague in India, PP* 1897 (C. 8386; C. 8511).

13. Prashant Kidambi, *The Making of an Indian Metropolis: Colonial Governance and Public Culture in Bombay, 1890–1920* (Hampshire: Ashgate, 2007), pp. 49–71; '"An Infection of Locality": Plague, Pythogenesis and the Poor in Bombay, c. 1896–1905', *Urban History* 31, no. 2 (2004): 249–67.

14. See, for instance, *Abstract of the Report of the Health Officer of Bombay for 1874*, in *RSM 1874–75* (C. 1615), pp. 124–6.

15. *Abstract of the Report of the Health Officer of Bombay for* 1874, pp. 124–6; *PP* 1897 (C. 8386); M.E. Couchman, *Account of Plague Administration in the Bombay Presidency from September 1896 till May 1897*, part I, chapter 1, Bombay, 1897; I.J. Catanach, '"Who Are Your Leaders?" Plague, the Raj and the "Communities" in Bombay, 1896–1901', in *Society and Ideology: Essays in South Asian History Presented to Prof. K.A. Ballhatchet*, edited by Peter Robb (Delhi: Oxford University Press, 1993), pp. 196–221.

16. Patell, *The Plague in Bombay*, p. 27.

17. P.C.H. Snow, *Report on the Outbreak of Bubonic Plague in Bombay, 1896–97* (Bombay, 1897), p. 5; Couchman, *Account of Plague Administration*, vol. 1, chapter 1; *Bombay Gazette*, 8 October 1896.

18. *Bombay Gazette*, 8 October 1896; See David Arnold, *Colonizing the Body: State Medicine and Epidemic Disease in Nineteenth-Century India* (California: University of California Press, 1993, pp. 219–20) for an account of the role of rumours in the spread of the plague panic.

19. *Bombay Gazette*, 30 October 1896; *Times of India*, 30 October 1896.

20. Snow, *Report on the Outbreak of Bubonic Plague*, pp. 6–7.

21. Snow, *Report on the Outbreak of Bubonic Plague*, pp. 6–7.

22. Snow, *Report on the Outbreak of Bubonic Plague*, p. 9.

23. Report from Brigade-Surgeon-Lieutenant-Colonel T.S. Weir, Executive Health Officer, IOR V/27/856/7–10; Snow, *Report on the Outbreak of Bubonic Plague*, p. 75.

24. *Times of India*, 2 April 1897.

25. *Times of India*, 7 April 1897.

26. *Times of India*, 8 April 1897.

27. Report by R.H. Vincent, Commissioner of Police, no. 2364/6R, to Judicial Department, Bombay, 1 April 1898, enclosed in Judicial Letter no. 6, 9 April 1898, IOR, L/P&J/3/959, OIOC.

28. Report by R.H. Vincent, Commissioner of Police, no. 2364/6R, to Judicial Department, Bombay, 1 April 1898, enclosed in Judicial Letter no. 6, 9 April 1898, IOR, L/P&J/3/959, OIOC.

29. Report by R.H. Vincent, Commissioner of Police, no. 2364/6R, to Judicial Department, Bombay, 1 April 1898, enclosed in Judicial Letter no. 6, 9 April 1898, IOR, L/P&J/3/959, OIOC; *Times of India*, 10 March 1898.

30. *Times of India*, 11 March 1898.

31. *Times of India*, 16 and 17 March 1898.

32. Catanach, 'Who Are Your Leaders?' pp. 217–18.

33. *Indian Spectator and the Voice of India*, 10 January 1897.

34. *Times of India*, 11 March 1898.

35. Patell, *The Plague in Bombay*, pp. 26–7, 32.

36. *Annual Report of Bombay Millowners' Association*, 1896, p. 2.

37. *Annual Report of Bombay Millowners' Association*, 1897, p. 2.

38. Rajnarayan Chandavarkar, *Imperial Power and Popular Politics: Class, Resistance and the State in India, c. 1850–1950* (Cambridge: Cambridge University Press, 1998).

39. Morris David Morris, *The Emergence of an Industrial Labour Force in India: A Study of the Bombay Cotton Mills, 1854–1947* (Berkeley: University of California Press, 1965).

40. Chandavarkar, *The Origins of Industrial Capitalism*.

41. Prashant Kidambi, 'State, Society and Labour in Colonial Bombay, c.1893–1918', unpublished PhD dissertation (Oxford, 2001), pp. 37–46.

42. Kidambi, 'State, Society and Labour in Colonial Bombay, c.1893–1918'. Also see Kidambi, 'Contestation and Conflict: Workers' Resistance and the "Labour Problem" in the Bombay Cotton Mills, c. 1898–1919', in *Labour Matters: Towards Global Histories [Essays in Honour of Sabyasachi Bhattacharya]*, edited by Marcel van der Linden and Prabhu Mohapatra (New Delhi: Tulika, 2009), pp. 106–28.

43. Kidambi, 'Contestation and Conflict'. See also Sandeep Hazareesingh, *The Colonial City and the Challenge of Modernity: Urban Hegemonies and Civic Contestations in Bombay, 1900–1925* (Hyderabad: Orient Longman, 2007).

44. Braudel had famously disparaged the concern of an older generation of historians with the 'flotsam' of historical events, which he saw as ephemeral and superficial, producing illusory excitements that dissembled the vast structures that underlay social life, structures that only change slowly and are impervious to events and individuals. In the context of conventional 'event-oriented' histories, anchored to the decisions of monarchs and political leaders,

his disparagement was fully justified. However, in strictly conceptual terms, and especially when considering histories plotted on a less grand, civilizational scale than that mapped by Braudel, it may well be necessary to reconsider the relations between structure, conjuncture, and event in ways that run counter to his order of priority.

45. These reflections are obviously inspired by Alain Badiou's understanding of the event as that which suspends the 'normal' order of 'Being', by releasing a new 'historical sequence' which only makes narrative sense in the light of this rupture. Thus, for instance, an authentic political revolution is not measured by the scale of its immediate break with circumstances—this break may well be, and in fact usually has to be, extremely limited. Its 'event-ness' consists, rather, in its introduction of a new sequence of actions, decisions, desires, and dreams that is *heterogeneous* to the situation from which it is born. An event, in this sense, marks the birth of the new, but in ways that are rarely immediately transparent. Slavoj Žižek has extended Badiou's considerations by clarifying their apparent temporal paradox: a historical event only *becomes* so retroactively, in the light of the sequence it initiates. But this does not mark a 'consequentialist' account of the event, for in a peculiar way the forces released by the event also have to be grasped as immanent to the event itself. The expectations, fears, hopes, and claims generated by the event in the medium or long term are, thus, both external to the event (they crystallize in its wake) and internal to it (the structure of the event itself, in its immediacy, foreshadows many of its future appropriations and 'consequences').

46. *Factory Report*, Bombay, 1897.

47. *Times of India*, 7 January 1897.

48. Snow, *Report*, pp. 219–20.

49. *Factory Report*, Bombay, 1897.

50. *Times of India*, 12 January 1897.

51. *Factory Report*, Bombay, 1897.

52. *Times of India*, 4 January 1897.

53. *Times of India*, 8 January 1897.

54. *Times of India*, 23 January 1897.

55. Circular from John Marshall, Secretary of BMOA, to Agents and Owners of Cotton Spinning and Weaving Mills in Bombay, listing scale of wages decided by Committee, in *Annual Report of Bombay Millowners' Association*, 1896, Appendix B: The Bubonic Plague.

56. *Times of India*, 9 March 1897.

57. *Times of India*, 9 March 1897.

58. *Times of India*, 9 March 1897.

59. Proceedings of Special General Meeting of the BMOA, 27 April 1897, for the purpose of considering the question of resuming monthly, instead of daily,

wages to millhands, in *Annual Report of Bombay Millowners' Association*, 1896, pp. 141–6.

60. *Factory Report*, Bombay, 1897.
61. *Times of India*, 12 January 1897.
62. *Bombay Gazette*, 30 April 1897.
63. *Factory Report*, Bombay, 1897.
64. *Times of India*, 10 May 1897.
65. *Factory Report*, Bombay, 1897.
66. *Factory Report*, Bombay, 1897.
67. *Times of India*, 10 May 1897.
68. *Times of India*, 5 February 1897.
69. *Times of India*, 5 February 1897.
70. *Times of India*, 5 February 1897.
71. *Times of India*, 2 June 1897.
72. *Times of India*, 3 and 4 June 1897.
73. *Times of India*, 3 and 4 June 1897.
74. *Times of India*, 4 June 1897.
75. *Factory Report*, Bombay, 1897.
76. *Factory Report*, Bombay, 1897.
77. *Factory Report*, Bombay, 1897.
78. *Factory Report*, Bombay, 1897; *TOI*, July 1897.
79. *Times of India*, 24 August 1897.
80. *Factory Report*, Bombay, 1897.
81. Abstracts of Proceedings, GD (Misc), 15 October 1888, IOR/P/3336, OIOC; *Annual Report of Bombay Millowners' Association for 1888*, Appendix G.
82. *Annual Report of Bombay Millowners' Association for 1892*.
83. J.N. Tata, 'Imported Labour for the Bombay Mills', Bombay, 26 May 1897, enclosed in *Annual Report of the Bombay Millowners' Association*, 1896, p. 156.
84. Tata, 'Imported Labour for the Bombay Mills', p. 157.
85. Letter from Tata and Sons to John Marshall, Secretary, Millowners' Association, Bombay, 11 May 1897, enclosed in *Annual Report of the Bombay Millowners' Association*, 1896, pp. 158–60.
86. *Times of India*, 10 May 1897.
87. *Times of India*, 3 June 1897.
88. *Annual Report of the Bombay Millowners' Association, 1897*, pp. 5–6.
89. Ashok V. Desai, 'The Origins of Parsi Enterprise', in *Entrepreneurship and Industry in India, 1800–1947*, edited by Rajat K. Ray (Oxford: Oxford University Press, 1992), pp. 99–108.
90. Proceedings of Annual General Meeting of Bombay Millowners' Association, 6 July 1897.
91. *Factory Report*, Bombay, 1897.

92. Proceedings of Annual General Meeting of Bombay Millowners' Association, 6 July 1897; *Factory Report*, 1897.

93. Proceedings of Annual General Meeting of Bombay Millowners' Association, 6 July 1897.

94. Proceedings of Annual General Meeting of Bombay Millowners' Association, 6 July 1897.

95. See Kidambi, *The Making of an Indian Metropolis*, pp. 71–115, for an account of the operations of the Bombay Improvement Trust.

96. I am grateful to Vanessa Caru for sharing her unpublished work on Bombay working-class housing with me.

97. Morris D. Morris, 'The Growth of Large-Scale Industry to 1947', in *The Cambridge Economic History of India*, vol. 2: c.1757–c.1970, edited by Dharma Kumar and Meghnad Desai (Cambridge, 1983; henceforth *CEHI*), p. 577.

98. S.M. Edwardes, *Bombay City Police: A Historical Sketch 1672–1916* (Bombay, 1923); Kidambi, *The Making of an Industrial Metropolis*, pp. 115–57.

99. Edwardes, *Bombay City Police*; Kidambi, *The Making of an Industrial Metropolis*.

100. Home (Judicial) A, March 1899, nos 457–615, NAI.

101. Home (Judicial) A, March 1899, nos 457–615, NAI.

102. No. 1576, Calcutta, 17 December 1896, Home Dept (Judicial), L.M. Thornton, Deputy Secretary to GOI, to Government of Bombay, in G.D., 1898, vol. 37, MSA.

103. No. F.I.–77, GD, no. 37, 4 February 1898, MSA.

104. No. F.I.–69, GD, no. 37, 1 February 1898, MSA [emphasis mine].

105. No. F.I.–69, GD, no. 37, 1 February 1898, MSA.

Conclusion

This book has been a study of the emergence, elaboration, and crisis of a regime of industrial relations centred on the cotton mills of Bombay in the late nineteenth century. I have tried to grasp the early history of factory regulation as a many-sided process with deeply contradictory outcomes. The politics of social control as adumbrated through factory law has been one arm of analysis; the fin de siècle emergence of a 'labour question', in the form of militant working-class agitation, has been the other.

These themes were, I felt from the outset of my research, best explored through a narrative history that 'followed' the law through different realms of administration, ideological articulation, social practices, and events. Only a tightly bound narrative, not necessarily tethered to distinctly mapped-out 'themes', could convey the character of change and continuity in the worlds of labour regulation and conflict. This insight governed the writing of this book. A narrow, almost micro-historical temporal focus resulted from this. This allowed me to track the emergence, at various sites, of ideologies of factory reform, of the politics of the administration of labour regulation, and the rhythms of industrial conflict as they unfolded in concrete contexts.

Factory law entered India through two channels. The first of these was ideological enterprise: Mary Carpenter, in her visits between 1866 and 1874, developed an interest in industrial workers which stands at the fountainhead of a long sequence of labour reform formulated by individual activists. The second was the domain of commercial politics. Bombay and Lancashire, the centres of the world's newest and oldest major textile industries in the era of modern textile capitalism, were the stages upon which the project of legislatively constricting the operations of Indian industrial employers took place. I have tried to show that this was not, as has commonly been supposed, a straightforward commercial rivalry. It was, rather, principally an ideological consequence of the differing political situations in which the textile capitalisms of metropole and colony found themselves from the 1870s—the onset of prolonged economic uncertainty in the former, the weight of a wayward yet frenetic industrial growth in the latter. The Bombay cotton textile industry, throughout the late nineteenth century, would remain the chief point of reference for factory legislation, but this was only indirectly a consequence of Lancashire's predicaments. I have argued that while, to an extent, Lancashire determined the *fact* of Indian factory legislation in 1881 and 1891, the *content* of factory law followed a different historical sequence.

So how, then, can the development of factory law best be comprehended? My attempt to answer this began with a micro-historical approach to the question, focusing minutely on a series of tensions disclosed by 'small' events in the internal life of the Factory Act of 1881. The death of Radhoo Saitoo, the singular inspectorial attention devoted to the Nadiad Mill, Meade-King's interventions, the scandals around the certification of mill children, the politics of the Factory Commission of 1875 which initially set the legislative ball rolling—these stories served several purposes simultaneously. First, they helped understand how a field of force emerged around Bombay's mills, which involved distinct sets of historical actors and interests—competing fractions of capitalists, labour reformers and activists, and the newly established machinery of factory inspection. This constituted a field of industrial relations *avant la lettre*. Factory legislation made up the principal matter of this field: it generated the principles which authorized—or forbade—the state's regulation of factory matters; it opened up certain questions, such as working time, and closed off others, such as wages. Second, the episodic form in which I explored these questions allowed me to show parallel ways in which the Factory Act developed (and unravelled), and to identify the cracks that emerged, which marked the outer limits of factory reform. Constantly, mill owners and state officials struggled to control the boundaries of the regulative norms intended to govern factory industry. These boundaries, I demonstrated, were continually disturbed by the protrusion of new dilemmas that disclosed a tense dialectic between the dynamics of Bombay's industrial growth, both extensive and fractured, and the emergence of new demands and debates centred on labour.

This was the point at which the overall narrative of the book moved away from the ideological, political, and economic constitution of the putative regime of industrial relations which emerged in the 1870s and 1880s, and began to consider the ways in which this field of force was undone. Here, again, we find a tangled skein of developments: the resumption of Lancashire–Bombay competition at the end of the 1880s; the flashpoint of the Royal Congress of Hygiene and Demography where Bahadhurji and Holt-Hallett faced off; the sacking of the women millworkers of Ahmedabad in 1892; the emergence and significance of Lokhande; the emergence of new capitalist strategies in response to new economic difficulties; and the first strike wave in the textile industry in 1892–3. This last development was of particular importance, since it dramatized the passage from one structure of industrial relations to another, from a period characterized by relative industrial peace to one marked by continuous strife, both active and latent. The early 1890s, in a strict sense, mark the first major stirrings of Bombay's labour movement. But there was also another dimension to this shift—it marked the emergence of a distinct wage-question upon Bombay's industrial scene. This, in turn, illuminated the overall structure of industrial control in the mills, which, I argued, was based upon the strict separation of the realm of production from the realm of the social reproduction of the workplace. This was achieved through a rolling system of wage-arrears compounded by structural working-class debt to local moneylenders, an area neither the state nor the Bombay Millowners' Association (BMOA) were able to, or sought to, intervene in.

It is the temporary but extremely consequential collapse of this structure of industrial control, upon the arrival of the plague pandemic in 1896–7, which my last chapter explored. The plague years, I have argued, were a crucial turning point, marking the growth of workers' bargaining power, and also of a new *figure* of the worker. In the 1870s and 1880s, government, factory officials, mill owners, and public activists had formulated paternalist idioms of industrial relations that hinged on the harmonious relationship between capital and labour. The work of factory legislation itself unwittingly problematized this normative structure, and the industrial practices of Bombay's mills increasingly made it hard to sustain. It was the conjuncture of 1896–8, however, which saw the emergence of what the Factory Inspector described as 'the Labour Question'. From this point, the idiom in which industrial relations were understood changed permanently, as workers, capitalists, and state increasingly inhabited states of siege.

Through the early twentieth century, millworkers would stamp themselves with increasing force and visibility upon the lived politics of Bombay's streets and neighbourhoods. They would also respond to rapidly changing conditions within the mills. Industrial relations were consequently remade, as workers' protests, which were getting more and more organized and militant, became increasingly visible and threatening. For Chandavarkar, Newman, and other historians of Bombay's industrial politics, this is a process that really begins with the war years. This was marked by the upswing of the textile industry, the rising prices of commodities, and the beginnings, in the 1920s, of a powerful, unionized labour movement that would move radically leftwards. This was a process sustained, unevenly but discernibly, between the 1920s and the 1960s, and it can be argued that the 'labour movement proper' belongs to these decades.[1]

Chandavarkar's path-breaking work, while illuminating the conflicts of the 1920s and 1930s, tends to relegate their prehistory to the status of a more or less passive historical backcloth: the real story of labour, here and elsewhere, begins in the aftermath of the First World War, even if it is acknowledged that their roots were deeper.[2] Kidambi has tried to redress this balance, and has offered a provocative hypothesis: what if the enhanced bargaining power of the working classes, and particularly the mill population, between 1893 and 1918, which was founded on an unprecedented—and unreplicated—advantage in the labour market for most of these years, was actually an experience that *ended* with the economic recovery of the mills? In that case, the unionizations of the 1920s, and the growing penchant for labour organization that is visible from the end of the war, would signify not the growing power, but actually the growing *vulnerability* of millworkers in this time?

Kidambi's is an intriguing suggestion, though unfortunately one that is beyond the remit of my investigations. It is clearly intended as a provocation to stimulate further inquiry, and it succeeds in problematizing an equation commonly made between expanding labour organization and greater working-class strength. Kidambi counter-intuitively inverts this assumption by arguing that 'workers' receptivity to trade unions in the inter-war years appears not as the expression of a more evolved working-class consciousness, but rather as a reflection of the growing vulnerability of labour'.[3] One is tempted to ask—why not both? Are these possibilities the poles of a binary opposition or are they logical moments of a dialectic where working-class consciousness and vulnerability grew simultaneously? Whatever the answer to this, the achievement of Kidambi's argument is to compel the recognition of the relationship of pre-war and post-war labour histories as a serious historical problem.

The events of 1905–11 marked, in many ways, the first time millworkers engaged in sustained, massive industrial action over an extended, though not unbroken, period of time. As with the plague years, and perhaps as their consequence, we find the industrial landscape largely unmarked by effective regulation. Lovat Fraser, the Editor of the *Times of India*, who carried out a long investigation of working conditions in mills in 1905, observed:

> At the beginning of 1905 the system of factory inspection in India had partly broken down. There was a Factory Act, but in certain respects it had become almost a dead letter. The Government were meticulous in insisting upon the fencing of machinery, but seemed to think that their responsibility ended at that point.... The 'Chief Inspector of Factories' was the Assistant Collector, usually a young civil servant. In 1905 the post was held by six different men, all inexperienced, and generally indisposed to regard factory inspection as a serious part of their manifold duties.[4]

Fraser attributed this to the growth of electric light used by mill owners to work the mills at night, which increased, and in some cases nearly doubled, the working time of legally unprotected adult men in factories. By 1905, according to his enumeration, there were thirty-nine mills using electric light, and working between 5 a.m. and 8 p.m., or fifteen hours a day. The context for this was the mill industry's recovery from the slump that had set in during the 1890s, with mill shares and profits rising exponentially, and the competition, in Fraser's words, 'so intense there seemed to be no limit to the hours worked'.[5]

The link between the breakdown of factory regulation and the deterioration of factory conditions signals a withdrawal of the state from the responsibilities it had reluctantly acquired in 1881. This was a long process, beginning, as I have indicated, in the early 1890s, but really crystallizing in the plague years, as mill owners and the state alike found themselves compelled to confront workers on more openly contested grounds. This was a pattern reversed again in the second half of the 1900s, and one dimension of this change was certainly Fraser's campaign. Fraser, like Bengali and Lokhande before him, instituted a politics of reformist negotiation and public, press-mediated pressure upon the government over the issue of a limitation of working hours.[6] This finally made the consideration of factory legislation that engrossed *all* categories of workers, including 'adult' males, possible. A regulated working day and week for all workers, ideas which would have been heresy two decades ago, could now legitimately be placed upon the table. In 1911, a new Factory Act was passed, instituting a compulsory limitation of hours for all workers, including adult males.

The actions of mill-workers, though, were much more important in triggering this fresh legislative change. These took, principally, the form of sustained strikes against the lengthening of the working day, many of which in the case of individual mills proved effective. The months of September and October 1905 were marked by large-scale strikes and mass picketing, which often turned violent: in one incident at the Phoenix Mills, the timekeeper's record books were torn up by workers protesting against long working hours.[7] These strikes, which continued in periodic sustained bursts for the next five years, were marked by a pervasive threat of violence and disorder that led the Police Commissioner to remark to the BMOA that he could not guarantee the safety of mill owners unless there was 'uniformity in the hours of closing'.[8] The alarm produced by events like this led, eventually, to the mill owners' reluctant agreement to first voluntarily reduce working hours, and then, in 1911, assent to a new Factory Act.[9]

The increasingly threatening links between the factory and the street, made explicit in the riots of 1893 and even more powerfully in the plague crisis of 1898, dominated the concerns of both the state and the industrial employers in Bombay in these years. Civic and industrial tensions coincided in more ways than one: besides the incidents of stone-throwing and aggressive picketing that were regularly reported in the 1900s, Bombay also witnessed an enormous general strike in 1908 on the occasion of the conviction and imprisonment of the nationalist leader Bal Gangadhar Tilak. Fraser, who brokered the agreement of 1911, cited the riot as a relevant context for protective legislation.[10]

With this enactment, a form of legislation that had primarily been conceived as a means of identifying the sources and bearers of 'special vulnerability' made the transition to a putatively universal regime of protection. This was a complex historical movement. Factory legislation was long eschewed for 'adult' males because they were deemed to be responsible economic actors entering into free contracts with which the state should not interfere. Legislative protection entered their working lives partly as a result of commercial rivalries, partly as a consequence of inspectorial intervention, and partly as a concession made to reformer-activists who spoke in their name and occasionally mobilized their support. Under the impact of the plague years, adult males came to be seen instead, or rather once again, as capable of protecting themselves, but collectively, as a working class or a 'labour question', to which strategies of both concession and pacification were appropriate.

The loop was completed in the early twentieth century, as the technological and competitive opportunities and pressures that confronted mill owners and rendered working conditions unbearable also began to threaten the existing structures of industrial relations. In this new conjuncture, with labour commanding unprecedented bargaining power and workers demonstrating their strength on the streets, factory legislation—in the form of a universal restriction of working hours—emerged from the shadows as a mediator, as it had in the 1870s. This time, though, the industrial relations that were being mediated were significantly different.

A fuller description of these developments is beyond the remit of this book. What is incontrovertible, though, is that the relationship between factory legislation, industrial relations, and urban politics changed decisively in these years. Emerging as an outcrop of commercial, ideological, and philanthropic middle-class political pressures in the 1870s and 1880s, factory law by 1911 was part of a significantly different landscape of industrial relations, marked by organized working-class strength, evident in a range of ways on the new battlegrounds of urban politics.

At a basic level, this has been a book about the connection, in a specific historical context, between a piece of social legislation and the social relations in which it intervened. What were the links between law and social power? Which social interests were best served—or limited—by factory legislation? This, in turn, raises the big question of the social consequences of the rule of law in a particular domain of social experience. And here there are conceptual issues involved which may be worth addressing briefly.

There is a long tradition of left-wing thinking about the rule of law, within which the arguments of this book are situated. Yet, this is a tradition riven at the root, composed of irreducible oppositions, as well as ceaseless oscillations, between a fundamentally optimistic image of law and a perspective which sees legal forms as unalterably bound up with the exercise of class power. Radical thought about the rule of law has usually taken one of two opposed forms. First, there is a tradition that tends to identify the rule of law with ideology, in the precise sense of a structure of belief which props up established orders of domination and repression. In some of its formulations, this mode of thought draws upon Marx's critique of the 'equivalences' of the commodity-form in bourgeois society. It derives legal equality under capitalism, as well as the constitution of legal subjects, from the equality of commodities in the world of market exchange, submitted as they are to a common and abstract measure of value. The work of the Soviet jurist Evgeny Pashukanis offers one of the earliest and most illuminating modulations of this line of thought. More recent legatees of this sceptical tradition, who draw in equal measure upon Marx, Althusser, and Foucault, are to be found in the chiefly American tradition of Critical Legal Studies (CLS). Its practitioners, while in general not denying the *strategic* uses of legal engagement for the work of social emancipation, nevertheless seek to inhabit a critical and negative relationship to the law in general—in Duncan Kennedy's striking formulation, the work of CLS is best conceived as 'viral' rather than 'constructive'.[11] Law is—when one gets down to it—an instrument for the perpetuation and defence of unequal social orders. It is ultimately made by and for the purposes of constituted power, however important its contingent uses as a weapon of the weak might be. This is the burden of the critical–legal approach, which seeks to deconstruct and demystify the law as a crucial support system (both coercive and ideological) for capitalist authority.

The other, and opposed, tradition of radical engagements with the rule of law was articulated most powerfully by E.P. Thompson, although it arguably also forms the implicit backdrop of most *practical* left-wing engagements with the law. Thompson's exposition of this, in the conclusion to his justly acclaimed *Whigs and Hunters*, emphatically affirms the rule of law as an 'absolute human good'.[12] The rich, he argues, have no real *use* for the rule of law—how would they benefit from a system of legal constraints? They submit to it on the whole reluctantly.

Conversely, it is the poor and disempowered who actually *need* law to protect them in their everyday lives. The rule of law, rather than by itself marking the tyranny of capital and state, actually delineates the point at which constituted power is compelled to recognize the force of those it rules and subjugates. The only real alternative to the rule of law is arbitrary power unchecked by any formal constraints.

These two traditions have not often spoken to each other. A rare exception to this is an angry and uncharitable review of *Whigs and Hunters* by the American critical legal historian Morton Horwitz.[13] Not unpredictably, Horwitz's conclusion was that Thompson had taken a 'conservative' turn with this work, and that, cut it where you will, the rule of law ultimately conserves rather than questions unequal social authority. My purpose is, in a sense, the reverse. The question I raise is whether or not these two traditions, despite their obvious incompatibility, can perhaps be brought together in a coherent way and made to animate one another; whether, in short, their insights can be articulated with one another without risking a lazy eclecticism.

There are certain productive tensions within Thompson's arguments, I think, which indicate that they can. Thompson's moving description of the rule of law as an 'absolute human good' is perhaps more ambiguous than it appears at first. His endorsement, in the first place, flows from three powerful but logically distinct propositions:

1. It is impossible to strictly separate the domains of law and social practice—least of all along the orthodox Marxist division into the 'levels' of base and superstructure. Law sets the very boundaries of much social experience, and thus directly constitutes it. As Thompson put it eloquently, law is 'at *every* bloody level'.[14]
2. It is impossible to imagine a society—even a socialist utopia—which will be able to part fully with the rule of law as a constraining force upon arbitrary power. This insight flowed from Thompson's profound rejection of Stalinism, and also of radical-left traditions which derided law as bourgeois ideology, only to find themselves defenceless in the face of new, nominally 'socialist' regimes of arbitrary and brutal power.
3. Ordinary people—workers, peasants, plebeians—have struggled momentously not just *against* the law but also *with* it, within its terms, which they infused with new and unexpected meanings.

> While historical forms of the rule of law may invariably have been hijacked by the powerful, law's secret treasure is its ceaseless appropriation by the poor, and the horizons of expectation which legal rights enshrine.

It is necessary to register a distinction between two senses of law which animated Thompson's work throughout his life. First, we have the 'rule of law' which he celebrates as a necessary if flawed weapon of the weak, a constraint upon arbitrary power, a space where the poor can press their claims upon the powerful. Here we have law as an unavoidable, and on the whole virtuous, fiction of neutrality and impartiality which *must* govern empirical instances of non-revolutionary conflict if justice is to have any meaning in any constellation of politics or society. Second, there is the notion of law Thompson militated *against*: law as 'the order of being', as 'the laws of history', as a code word for the invariant socio-economic structures which, according to orthodox Marxists, govern all historical situations. Thompson rejected the idea of law as the iron grip of historical or social *necessity*. It was, indeed, the very refusal of determinate, historically necessary 'laws of motion' which cleared the ground for his endorsement of the rule of law. This can, among other things, help us grasp what would otherwise appear as a contradiction in Thompson's work, namely that his resolute defence of the rule of law did not prevent him from equally enthusiastically endorsing the great antinomian William Blake, who opposed 'law' and 'love' to each other as eternal opponents in his visionary poetry.[15] In a strange but not inconsistent way, Thompson's appreciation of the rule of law and his deep love for antinomian thought ran together.

But there is arguably a graver tension in Thompson's belief in the *principle* of an—empirically unrealized—world of formal justice administered by law. Given the undeniable barricading of the law by the interests that compose it, can the rule of law as an absolute human good be anything other than something approached asymptotically, as a horizon never fully reached but, nevertheless, virtuously regulating social practice? Here it might be apposite to recall the peculiar, dualistic split in the structure of argument in *Whigs and Hunters*. That book, above all, offered a stinging critique of the work of law in eighteenth-century England, of the way the Black Act of 1723 rendered innocuous offences against property into capital crimes and acted in the interests of extreme social oppression. The abuses sanctioned by law were the explicit focus of Thompson's book. The sudden swerve he made in his magnificent conclusion and the persuasive defence of the rule of law 'in principle' masks an insufficiently mediated movement in his argument. There is something, in other words, in his defence of the rule of law which has a *transcendental* character. Thompson moves from (*a*) law as an instrument of power to (*b*) law as a site of struggle and ultimately to (*c*) the rule of law as a necessary good in all social life. An *empirical* account of law's abuses is thus sublated by a *transcendental* account of law-as-justice. It is the form of Thompson's historical investigation which gives rise to this peculiar progression of arguments, for he is able to move from a *bad* law to the virtue of the *principle* of law.

What, however, if the terms were reversed? What if the story in question were that of a 'good' law, necessary to protect and defend workers against their masters? In short, something like the Factory Acts. And what if the 'transcendental' principle that blocks the realization of *this* law in a full sense is not just about contingent 'failures' of implementation, but has something fundamental to tell us about the role and nature of law in an unequally and unjustly structured social order?

There is another dimension to this, something which we might describe as the *specific efficiency* of factory law. Legislation is commonsensically understood as a response to a determinate set of problems. Crime exists; laws exist to punish and restrain it. Contracts need enforcement; law steps in to regulate them. Public morality is threatened; law issues the appropriate interdictions and permissions which guard it. In all these cases, we apparently have law-making standing in a direct relation with the legal object it addresses.

However, there are ways in which these axioms can be modified. First, what about the role law plays in constructing its own objects, assembling and reproducing them? Such a query is substantially similar to Foucault's formulations about the functions of social power. There is also a Marxist approach to this question available. In his essay on 'the Jewish question', Marx remarks, apropos of Bauer's pleas against religion, that 'to pose the problem is to have already solved it'. Law, it can often be seen, works exactly in this way—it posits the very problem it seeks to contain, by constituting it and giving it substance, depth, and limit.

Further, what if law and the law-making *subject* are actually radically unmoored from each other? Paradigms of social construction tend to presuppose a strong—or at least determinate—set of interests *behind* the law. The rationality of law-making agents (states, legislators, officials) is understood to directly determine the shape of law. The corollary to this is that someone, or some determinate social interest, actively *wants* this law to exist, and the existence of the law in question is testament to the power commanded by this interest.

In the case of factory legislation, however, I have tried to show that something quite distinct from this logical sequence took place. In a strong sense, the Factory Acts of late-nineteenth-century colonial India were inadequate answers to non-existent questions. Factory law, unlike in the British case, did not emerge from within the interests which composed Indian—specifically Bombay's—capitalist activity. It emphatically was not, till the early twentieth century, designed as a response to workers' own demands. And while it was deeply related to the commercial relations between Lancashire's and Bombay's textile industrialists, it was, in no sense, a reflex of Lancashire's economic interests. So, factory law did not *originate* in coherent, concrete interests, but rather through indirect pathways—one of the reasons why individual, independent reformers played such a major role in its initial elaboration. In fact, the Factory Acts came to *acquire* such concrete interests as they began to be played out in discrete spheres of industrial life. Its trajectories, therefore, were necessarily indirect—an indirection of both causes and consequences.

My narrative of factory legislation has *not* sought to reverse Thompson's appreciation of the rule of law with a CLS-inspired denunciation of the same, but, rather, to clarify a certain irreducible split at the heart of legal order itself. We, thus, have the story of a law which perpetually twists between its 'progressive' and 'reactionary' uses, creating fresh problems along the way for those caught up in its exercise—state officials, industrialists, managers, reformers, workers. Factory law intensified, rather than resolved, the social problems it set out to redress. This was its historical achievement.

Notes

1. Rajnarayan Chandavarkar, *The Origins of Industrial Capitalism in India: Business Strategies and the Working Classes in Bombay, 1900–1940* (Cambridge: Cambridge University Press, 1994). Important exceptions to this general trend are the work of Shashi Bhushan Upadhyay, *Existence, Identity and Mobilization:*

The Cotton Millworkers of Bombay, 1898–1919 (New Delhi: Manohar, 2004), and Prashant Kidambi, 'Contestation and Conflict: Workers' Resistance and the "Labour Problem" in the Bombay Cotton Mills, c. 1898–1919', in *Labour Matters: Towards Global Histories [Essays in Honour of Sabyasachi Bhattacharya]*, edited by Marcel van der Linden and Prabhu Mohapatra (New Delhi: Tulika, 2009).

2. Kidambi, 'Contestation and Conflict', pp. 106–28.

3. Kidambi, 'Contestation and Conflict', p. 122.

4. Lovat Fraser, *India Under Curzon and After* (London: William Heinemann, 1911), p. 330.

5. Fraser, *India Under Curzon and After*, p. 332.

6. Fraser, *India Under Curzon and After*, pp. 333–6

7. *Times of India*, 10 October 1905. See Kidambi, 'Contestation and Conflict' and Upadhyay, *Existence, Identity and Mobilization*, pp. 170–209 for more detailed descriptions and analyses of the strikes in this period.

8. *Annual Report of Bombay Millowners' Association*, 1905, p. 8.

9. Fraser, *India Under Curzon and After*, p. 336.

10. Fraser, *India Under Curzon and After*, p. 336.

11. Duncan Kennedy, *A Critique of Adjudication* (Cambridge, MA: Harvard University Press, 1997).

12. E.P. Thompson, *Whigs and Hunters: The Origin of the Black Act* (New York: Pantheon Books, 1975).

13. Morton Horwitz, 'The Rule of Law: An Unqualified Human Good?' *Yale Law Journal* 86, 1976–7: 561–6.

14. Thompson, *Whigs and Hunters*, p. 263.

15. See E.P. Thompson, *Witness against the Beast: William Blake and the Moral Law* (Cambridge: Cambridge University Press, 1994).

Select Bibliography

Government Records

Maharashtra State Archives, Bombay

Records of the Government of Bombay: General, Judicial, Home, and Legislative Departments.

National Archives of India, New Delhi

Records of the Government of India: Home Department, Commerce and Industries Department.

Oriental and India Office Collection, British Library, London

Abstracts of Proceedings of the Government of Bombay: General, Legislative, and Judicial Departments.

Abstracts of Proceedings of the Government of India: Home, Legislative, Commerce and Industries Department.

Public and Judicial Department: Annual Files.

Official Publications

Abstract of the Proceedings of the Council of the Governor General of India, assembled for the purpose of making Laws and Regulations under the provisions of the Act of Parliament.

Administration Report of the Cotton Department in the Bombay Presidency for 1872–73.

Annual Report on the Administration of the Indian Factories Act in Bombay Presidency, 1892–1910.

Annual Report of the Municipal Commissioner for the City of Bombay.

Census of the City of Bombay taken on 17 February, 1881, by T.S. Weir. Bombay, 1883.

Census of India, 1891, vol. VII: Bombay and Its Feudatories. Bombay, 1892.

Census of India, 1901, vols. X and XI. Bombay, 1901.

Condon, J.K. *The Bombay Plague, Being a History of the Progress of Plague in the Bombay Presidency from September 1896 to June 1899*. Bombay, 1900.

Couchman, M.E. *Account of Plague Administration in the Bombay Presidency from September 1896 till May 1897*. Bombay, 1897.

Gazetteer of the Bombay Presidency, vol. X: *Ratnagiri and Savantwadi*. Bombay, 1880.

Gazetteer of Bombay City and Island, 3 vols. Bombay, 1909.

Hansard's Parliamentary Debates: House of Commons and House of Lords.

Imperial Gazetteer of India, Bombay Presidency, 3 vols. Calcutta, 1908.

Report and Proceedings of the Bombay Factory Commission. Bombay, 1875.

Reports from the United States Consuls in the Several Countries of Europe on the State of Labour in Europe. Washington, 1878.

Report of W.O. Meade-King on the Working of the Indian Factories Act in Bombay together with Certain Suggestions and Proposals. Bombay, 1882.

Report and Proceedings of the Commission Appointed to Consider the Working of Factories in the Bombay Presidency, 1884–85. Bombay, 1888.

Report of the Indian Factory Commission, Appointed in September 1890, under the Orders of His Excellency, the Governor-General in Council, with Proceedings and Appendices. Calcutta, 1890.

Report of the Bombay Plague Committee, 1897–98.

Report and Proceedings of the Textile Factories Labour Committee, 1906–07.

Report of the Indian Factory Labour Commission, 1908, 2 vols. Simla, 1908.

Report on the Native Newspapers in the Bombay Presidency.

Snow, P.C.H. *Report on the Outbreak of Bubonic Plague in Bombay, 1896–97*. Bombay, 1897.

Parliamentary Papers

Chief Inspector of Factories and Workshops Report, 1888 (C. 5328).

Correspondence with Government of India on Inspection of Factories and Factory Inspectors' Reports, 1894 (108).

Correspondence Relating to Indian Tariff Act, 1875, 1876 (56) (C. 1515).

Correspondence Relating to Amendment of Indian Factory Act, 1881, 1889 (162), 1890–91 (224).

Correspondence Respecting the Proposed Labour Conference at Berlin, 1890 (C. 5914); (C. 6042).

Despatches from Secretary of State to Government of India, May and July 1890, Relating to Amendment of Indian Factory Act, 1890–91 (120).

Papers Relating to Import Duties on Cotton Goods and other Articles of Tariff in India, 1878–79 (241).

Papers Relating to Outbreak of Bubonic Plague in India, 1897 (C. 8386), (C. 8511).

Reports of Inspectors of Factories to Secretary of State for Home Department, 1875 (C. 1184).

Report of J.S. Davy, Assistant Local Government Board Inspector, on Strike of Cotton Operatives in Town of Bolton, September and October 1877, 1878 (286).

Report to Marquis of Salisbury by Miss M. Carpenter on Prison Discipline and Female Education in India, 1877 (185).
Reports from Her Majesty's Representatives Abroad Relative to the Recommendations of the Berlin Labour Conference, 1890–91 (C. 5371).
Reports on Working of Indian Factory Act to Government of India, 1889 (124).
Royal Commission on Labour, Foreign Reports, vol. II, *The Colonies and the Indian Empire with an Appendix on the Migration of Labour*, 1892 (C. 6795-XI).
Report on Sanitary Measures in India, 1874–75 (C. 1615); *1896–97* (C. 9111); *1897–98* (C. 9549).
Statement of Moral and Material Progress and Condition of India, 1875–1885.
Statistical Abstracts Relating to British India, 1875–85, 1886 (C. 4730).

Non-official Reports and Publications

Annual Reports of the Bombay Millowners' Association.
The Bombay Riots of 1893: Reprinted from the Times of India. Bombay, 1893.
Manchester Chamber of Commerce, *Bombay and Lancashire: Cotton Spinning Inquiry: Minutes and Evidence*. Manchester, 1888.
Tracts Relating to Finance and Trade, 1796–1883. OIOC, London.

Newspapers and Periodicals

Bharat-Sramajibi
Bombay Gazette
Dnyanodyaya
Indian Spectator and Voice of India
Indian Textile Journal
Journal of the National Indian Association
Reports on Native Newspapers
Times, The
Times of India, The

Private Papers

'Bombay during the Plague, 1897–8: Extracts from the letters of Hesther Mary Dowson, Plague Hospital Sister under Government', MSS Eur.B.385, OIOC.
Letters, 1896–7, from Ernest Walter Saxton, Indian P.O., 1890–1921, to Rose Sophia Goldswain, MSS Eur.B.261, OIOC.

Diary of Vithaldas Damodar Thackersey, 1896–98, Indian Merchants' Chamber Library, OIOC.

Books, Articles, and Pamphlets

Adarkar, N. and M. Menon. *One Hundred Years, One Hundred Voices: The Millworkers of Girangaon: An Oral History*. Calcutta: Seagull Books, 2004.

Ahuja, R. 'Labour Relations in an Early Colonial Context: Madras, c. 1750–1800'. *Modern Asian Studies* 36, no. 4 (2002): 793–826.

Alborn, T.L. 'Age and Empire in the Indian Census, 1871–1931'. *Journal of Interdisciplinary History* 30, no. 1 (1999): 61–89.

Alexander, J.T. 'Catherine II, Bubonic Plague, and the Problem of Industry in Moscow'. *The American Historical Review* 79, no. 3 (1974): 637–71.

Alger, G.W. 'The Courts and Factory Legislation'. *The American Journal of Sociology* 6, no. 3 (1900): 396–406.

Andeson, G.M., R.B. Ekelund, and R.D. Tollison. 'Nassau Senior as Economic Consultant: The Factory Acts Reconsidered'. *Economica*, New Series 56, no. 221 (1989): 71–81.

Apte, M.L. 'Lokahitavadi and V.K. Chiplunkar: Spokesmen of Change in Nineteenth-Century Maharashtra'. *Modern Asian Studies* 7, no. 2 (1973): 193–208.

Arnold, D. 'Industrial Violence in Colonial India'. *Comparative Studies in Society and History* 22, no. 2 (1980): 234–55.

———. 'Touching the Body: Perspectives on the Indian Plague, 1896–1900'. In *Subaltern Studies* V, edited by R. Guha, 55–90. Delhi: Oxford University Press, 1987.

———. *Colonizing the Body: State Medicine and Epidemic Disease in Nineteenth-Century India*. California: University of California Press, 1993.

Asher, R. 'Experience Counts: British Workers, Accident Prevention and Compensation, and the Origins of the Welfare State'. *The Journal of Policy History* 15, no. 4 (2003): 359–88.

Bagchi, A.K. *Private Investment in India, 1900–1939*. Cambridge: Cambridge University Press, 1972.

———. 'Colonialism and the Nature of "Capitalist" Enterprise in India'. *Economic and Political Weekly* 23, no. 31 (1988): PE38–PE50.

Banerjee, A.R. *An Indian Pathfinder: Being the Memoirs of Sevabrata Sasipada Banerji, 1840–1924*. Oxford: Kemp Hall Press,1934.

Barker, D.A. 'Factory Legislation in India'. *The Economic Journal* 21, no. 84 (1911): 643–8.

Bartrip, P. 'Success of Failure? The Prosecution of the Early Factory Acts'. *The Economic History Review*, New Series 38, no. 3 (1985): 423–7.

Bartrip, P.W.J. and P.T. Fenn. 'The Evolution of Regulatory Style in the Nineteenth-Century British Factory Inspectorate'. *Journal of Law and Society* 10, no. 2 (1983): 201–22.

Basu, S. *Does Class Matter? Colonial Capital and Workers' Resistance in Bengal, 1890–1927*. Delhi: Oxford University Press, 2004.

Battiscombe, G. *Shaftesbury*. London: Constable, 1974.

Beales, D. *From Castlereagh to Gladstone, 1815–1885*. London: Nelson, 1969.

Bender, D.E. 'Inspecting Workers: Medical Examination, Labor Organizing, and the Evidence of Sexual Difference'. *Radical History Review* 80 (2001): 51–75.

Benenson, H. 'Patriarchal Constraints on Women Workers' Mobilization: The Lancashire Female Cotton Operatives 1842–1919'. *The British Journal of Sociology* 44, no. 4 (1993): 613–33.

Bengallee, N.S. *The Life of Sorabjee Shapoorjee Bengallee, C.I.E., (With illustrations, Letters and a Sketch in English)*. Bombay, n.d.

Bhattacharya, S. 'Capital and Labour in Bombay City, 1928–29'. *Economic and Political Weekly* 16, no. 42/43 (1981): PE36–PE44.

Bienefield, M.A. *Working Hours in British Industry: An Economic History*. Wiltshire: Weidenfeld & Nicolson, 1972.

Breman, J. 'A Dualistic Labour System? A Critique of the "Informal Sector" Concept'. *Economic and Political Weekly* 11, no. 48–50 (1976): 1870–6, 1905–8, 1939–44.

Broughton, G.M. *Labour in Indian Industries*. London, 1924.

Buchanan, D.H. *The Development of Capitalist Enterprise in India*. London: Macmillan , 1934.

Burnett-Hurst, A.R. 'Lancashire and the Indian Market'. *Journal of the Royal Statistical Society* 95, no. 3 (1932): 395–454.

Burton, A. 'Fearful Bodies into Disciplined Subjects: Pleasure, Romance, and the Family Drama of Colonial Reform in Mary Carpenter's *Six Months in India*'. *Signs* 20, no. 3 (1995): 545–74.

Carpenter, J.E. *The Life and Work of Mary Carpenter*. London: Macmillan, 1879.

Carpenter, M. *Reformatory Schools for the Children of the Perishing and Dangerous Classes*. Bristol: C. Gilpin, 1851.

———. 'On the Importance of Statistics to the Reformatory Movement, with Returns from Female Reformatories, and Remarks on Them'. *Journal of the Statistical Society of London* 20, no. 1 (1857): 33–40.

———. 'On the Treatment of Female Convicts'. *Fraser's Magazine for Town and Country* 67, no. 397 (1863): 31–46.

———. *Our Convicts*, two volumes. London: Longman, 1864.

———. *Six Months in India*, two volumes. London: Spottiswoode & Co., 1868.

Carson, W.G. 'Some Sociological Aspects of Strict Liability and the Enforcement of Factory Legislation'. *The Modern Law Review* 33, no. 4 (1970): 396–412.

Catanach, I.J. '"Who Are Your Leaders?" Plague, the Raj and the "Communities" in Bombay, 1896–1901'. In *Society and Ideology: Essays in South Asian History Presented to Prof. K.A. Ballhatchet*, edited by P. Robb, 196–221. Delhi: Oxford University Press, 1993.

———. 'The "Globalization" of Disease? India and the Plague'. *Journal of World History* 12, no. 1 (2001): 131–53.

Chakrabarty, D. 'Sasipada Banerjee: A Study in the Nature of the First Contact of the Bengali Bhadralok with the Working Classes of Bengal'. *Indian Historical Review* 2, no. 2 (1976): 339–64.

———. 'On Deifying and Defying Authority: Managers and Workers in the Jute Mills of Bengal, Circa 1890–1940'. *Past and Present* 100 (1983): 124–46.

———. *Rethinking Working Class History: Bengal, 1890–1940*. Princeton: Princeton University Press, 1989.

Chambers-Schiller, L. 'The Single Woman Reformer: Conflicts between Family and Vocation, 1830–1860'. *Frontiers: A Journal of Women Studies* 3, no. 3 (1978): 41–8.

Chandavarkar, R. *The Origins of Industrial Capitalism in India: Business Strategies and the Working Classes in Bombay, 1900–1940*. Cambridge: Cambridge University Press, 1994.

———. *Imperial Power and Popular Politics: Class, Resistance and the State in India, c. 1850–1950*. Cambridge: Cambridge University Press, 1998.

———. 'Questions of Class: The General Strikes in Bombay, 1928–29'. In *Contributions to Indian Sociology* 33, nos 1 and 2, edited by J.P. Parry, J. Breman, and K. Kapadia. 1999.

———. The Decline and Fall of the Jobber System in the Bombay Cotton Textile Industry, 1870–1955. *Modern Asian Studies* 42, no. 1 (2008): 1–94.

Chandra, B. *The Rise and Growth of Indian Nationalism*. Delhi: People's Publishing House, 1966.

Chatterji, Basudev. *Trade, Tariffs and Empire: Lancashire and British Policy in India, 1919–1939*. Delhi: Oxford University Press, 1992.

Clark, G. 'Factory Discipline'. *The Journal of Economic History* 54, no. 1 (1994): 128–63.

Clark, L. *Women and Achievement in Nineteenth-Century Europe*. Cambridge: Cambridge University Press, 2008.

Clarke, P.F. 'The End of Laissez Faire and the Politics of Cotton'. *The Historical Journal* 15, no. 3 (1972): 493–512.

Clay, W.G. 'The Law of Employers' Liability and Insurance against Accidents'. *Journal of the Society of Comparative Legislation* 2 (1897): 1–111.

Cola, P.R. *How to Develop Productive Industry in India and the East*. London: Virtue & Co., 1867.

Cottrell, J. '"Indian Judicial Activism, the Company and the Worker: A Note on National Textile Workers" Union v. Ramakrishnan'. *The International and Comparative Law Quarterly* 39, no. 2 (1990): 433–51.

Crawford, D.G. *A History of the Indian Medical Service*. London: W. Thacker, 1914.

Dantwalla, M.L. *A Hundred Years of Indian Cotton*. Bombay: Orient Longmans, 1948.

Darukhanawalla, H.D. *Parsi Lustre on Indian Soil*. Bombay: G. Claridge & Co., 1939.

Darwin, J. 'Imperialism and the Victorians: The Dynamics of Territorial Expansion'. *The English Historical Review* 112, no. 447 (1997): 614–42.

Das, R.K. *Factory Labour in India*. Berlin, 1923.

———. *History of Indian Labour Legislation*. Calcutta: University of Calcutta, 1941.

de Graffenried, C. 'Child Labor'. *Publications of the American Economic Association* 5, no. 2 (1890): 71–149.

Desai, A.V. 'The Origins of Parsi Enterprise'. In *Entrepreneurship and Industry in India, 1800*–1947, edited by R.K. Ray. Oxford: Oxford University Press, 1992.

Divekar, V.D. 'The Emergence of an Indigenous Business Class in Maharashtra in the Eighteenth Century'. *Modern Asian Studies* 16, no. 3 (1982): 427–43.

Dossal, M. *Imperial Designs and Indian Realities: The Planning of Bombay City, 1845–1875*. Oxford: Oxford University Press, 1991.

Douglas, J. *Bombay and Western India: A Series of Stray Papers,* 2 vols. Bombay, 1893.

———. *Glimpses of Old Bombay and Western India, with Other Papers*. London, 1900.

Dutton, H.I., and J.E. King. 'The Limits of Paternalism: The Cotton Tyrants of North Lancashire, 1836–54'. *Social History* 7, no. 1 (1982): 59–74.

Eagles, J. *The Bristol Riots: Their Causes, Progress and Consequences, by a Citizen*. Bristol, 1832.

Echenberg, M. 'Pestis Redux: The Initial Years of the Third Bubonic Plague Pandemic, 1894–1901'. *Journal of World History* 13, no. 2 (2002): 429–49.

———. *Plague Ports: The Global Urban Impact of Bubonic Plague, 1894–1901*. New York: New York University Press, 2007.

Edwardes, S.M. *The Rise of Bombay: A Retrospect*. Bombay: Times of India Press, 1902.

———. *The Bombay City Police, 1672–1916: An Historical Sketch*. London: Oxford University Press, 1923.

Engels, F. *The Condition of the Working Class in England*. London: Swan Sonnenschein, 1892.

Epstein, S. 'District Officers in Decline: The Erosion of British Authority in the Bombay Countryside, 1919 to 1947'. *Modern Asian Studies* 16, no. 3 (1982): 493–518.

Field, S. 'Without the Law? Professor Arthurs and the Early Factory Inspectorate'. *Journal of Law and Society* 17, no. 4 (1990): 445–68.

Forsey, E. 'A Note on the Dominion Factory Bills of the Eighteen-Eighties'. *The Canadian Journal of Economics and Political Science* 13, no. 4 (1947): 580–3.

Foucault, M. *Discipline and Punish*. New York: Random House, 1977.

Fraser, L. *India Under Curzon and After*. London: William Heinemann, 1911.

Freedgood, E. *Factory Production in Nineteenth-Century Britain*. Oxford: Oxford University Press, 2003.

Fry, A.A. 'Report of the Inspectors of Factories on the Effects of the Educational Provisions of the Factories' Act'. *Journal of the Statistical Society of London* 2, no. 3 (1839): 173–81.

Gadgil, D.R. *The Industrial Evolution of India in Recent Times, 1860–1939*. Bombay: Oxford University Press, 1971.

Gallagher, J. and R. Robinson. 'The Imperialism of Free Trade'. *The Economic History Review*, New Series 6, no. 1 (1953): 1–15.

Garratt, G.T. 'The Indian Industrial Worker'. *The Economic Journal* 42, no. 167 (1932): 399–406.

Geary, D., ed. *Labour and Socialist Movements in Europe before 1914*. Oxford: Oxford University Press, 1989.

Goldingham, J. 'Of the Geographical Situation of the Three Presidencies, Calcutta, Madras and Bombay, in the East Indies'. *Philosophical Transactions of the Royal Society of London* 112 (1882): 408–30.

Gopal, S. *British Policy in India, 1858–1905*. Cambridge: Cambridge University Press, 1965.

Gordon, A.D. *Businessmen and Politics: Rising Nationalism and a Modernizing Economy, 1918–1933*. Delhi: Manohar, 1979.

Greer, D. and J.W. Nicolson. *The Factory Acts in Ireland: 1802–1914*. Dublin: Four Courts Press, 2003.

Guha, R., ed. *Subaltern Studies II*. Delhi: Oxford University Press, 1983.

Gumperz, E.M. 'City-Hinterland Relations and the Development of a Regional Elite in Nineteenth-Century Bombay'. *The Journal of Asian Studies* 33, no. 4 (1974): 581–601.

Gupta, R.D. 'A Labour History of Social Security and Mutual Assistance in India'. *Economic and Political Weekly* 29, no. 11 (1994): 612–20.

———. 'Indian Working Class and Some Recent Historiographical Issues'. *Economic and Political Weekly* 31, no. 8 (1996): L27–L31.

Gupta, U.D. 'The Indian Press 1870–1880: A Small World of Journalism'. *Modern Asian Studies* 11, no. 2 (1977): 213–35.

Halevy, E. *Imperialism and the Rise of Labour, 1895–1905*. New York: Barnes and Noble, 1926.

Hall, C. *White, Male and Middle Class: Explorations in Feminism and History*. Cambridge: Polity Press, 1992.

Hammond, J.L. and B. Hammond. *Lord Shaftesbury*. London: Constable, 1923.

———. *The Rise of Modern Industry*. London: Methuen, 1925.

Hardiman, D. *Peasant Nationalists of Gujarat: Kheda District 1917–1934*. Delhi: Methuen, 1981.

Harnetty, P. 'The Imperialism of Free Trade: Lancashire and the Indian Cotton Duties, 1859–1862'. *The Economic History Review*, New Series 18, no. 2 (1965): 333–49.

———. *Imperialism and Free Trade: Lancashire and India in the Mid-Nineteenth Century*. Vancouver: University of British Columbia Press, 1972.

Harrison, M. *Public Health in British India: Anglo-Indian Preventive Medicine, 1859–1914*. Cambridge: Cambridge University Press, 1994.

Hattam, V.C. *Labour Visions and State Power: The Origins of Business Unionism in the United States*. New Jersey: Princeton University Press, 1993.

Haynes, Douglas E. *Small-Town Capitalism in Western India: Artisans, Merchants, and the Making of the Informal Economy, 1870–1960*. Cambridge: Cambridge University Press, 2012.

Hays, J.N. *The Burdens of Disease: Epidemics and Human Response in Western History*. New Jersey: Rutgers University Press, 2003.

Hazareesingh, S. 'The Quest for Urban Citizenship: Civic Rights, Public Opinion, and Colonial Resistance in Early Twentieth-Century Bombay'. *Modern Asian Studies*, no. 4 (2000): 797–829.

———. 'Colonial Modernism and the Flawed Paradigms of Urban Renewal: Uneven Development in Bombay, 1900–25'. *Urban History* 28, no. 2 (2001): 235–55.

———. '"Chasing Commodities over the Surface of the Globe": Shipping, Port Development and the Making of Networks Between Glasgow and Bombay, c. 1850–1880', *Commodities of Empire Working Paper No. 1*, Ferguson Centre for African and Asian Studies, The Open University. London, 2007.

———. *The Colonial City and the Challenge of Modernity: Urban Hegemonies and Civic Contestations in Bombay, 1900–1925*. Hyderabad: Orient Longman, 2007.

Heck, E.J. '"Hard Times": The Handwriting on the Factory Wall'. *The English Journal* 61, no. 1 (1972): 23–7.

Helm, E. 'The Recent Wages Dispute in the Lancashire Cotton-Spinning Industry'. *The Economic Journal* 3, no. 10 (1893): 342–5.

———. 'An International Survey of the Cotton Industry'. *The Quarterly Journal of Economics* 17, no. 3 (1903): 417–37.

Hobsbawm, E. *Industry and Empire: An Economic History of Britain since 1750*. New York: The New Press, 1968.

———. *The Age of Empire, 1875–1914*. London: Weidenfeld and Nicolson, 1987.

Howells, R.W.L. 'New Wave of Interpretations of the Factories Acts'. *The Modern Law Review* 25, no. 1 (1962): 98–108.

———. 'Priestley v. Fowler and the Factory Acts'. *The Modern Law Review* 26, no. 4 (1963): 367–95.

Humphries, J. 'Protective Legislation, the Capitalist State, and Working Class Men: The Case of the 1842 Mines Regulation Act'. *Feminist Review* 7 (1981): 1–33.

Hunt, E.H. *British Labour History, 1815–1914*. London: Weidenfeld and Nicolson, 1981.

Hunter, K.M. 'Fighting the Bubonic Plague in India'. *The Nineteenth Century: A Monthly Review* 43, no. 256 (1898): 1008–16.

Hunter, W.W. *Bombay, 1885–1890: A Study in Indian Administration*. London: Henry Frowde, 1892.

Hutchins, B.L. 'Gaps in Our Factory Legislation'. *The Economic Journal* 18, no. 70 (1908): 221–30.

Hutchins, B.L., and A. Harrison. *A History of Factory Legislation*. London: P.S. King & Son, 1903.

Ignatieff, M. *A Just Measure of Pain*. New York: Pantheon, 1978.

Jackson, R.R. 'India and Lancashire'. *Fortnightly Review* 19, no. 114 (1876): 877–96.

James, R.C. 'Discrimination against Women in Bombay Textiles'. *Industrial and Labor Relations Review* 15, no. 2 (1962): 209–20.

Johnson, R. 'Educational Policy and Social Control in Early Victorian England'. *Past and Present* 49 (1970): 96–119.

Joshi, C. 'Bonds of Community, Ties of Religion: Kanpur Textile Workers in the Early Twentieth Century'. In *Unions in Conflict: A Comparative Study of Four South Indian Textile Centres, 1918–1939*, edited by E.D. Murphy. Delhi, 1981.

———. 'Kanpur Textile Labour: Some Structural Features of Formative Years'. *Economic and Political Weekly* 16, nos 44–6 (1981): 1823–38.

———. *Lost Worlds: Indian Labour and Its Forgotten Histories*. New Delhi: Permanent Black, 2003.

Joyce, P. 'The Factory Politics of Lancashire in the Later Nineteenth Century'. *The Historical Journal* 18, no. 3 (1975): 525–53.

———. *Work, Society and Politics: The Culture of the Factory in Later Victorian England*. Brighton: Harvester Press, 1980.

Kannangara, A.P. 'Indian Millowners and Indian Nationalism before 1914'. *Past and Present* 40 (1968): 147–64.

Kapadia, K. 'Indian Industrial Labour Today: An Agenda for Research'. *Economic and Political Weekly* 33, no. 52 (1998–9): 3305–8.

Karkaria, R.P. *The Charm of Bombay: An Anthology of Writings in Praise of the First City in India*. Bombay: D.B. Taraporevala, 1915.

Karnik, V.B. *Strikes in India*. Bombay: L Manaktalas, 1967.

Kelman, J.H. *Labour in India: A Study of the Conditions of Indian Women in Modern Industry*. London: George Allen & Unwin, 1923.

Kennedy, D. *A Critique of Adjudication*. Cambridge, MA: Harvard University Press, 1997.

Kerr, I.J. *Building the Railways of the Raj, 1850 to 1900*. New Delhi: Oxford University Press, 1995.

———. 'Labour Control and Labour Legislation in Colonial India: A Tale of Two Mid-Nineteenth Century Acts'. *South Asia: Journal of South Asian Studies* 27, no. 1 (2004): 7–25.

Kidambi, P. '"An Infection of Locality": Plague, Pythogenesis and the Poor in Bombay, c. 1896–1905'. *Urban History* 31, no. 2 (2004): 249–67.

———. *The Making of an Indian Metropolis: Colonial Governance and Public Culture in Bombay, 1890–1920*. Hampshire: Ashgate, 2007.

———. 'Contestation and Conflict: Workers' Resistance and the "Labour Problem" in the Bombay Cotton Mills, c. 1898–1919', in *Labour Matters: Towards Global Histories [Essays in Honour of Sabyasachi Bhattacharya]*, edited by P. Mohapatra, and M. van der Linden, 106–28. New Delhi: Tulika, 2009.

Kilmuir, Lord. 'The Shaftesbury Tradition in Conservative Politics'. *Journal of Law and Economics* 3 (1960): 70–4.

Kirkwood, T.M. 'The Impending Famine'. *Fortnightly Review* 60, no. 360 (1896): 856–68.

Klein, I. 'English Free Traders and Indian Tariffs, 1874–96'. *Modern Asian Studies* 5, no. 3 (1971): 251–71.

———. 'Urban Development and Death: Bombay City, 1870–1914'. *Modern Asian Studies* 20, no. 4 (1986): 725–54.

———. 'Plague, Policy and Popular Unrest in British India'. *Modern Asian Studies* 22, no. 4 (1988): 723–55.

Koditschek, T. 'The Gendering of the British Working Class'. *Gender and History* 9, no. 2 (1997): 333–63.

Kooiman, D. 'Jobbers and the Emergence of Trade Unions in Bombay City'. *International Review of Social History* 22, no. 3 (1977): 313–28.

———. 'Bombay Communists and the 1924 Textile Strike'. *Economic and Political Weekly* 15, no. 29 (1980): 1223–5, 1227–36.

———. 'Labour Legislation and Working Class Movement: Case of Bombay Labour Office, 1934–37'. *Economic and Political Weekly* 16, no. 44/46 (1981): 1807–9, 1811, 1813, 1815–17, 1819, 1821–2.

———. *Bombay Textile Labour: Managers, Trade Unionists and Officials*. Delhi: Manohar, 1989.

Kosambi, M. 'Commerce, Conquest and the Colonial City: Role of Locational Factors in Rise of Bombay'. *Economic and Political Weekly* 20, no. 1 (1985): 32–7.

Koven, S. and S. Michel. 'Womanly Duties: Maternalist Politics and the Origins of Welfare States in France, Germany, Great Britain, and the United States, 1880–1920'. *The American Historical Review* 95, no. 4 (1990): 1076–108.

———. , eds. *Mothers of a New World: Maternalist Politics and the Emergence of Welfare States*. New York: Routledge, 1993.

Kulkarni, V.B. *History of the Indian Cotton Textile Industry*. Bombay: Bombay Millowners' Association, 1979.

Kumar, D., and M. Desai, eds. *The Cambridge Economic History of India*, vol. 2: *c.1757–c.1970*. Cambridge: Cambridge University Press, 1983.

Kumar, R. 'City Lives: Workers' Housing and Rent in Bombay, 1911–47'. *Economic and Political Weekly* 22, no. 30 (1987): PE47–PE56.

Kydd, J.C. *A History of Factory Legislation in India*. Calcutta: Calcutta University Press, 1920.

Lamb, H.B. 'The Indian Business Communities and the Evolution of an Industrial Class'. *Pacific Affairs* 28, no. 2 (1955): 101–16.

Landes, D.S. *The Unbound Prometheus: Technological Change and Industrial Development in Western Europe from 1750 to the Present*. Cambridge: Cambridge University Press, 1969.

Lefebvre, H. *The Production of Space*. Oxford: Blackwell, 1974.

Lucy, H.W. 'The Liverpool of India'. *Belgravia: A London Magazine* 53, no. 210 (1884): 210–17.

MacGregor, D. *Hegel, Marx and the English State*. Toronto: Westview Press, 1992.

Maclean, J.M. *A Guide to Bombay*. Bombay: The 'Bombay Gazette' Steam Press, 1880.

Mandler, P. 'Cain and Abel: Two Aristocrats and the Early Victorian Factory Acts'. *The Historical Journal* 27, no. 1 (1984): 83–109.

Manton, J. *Mary Carpenter and the Children of the Streets*. London: Heinemann Educational, 1976.

Mantoux, P. *The Industrial Revolution in the Eighteenth Century*. London: Methuen Press, 1928.

Markovits, C. *Merchants, Traders, Entrepreneurs: Indian Business in the Colonial Era*. Ranikhet: Permanent Black, 2008.

Marvel, H.P. 'Factory Regulation: A Reinterpretation of Early English Experience'. *Journal of Law and Economics* 20, no. 2 (1977): 379–402.

Marx, K. *Early Writings*. Harmondsworth: Penguin, 1975.

———. *Capital: A Critique of Political Economy*, volume 1. Harmondsworth: Penguin Books, 1976.

Masselos, J. 'Social Segregation and Crowd Cohesion: Reflections around Some Preliminary Data from 19th-Century Bombay City'. *Contributions to Indian Sociology*, New Series 13, no. 2 (1979): 145–67.

———. 'Jobs and Jobbery: The Sweeper in Bombay under the Raj'. *Indian Economic Social History Review* 19, no. 2 (1982): 101–39.

———. 'The City as Represented in Crowd Action: Bombay, 1893'. *Economic and Political Weekly* 28, no. 5 (1993): 182–8.

———. *The City in Action: Bombay Struggles for Power*. New Delhi: Oxford University Press, 2007.

Matherly, W.J. 'The Emergence of Factory Labor'. *Social Forces* 4, no. 1 (1925): 175–83.

Mayhew, H. *London Labour and the London Poor*. London: George Woodfall & Son, 1849.

Mazumdar, D. 'Labour Supply in Early Industrialization: The Case of the Bombay Textile Industry'. *The Economic History Review*, New Series 26, no. 3 (1973): 477–96.

McAlpin, M.B. 'Famines, Epidemics, and Population Growth: The Case of India'. *Journal of Interdisciplinary History* 14, no. 2 (1983): 351–66.

McDonald, E.E. 'English Education and Social Reform in Late Nineteenth Century Bombay: A Case Study in the Transmission of a Cultural Ideal'. *The Journal of Asian Studies* 25, no. 3 (1966): 453–70.

Mehta, S.D. *The Cotton Mills of India*. Bombay: Textile Association, 1954.

Misra, A.M. '"Business Culture" and Entrepreneurship in British India, 1860–1950'. *Modern Asian Studies* 34, no. 2 (2000): 333–48.

Misra, B. 'Factory Labour during the Early Years of Industrialization: An Appraisal in the Light of the Indian Factory Labour Commission, 1890'. *Indian Economic and Social History Review* 12, no. 3 (1975): 203–28.

Mohapatra, P. *Situating the Renewal: Reflections on Labour Studies in India*. Noida: V.V. Giri National Labour Institute, 1998.

Mohapatra, P., and M. van der Linden, eds. *Labour Matters: Towards Global Histories [Essays in Honour of Sabyasachi Bhattacharya]*. New Delhi: Tulika Books , 2009.

Morris, M.D. *The Emergence of an Industrial Labour Force in India: A Study of the Bombay Cotton Mills, 1854–1947*. Berkeley: University of California Press, 1965.

Mukhtar, Ahmad. *Factory Labour in India*. Chidambaram: Annamalai University Press, 1930.

Mundella, A.J. 'What Are the Conditions on which the Commercial and Manufacturing Supremacy of Great Britain Depend, and Is There Any Reason to Think They Have Been, or May Be, Endangered?'. *Journal of the Statistical Society of London* 41, no. 1 (1878): 87–134.

Nair, J. *Miners and Millhands: Work, Culture and Politics in Princely Mysore*. Delhi: SAGE, 1998.

Nardinelli, C. 'The Successful Prosecution of the Factory Acts: A Suggested Explanation'. *The Economic History Review*, New Series 38, no. 3 (1985): 428–30.

Newman, R. *Workers and Unions in Bombay, 1918–1929: A Study of Organization in the Cotton Mills*. Canberra: Australian National University, 1981.

O'Hanlon, R. 'Maratha History as Polemic: Low Caste Ideology and Political Debate in Late Nineteenth-Century Western India'. *Modern Asian Studies* 17, no. 1 (1983): 1–33.

———. *Caste, Conflict and Ideology: Mahatma Jotirao Phule and Low Caste Protest in Nineteenth-Century Western India*. Cambridge: Cambridge University Press, 1985.

Omvedt, G. 'Non-Brahmans and Communists in Bombay'. *Economic and Political Weekly* 8, no. 16–17 (1973): 749–59, 800–5.

Oonk, G. 'Motor or Millstone? The Managing Agency System in Bombay and Ahmedabad, 1850–1930'. *Indian Economic and Social History Review* 38, no. 4 (2001): 419–52.

Pahl, R. E., ed. *On Work: Historical, Comparative and Theoretical Approaches*. Oxford: Blackwell, 1988.

Panandikar, S.G. *Industrial Labour in India*. London: Longmans, Green and Co., 1933.

Pandit, N. 'Narayan Meghaji Lokhande: The Father of Trade Union Movement in India'. *Economic and Political Weekly* 32, no. 7 (1997): 327–9.

Parry, J.P., J. Breman, and K. Kapadia, eds. *The Worlds of Indian Industrial Labour*. New Delhi: SAGE, 1996.

Patell, B.F. *History of the Plague in Bombay*. Bombay, n.d.

Peacock, A.E. 'The Successful Prosecution of the Factory Acts, 1833–55'. *Economic History Review*, vol. 37, no. 2 (1984): 197–210.

Prakash, P. 'The Making of Bombay: Social, Cultural and Political Dimensions'. *Economic and Political Weekly* 28, no. 40 (1993): 2119–21.

Punekar, S.D., and R. Varickayil, eds. *Labour Movement in India: Documents 1891–1917*. New Delhi: Indian Council of Historical Research, 1990.

Rabitoy, N. 'The Control of Fate and Fortune: The Origins of the Market Mentality in British Administrative Thought in South Asia'. *Modern Asian Studies* 25, no. 4 (1991): 737–64.

Rae, J. 'The New East India Factory Act'. *The Economic Journal* 1, no. 4 (1891): 803–6.

Ramanna, M. 'Social Background of the Educated in Bombay City: 1824–58'. *Economic and Political Weekly* 24, no. 4 (1989): 203–11.

———. 'Profiles of English Educated Indians: Early Nineteenth-Century Bombay City'. *Economic and Political Weekly* 27, no. 14 (1992): 716–24.

Ranciere, J. *The Nights of Labour: The Workers' Dream in Nineteenth-Century France*. Philadelphia: Temple University Press, 1989.

Ranganathan, M., trans. and ed. *Govind Narayan's Mumbai: An Urban Biography from 1863*. London: Anthem, 2008.

Raychaudhuri, S. 'Colonialism, Indigenous Elites and the Transformation of Cities in the Non-Western World: Ahmedabad (Western India), 1890–1947'. *Modern Asian Studies* 35, no. 3 (2001): 677–726.

Reid, D. 'Industrial Paternalism: Discourse and Practice in Nineteenth-Century French Mining and Metallurgy'. *Comparative Studies in Society and History* 27, no. 4 (1985): 579–607.

Richards, P. 'R. A. Slaney, the Industrial Town, and Early Victorian Social Policy'. *Social History* 4, no. 1 (1979): 85–101.

Richey, R.E. 'From Puritanism to Unitarianism in England: A Study in Candour'. *Journal of the American Academy of Religion* 41, no. 3 (1973): 371–85.

Robb, P., ed. *Dalit Movements and the Meanings of Labour in India*. Oxford: Oxford University Press, 1993.

Roberts, C. 'The Physical Requirements of Factory Children'. *Journal of the Statistical Society of London* 39, no. 4 (1876): 681–733.

Rodger, R. 'Mid-Victorian Employers' Attitudes'. *Social History* 11, no. 1 (1986): 77–80.

Roy, T. *Traditional Industry in the Economy of Colonial India*. Cambridge: Cambridge University Press, 1999.

———. 'Apprenticeship and Industrialization in India 1890–1930'. Paper presented at S.R. Epstein Memorial Conference on 'Technology and Human Capital Formation in the East and West', London School of Economics, 19–21 June 2008.

Rungta, R.S. *Business Corporations in India, 1851–1900*. Cambridge: Cambridge University Press, 1970.

Rutnagar, S.M. *Bombay Industries: The Cotton Mills: A Review of the Progress of the Textile Industry in Bombay from 1850 to 1926 and the Present Constitution, Management and Financial Position of Spinning and Weaving Factories*. Bombay: The Indian Textile Association Ltd, 1927.

San Juan Jr., E. 'Toward a Definition of Victorian Activism'. *Studies in English Literature, 1500–1900* 4, no. 4 (1964): 583–600.

Sanderson, M. 'Education and the Factory in Industrial Lancashire, 1780–1840'. *The Economic History Review*, New Series 20, no. 2 (1967): 266–70.

Sarkar, S. *Modern India, 1885–1947*. Delhi: Macmillan, 1983.

Sarkar, T. *Hindu Wife, Hindu Nation: Community, Religion and Cultural Nationalism*. Ranikhet: Permanent Black, 2001.

Schaffner, M.A. 'Factory Legislation—India'. *The American Political Science Review* 3, no. 4 (1909): 556.

Schupf, H.W. 'Education for the Neglected: Ragged Schools in Nineteenth-Century England'. *History of Education Quarterly* 12, no. 2 (1972): 162–83.

Sen, N. *India in the International Economy, 1858–1913: Some Aspects of Trade and Finance*. Calcutta: Orient Longman, 1992.

Shah, J.J. 'A Comparative Analysis of Two Major Cotton Textile Centres of India: Bombay & Ahmedabad'. *Treballs de la Societat Catalana de Geografica* 3 (1985): 87–106.

Sheth, N.R. 'The Problem of Labour Commitment'. *Economic and Political Weekly* 6, no. 9 (1971): M35–M39.

Silver, A. *Manchester Men and Indian Cotton, 1847–1872*. Manchester: Manchester University Press, 1966.

Simeon, D. *The Politics of Labour under Late Colonialism: Workers, Unions and the State in Chota Nagpur, 1928–1939*. Delhi: Manohar, 1995.

Simmons, C. '"De-Industrialization", Industrialization and the Indian Economy, c. 1850–1947'. *Modern Asian Studies* 19, no. 3 (1985): 593–622.

Singh, V.B., ed. *The Economic History of India, 1857–1956*. New Delhi: Allied Publishers, 1965.

Singha, R. *A Despotism of Law: Crime and Justice in Early Colonial India*. New Delhi: Oxford University Press, 1998.

Smitha, S.M. 'Blue Books and Victorian Novelists'. *The Review of English Studies*, New Series 21, no. 81 (1970): 23–40.

Stedman Jones, G. *Outcast London: A Study in the Relationship between Classes in Victorian Society*. London: Oxford University Press, 1971.

———. *Languages of Class: Studies in English Working Class History 1832–1982*. Cambridge: Cambridge University Press, 1983.

Steedman, C. *Strange Dislocations: Childhood and the Idea of Human Interiority, 1780–1930*. Cambridge, MA: Harvard University Press, 1995.

———. *Dust*. Manchester: Manchester University Press, 2001.

———. 'The Servant's Labour: The Business of Life, England, 1760–1820'. *Social History* 29, no. 1 (2004): 1–29.

Steinfeld, R. *Coercion, Contract and Free Labour in the Nineteenth Century*. Cambridge: Cambridge University Press, 2001.

Stewart, R. 'The Ten Hours and Sugar Crises of 1844: Government and the House of Commons in the Age of Reform'. *The Historical Journal* 12, no. 1 (1969): 35–57.

Subramaniam, K.N. *Labour-Management Relations in India*. New Delhi: Asia Publishing House, 1967.

Talcherkar, V.A. *Our Mill-hands and the Factory Labour Agitation*. Bombay, 1909.

Tattvabhushan, S. *Sasipada Banerji's Life and Life Work*. Calcutta, 1919.

Thomas, M.W. *The Early Factory Legislation: A Study in Legislative and Administrative Evolution*. Leigh-On-Sea: Thames Bank Publishing, 1948.

Thompson, E.P. *The Making of the English Working Class*. New York: Pantheon, 1963.

———. 'Time, Work-Discipline and Industrial Capitalism'. *Past and Present* 38 (1967): 56–97.

———. 'The Moral Economy of the English Crowd in the Eighteenth Century'. *Past and Present* 50 (1971): 76–136.

———. *Whigs and Hunters: The Origin of the Black Act*. Harmondsworth: Penguin, 1975.

———. *Customs in Common*. New York: The New Press, 1991.

Trant, W. 'Trade Unionism in India'. *Fortnightly Review* 26, no. 152 (1879): 261–77.

Turner, M.J. 'The "Bonaparte of Free Trade" and the Anti-Corn Law League'. *The Historical Journal* 41, no. 4 (1998): 1011–34.

Upadhyay, S.B. 'Communalism and Working Class-Riot of 1893 in Bombay City'. *Economic and Political Weekly* 24, no. 30 (July 1989).

———. 'Cotton Mill Workers in Bombay, 1875 to 1918: Conditions of Work and Life'. *Economic and Political Weekly*, 25, no. 30 (1990): PE87–PE99.

———. *Existence, Identity and Mobilization: The Cotton Millworkers of Bombay 1890–1919*. New Delhi: Manohar, 2004.

Valenze, D. *The First Industrial Woman*. Oxford: Oxford University Press, 1995.

von Laue, T.H. 'Factory Inspection under the "Witte System": 1892–1903'. *American Slavic and East European Review* 19, no. 3 (1960): 347–62.

Vorspan, R. 'Vagrancy and the New Poor Law in Late-Victorian and Edwardian England'. *The English Historical Review* 92, no. 362 (1977): 59–81.

Wacha, D.E. *A Financial Chapter in the History of Bombay City*. Bombay: The Commercial Press, 1910.

———. *Shells from the Sands of Bombay: Being My Recollections and Reminiscences—1860–1875*. Bombay: Bombay Chronicle Press, 1920.

Ward, J.T. *The Factory Movement, 1830–1855*. London: Macmillan, 1962.

Warm-Schupf, H. 'Single Women and Social Reform in Mid-Nineteenth Century England'. *Victorian Studies* 17, no. 3 (1974): 301–17.

Waters, G. *Plague in Bombay. A Lecture Delivered at the Sassoon Mechanics' Institute, Bombay*. Bombay, 1897.

Webb, R.K. 'A Crisis of Authority: Early Nineteenth-Century British Thought'. *Albion: A Quarterly Journal Concerned with British Studies* 24, no. 1 (1992): 1–16.

Williams, Raymond. *Keywords: A Vocabulary of Culture and Society*. New York: Oxford University Press, 1976.

Wood, G.H. 'Factory Legislation, Considered with Reference to the Wages, & c., of the Operatives Protected Thereby'. *Journal of the Royal Statistical Society* 65, no. 2 (1902): 284–324.

Woods, K.P. 'Accidents in Factories and Elsewhere'. *Publications of the American Statistical Association* 4, no. 32 (1895): 303–21.

Yamin, G. 'Character and Origins of Labour Migration from Ratnagiri District'. *South Asia Research* 9, no. 1 (1989): 33–53.

Young, G.M. *Portrait of an Age*. London: Oxford University Press , 1936.

Zandy, J. *Hands: Physical Labor, Class, and Cultural Work*. New Brunswick: Rutgers University Press , 2004.

Zastoupil, Lynn. *Rammohun Roy and the Making of Victorian England*. New York: Palgrave Macmillan, 2010.

Zeitlin, J. 'From Labour History to the History of Industrial Relations'. *The Economic History Review*, New Series 40, no. 2 (1987): 159–84.

Žižek, S. *The Sublime Object of Ideology*. London: Verso, 1989.

———. *The Parallax View*. London: Verso, 2006.

———. *Less Than Nothing: Hegel and the Shadow of Dialectical Materialism*. London: Verso, 2013.

Unpublished Dissertations

Asher, T.F. 'Bombay Dyeing and the Future of Laborers Past: Politics and Social Welfare in the Bombay Cotton Mills, 1918', unpublished PhD dissertation, University of Chicago, 2006.

Chopra, P. 'The City and Its Fragments: Colonial Bombay, 1854–1918', unpublished PhD dissertation, University of California, Berkeley, 2003.

Kidambi, P. 'State, Society and Labour in Colonial Bombay, c. 1893–1918', unpublished PhD dissertation, Oxford, 2001.

Krishnaswamy, S. 'A Riot in Bombay, August 11, 1893: A Study in Hindu-Muslim Relations in Western India during the Late Nineteenth Century', unpublished PhD dissertation, University of Chicago, Chicago, 1966.

Kumar, R. 'City Lives: Women Workers in the Bombay Cotton Textile Industry, 1911–1947', unpublished PhD dissertation, Jawaharlal Nehru University, New Delhi, 1991.

Kumar, S. 'Imperial Power and the Law of Vulnerability: Childhood, Labour and the Evolution of Social Law in the 19th Century', unpublished MPhil dissertation, University of Delhi, 2013.

Schroeder, J.E. 'The Public Voice in Victorian Feminist Speech and Writing', unpublished PhD dissertation, University of Alberta, 2002.

Index

About the Author

Aditya Sarkar teaches history at the University of Warwick, UK. His current research interests include the long history of labour movements in colonial and post-colonial India, and the history of the Indian left. He has previously published articles on factory law in the 1880s, and the social and political ramifications of the plague crisis in Bombay at the end of the nineteenth century.